BIRD OF PARADISE

The Blog

Part 1

November 20, 2004-September 11, 2005

A Compilation by

James A. Tweedie

Duncrest Press

Bird of Paradise—The Blog—Part 1

Credits

Cover Design © by James Tweedie

Printed in USA by Dunecrest Press, Long Beach, WA 98631

ISBN: 978-1-945539-15-2

Preface

Bird of Paradise (the blog) was inspired by talk radio host Hugh Hewitt, who urged his listeners to enter the emerging world of blogging and engage the internet community in whatever topics they were passionate about. As one of Hugh's fans, I took the bait and opened up a free site hosted by blogspot.com. I chose the name "Bird of Paradise" because at the time I was a "Tweedie-bird in paradise" (i.e. Hawaii). My email address at the time was "tbirdofparadise" for the same reason.

I used the blog as a venue for expressing my feelings and opinions on a wide variety of subjects with special attention to politics (strongly supportive of Republican/conservative views), the war on terror (of personal interest since I was serving a congregation—Mililani Presbyterian Church—with a strong military membership including a significant number of men and women deployed to Afghanistan and Iraq), and theology (especially in regards to reflections on my own ministry as well as Islam in general and radical Islam in particular). As pastor to a politically diverse congregation I felt constrained to keep many of my personal opinions to myself. My blog gave me a semi-anonymous venue to speak my mind more openly than I could otherwise

My blogsite masthead described my intentions as follows

WHEN I HAVE THOUGHTS ON MATTERS OF FAITH, NEWS, PERSONAL ENCOUNTERS, OR...SIMPLY THOUGHTS BY THEMSELVES, I WRITE THEM DOWN AND GET THEM OFF OF MY CHEST AND ONTO SOMEONE ELSE'S

My first blog entry was dated Saturday, November 20, 2004 and—although there were a few scattered posts later—my final posts were written in May, 2007. My earliest blogs were not illustrated, mostly because I had not yet mastered the HTML coding and use of URLs necessary to make my site more attractive.

As time went by, my readership grew to 400 to 600 hits each week. I networked and posted on other sites on the web and grew a following of folks who read my postings each day and occasionally linked back to them. Recently, as I compiled my posts for publication, I was surprised to discover how much I had written for the blog.

Highlights of my shortlived blogging career included being quoted by and linked to such major national sites as *Hugh Hewitt*, *Rush Limbaugh*, and *Powerline*. My article on the passing of Coretta Scott King was honored as "Culture Pick of the Week" by a major blogging aggregate. One picture I posted in reference to a major international event went viral; ranking third highest on Google search and getting so many hits that it shut down my Photobucket account. My article honoring a firefighter who died in the collapse of the World Trade Center towers received comments from members of his family who expressed gratitude for my kind words. My postings on matters related to Islam generated many comments from Muslims eager to criticize and challenge my views. I entered into these dialogues with enthusiasm, insofar as they gave me an opportunity to defend the Christian faith, raise questions concerning Islam, and articulate the Gospel to those who were standing in opposition to it.

Now, ten years later, I find myself more or less disenfranchised by both of our nation's major political parties. While I may still be inclined to be more "conservative" than "progressive," I am now less conservative than I was when I was blogging. This three-volume collection of my blog posts represents a snapshot of my thoughts at a particular time of my life. Even so, I still "own" what I wrote back then, even though any given post may or may not represent my thoughts and opinions today.

Back in the first decade of the 21st century blogging was still in its "Wild West" stage of development, inventing itself as it went along while going through the the process of figuring out its ethics and protocols. "Hat tips" or "HTs" were a way of acknowledging the original source of information culled from other bloggers. I, along with everyone else, infringed on copyright in my use of other people's photographs and I would now have second thoughts about posting so many photographs of adults and children in my congregation without their permission. I did, however, consciously make an effort to never mention the name of my congregation by name, or to mention the name "Tweedie" or the names of my wife or three daughters in the text of my posts. This was done to prevent anyone searching for these names on the internet to link them with my blog.

I did most of my writing in the evenings after my wife had gone to bed for the night and my attempts to create articulate postings on the fly improved my writing skills immensely. For better or worse I have preserved every blog I posted, along with every error in spelling and grammar. Unfortunately, some of the photographs that once adorned these posts disappeared over time as html links were broken. Other photos were censored by Photobucket (such as my posting of the infamous Danish Mohammed cartoons) and still others evaporated after apparently offending somebody with enough clout to delete them (or have others delete them) from my Blogspot or Photobucket accounts. For the life of me, I do not understand the logic behind these deletions—such is the world in which we now live.

I have taken the time and effort to preserve my ***Bird of Paradise*** blog postings for the same reason that people create photo albums: To preserve a memory of the past and create a historical record of who we once were and the way things used to be. The entire blog is, of course, still available on-line at www.tbirdofparadise.blogspot.com.

I do not expect anyone to ever read these three volumes of blog postings, but I would be pleased if someone did. If you happen to be that brave person, I hereby welcome you to ***Bird of Paradise*** and invite you to enter the world of my thoughts, such as they were from 2004-2007.

James A. Tweedie
Long Beach, Washington
December 2017

BIRD OF PARADISE

WHEN I HAVE THOUGHTS ON MATTERS OF FAITH, NEWS, PERSONAL ENCOUNTERS, OR...SIMPLY THOUGHTS BY THEMSELVES, I WRITE THEM DOWN AND GET THEM OFF OF MY CHEST AND ONTO SOMEONE ELSE'S

About me

Gender	MALE
Industry	Religion
Occupation	Pastor
Location	Hawaii, United States
Introduction	I'm a Christian Pastor in Hawaii. Married with three daughters who are either in high school (1) or college (2). I do not know how to surf except on the internet. Like most Christians I am an optimist and have a sense of humor. My wife is wonderful.
Interests	philospphy, religion, Jesus, Christianity, science, music, literature, sports, world events
Favorite Movies	Lawrence of Arabia, Gandhi, Patton, Star Wars (episodes 4 & 5...the first two), LOTR, most of Monty Python and the Holy Grail, Princess Bride, most of Mel Brooks, Secondhand Lions, most of the "classics" such as W of Oz, Casablanca, etc.
Favorite Music	Anything by J.S. Bach, most other pre-20th century renaissance/baroque/classical composers, Manhattan Transfer, Beatles, and favorite selections from many other groups, including rock, jazz, country, big band...any music that is good!
Favorite Books	The Bible, Lord of the Rings, anything by CS Lewis, all four of the Hitchiker's Guide to the Universe trilogy, and most, but not all, of what are considered to be, "classic" works of literature, I have discovered that they are, considered "classics" because they are really, truly good, (except for Jane Austin who's humor escapes me entirely)

BIRD OF PARADISE

Part 1

THE BEGINNING

November 20, 2004-September 11, 2005

SATURDAY, NOVEMBER 20, 2004

Hello World

Blogspot was kind enough to offer a blogsite when I wasn't looking for one! So here I am, led by the nose to a new adventure unsought for. Much of life is like that, I think. Life is sort of like reading a book. Each day you turn a new page, not knowing exactly what to expect. When the day is done and the page has been read the mystery of tomorrow and the following "page" remain, filling us with either hope or foreboding with what may next appear.

Much of what we read we have predetermined by our choices and actions. At the least, what we have chosen and done today will limit the parameters in which our life will unfold tomorrow.

The adventure of my life, as that of history and world events on the larger stage, is always one of mystery, wonder and anticipation of what may happen next. Insofar as it is within my power to shape tomorrow I am free to do so in whatever manner I shall choose, either for good or ill (what may be "good" or "ill," of course, will depend on any one's personal point of reference).

My chosen point of reference is that of Jesus Christ. It is from the perspective of his teachings and example I choose to discern right and wrong, good and evil. The distinction (in a sinful world) is not always as clear as I would like. Even so, God has promised that by his Spirit he will lead me, more often than not, towards that which is right and good in God's eyes--If I am genuine in my desire to "be conformed to the image of God's Son."

Being a Christian does not mean that I know what will appear on the next page of my life's story. But it does mean that I have been given a peek at how the story will end in the end. And, yes, my story will have a happy ending (at least from God's point of view) because of Jesus. His teachings and promises have been affirmed and confirmed by the historic events of his life, death, resurrection and ascension. My story may end suddenly tomorrow or it may wander through existential terrors like a novel by Dostoevsky. It may also be filled with pain and suffering, ecstasy and joy or all of these mixed together. So shall it be. I will be content with what shall come.

Yet through it all I will be an optimist. Because I know that there will be a victory in the end....and the life of love, forgiveness, mercy, justice, righteousness and hope that I have chosen will triumph...because they are of God...who is the beginning and the end of my present story...and the never-beginning, never-ending God of eternity in my upcoming sequel.

Nice to meet you all. In the words of most bloggers I have read..."more later.."

God and American Democracy

Note: This post was originally written as a response to the argument that American democracy was largely founded on classical models such as Athens.

I was disappointed that no one followed up on PresbyPoet's comments posted earlier today at The Belmont Club. His point is important. Until John Calvin, there had been little or no Biblical/theological rationale for overthrowing an "ordained by God" monarch. If, as the Medieval Church had held (and the Bible supported--see Romans 13), a monarch's authority was given by God, then any opposition to a king/queen was identical to opposition to God.

Calvin, however, showed that a "magistrate" (here read "monarch" or "any political leader") was granted authority by God solely for the purpose of protecting his/her people from injustice and oppression. Calvin speculated that, should the magistrate violate his covenant with God and become a vehicle for injustice and oppression, then the people, calling on God's mercy, had the "right" to remove or overthrow the one whose misuse of authority had proven their personal rejection of God's favor.

As PresbyPoet pointed out, this theological approach was put to practical use by Calvin's student, John Knox of Scotland. Knox confronted the "authority" of Mary, Queen of Scots and, in the end, prevailed against her. Her son, James the VI of Scotland was raised as a reformed protestant and carried this faith with him when he united the kingdoms of England and Scotland, becoming King James I of England. Scotland, meanwhile, had established a form of representative democracy overseen by representative Lairds on the civil side and church ministers and elders on the spiritual side (aka the Church of Scotland).

James I carried the Calvinist fervor into England. He was the one who commissioned the translation of the Bible into a uniform, scholarly, literate and contemporary form. In many ways, he reflected a certain attitude of humility and service as befitted his Calvinist upbringing.

His son and successor Charles I, however, regressed into magisterial despotism. His pandering to selected royals was divisive and utterly rejected by the growing number of "puritans" among the English population. (Puritans were "Anglicans" who desired that the faith be kept "pure" from the corruptions emerging from a national church under the authority of a self-centered monarch.) A national revolt was begun (justified by the rationale proposed by Calvin) headed by Oliver Cromwell and his Roundhead army.

In the end, London was successfully besieged, Charles I arrested, tried and subsequently beheaded. Cromwell set up a "commonwealth" government loosely based on Calvinist principals. At his command, Calvinist and other selected religious representatives from England were called to a convocation in Westminster Hall (referred to as the Westminster Assembly of "Divines") and ordered to create a comprehensive Confession of Faith and Catechism that would unite the people of England around one standard set of beliefs. Among other things, this Assembly produced the Westminster Confession of Faith and the Larger and Shorter Catechisms. These documents became the standing interpretation of Scriptural doctrine for faith and life among Reformed Protestants throughout Europe and the emerging New World.

Cromwell, of course, fell into his own form of despotism and, following his death and the short rule of his son and successor, the public demanded the return of the monarchy. This was accomplished with the coronation of Charles II.

What this has to do with today's topic is this: A hundred years or so later, as American colonists sought a way to separate themselves from the often reactionary governance of the English monarchy, they did not have to look very far to find their justification. It did not hurt that the largest "religious group" represented by delegates in Philadelphia in 1776 were Calvinist Presbyterians (including the only minister to sign the resulting Declaration of Independence, Rev. Dr. John Witherspoon, then President of Princeton College in New Jersey, founded as a school for educating Presbyterian pastors and later to become Princeton University.)

(Note that in colonial times the term "religion" was commonly used in the sense that we now use the word "denominations." What we would call world "religions" today were not generally granted the privilege of that term. Other faiths were "pagan." Christianity was the one true "religion." Keep this in mind as you read the first amendment and its reference to the "establishment of religion"--a clear assertion that the "United States" would not endorse one form of Christianity over another...something that had caused so much death and destruction and destabilization in Europe for the previous two centuries).

Jefferson, who was commissioned to write the first draft of the "Declaration of Independence," made explicit use of the "Calvinist loophole" for overthrowing the rule of a magistrate. This does not mean for a moment, of course, that Thomas Jefferson believed in any form of Calvinism personally. In fact, I'm sure he didn't. He was, in a uniquely "American" sense, a product of the European "enlightenment." Nonetheless, Jefferson found this approach to be the most useful way to justify the colonial cause, give it a theological foundation (which was historically familiar to the English and credible among the deeply religious colonists) and unifying for the colonial delegations in Philadelphia who were seeking some form of consensus for independence.

It is not coincidental that the ensuing American Revolution was, on several occasions, described in the English Parliament as "that Presbyterian revolt."

Whereas the Declaration of Independence was explicitly religious/theological in tone the subsequent U.S. Constitution was deliberately secular in language (although philosophically based far more on ideas derived from Calvinism than from Enlightenment philosophy as can be determined from the arguments--which largely prevailed--so eloquently expressed in the "Federalist Papers.")

Although the "founding fathers" were well versed in classical philosophy and literature, I do not believe that their political philosophies were greatly shaped by them. The influence of the Protestant Reformation in general, recent European history, Calvinism and the Bible in particular, provided the primary theoretical foundations for both the Declaration and the Constitution (any reading of the original transcripts of proceedings will bear this out).

It is also not coincidental that the Presbyterian Church wrote its first Constitution as a national body meeting in General Assembly in Philadelphia in 1789--concurrently with the creation and adoption of the U.S. Constitution in the same location in the same year.

My argument is thus: The peculiar form of a democratic republic which was established in the United States of America is primarily founded on Christian civil/theological premises originating from John Calvin (who was an excellent classicist himself, personally writing his great "Institutes of the Christian Religion" in both French and Latin). If one is ignorant of the facts I have presented then one will most certainly be forced to grasp at Iroquois or Greek precedents to explain the origins of the Declaration of Independence and the U.S. Constitution. Knowing what they knew, the "founding fathers" had no need to reach that far. Nor did they.

MONDAY, NOVEMBER 22, 2004

Conversation With Soldier Home From Iraq

I am not a soldier. Nor have I ever been one. But the work I do has led me into personal friendships with many of them. Currently I know 12 men and women deployed in Iraq or

Afghanistan, one who has just returned and two who have been "adopted" by my local church because they did not have any "home support" from family or friends.

Today I had coffee at Starbucks with a man home for two weeks on R & R from Mosul. We have emailed back and forth during these first 10 months of deployment. He has seen the worst of it over there. As a volunteer on the "rescue" team he was sent out to secure and recover damaged military vehicles and soldiers killed or injured by roadside bombs, ambushes and suicide car bombers. One victim was his base chaplain who later died of his injuries in Germany. At least one person from every unit in his base has died in Iraq except for his own unit. The tension is high as they realize that the odds are against their keeping a 100% casualty-clean record before they return home for good at the end of January.

At the front gate to the base, where he meets the local Iraqis employed by his unit he has watched as a woman driving a truck blew herself and two Iraqi bystanders to bits in a suicide explosion. One day, while standing guard duty 6 months ago, he counted 15 rpgs (rocket-propelled grenades) sail over his head directed at the base.

More recently he has stopped volunteering to collect the dead and wounded and has begun the difficult transition to begin thinking about the end of his deployment and a return to some measure of normalcy with his wife and two children, one of whom was not yet walking when he left for Iraq.

He tells me that at first he "hated" all Iraqis even though his Christian faith told him otherwise. As he has come to know many Iraqis personally both at work and in various community settings he has learned to appreciate the fact that most Iraqis are not hateful or violent and, in a confused sort of way, appreciative and supportive of not only the American troops but of President Bush in particular. Although he has seen much improvement in security over the past 10 months he is not convinced that the "jihadis" will disappear any time soon and that the desire to die in jihad, with its promise of guaranteed and instant entrance to paradise will continue to attract eager new volunteers almost as fast at others are killed or captured.

Although he did not support the political decision to enter Iraq in the first place he is both a good patriot and a good soldier. He knows that 9 to 11 months after his return he will likely be deployed back to Iraq for another tour of duty. If he had any say in the matter he would eagerly choose not to return. But he will fulfill his commitment and, I have no doubt, fulfill it well.

This will be the third time he has headed off to Iraq (due to a family crisis this has been his second "R & R" visit). Each time I have spoken and prayed with him and each time I have wondered whether he will come home alive or in one piece. I know his wife and children very well and I am amazed at her ability to cope with this reality. Our nation is indeed blessed by wonderful men and women giving all they have in service to our country. Their husbands, wives, children, parents, brothers, sisters, lovers and friends also share in this sacrifice and, remarkably, have also demonstrated an almost heroic ability to bear the stress with courage and with grace.

Every one of the deployed soldiers I know is a committed follower of Jesus Christ as their Lord and Savior. I have no doubt that this faith enables each of them to see this particular conflict in the larger context of history where God has already won the victory over evil, sin and death. To a one they are, as every Christian should be, optimists, seeking to keep their eyes open for the good they may do and giving thanks for any sign of good they might spot in the emerging nation struggling to "breathe free" as a democracy.

These soldiers carry a deep and profound sense of decency and high standards of personal moral integrity. I know through my correspondence with them that they struggle often with the Christian obligation to "love your enemies and pray for those who persecute you." Like myself and so many other Americans, they want only the highest and the best for the people of Iraq. Along with them we should pray daily that the Iraqi people will also desire this same ideal for themselves....and find the courage and determination to seize it while the window of opportunity is open.

Just before we left Starbucks my friend on leave from Mosul said something that caught me off guard. He said that he and his buddies had been watching the movie, "Band of Brothers." After comparing what they were experiencing in Iraq with what the survivors featured in the movie had experienced he said...well...he said that it made him feel like a wimp.

I must say that I was more than humbled by this man today. I count it a great privilege to count him as a friend.

Thanksgiving

This year there were 34 people at our home for Thanksgiving dinner. Since we are too far away to spend the holiday with our own family in California we invite members of our church family to share the day together with us. Every generation was present and accounted for from seniors to babies. Between the rain showers the children blew bubbles, drew chalk pictures on our driveway and set up a beauty salon on the front porch. Most of the adults were too stuffed to move out of the house so card games kept everyone busy and laughing. JJ proved to be an addict for UNO. She kept Ryan busy in the back room long after the others had quit and gone home.

Only a small amount of meat was left from our 21 pound turkey. I finished it off today for lunch along with stuffing and cranberry sauce.

I can't say that I really like being in the middle of a crowd of people, but having an empty house would be far less appealing for a holiday such as Thanksgiving. On the other hand having to walk sideways to squeeze across from one room to another has become almost a sacred ritual as it stirs up so many memories of crowded family holiday gatherings in years past.

As I told several of our friends, I'm glad they all came. And I'll be glad when they have all gone back to their own homes, too. They all understood what I meant by that. Now the house is quiet. I have talked to middle daughter *en route* back to Seattle Pacific University after spending the holiday with my mother, brother (& wife), sister (& husband), aunt, uncle, nephews, two niece-in-laws, one grandniece and one grand nephew. My daughter enjoyed getting to hold little Lizzie for the first time, something the rest of her Hawaii family hasn't been able to do yet.

Sunday is tomorrow and Advent begins. Christmas is on the way. In the evening our church will decorate the Worship Center together as we sing carols and "get into the Christmas spirit." I don't know if God really cares all that much about our celebration of Christmas each year. But I am convinced that it is good for us to remember the One who came to live and die and live again for us. We must not forget. The world would like to keep Christmas and get rid of Jesus in the same way that they are expunging him from American and world history. By themselves the glitz and glitter and even the Thanksgiving turkey are shallow and empty; each in their own way becoming an empty carcass by the time the season has past.

With Jesus the joy of the season never passes away. He is here. He is yesterday, today and forever. He is family and friends and celebration that never ends. Apart from him there would be no thanks at all. Except, perhaps, for my wife, Jeanine, who took on a difficult challenge and, as always, made it look easy.

SATURDAY, NOVEMBER 27, 2004

Jeff Hall

I first met Jeff when I arrived in Hawaii in 1993. He was then our church custodian and groundskeeper. Until he was replaced by a custodial service in 1998 Jeff was a friend as well as an employee.

Jeff taught me everything I know about surfing.....as a spectator! When the surf was up and pounding on the North Shore I would call out to Jeff, "Want to drive up and see what's going on?" and Jeff would say, "Sure." We'd watch the 15 footers rolling into Haleiwa or the 20 footers sweeping into Waimea Bay and I would have a "small wave" expert explaining every move and maneuver.

Jeff didn't like to surf in anything much larger than 7 feet. He enjoyed hanging in the line, taking his turn simply for the sheer joy of the thing.

At Waikiki he made some money giving surfing lessons to tourists using some old boards he had collected. I'm sure that Jeff became one those special, personal memories taken back home from the islands by every one who met him. His weathered face and smile undoubtedly still stare out from the pages of many a dusty photo album commemorating a treasured Hawaii vacation.

Jeff was born in Korea but raised by an American couple who adopted him and another Korean boy. The couple added a few of their own children to the mix so there was a definite sense of being a part of a family.

Jeff took up dance and eventually joined a professional dance company that performed at the "Festival of the American West" in Logan, Utah, when I was living there in the early 1980's. The last time I saw Jeff he was once again back on stage at Leeward Community College dancing the role of the Mouse King in the Nutcracker.

On Friday, November 12, Jeff called a taxi to take him to Queen's Hospital where he was admitted. He passed away the following Sunday morning. I am not clear on what he suffered from although his brother has indicated that it might have been colon cancer. The hospital contacted me after his death since the only personal "contact" they could find was in an old medical file that listed the church as a former employer. It took over a week before his brother finally heard the news and came forward as a relative to claim the body.

A brief memorial service will be held on Wednesday, Thursday or Friday morning of next week. His other brother and sister will be flying out from California. His "beachboy" friends have offered to carry his ashes out to the Waikiki reef where they will be scattered. Jeff, I think, would be pleased, but maybe just a little bit embarassed by all the attention.

All Praise To God Who Strengthens and Sustains Me

As part of a women's gathering at her church in Daly City, California, my sister, along with the other women, wrote a two line Psalm modeled after the opening two lines of the great hymn, "How Great Thou Art." My sister wrote, "All praise to God, who strengthens and sustains me, To Thee I pray, and thank Thee for thy love." When I read this in her church newsletter I liked it and felt it needed to be added to somewhat. What follows is the "rest" of the poem (which can be sung to "How Great Thou Art" if you really feel like it).

"All Praise to God, Who Strengthens and Sustains Me"

To be sung to the tune of "How Great Thou Art

1. All praise to God, who strengthens and sustains me;
To you I pray, and thank you for your love.
When shadows fall and stress and worry pains me
Your Spirit comes with healing from above.
You are my Rock, my Fortress and my Might;
Where you abide no shadows fall.
You are my Friend, my Savior and my Light;
You are my Lord, my Life, my All.

2. When I consider all that you created;
The sun and moon and stars high in the sky.
All things reflect your greatness unabated;
I see it all, and wonder, "Who am I?"
And yet of all the creatures of the earth
You've chosen me to be your own.
You formed me, knew me, long before my birth;
I am not mine, but yours alone.

3. One day my life will fade beyond a whisper
And then my spirit will return to you.
That day I'll be more than a brother, sister;
I'll be your own, for I'll be born anew.
Because you died and rose so I might live
I'll walk that shadowed vale no more.
As you have given, so I, too, shall give
All praise to you forevermore.

SUNDAY, NOVEMBER 28, 2004

Best Part of the Wedding

I attended a wedding this afternoon for a friend. Along with most of the other men I wore a nice "aloha" shirt. Standing in line to sign the guest book a women said to me, "I really like your shirt." The man in front of me turned, thinking she was speaking to him. Seeing this the woman said to him, "You're wearing a nice shirt, too." Then she decided to lift her foot up and place it in her mouth up to her ankle. "It's an old shirt, isn't it? I just love old shirts. They don't make them like that anymore. They're so 'retro!' My son found one just like yours at a thrift shop. He brought it home and used it to cover a chair." While I tried to keep from laughing out loud the man graciously replied with a smile, "I guess it's an old shirt for an old guy." Mercifully, the woman bit down hard, kept her mouth shut and kept any further thoughts to herself.

The marriage ceremony which followed, while nice, had to settle for being my second favorite part of the wedding.

Hanging of the Greens

This evening of the first Sunday in Advent is always one of my favorite times. The church, in the space of thirty minutes, decorates the entire Worship Center for the Christmas season. Everyone attending helps to put up banners, bows, garlands, wreaths, lights, artificial poinsettas, tree ornaments and a nativity scene on the communion table while singing Christmas carols and listening to special music from the choir. At the end we turn off all the lights and sing Silent Night. After that we eat the brownies, cookies and other goodies out on the church lanai.

Tonight, possibly due to the heavy rain, only one child from our preschool showed up to sing their special song. So....all the preschool teachers came up and sang the children's song with her so she could sing along, too! The teachers sang and did the hand motions very well. The little girl did what preschool children always do when they "perform:" She smiled and waved at her parents the entire time. It was perfect!

The church children decorated the tree, of course. For the 1-year olds it was their first Christmas. They toddled about during the whole service, touching and exploring everything they could reach. The wonder in their eyes and the tipsy wobbling of their uncertain footsteps captured the essence of the Christmas story for me. They reminded me that Jesus came into the world as a baby just like them and, as he grew, the Savior of the world toddled along with the other children, wide-eyed with wonder at the world he had once created.

It's funny how we all change as we grow older. When I was younger, if a baby cried during worship I'd go nuts. The noise would distract me from the business of worship and I'd be bothered by it all. Now, however, ever since I have had children of my own (and the youngest is now half-way through her teenage years) I am no longer bothered by the cry of a baby. I cannot even imagine how boring worship would be without them. How dull are the churches that have no children or babies in worship! If the Good News of the Gospel of Jesus Christ has anything at all to do with life, then it must have a great deal to do with babies. Surely, they are more closely formed in the image of their Creator than we are as adults!

Even so, I am glad when a parent eventually takes their complaining child outside and gives them a less public place to finish their crying. Jesus said, "Let the children come to me." He didn't say they could stay all day!

TUESDAY, NOVEMBER 30, 2004

Killing Babies In the Netherlands

Some years ago doctors in the Netherlands began killing terminally ill elderly patients (some with, some without, their consent) even though it was against the law. They were never prosecuted. Instead, the law was changed to make what they had been doing legal.

Now, doctors in the Netherlands are killing newborn babies...Not a lot of them...Only a few...So they tell us...And of course we believe them. As history repeats itself we find that killing babies is against the law in the Netherlands. But, once again, rather than prosecuting the doctors the parliament is debating whether to make this "procedure" legal as well.

The doctors have recommended a process of selection they call "the Groningen Protocol." This would involve a "committee" that would be given the authority to give a "thumbs up" or a "thumbs down" on whether a baby with a terminal or painful condition should live or die. This "protocol" would also extend to any person, child or adult, who is unable to make such a decision for him/herself...such as elderly with dementia, those in comas, uncommunicative persons on life-support, etc.

This reminds me of the jury in California that today began deliberation of whether convicted murderer Scott Peterson should receive the death penalty or not. The difference is that in the Netherlands you don't have to be guilty of anything except the natural effects of age, illness or disability to be put on "trial" for your life by a jury of your peers. It is ironic that the Netherlands takes pride in their high moral position of not allowing the death penalty in criminal cases.

It appears that, in the Netherlands, you can ritually slaughter a movie maker on the street because he has offended your religious sensibilities and not worry about receiving a death sentence. The government will protect your "right to life."

But woe to you who have committed no crime at all except to face a terminal illness with a muddled mind. It appears that, under such circumstances, you have offended society to such a degree that you have been deemed to have forfeited that right. How dare you keep on living! Like Jesus and Barabbas, the innocent dies and the guilty goes free.

If this is what post-Christian European morality leads us to then I think we should think long and hard before we allow this type of thinking to become socially "acceptable and respectable " in America. The "slippery slope" arguement has now been proven true over and over again. Each one of us should challenge, confront and refute this idea whenever and wherever we hear it being suggested or presented in a positive manner.

The one positive note in all this is that some in the Netherlands, apparently, still have enough of a moral compass to have gathered in mass protest against their goverment's consideration of this new policy. Perhaps some of them are old enough to remember when Hitler instituted his own "protocol" for determining who was worth keeping alive and who wasn't.

No true follower of Jesus would ever support the legitimization of anyone determining whether another person, soley for reasons of the status of their health, should live or die. When we submit the value of human life to a tribunal's interpretation of a "protocol" then we have taken the final step in abandoning our God-given, unalienable right to life, liberty and the pursuit of happiness.

The Dutch are feasting on "forbidden fruit" and, to their surprise, will wonder why the Garden of Eden has moved so far away. They will probably not even realize that the cherubim with the flaming swords are God's judgment upon their rejection of the very rights and freedoms their deluded minds and corrupted consciences sincerely believe they are defending.

Jewish/Christian tradition claims that Adam and Eve wept as they were cast out of the garden. There will be no hope for the Netherlands until there is a national weeping, mourning and repentence for what they have done. Until then, we will have to do their weeping for them.

WEDNESDAY, DECEMBER 01, 2004

Rats In the Belfry?

Today Colleen, one of our church preschool teachers, asked me if I had put out any rat poison lately. When I said, "Yes," she told me a story of remarkable personal courage.

Yesterday afternoon, while looking out on the decking of the lanai behind her classroom, she saw a large rat, a foot long from nose to tail, sitting and drinking from some standing rainwater. Sensing that there was something not quite right with the rat she grabbed a large glass jar, walked quietly up behind the rat and scooped it into the jar...all but the tail that still stuck out, wriggling against her arm. Once in the jar the rat became more active, thrashing about and giving her chicken skin all over (that's "goose bumps" for you mainland types). After shoving in the tail and securing the lid she rushed across the school to the church office where she gave it over to Roger for disposal.

She says she had trouble sleeping last night because any thought of that rat gave her the creeps. She also added that, since yesterday, she has been washing her hands far more often than usual.

I'm not sure, but I sincerely doubt that "rat catcher" is in Colleen's job description. In any case I am proud of her. She told me she did it only because of the children. She did not want that rat to get away. It appears that "courage" does indeed "rise with danger." In her own small way she acted selflessly and heroically. If it had been "Fear Factor" she would have won the day.

THURSDAY, DECEMBER 02, 2004

A Solution to the UN's Problems

While the United Nations continues to "rope-a-dope" the largest financial scandal in world history I have not only been doing some creative thinking but have hit upon a brilliant solution.

I propose that the United Nations headquarters be moved from New York City to Yamoussoukro. "Huh?" you may ask. "What the heck is a Yamoussoukro?"
Although it sounds like the name of an Iraqi automobile (as in "I just love driving through Fallujah in my Yamoussoukro") it is, in fact, the capital city of that tropical paradise known as Cote d'Ivoire or, for those water-drinking, bath-taking Americans, the Ivory Coast.

The genius of my idea goes like this:

1. The Ivory Coast used to be a colony of France and, in independence, continues to enjoy the many positive political, religious and cultural values it inherited from the mother country which gave it birth

2. They speak the French language there which means it is a very cultured place. (French is, of course, one of the official languages of the United Nations. This, by itself, should be enough to commend this lush and verdant land as a logical place for the representative leaders of the

nations of the world to gather for their deliberations on how to spread peace and happiness to all people everywhere.

3. It has offshore oil reserves (useful for trading for food, etc.)

4. It is far, far away from everywhere.

This last point is the most important since it appears to me that the biggest problem facing the United Nations is having its headquarters in New York City. New York simply has too many tempting restaurants, showplaces and activities to distract and dazzle the otherwise sober and serious work of international diplomacy for which the UN is renowned.

Even more of a concern is that New York is such a good place to enjoy diplomatic privileges (such as legal "immunity") that the best representatives of world nations get shoved aside by aggressive, self-centered prigs who consider that being a national delegate to the United Nations in New York City would be a real "plum" job. Even more tempting, such a job provides a wonderful, all-expenses paid opportunity for most of them to leave their corrupt, violent, scandal-ridden, backward and bankrupt countries behind and bask, instead, in a life of opulent luxury covered by extravagant expense accounts.

In New York City even the delegates from the poorest countries get the chance to pretend that they are equal to the "big boys." In General Assembly their vote counts as much as everyone else's and, when their turn comes to rotate through the Security Council they can hold the rich countries hostage and blackmail them (diplomatically, of course) for their kind words, support and votes.

The New York media loves to publish every squeak and squeal uttered by these diplomats, especially if they contain some condemnation of either Israel or the United States. This also makes the delegates from the smaller countries feel important and, of course, further distracts them from the always urgent demands of negotiating peace with everyone engaged in domestic or international conflict.

If the UN Headquarters were moved to Yamoussoukro, however, none of the self-centered prigs would want to go, leaving the delegate positions vacant to be filled with career diplomats who might possibly have ideas for peace that might actually work.

Every squeak and squeal would be quoted in the local Yamoussoukro news media and would be read by hardly anyone anywhere because the news would be printed or aired in French.

And, best of all, foreign diplomats will be spared the hypocrisy of enjoying the benefits of living in America while, at the same time, constantly condemning it as a vile, hate-mongering, imperialist and morally-challenged Great Satan.

From Yamoussoukro they can be free to express their contempt for the United States without having to deal with the burden of guilt that they must have felt when they were enjoying living here so much.

Finally, the warm feelings of the Cote d'Ivoirians toward France would help France overcome its feelings of low self-esteem in the world. Video of French tanks, armored troop carriers and snipers slaughtering unarmed groups of local citizens will also persuade even the most skeptical nations of France's unequaled ability to negotiate, implement, maintain and preserve peace throughout the world.

My guess is that if the UN Headquarters were moved to Yamoussoukro no one would even bother to show up for meetings, the UN would shrivel up and die, and the aggressive, self-centered prigs of the world of nations would dream up a new organization to assure world peace. After much deliberation they would, I suspect, reluctantly agree to have it headquartered in New York City.

FRIDAY, DECEMBER 03, 2004

Burial at Sea Off Waikiki

Jeff Hall, who I wrote about several days ago, was buried today off of Waikiki Beach. The "beachboys" (yes, there really are beachboys) paddled his ashes out to the reef in their catamaran at 6:30 am just as the sun was rising over Diamond Head. The surf was unexpectedly high today, unusual for this time of year when the North Shore gets the big waves and the South Shore is almost flat. Jeff's local brother set the whole thing up with Jeff's Waikiki friends. Another brother and a niece came all the way from California to be here today.

Everyone was friendly but I was clearly the only tall, white, non-pidgin speaking haole in attendence. Even so, being a minister (or kahu), as well as being a friend and former employer of Jeff, generated toleration, if not respect, for my being there. After we had pulled the catamaran up on the beach we all gathered around Jeff's brother. He introduced me, I said a few words about Jeff and offered a short prayer. Then a letter, written for the occasion by Jeff's mother was read.

Afterwards we talked story and shared pupus on the beach. One woman who had known Jeff worked at a photography place on the beach. She did not have a lot of money and had recently had a baby girl. Jeff had often stopped by the shop and given her a package of diapers. "He was always doing nice things like that," she said.One by one folks left to go to work or to do whatever else they had to do.

I was unable to get my valet parking ticket validated at the Sheraton Moana so, instead I had a cup of "for guests only" coffee and went to pick my car.

The valet guys didn't look too happy when I gave them an unvalidated ticket so I explained that I was there for a beach funeral and couldn't find anyone to validate it. They sort of shook their heads, said "Merry Christmas" and only charged me $5. I gave them $10 instead and said, "Thanks, and Merry Christmas to you, too."

The unseasonal waves seemed to strike everyone as a sign that nature was smiling on Jeff today. I suppose it is a good thing to go out when the surf is up!

SUNDAY, DECEMBER 05, 2004

Hawaii Football Wow!

Last night my oldest daughter took me to the University of Hawaii 6-5) vs. Michigan State (5-6) football game. The tickets were a promised gift from my birthday back in May. I was allowed to choose the game and I chose what I thought would be the best matchup of the year in Aloha Stadium this year. I made a good choice. After blow-out losses to Boise State and Fresno, UH had to win its final three games to become eligible for the Christmas Day Hawaii Bowl. Last week they upset Big 10 Northwestern and now, the final game of the regular season was their last hope for a post-season game.

Although broadcast live on ESPN (not blacked out in Hawaii) the stadium was about as filled as it ever gets...even for the Pro Bowl each February. Lots of MSU fans were strolling about. You could easily spot them. They were the ones wearing tank tops, shorts and slippers...glad to be in a warm place and determined to enjoy it to the full. With heavy rain showers, strong wind and lower than usual temperatures the local Hawaii folks were clad in ponchos, jackets, long pants and shoes.

The predominant color for both schools is green so there was a pleasant uniformity to the stadium crowd. As we munched nachos and andagi my daughter commented on how unique college football is in Hawaii. What other football stadiums sell teryaki beef cooked over kiawe coals, ginger-marinated chicken, and, in the stands during the game, tako poke! (Not to mention the national side dishes of Hawaii, "two scoop rice & mac salad!")

As it turned out, UH made mac salad out of MSU for their second win over a Big 10 team in two weeks. The final score was UH 41 MSU 38. Michigan State led by 28-0 in the second quarter but Hawaii methodically came back to take a lead of 41-31 in the last part of the final quarter. MSU scored a desperation TD with 1:30 left but, after UH recovered the ensuing on-side kick and with MSU left with only one time-out the game was essentially over.

As we left the stadium to return home on the bus I turned to my daughter and said, "I sure like a good story. Especially one like this that has a happy ending!"

Having a daughter old enough (22) and wise enough to buy football tickets for her father and accompany him to the game was the best part of the whole deal. The game and the upset victory were simply icing on the cake! Go Bows! (oops! I mean...) Go *Warriors*!

MONDAY, DECEMBER 06, 2004

The Family Christmas Letter

Daisy Allsmall, our family dog, sat down and wrote this year's family Christmas letter. She has done this for the past four or five years. Before that our youngest child wrote the letter each year going back to our eldest daughter's birth year of 1982.

Both the dog and the daughters have had a ghost writer, of course, who, like the Wizard of Oz, is happy to shout, "Pay no attention to the man behind the curtain!"

In recent years the family letter has been written around this first week of December. For some unknown reason, however, the letter has not been mailed out until Christmas week or after. Time will tell if this year will be any different than any other.

Daisy the Beagle has done her part. I guess the rest is up to "the man behind the curtain!"

TUESDAY, DECEMBER 07, 2004

Buying the Tree

I picked up my youngest daughter from the High School and drove straight over to WalMart to buy our Christmas tree, just like we do each year.

Christmas trees are a big deal in Hawaii and the Season does not officially start until a Matson container ship arrives with the first shipment of trees from the mainland. This is usually the week after Thanksgiving.

For some reason many folks in Hawaii like to buy their tree from the first shipment. These trees, mostly from the Pacific Northwest, were probably cut in early to mid-November, shipped to Seattle, Portland or Oakland by train or by truck, loaded into containers and then loaded onto the ship and then spend 5 days sailing half-way across one of the seven seas to Hawaii. It is amazing that the needles are still on the trees when they arrive. But there they are, green and smelling like Christmas in the Cascades.

After sitting in a house for four weeks, these trees, having already dried out in shipping, begin dropping their needles like the raindrops in a tropical shower.

By the time they are hauled off to the dump or picked up by the Boy Scouts for recycling (they are used for fuel in a county-owned refuse fueled electric power plant) many have already turned into skeletons, like a New England maple in mid-winter.

Daughter #3 and I had to drive all the way to Waipahu for a tree this year since the WalMart lot was already closed and the Lutheran Church across the street wasn't selling them either this year.

In any case, we have the tree set up in the living room. Tomorrow I will string up the lights but we will not decorate it until Daughter #2 arrives on Thursday, home on Christmas break from her college in Seattle.

The outside lights went up last Saturday and our basket is starting to fill up with Christmas cards. For us the Season did not begin with the arrival of the trees. But it won't really arrive until Daughter #2 is home and we are all together as a family again... at least for a few weeks.

WEDNESDAY, DECEMBER 08, 2004

Martha Again

It seems that we can't get rid of Martha Stewart.

Apparently the producers of the "Survivor" TV show have met with representatives of Martha Stewart in hopes of turning her problems into a profit. Since Martha knows how to profit from almost anything this story would appear to have K-Mart sponsorship written all over it.

On the other hand, do we really want to watch a "real life" TV series to see which incarcerated criminal in San Quentin can go the longest without being raped, stabbed or caught with drugs? Would the winner get a free weekend pass for good behavior?

Or would the TV series involve ten people dropped deep into the Amazon Basin vying to see who can create the best "piranha party," tastiest "turtle souffle" or the cutest wedding invitations made from dried banana peels, colored with squashed aphids and trimmed out with lace carefully removed from someone's brassiere?"

If Martha is as smart as she seems she should drop this idea like a hot rock (which can, by the way, be useful for steaming shellfish right on the beach). Instead, she should release a new line of horizontally-striped black and white curtains, towels and bed linens. This touch of humor and irony would not only continue to endear her to frazzled women everywhere but would demonstrate that even everyday clothing can be recycled into practical, yet tasteful, interior decoration.

FRIDAY, DECEMBER 10, 2004

Whatever Happened To Afghanistan?

Charles Krauthammer had an article in today's **Washington Post** reminding us of the near miraculous change in the political landscape of Afghanistan during the past three years. The American media has seemingly lost interest in this corner of the world. Why?

Perhaps journalists are attracted to where the highest American casualties are taking place...Iraq. Perhaps the hotels in Baghdad are nicer than in Kabul.

Perhaps photographs of a peaceful and pacified Afghanistan, the voluntary surrender of disspirited Taliban mujahadin, the ongoing creation of a federal system of government with legislation controlling the regulation of trade, finance, education, elections, economics, etc. simply do not provide a photo-op dramatic enough to be featured in the daily paper or the evening network news broadcast.

After all, the creation of electrical grids, power plants, sewage treatment systems and communications networks are, from a news standpoint, boring, boring, boring.

So it was that I was not surprised when the inauguration of newly-elected President Karzai this week was buried in a small three paragraph side-bar on page three of the *Honolulu Advertiser*.

As I have watched these events unfold I have gotten the feeling that Afghanistan was not "conquered" by the United States, at least not in the usual sense of the world. It would, instead, appear that the expulsion of the Taliban has released Afghanistan from its historic isolation from the world and provided the local chieftains and warlords an alternative to the internal, warring, provincial feudalism of the past. For the first time, the people have been able to taste and smell and touch and see the first fruits of freedom: Hope for peace and a more prosperous tomorrow.

Ironically, the historic isolation and "emptiness" of Afghanistan which, in the past, provided a haven for those intent on imposing terror and tyranny, has now become the cause of their swift destruction. With modern methods of surveillance and intelligence gathering there is literally no place to hide. The lack of urban population centers, such as are found in Iraq, allow for little or no opportunity for foreign fighters or remnants of the Taliban to blend in with the local population.

Even so, there are many of the former Taliban and Al Qaeda leaders and fighters lying in wait across the borders in Iran and Pakistan, waiting for a chance to reclaim the power that was once theirs. Political realities prohibit American or other coalition troops from crossing those borders for reasons of search or pursuit. Given this reality I do not expect to see Osama bin Laden or his ilk capt ured and brought to justice any time soon. More likely, in the next few years there will be a betrayal leading to an assassination or a pinpoint missile attack. The cat often must stand still for a long time before snatching its prey. In this case, America's intensely focused patience will sooner or later bring Osama to his inevitable destruction.

This week one of our church elders who has spent the past eight months in Afghanistan has come home for a two-week R & R. On Tuesday he arrived and met his three-month old son for the first time. I hope to have coffee with him and with several others who will be returning for brief visits over the next few weeks. From them I will get a view from the ground as to what the reality of the new Afghanistan is like.

The only Afghani I have ever met (a cab driver in Walnut Creek, California) was glad that the United States had kicked out the Taliban. His mother, sisters and brothers in Kabul were glad, too, he said. When things settled down he hoped to return for a visit and, if possible, bring the rest of his family back to the United States to join him, his wife and two children. When pressed he wasn't sure that they would actually want to leave if things improved.

If this man is any indication of what other Afghanis are thinking and feeling these days I should expect the situation there to continue to improve, step by step, until, by God's grace, a new and peaceful way of life can become the norm throughout the country.

Good news from a distant, dry and dreary land does not sell newspapers or generate advertising sponsorship for the evening news. But it is still "good" regardless of whether we hear about it or not.

I am glad that I know some of the men and women who have made this "good" thing possible. And I am glad that writers like Charles Krauthammer continue to make the effort to remind us of it every so often.

SUNDAY, DECEMBER 12, 2004

Morning Worship

Today was the third Sunday in Advent and the theme was "Joy." The third Advent candle was lit. This candle is pink while the others are purple. There is a reason for this candle being pink but I can never remember what it is! Ah, tradition...!

CE Director Miss Kathryn let "Uncle Geoff" give the Children's Sermon today. He used the candy cane to tell the story of Christmas and Easter to the children. He did not make the common internet error of saying that this symbolism was completely intentional for which I was most pleased. He did show how the cane can represent the letter "J" for Jesus, can be a shepherd's crook or, in a pinch, be used to pull Pastor Jim from the pulpit when he tells a bad joke!

Our Children's Choir sang next, full of enthusiasm, singing like I have always wished our non-choir adults would sing (but don't...sigh). Isabella's artificial flower lei (worn by all choir members) was a bit too big for her and twice slipped off her shoulders, over her arms and all the way to the floor. Each time she put it back on by trying to pull it straight up her entire body. It caught on her dress and lifted it up. Of course she was totally oblivious to this and, with the innocence of childhood, never missed a note of the song. I was sitting behind the choir and started to laugh so hard I had to put my hand over my mouth to hold it in. I kept on thinking that the service theme was "Joy" and decided that a few uncontrolled smiles in worship was not necessarily a bad thing.

Next came the baptisms of three-month old Carrie and David. David's father had just arrived for a short R&R from deployment in Afghanistan and had just met his son for the first time last week. Carrie's father was preparing for his own 6-month deployment to Kuwait soon after Christmas. In any case, Cassie was very unhappy to be up in front but, miracle of miracles, when I took her from her Mom she stopped the "boo-hooing" immediately and started to stare at everybody in the church. More "Joy" and smiles from everyone. Usually the babies begin to cry when I take them from their parents for baptism! The baptisms went fine otherwise except that David got caught in my robe sleeve when I tried to hand him back to his mom. For a moment his head (and most of the rest of him) completley disappeared into the tangle. More smiles from everyone and, of course, more "Joy" than could have been generated by anything other than spontaneity.

Next, Charles, a retired minister, told how little he had earned when he served congregations in Missouri, Utah and Alaska. He was greatful for the extra $300 dollars he was now receiving each month as a pension supplement because of our denomination's Christmas Joy Offering and urged us all to give generously this year. As he sat down he added, "Speaking of joy, did you hear about the lady who only had two teeth? She gave thanks to God every day because they "hit!"

I was tempted to use "Uncle Geoff's" big white candy cane to haul Charles right out of the sanctuary! But the theme of "Joy" seemed to be contageous.

My sermon was brief, explaining that "Joy" is central to our faith but not unique to it. What is unique about Joy for a Christian is that we are the only major religion whose adherents are commanded to find Joy even in suffering (James 1:2). Our sense of Joy is grounded in God's victory over sin, suffering and death. Our own suffering and difficulties in life give us the opportunity to put our trust and reliance in Jesus to the test. The suffering itself isn't good, of course, but insofar as it reminds us that Jesus has already "been there, done that" for us, we can rejoice because we are "convinced that neither death nor life, neither angels nor demons, neither the present nor the future, nor any powers, neither height nor depth, nor anything else in all creation, will be able to separate us from the love of God that is in Christ Jesus our Lord." (Romans 8:38-39)

Later, as I helped lead the adult women's class, each person shared how they have experienced joy in their lives. The birth of children and the raising of children was the most common response. But stories of joy in the midst of miscarriages and other dark moments were also shared. As one of our new Elders put it, "The darker it is the brighter the light (of God's loving presence) seems to shine."

I couldn't have said it any better. So I'll leave it at that.

MONDAY, DECEMBER 13, 2004

More Joy

After yesterday's worship service with its focus on "Joy" I find that I can't seem to get it out of my mind. In Bible Study this morning there were even references to it in the book of Job. In Job 8:21 "Bildad the Shuhite" (sometimes referred to as the shortest man in the Bible...get it? "Shoe-height?") tells Job that if he acts righteously he will be rewarded by more blessing that he had ever had before. In this he would find "joy." In Job 9:25 Job replies that since his sufferings began joy has eluded him completely. It is not joy or prosperity that he desires but justice...some explanation of why this suffering has come upon him. Later, in 10:20 Job wishes that God, who he believes is the source of his suffering, would just leave him alone he might experience some measure of joy again before he dies.

We pondered this exchange for a while until it dawned on us that Job was not a Christian, but an Old Testament Jew living under the covenant law of Moses. The Law promised blessings in return for obedience and the witholding of blessings for violation of the covenant commands. In otherwords, as Irna pointed out, a *quid pro quo*. "You get what you deserve" is the way that Job understood his relationship with God.

According to the New Testament gospel of Jesus, however, the whole point of the Law was to teach us that we could never ever be obedient or good enough to "earn" God's blessings. According to Genesis 12:17 the "fruit" of disobedience is death. Since "all have sinned and fall short of the glory of God" (Romans 3:23) we all deserve to die, no matter how good we might try to be or think we are.

Jesus and the Christian faith answers Job in this way: Obeying the Law does not "earn" us the right to life, health or prosperity. Often, according to Jesus, being obedient to God will bring just the opposite...unjust persecution and suffering. Suffering comes with being human. It is the inevitible consequence of sin permeating the world. "Job," Jesus would say, "although bad behavior often has bad consequences, in your case you are not suffering because of anything you have done. The very fact that you are still alive should be evidence of God's mercy at work. Trust in God. He sends his rain on the just and the unjust equally (Matthew 5:45) and, remember those men who died when the scaffolding fell the other day while they were repairing the Jerusalem wall? (Luke 13:4) Were they greater sinners than any of the rest of you that they deserved to die? Was this man born blind because he had sinned? Or because his parents had sinned? (John 9:1-3) Of course not! God is a God who creates, not destroys; who heals, not inflicts disease; who makes the lame to walk, the blind to see and the dead to rise! A weak man can tear down a house. It takes a strong and patient man to rebuild it again from the rubble."

Only God can save us from sin and death. "By grace you have been saved through faith, and not by works, lest any one should boast." (Ephesians 2:8-9)

Job, of course, never got the clear answer from God that he demanded. Why did he deserve to suffer so badly? In Jesus we understand that we all deserve to suffer for our sin. But thank God we have been saved from our sin. And our Savior is Jesus. That is why we can have "Joy" in all circumstances...even in suffering.

Thinking about this again today has brightened me considerably. Not all the issues I have to deal with each day are happy ones. But my sense of joy remains full and undiminished. Because of Jesus. For me that is very good news. What about you?

TUESDAY, DECEMBER 14, 2004

Newsweek's "The Birth of Jesus": A Muddled Collage

In the December 13th issue, *Newsweek* Managing Editor Jon Meacham has written a cover story in which he ponders the origin and reliability of the Gospel narratives of Jesus' birth.

Others, such as Dr. Mark D. Roberts and Dr. Albert Mohler have already done a wonderful job of responding to the various assertions, opinions and insinuations presented in the article. I will not try to compete with their knowledge and scholarship. A large number of blogger responses to this article have been compiled by Hugh Hewitt (under the heading, "Vox Blogoli Vi") and are also worth reading.

All I wish to add to this conversation is to observe that Mr. Meacham has made the undergraduate level mistake of collecting various competing and contradictory opinions of unequal value and laying them alongside one another. Mr. Meacham then arrives at the only conclusion that can be reached from this methodology: That, because there is no consensus of opinion, and because one way of looking at the subject is as good as another, therefore the truth of the matter cannot be known with any confidence one way or the other. Further, Mr. Meacham speculates that the existence of many different opinions is evidence that the traditional understanding of the Birth of Jesus is most likely fabricated either in part or in its entirety.

The logic in all of this escapes me entirely. But I am not surprised. The purpose of the article is clearly not to inform but to exploit the season of Christmas to sell copies of *Newsweek*.

The image of a collage comes to mind. If a person wanted to present an image of what life in the United States is like they could collect many different magazines, cut out eye-catching pictures (from ads and articles) showing Americans at work or play, and pasting them all together on poster board.

The result would be a hodge-podge of images that may or may not have anything to tell us about what life in the United States is like. Further, the impact of the collage would be largely predetermined whatever bias the person brought to the project in the first place. The collage itself would give us no way to judge which pictures are actually representative of American life and which are commercial stereotypes. Nor would we know whether pictures of any one subjectg (such as violence, for example) are over-represented or under-represented.

The *Newsweek* article struck me as sort of like a collage made up of snippets of fact and fancy, fringe theology and orthodoxy, fact and conjecture all thrown together leaving an impression of uncertainty, controversy and confusion.

When the literary and historical evidence of Jesus' birth is laid bare, however, we find that there is a massive critical consensus as to what the Bible says, who said it, when it was said, and how it was received, believed and validated by contemporaries who could tell a fabrication from a fact and who could have easily discredited a fabrication had there been one.

Dr. Robert's list of 15 common elements in the birth narratives of Matthew and Luke (two independent sources) are not only convincing evidence for the historical reality of the "virgin birth" and other details surrounding Jesus' incarnation but also reveal an early consensus as to what these details, when added together, meant to the first century Christian Church.

In 2 Peter 3:16 we read how the earliest Christian writings were sometimes "hard to understand." It was easy then and it is easy today for "ignorant and unstable people" to "distort" the meaning of these scriptures.

The sad part of all this is the pretentiousness of magazines like *Newsweek* when they pretend to be presenting a reasoned and balanced view when they are not. In this case, the vast majority of Christians who read this article will just shake their heads and set it aside. Many, however, who do not know any better, will be deceived by the deception. It would appear that this is just one more example of the mainstream media being more interested in creating a "story" than they are in presenting the "facts."

The best antidote to all this is, of course, to take the time to read the New Testament in a good study Bible, check out all the Old Testament citations and ask yourself if it sounds like a fabrication or not. When read on its own terms, the Bible (including the narratives of Jesus' birth) holds up quite well, thank you very much!

WEDNESDAY, DECEMBER 15, 2004

High Surf, Waimea and Eddie Aikau

Photo courtesy Quiksilver
Kaua'i's Bruce Irons said he caught the biggest waves of his life in winning the Quiksilver In Memory of Eddie Aikau Big Wave Invitational.

Exceptionally large North Shore surf was expected at high tide this morning (6:30 am). Waves as high as 50 feet (25 feet Hawaii scale) were expected. At Waimea Bay the grandstand went up in anticipation of the Quiksilver Eddie Aikau Big Wave competition. This event is only held at Waimea when clean, steady surf of at least 20 feet (Hawaii scale) is expected. These conditions only appear about once every other year so it is a Big Deal here in Hawaii. All the greatest surfers in the world are already on island for the last three events of the world surfing tour (at the moment they are in the midst of the final event, the Pipeline Masters) and only the top 24 big wave surfers are invited to participate in the Eddie Aikau.

With my wife's help I woke up earlier than usual, threw together some snacks and a beverage in a backpack, grabbed my binoculars and drove to North Shore. I got half-way between Chun's Beach and Waimea before having to park on the side of the road. The traffic was virtually stopped dead in its tracks. Along with many others I walked the final mile and arrived at the the Waimea Bay overlook at 7:50 am. The morning competition was over by the time I arrived, the high surf had never gotten much above 25 feet and had dropped below that by the time I arrived. A second one-hour heat was scheduled for the afternoon.

The swells were still large enough to produce waves on the outer reef and thirty or more surfers and boogie boarders were swarming around hoping to catch a stray "big one." Funny to say, the largest wave I saw this morning was missed by every single surfer. One guy almost made it but when the wave broke past him several thousand spectators audibly groaned in unison.

Events like this are an "only in Hawaii" sort of thing...like a minor Woodstock Festival but with more spontaneity. Families with children, single women with dogs, North Shore counter-culture types with the fragrance of pakalolo, guys on bicycles, and even a few carrying surfboards all heading in the same direction with slippahs on their feet. People stuck in the traffic are patient and polite and, in spite of the lack of parking (by the time I left people were walking 2 miles to get to Waimea) private driveways, fire plugs and bus stops were respected. The spirit of Aloha is tangible at these events. The man next to me was trying to take pictures but a long shoot from a kiawe bush kept getting in his way. Another man, below us, saw this and bent the branch over and put his bag on it to hold it down.

After about 20 minutes or so I walked back to my car and headed back to the church to start the day. I had seen some interesting people, been part of a cultural event unique to Hawaii, saw one terrific wipe-out and got in two miles of walking exercise as a bonus.

For those of you who may not know who Eddie Aikau was, here is a brief bio: Eddie was a native Hawaiian Big Wave surfer and North Shore lifeguard (a Big Deal in Hawaii). He was also heavily involved in the renaissance of Hawaiian culture in the early 1970s. In 1978, while serving as crew on the Hokule'a (Hawaiian voyaging canoe), the ship capsized in inter-island waters. As the ship and crew floundered helplessly Eddie offered to paddle his board an estimated 12 miles to Lanai for help. After much discussion he was allowed to go. He was never seen again. Today a common bumper sticker reads simply, "Eddie would go!" His legacy continues to provide a good role model of a good man sacrificing himself for others. There is a monument to him at Waimea Bay and when the Big Wave contest is held there it bears his name as a tribute.

Update: Bruce Irons of Kauai won the 2004 Eddie Aikau Big Wave competition with 370 points out of a possible 400 (the four highest scoring rides are added up, each with a possible 100). Among his scores was a 99 and a perfect 100 (a 40 footer which he rode all the way to the beach and finished with a barrel ride in the dangerous shore break).

THURSDAY, DECEMBER 16, 2004

Christmas Eve Music

Last night I finished editing my Christmas Eve music for this year. Each year I compose a vocal piece which then illustrates my sermon message. Some years I have reached back and reused an old one but this year's will be original.

At last Tuesday's Worship Team meeting our Music Director asked if my music was ready and did I want her to sing it this year (as she did last year). I said, "Yes, I wrote it with you in mind." Now the song is made up of a short musical comment from Joseph to baby Jesus and then another from Mary. At the end the two melodies are sung together. I had planned on singing the Joseph part but, "Praise the Lord," Jen's husband will be home for Christmas on leave from his deployment in Afghanistan. I asked her if he might be willing to sing the Joseph part. She immediately replied, "Yes, of course he will! I'll make sure that he does!" All this enthusiasm for music she hasn't even seen yet. I felt complimented (which is not a common thing with musicians!).

In any case the music is now finished and printed out more or less legibly on my MusicTime

Deluxe computer program. Unlike some years, when I feel I have tried too hard to make my music too elaborate, this year's piece is short, simple and elegant...sort of like the Christmas story in the gospels of Matthew and Luke. I can't wait to hear Jen and Jaime sing it together. After all the miles and all the dangers of the past eight months of separation just having them stand up together in worship will be more sweet than the music itself.

FRIDAY, DECEMBER 17, 2004

Gifts

Today the church office staff gave me a $100 gift certificate good for any performance at the Neil Blaisdell Arena/Auditorium. They want Jeanine and I to enjoy a night out on their dime and with their blessing.

For me, gifts are just that: blessings.

Gifts are a way of saying, "You are important to me and I honor you with this gift and wish you well."

In the Bible Jacob could have blessed his brother Esau by giving him the bowl of soup as a gift. Instead he teasingly offered to sell it to him for his birthright. Esau "despised" that birthright by throwing it away for a mess of lentils.

That birthright was not a blessing for Jacob, either. It had not been gifted to him with any love, appreciation or respect. Neither brother was worthy of it but, through a legal technicality involving deceit, Jacob came out owning the prize and receiving a misdirected blessing from his father. For his trouble he had to flee his brother and family for his life. Some blessing!

The true blessing for Jacob came when, after 14 years, he returned home with two wives, children, servants and flocks of his own. Although he was convinced that his brother would seek revenge on him he was shocked when, instead of a blow to the head, Esau embraced him, forgave him and welcomed him back.

No amount of bribery, no amount of trickery, no amount of deception could have squeezed that forgiveness out of Esau. Nor could it have ever been earned, even with a lifetime of penance, repentance and restitution.

Esau's forgiveness could have only come as a gift of grace; unearned and undeserved. For Jacob, this was the first true blessing he had ever received. It humbled him and changed him completely. Ironically, it was not the blessing he had stolen from his father, Isaac, that unltimately bestowed honor upon him as a patriarch. Instead, it was the free gift of love extended by his brother that set him free to fulfill God's plan in his life.

Every Christmas gift that I give each year, whether to my family, friends or our church elders, deacons, Stephen Ministry team and staff, is intended as a blessing from me to them. With each gift I am saying, "You are important to me, I honor you with this gift and wish you well."

At Christmas we sometimes describe Jesus as God's gift of himself to us. Could it be that God is saying to us, "You are important to me and I honor you with this gift and wish you well?"

Like Jacob, burdened with a heavy load of guilt and sin; by any stretch of the imagination, "unworthy;" we, too, have received forgiveness and a welcome home from God.

No amount of bribery, no amount of trickery, no amount of deception could have squeezed that forgiveness out of God. Nor could it have ever been earned, even with a lifetime of penance, repentance and restitution.

It is a gift. A blessing. Just like Christmas.

SATURDAY, DECEMBER 18, 2004

A Beautiful Wedding: Reflections on Tolerance

This afternoon I officiated at the wedding of Anne and David. I have known Anne and her family for over 11 years. When her father passed away 8 years ago I sat with the family at the hospital for 14 hours and later officiated at his funeral. The entire family came to faith in Jesus Christ during the ministry of a former pastor of the church. Herb, Grace and their four children (including Anne) were all baptized on the same Sunday morning.

Anne and David chose to be married in front of the Byodo-In Temple in Valley of the Temples, Kaneohe. The temple is a beautiful exact replica of a historic and ancient Buddhist temple in Uji, Japan. It stands, surrounded by a carp-filled pond and lush trees and shrubs, against the backdrop of the sheer Pali cliffs.

I do not normally take pictures at the weddings I perform but today's was an exception. Both before and after the ceremony I snapped photos of the bride and groom, the temple and grounds.

For some reason I did not feel uncomfortable performing a Christian wedding on the grounds of a Buddhist temple. Buddha has long since passed from the earth but Jesus remains, risen and alive in all his ascended glory. All things are his by right and even the things commonly called "pagan" can be transformed into something holy when they are offered to him and used for a good and pleasing purpose. (see I Corinthians 8:4-6)

Out of courtesy to those of the Buddhist faith we showed proper respect for their beliefs and traditions as well as the precincts of the temple and grounds. One does not need to either worship or believe in something in order to show respect. It was God, the Father of our Lord Jesus Christ, risen and present by his Holy Spirit who was worshipped, praised and glorified today.

As followers of Jesus we must always respect the beliefs of others whether we are a majority or a minority of the population. Our faith is never to be imposed on others for God has given each of us the freedom to either love and serve him or to turn elsewhere for meaning and purpose in our lives. We are called to live in peace with all people and, if the Buddhists are kind enough to allow us to celebrate Christian marriage on their property. then we can and should be grateful to them for the tolerance and respect they have shown to us.

Certainly there are those whose beliefs and practices may be destructive of the God-given rights and freedoms of others. Such beliefs may serve to erode the social order that allows us to live in peace with one another. Such peace is to be highly valued and, ironically, is worth fighting for to preserve, even at the cost of limiting the freedoms of those who would weaken it.

This respect and toleration of others is a fundamental tenet of the Christian faith (which has not always been lived out very well when Christianity and "Christendom" have formed unholy historical alliances in the past.)

We are glad to share this same understanding of tolerance with our Jewish brothers and sisters as well as most Buddhists and Hindu. Islam, however, is more complex insofar as it affirms peace and tolerance when a minority but expects Islamic "law" to be enforced over everyone when becoming a majority of the population.

Some have said, "It doesn't matter what you believe. All faiths lead us in the same direction towards the same destination. Like different rivers flowing into the same ocean."

Nonsense! In most Muslim countries neither Buddhists nor Christians could have enjoyed today's events in the open, public way we did this afternoon.

The retired Buddhist Bishop who oversees the Byodo-In Temple and grounds spoke words of blessing on the wedding party as we processed passed where he was standing. I quietly offered a blessing for him in return. It was, after all, Jesus himself who said, "Those who are not against us are for us." Amen.

MONDAY, DECEMBER 20, 2004

A Military Funeral at Punchbowl

Today I officiated at the funeral of a man who had been dead for seven years. His daughter and first wife had waited that long before they had been financially and emotionally ready to bring his ashes to Hawaii where they had last been a happy family.

The inurnment was at the National Memorial Cemetery of the Pacific, more commonly referred to as the Punchbowl Cemetery. This is one of the major national cemeteries for WW II Pacific casualties and Korean War dead, especially the unprecedented number of unidentified/unknowns from what has been called "the forgotten war."

Famous people are buried here. Many of the casualties from the December 7, 1943 attack on Pearl harbor, including many from the USS Arizona that did not sink with the ship, lay at rest in the central part of the cemetery. Nearby lie the bodies of famed WW II journalist Ernie Pyle (who was killed on Okinawa) and Hawaii-born Ellison S. Onizuka who perished in the Space Shuttle Challenger tragedy in 1986.

Although all ground plots are now filled or "owned," a limited number of niches have been built for cremated remains. Accordingly, grave-side burials are few and far between these days. An exception was recently made for Lance Cpl. Blake Magaoay of Pearl City, killed last month (November 29) in Iraq. Someone graciously released their gravesite so he might be honored with burial here.

The man I trusted to "the care and mercy of almighty God" today had moved to Hawaii with his wife and daughter when he began his tour of duty in Vietnam, where he served with distinction. Upon his return he became the commander of the famed 100th Battalion/442nd Regimental Combat Team which had earlier been redesignated as a Reserve Unit (and which has now been activated for deployment to Iraq in several weeks).

While in Hawaii he and his wife had been members of the church I now serve as Pastor. It was for this reason that I was invited by the family to officiate today.

Several former friends who had served with him in Vietnam and with the 442 (including one now a 2-star general) came to pay their respects. Several members of my congregation who had known the family back in the early 1980's also attended. There were full military honors with taps and the presentation of the American flag to his family. Two bagpipers from the Honolulu Police Department Bagpipe Band were present and played "Amazing Grace" and the well-known "Going Home" motif from Dvorak's "New World Symphony."

As always, I returned to my car by way of the area set apart for the several hundred graves marked simply, "Unknown-Korea." As always I felt tremendous emotion for these young American men who had perished so far from home, their identities lost, but their bodies laid to rest with respect and honor. Unknown, but not forgotten. As always, I paused at several of them to imagine the person whose mortal remains were buried their. I imagined where they might have been born, who their parents might have been, brothers and sisters, school and church, hopes and dreams, hobbies, interests and their final thoughts and emotions on the day they perished. As always, I offered a prayer of remembrance and gratitude to God for their lives and for the families that never had the satisfaction of knowing either the soldiers fate or final resting place.

One of the men in my church helps administer the forensic lab in Hawaii that tests remains of "unknown" soldiers and attempts to identify them by matching their DNA them with surviving family members. Remains of MIAs are regularly being identified from Vietnam, South Pacific Islands, New Guinea, Europe and many other places where lost planes, ships, previously unknown burial sites and other "hot" or "cold" war artifacts have been recovered.

The lab is also systematically testing the remains of those many Korean War unknowns buried in Punchbowl. Happily, they have identified many of them who, at long last, have been returned to their families and reinterred closer to home on the mainland.

In Arlington National cemetery, across the Potomac River from Washington DC, the Tomb of the Unknown Soldiers bears these words, "Known but to God."

I shared those words today, pointing to the Korean War "unknowns" and then gesturing toward the remains of the one being inurned today. "Time and history may obliterate this cemetery someday," I observed. "But God will not forget any of them. He will not forget any of us. This is his promise to us in Jesus Christ."

Regardless of how my own life will one day end I, too, am comforted in knowing that God will remember me. My old body will "rest in peace" but, with a new body, I will be raised with Jesus to eternal life.

An Unusual (for me) Baptism

Yesterday I stayed after Sunday morning worship and Sunday School to attend the 12 Noon worship of the Hanmi Presbyterian Church (Korean speaking) that "nests" in our facilities. A Korean woman, married to an American, has been attending my congregation, staying for Sunday School along with her children and then attending the Korean service after that.

Recently she completed a "new members" class that I offer several times each year. After several years of study and prayer she decided to accept Jesus Christ as her personal Lord and Savior and receive the Sacrament of Baptism.

She hesitantly expressed some uncertainty to me about in which congregation she should be baptized. Clearly, she didn't want to hurt anyone's feelings! I mentioned this situation to the Korean pastor (who is also a close friend) and suggested that he speak with her and assure her that we were both delighted in her commitment to Christ and would both be present at whatever worship service or congregation she decided to be baptized in.

As it turned out, she chose the Korean congregation (which I felt was her preference all along). Her baptism was to be yesterday so I made sure I would be present for the event. To my surprise I discovered that she and the Korean pastor had decided that I would officiate at her baptism. So, when the time came, I stood with her before the congregation, listened as she affirmed her faith in Korean and then baptized her in English (but using her Korean name).

Clearly God does not care what language is spoken. It is the heart that God listens to. And yesterday the heart of this young woman, the hearts of two pastors and the hearts of two very culturally different congregations were united as one in Jesus Christ. There was no doubt in my mind that this was a very good thing indeed.

TUESDAY, DECEMBER 21, 2004

Holding My Breath

When I woke this morning my wife, who is always up long before I begin to stir, told me that an explosion at a U.S. military base in Mosul had killed and/or injured over 50 soldiers.

Two of my church elders are currently stationed in Mosul. One is due to leave in just eight days. I have to confess that my heart skipped a beat as I quickly offered a silent prayer for the soldiers and their families. What I didn't know was whether there were now two new widows and three children without fathers in my congregation.

As it turned out both men are assigned to a base adjacent to the one hit by the mortar (or rocket) yesterday. They had already contacted their wives and said they were OK.

A base chaplain who blogs has written up his experience providing spiritual support among the dead, dying, wounded, traumatized and those providing medical care. You can read it **here**. It reads like a war novel from WW II or a real-life episode of M.A.S.H. but without the humor...well, there are one or two bits of humor. Finding any humor at all amidst the carnage is a real gift of grace. As T.S. Elliot once wrote, "Human kind cannot stand very much reality."

I am glad that there are chaplains tending to the needs of the troops. I know that my two elders in Mosul have been grateful for them, too. One chaplain in Mosul has already been killed this past year. The chaplain with the blog ended his entry with these words,

"The last count was 25 dead, and around 45 wounded. Nevertheless, our cause is just and God is in control even when the crap is a yard deep. I'm where God wants me and wouldn't change that for anything, even if it means death. After all, "to die is gain."

I have prayed often today for those whose hearts skipped a beat, for those who held their breaths and for those whose hearts and breath came to a complete and final halt yesterday in that mess tent in Mosul.

THURSDAY, DECEMBER 23, 2004

Pigs Fly As Hell Freezes Over

The impossible happened two weeks ago. Right here on Oahu. A major business admitted it was responsible for an accident!

It seems that a 1,000 pound boulder fell out of a rock quarry and landed in the right-hand lane of the H-1 freeway. A car hit the rock and two people were seriously hurt.

Grace Pacific, the company the owns the quarry, got to the scene of the accident before any of the state highway crews. They removed the rock before they even realized it was theirs. Soon after they discovered that the rock had become dislodged by the own workers who had been trying to secure a section of the quarry to prevent the very sort of rock-fall that had occurred. The President and CEO, Robert Wilkinson, said it was obvious that work at the quarry caused the rock to fall and issued a statement to that effect. Then, as Hugh Hewitt likes to say, comes the money quote:

"You can't demand integrity from your employees if you don't practice it from the top. Our situation wouldn't be any worse if we took responsibility right away. It's better than having lawyers argue over responsibility for months in court and then come to the same conclusion. If we're going to give out money, I'd rather give it to the victims than attorneys."

When asked about the unprecedented display of honesty, Wilkinson replied, "I'm a Midwest boy. I believe things will die down fast if you just tell people what happened and answer their questions up front."

What about the two women injured in the accident? "We sent them flowers in the hospital," Wilkinson said. "And," added VP Sidney Quintal, "we said we were sorry."

Note: All credit for this blog goes to Honolulu Advertiser columnist Lee Cataluna whose article in the December 18, 2004 edition has been liberally summarized and quoted.

MONDAY, DECEMBER 27, 2004

Christmas Past

I had a good Christmas with my family. Others, unfortunately, did not.

First: A man woke up at 8:00 am in Hilo and found his bedroom on fire. He escaped but his home was destroyed.

Second: A good Christian man. who also happened to be a Hall of Fame football player, died in his sleep after going to bed the day after Christmas. Reggie White, one of the best defensive players ever, had spent part of Christmas Day going to the movies and watching "Fat Albert." Alive and well one moment and gone the next. Already a legend at age 43. Among other things, Reggie White was an ordained Christian minister and founder of what has become a nationwide Christian athletes organization. I am 53 and cannot say that I have had anywhere near the impact of this man. He worked hard. He excelled. And he shared his Good News. Perhaps dying so young will elevate his memory to the "greater than life" status that comes with legend-hood. If so, this will only serve to enhance his value as a positive role model, especially for African-Americans who have seen too many of their "sports heroes" fall during the past few months.

Third: One man's death, even that of a very good man, pales when contrasted with death of 25,000-50,000 in the wake of the earthquake and tsunami that swept the Indian Ocean that same day. Somali fisherman who set out to sea that morning never returned. Tens of thousands were startled awake only to drown in the final few moments of life that remained to them. Early warning systems that have been installed and maintained throughout the Pacific Basin were felt to be too costly and unnecessary among the nations surrounding the Indian Ocean. Even so, some warnings were communicated via satellite to many countries who took a casual approach to the looming disaster, in some cases passing the information to coastal areas two hours after the massive waves had swept everything and everyone away.

Today's report indicated that only 3 people in Bangladesh had been reported killed in the tsunami. If the history of past flooding in Bangladesh is any indicator I fear that number will skyrocket into the tens of thousands in the coming days.

As Hugh Hewitt said on his radio broadcast today, these preliminary numbers represent the equivalent of more than 8 World Trade Center attacks. Relief needs will be overwhelming to the impoverished nations involved. People living in most of the areas impacted were already subsisting with sub-standard water supplies, inadequate sanitation, little food supply and few medical resources. Undoubtedly more will die from the effects of hunger and disease than by the first blast of the tsunami itself.

It will reflect well on us all, as Americans, to donate generously to agencies that can effectively direct emergency aid. World Vision, Church World Service and the International Red Cross come to mind. This is one of those times when even a small amount of money will almost guarantee that someone in some lonely, devastated spot, will live instead of die.

You can either buy a latte or save a life with the same amount of money spent. I suspect that far too many Americans, including Christians, will choose the latte. And God will weep.

WEDNESDAY, DECEMBER 29, 2004

Playing the Odds

Although I am supposed to be on vacation I am still at home and available. So last night, when I heard that 85 year old Hellen had been taken to the hospital with chest pain and a doctor's recommedation for triple by-pass surgery, I had to make a decision. As a "Pastor on vacation" should I just put Hellen out of my mind until next Monday or make the one-hour round-trip drive to the hospital? For me it was a no-brainer. Hellen is not just a member of my congregation but a friend who I greatly respect and admire. Not making a visit to Hellen in the hospital would be like not visiting my own mother!

So today, after dropping daughter #1 off at the Honolulu airport for a flight to California I headed off to the hospital to see Helen. Her son and two friends from church had just left. She lay on her bed in CCU looking very bored. She knew I was coming and was glad to see me. Among other things she told me that the heart surgeon had told her that, because of her age, she would only have a 10-15% chance of surviving the surgery successfully. These were very slim odds so she was debating whether or not to have the surgery or hope that medication would somehow keep the three main arteries to her heart open (all three were 90-95% closed).

She said that she was inclined to have the surgery and take her chances. The pain, shortness of breath and general discomfort and malaise she had been experiencing were not things she wanted to suffer through for the rest of whatever life remained for her.

From experience I had some misgivings about the accuracy of the "survival" odds she had quoted but I was, nonetheless, impressed with her willingness to stake all of her chips on such a risky roll of the dice. She was cool and composed throughout our conversation, injecting humor amidst the life-stories and *bon mots* she is so good at offering. I imagined her sitting at a poker table in Las Vegas, calculating the odds of winning with a pair of Queens and betting the house, partly out of boredom and partly out of tiring of the game. She would be a tough one to read. Someone I would want on my side if I were playing any sort of bluffing game!

When her general physician came in the room for a consultation I asked Hellen to tell him the survival odds she had been quoted. As I knew he would, the doctor explained that she had got it backwards. The 10-15% figures were for the estimated *failure* rate. The success rate would be 85-90%. After the doctor left Hellen turned to me and said, "Thank you. I'm glad you asked him that question!"

That good news further strengthened her inclination to go ahead with the surgery. After a short prayer I left the room as the heart surgeon entered to discuss whether or not she had decided on the surgery. I left the room before I heard her answer. If "yes" the surgery could come as early as tomorrow.

Once again I will have to face the decision of whether I will be on vacation or take the time to visit the hospital. As before it will not be a difficult choice. As I said to her during my visit this afternoon, "Hellen, I am not here as your pastor (even though I am your pastor). I am here as your friend."

Pastors can and should take vacations. But friendship isn't allowed to take time off. Even for good behavior.

Soldier from Afghanistan

Today I had coffee with one of my church members home on R&R from deployment in Afghanistan. He has been there for 8 months already, serving out of Kandahar.

I was impressed as this young officer shared his enthusiasm for what our coalition forces have accomplished and are still accomplishing in that ancient, diverse and relatively primitive corner of the world.

I was even more impressed by his throrough knowledge of the historical, cultural and political aspects of the place. He said he had begun researching this as soon as he had been told about his upcoming deployment...six months of reading and digesting everything he could find in books and on the internet.

I was even *more* impressed when he added that he had recommended three particularly helpful books for his enlisted troops to read before they were deployed. "Knowledge is power" and he shared numerous examples as to how this research had paid off, especially when he and his men/women interacted with the local population both in Kandahar and in isolated villages scattered in the hills, valleys and mountains along the southern Afghanistan/Pakistan border.

"The people are tired of war and conflict," he said. "They are ready for peace and quiet." So they supported the elections and participated in them with enthusiasm. For a country so recently oppressed by the Taliban he was happy to report that the Presidential candidate receiving the fourth highest number of votes was a woman! My comment was, "I can guess who voted for her!"

Although he had not yet been caught in a firefight he had several friends in other companies who had been killed. Two of these had been men of strong Christian faith. One, a sergeant, had brought the other, a corporal, to faith. The corporal, in turn, had brought several others in their company to faith. The fact that these two particular men were the ones killed in a vicious IED explosion raised many questions about God, life, death, faith and salvation among the members of this group. The conclusion was that there was a great purpose not only in the lives of these two men but in their deaths, as well. Because of them God was glorified and lives were changed for the better.

When the time comes when he will leave the military, this young officer wants very much to work in some government position where he can continue to support the fight against international terrorism. As is true for most military personnel I have known, he had developed a sincere respect and appreciation for the country in which he has served and sacrificed; in his case the nation and people of Afghanistan.

I must say that I enjoyed one of the most insightful, informed, interesting and intelligent conversations I have had in a long time. If he is in any way representative of the rest of the American officers and soldiers serving in Afghanistan then I would have to conclude that Dr. Karzai, his two vice-presidents, his evolving (and revolving) cabinet members and most everyone else in that country have every reason to be optimistic about their future. From what I heard this morning I might dare to guess that they are also grateful for those who have placed that future back into their hands as a gift.

After a short prayer we said our good-byes, knowing that, by God's grace, the next time we would see each other would be in April. Once again I come away feeling good about being an American....and glad that there are men like this serving in our armed forces.

THURSDAY, DECEMBER 30, 2004

End of the Year in Hawaii

Tomorrow is New Year's Eve. My wife and I will spend the night at a nearby resort to keep away from all the smoke of the "traditional" Hawaii New Year's Eve celebrations. Two of our children will stay home to keep the dog from losing her mind during the three to four hours of firecrackers, fireworks & sky rockets (which are illegal but, who pays any attention to that!) that begin around 9:00 pm and build to a deafening crescendo at around 11:45 pm. One local tradition is setting off what is called a string of "10,000 firecrackers." Actually, these long bundles have only around 7500 firecrackers each but they pack a wallop when they go off. They are strung up in the air on improvised mini-booms and lit from the bottom. Like a long popping, exploding fuse the crackers burn to the top where a small bundle of concentrated gunpowder goes off with a flash and a roar. I have seen the more serious celebrators tie two or more of these together with duct tape to enhance the thrill.

Walking through our neighborhood is like walking through a war zone (minus the lethality, of course). Smoke fills the streets in some places so thickly that cars can no longer see past their front bumper. Personally, I think it's kind of fun, in an antinomian, anarchistic sort of way! Although my three daughters are more of less ambivalent over the fireworks they at least enjoy the evening. My wife, however, finds that the smoke and noise causes her asthma to flare up. So, most years, we find a local resort and spend the night breathing some clean air in a calmer atmosphere.

I guess I'm sentimental but I like the idea of dividing time up into relatively short, yearly increments. In a sort of formal ritual, the past 12 months are relegated to history and the coming year enters with a clean slate, full of empty space and time to be filled with new tragedies and triumphs which will draw out both the best and worst that is within us.

The current crises of Iraq (with the upcoming elections) and the continuing tragedy of the South Asian tsunami will link past and future together in a way that will make the end of this year seem less final than usual. December 31 will slide seamlessly into January 1 and there will be sort of a blurry overlap between 2004/5.

If the past is any predictor of the future, my wife will fall asleep around 10 pm tomorrow night. I will stay up, quietly watching Dick Clark's evil twin, Regis Philbin, provide the necessary incantations to begin the sacred ritual of the "dropping of the ball" in New York's Times Square. Most years I have already seen this five hours earlier due to our mid-Pacific time zone. Instead, at midnight, I will probably be walking around the resort, listening to whatever distant sound of firecrackers are carried on the evening Trade Winds. I will then offer a short prayer of peace and thanksgiving to God, remembering our troops overseas, the people of Iraq and Afghanistan, and the millions of people suffering loss, uncertainty and instability in the wake of the tsunami.

In the morning I will awake, pack up, return home and watch football for the rest of the day, waiting eagerly and expectantly for the University of Oklahoma football team to celebrate their own ritual of the "dropping of the ball." Go USC!

SUNDAY, JANUARY 09, 2005

Seeing Something in a New Way

I sat in with the Men's Sunday School class this morning. I'm glad I did. They had read the Sermon on the Mount (Matthew -5-7) during the week and were sharing what had touched them personally. Towards the end of the class Roger drew our attention to Matthew 7:13-14 which he then read,

“Enter through the narrow gate. For wide is the gate and broad is the road that leads to destruction, and many enter through it. But small is the gate and narrow the road that leads to life, and only a few find it."

He then read a poetic reflection on this passage written by Sam Shoemaker called, "I Stand at the Door." In these words Shoemaker describes those who seek truth blindly in the dark, as though feeling their way along a wall, groping for something, anything that might give meaning and purpose to their lives. He declares that he will stand by the door, or "narrow gate," that leads to God and to life. (For a Christian, of course, the door or gate is Jesus Christ.)

Shoemaker's explains that his purpose in standing by the door is two-fold. 1. To grasp the arms of the seekers and lead them to the door so that they might go in, and 2. To meet those who, having entered the door, are in retreat due to fear or guilt and encourage them to trust the love and mercy of God and to continue with their journey through and beyond the door.

I have read these words from Matthew 7 many, many times. But never had I thought of them in terms of outreach and evangelism. But now my eyes have been opened!

It makes sense to me that the point Jesus was trying to make may have been this: Since the gate is small and narrow and few find it, it should be the responsibility of those who have already found it to lead others to it!

Shoemaker ends his reflections with these words, "I had rather be a door-keeper. So I stand by the door."

Twenty-five hundred years ago a Jewish poet wrote a similar sentiment when he said, "Better is one day in your courts than a thousand elsewhere; I would rather be a doorkeeper in the house of my God than dwell in the tents of the wicked." (Psalm 84:10)

As Alice (in Wonderland) discovered, sometimes the smallest doors can lead to the greatest wonders! To help lead others to find that door for themselves, I think, must make God smile. Thank you, Roger, for helping me to see something "old" in a new way.

TUESDAY, JANUARY 11, 2005

Pastor's Retreat

The past two days I have been at the annual Pastor's Retreat sponsored by Hawaiian Islands Ministry (aka HIM). This was the 11th time I have been a participant and it gets better every time.

This year over 60 pastors and staff from over 40 churches spent two days listening to Don Cousins, a co-founder and former Executive Pastor of the Willow Creek mega-church outside of Chicago. Don helped us refocus our call to ministry and helped walk us through matter of the heart, team building, truths and lies about serving God and what really determines whether a minister is "successful" or not. It was better than great. God showed up in the presentations, in the prayers, in the sharing, in the renewing of old friendships and the creation of new ones.

For the past five years the retreat has been held at St. Stephen's Diocesan Center *(that's the picture)* just off the Pali Highway, half-way up the Pali from the Kailua side. There are few more beautiful spots in the world and the sun shined the entire time!

I took copious notes and fear that I may have compiled enough material for at least three sermon series covering nearly four months worth of Sundays! It is all wonderful, biblical, life-changing, life-rearranging stuff. It helped touch the hearts of a bunch of tired and hungry pastors. I know it will do the same for the good folks in my congregation. After all, they get tired and hungry, too!

Rathergate

Well, the Dick Thornburgh and Louis D. Boccardi investigative report on the fraudulent Rathergate memos (purporting to be documents from President Bush's National Guard Service) was finally released while I was on retreat. These memos, immediately declared to be forgeries by internet bloggers (including, but not limited to Powerline, Jim Geraghty, Instapundit, RatherBiased, LittleGreenFootballs INDCJournal, Wizbang, and Hugh Hewitt) were aired on CBS just one month before the national election as evidence of W's purported absences from duty responsibilities back in the 1970.s.

Several investigative and news-vetting staffers were fired but the credibility of Dan Rather and CBS News President Andrew Heywood were covered and "preserved." Heywood not only got a pass but was commended for his tough insistence that the report be accurate and validated. According to the report his words of caution and instruction were ignored and not carried out.

As chief administrator of the news department, doesn't that imply that he had, through lack of oversight, discipline or guidance, allowed a culture of incompetence and rampant anarchy to matasticise throughout the news staff? How can he get off the hook so easily? Whatever happened to "the buck stops here?" We don't even get an apology from him like we did from good old Dan. I suspect that either his "golden parachute" is too big for CBS to afford or that he has enough "dirt" on the rest of the CBS executives to sink the entire ship should he be placed in a position to write a book or to "get even." My guess is that he will be allowed to hang in there for a year and then retire early or be transferred to some other CBS job where he will not be able to cause any more embarrassment to the network.

Clearly the blogosphere had the big hand in bringing this entire matter to the fore. Tens of thousands of bloggers and informed internet readers knew of the scandal even before the CBS folks woke up the day after the story was broadcast. Even if the bloggers had not raised the red flag when they did it is likely that the forgeries would have been noticed soon enough, but perhaps without enough pressure or outrage to have forced the sort of backbreaking contortions and spin that actually ensued at CBS.

While I would encourage the blogospere to continue to pursue the "missing links" in the report (especially the professional connections between CBS staffers and the Democratic Party...bias? what bias?) I think the one-eyed monster has been beaten into a respectable level of humiliation in the eyes of the American public. Let's just let Dan "go gentle into that good night" but keep up the "rage, rage against the dying of the light" wherever the truth is twisted, fabricated or ignored.

The "evil eye" winked at the truth once too often and got poked with a blog-stick. Perhaps a corrective lens would help the CBS news department see reality a little more clearly next time. I'll not be holding my breath.

WEDNESDAY, JANUARY 12, 2005

Proud Parents; Happy Daughter

Today was a good day. It was a day that many parents ponder as they stare in wonder and disbelief at their newborn child. No, not a wedding, but a *college graduation*! Such miracles do occur! I can attest to it. My eldest daughter did it this evening. Her name was called, loud and clear, from the platform of the Waikiki Shell in Honolulu's Kapiolani Park, and she walked across and received her BA degree in Psychology. At that moment she became an alumnae of Hawaii Pacific University (which will, starting later this year, begin asking her for financial contributions to the alumni/ae fund at ridiculously frequent intervals).

I sat out front next to my mother (visiting from California for the occasion), my daughter's best friend and my youngest daughter My. middle daughter, was back at college in Seattle braving winter snow while we were basking in mid-70s evening outdoor temperatures in our shirtsleeves.

My wonderful wife, who is a faculty member at Hawaii Pacific, not only marched in with the faculty and got a close-up view of the whole thing from the platform, but also enabled us to get a reserved parking place in the faculty parking area. All her years of study and teaching *finally* paid off!

Before the commencement we enjoyed a wonderful meal together. Afterwards my daughter and her friend headed off to a graduation party at a restaurant overlooking Waikiki Beach.

Her proud father (me) thought she looked beautiful and radiant tonight (two cliches that actually describe her perfectly). The Hawaiian custom of piling up floral leis on honored people on special occasions made many of the graduates look worrysomely top-heavy in a South Pacific, fragrant sort of way!

I thought my daughter wore her cap, her gown, her leis and her smile quite well. Her mother

even joined her in a little dance before the ceremony and her proud Grandma T joined them both in a happy photo op afterwards. Dad managed to wind up in a few pictures as well, but humility precluded him from posting anything with his face on it tonight.

Ah! One child down and two more to go! I haven't had to take out a second mortgage on our house, yet, and, by God's grace, will never have to. On the other hand, Daughter #1 is hoping to begin a graduate school program on the mainland next Fall. I'm proud of her for that, too. But I'm keeping my hand on the wallet in my back pocket!

FRIDAY, JANUARY 14, 2005

A Response to Article by the Moderator of the Presbyterian Church (USA) General Assembly

In the December 20/27, 2004 issue of The Presbyterian Outlook, the current Moderator of the Presbyterian Church (U.S.A.) General Assembly, Rick Ufford-Chase, delivered a message to the church.

The subject of his article is raised in the first sentence, "Brothers and Sisters in Christ, Is peace possible?"

In a rambling response, reading more like a journal entry than a carefully crafted theological reflection, he shares his complete lack of a clear and cogent answer to the question.

He first considers and rejects the idea that a "just war" approach can ever lead to "credible peacemaking." Here he also equates "just war" with something called "redemptive violence" and finds this also "problematic on both a theological and a pragmatic level." With these words the Moderator raises concepts not even taught by scripture. They are "straw men" arguments, artificially brought forward for the simple purpose of easily dismissing them.

Nowhere, for example, does scripture ever describe warfare or violence as being righteous and holy. In this sense war is never "just" as God is "just." Nowhere does scripture declare that the "the peace which passes understanding" can be inaugurated with the sword. Nowhere does the Bible teach the concept of "redemptive violence" except in the case of animal sacrifice in the Old Testament and the crucifixion of Jesus in the New.

My response to this first point is one of wonder...wonder as to whether he has ever read Romans

13:1-8. In this passage, the Apostle Paul declares that God has granted governmental authorities the power of the sword to assert order and justice within its bounds and to deter and repel those who would threaten the peace and security of its subjects from beyond its borders.

Under ordinary circumstances, scripture declares that the single-minded purpose of government-sanctioned violence is to resist and contain sin that threatens to corrupt or destroy the social fabric of an otherwise peaceful and secure nation.

In practice, war is not unlike biblical divorce. God permits divorce because of the "hardness of men's hearts" (Matthew 19:3-9). Even so, God does not "bless" divorce or declare it to be "just." On the contrary, the mind of God on this matter is very clear: "'I hate divorce,' says the Lord your God" (Malachi 2:16).

In the same way, God permits war because of the hardness of our hearts and the self-justified violence that ensues when rebellion against God leads to the intentional and wanton destruction of the life and liberty of others. Even so, God does not "bless" war or declare it to be "just." On the contrary, the mind of God on this matter is very clear: "Love one another as I have loved you:" (John 13:34). While this command for mutual, reciprocal love is specifically intended for individual followers of Jesus to put into practice, it is clear that it is also characteristic of God's rule over nations, kings and lords as well. The meaning of scripture is, or ought to be, clear: "God hates war."

Along with God, we, too, should hate both divorce and war. But we should keep in mind that God "permits" them both as merciful concessions to our sin and to grant us the means to resist the oppression that constantly threatens us as individuals and as nations in a fallen world.

We have only to turn to World War II for a simple example of war engaged for the purpose of resisting the oppression that threatened us at that time. While ultimate judgment against evil remains with God alone, it is questionable theology to assert that it is more righteous to stand by while sin devours the innocent than it is to resist that evil by any and all means, including force, when all else has failed or is deemed to be futile.

While the murderous slaughter of millions of people (both military and civilian) did not usher in the "peaceable kingdom" of the Realm of God it did have the effect of curbing evil and setting innumerable numbers of people (mostly civilians) free from the yoke of tyranny and bigotry. Ask any Jew if they think that WW II was a war worth fighting.

Secondly, Mr. Ufford-Chase then states that he "can no longer nuance the use of violence. It's increasingly difficult to distinguish between the good guys and the bad guys." He then proceeds to equate any act of violence which kills civilians, "whether they are the victims of terrorist attacks or well-executed military campaigns."

The Moderator has committed a common but grievous error by confusing two distinct issues. He has conflated the matters of purposeful intent (motive) and particular outcomes. It is as though a man entered my home and beat my child to death to keep them quiet while committing a burglary and to then equate that with a child crushed to death under the wheels of his mother's car as she backed out of the driveway.

While the outcome is identical (a dead child) the motives are clear and distinct from each other. To dismiss this distinction as a "nuance" is nothing short of outrageous as is the attempt to classify them as morally equivalent.

Using a different example: It might be important to debate whether pursuing a suspected robber or murderer in a high-speed car chase is worth the risk of life and limb to the police officers and to others who might be caught in between; but it would be foolish to assert that the moral intent of the pursuing officers was indistinguishable from that of the fleeing suspect.

The Bible declares that the Lord judges peoples *hearts*, not simply the consequences of their behavior. The Old Testament law is filled with examples of just how important the application of this "nuance" is to God. Motive and intent are not optional considerations in such things. Indeed, they form the veritable essence of morality.

Lastly, the Moderator proposes a "third way, the way of the cross." This "way of the cross" leads to "the kind of security that comes from upside-down, Gospel-inspired thinking." I would hope to think that Mr. Ufford-Chase would have rewritten his next sentence had he taken the time to proof-read it carefully: "Security, in Jesus' world, comes not at the point of a gun that protects us from our enemies but from the peace that can only be achieved when we all feel secure."

When this sentence is reduced to its simple noun, verb and subject essence, it reads: "Security comes when we all feel secure." It is from this tautological premise that the rest of the article proceeds...and fails either to persuade or to offer anything other than wishful thinking ("What if my own privilege didn't appear to come at the expense of another person's ability to provide for the most basic needs of her family?") and outrageous imaginings ("What if 200,000 Christians trained in nonviolence had gone to Afghanistan and Iraq in the aftermath of September 11, 2004?" (sic)).

Over the years I have seen many cars bearing a bumper sticker that reads, "Visualize World Peace." Our General Assembly Moderator and all of us would do well to do the same (not the bumper sticker but the thought!). But to think that this sentiment rises to the level of "practical theology" is less than compelling.

On the other hand I must affirm our Moderator's comment that "many believe I am naïve to think that one can follow Christ's witness and refuse to respond to violence with violence." My family heritage on my mother's side is Anabaptist pacifist. To avoid war and forced conscription is why they fled to American in the first place. Some were even slaughtered by Indians in 18th century Pennsylvania because they refused to use violence to defend themselves.

Christian pacifism is not naïve. It is a serious response to Jesus' call to introduce his kingdom into this world and live the fullness of the Christian life in a world that still operates in the context of sinful humanity.

While I respect this personal act of conscience among Christian believers I must disagree with any attempt to apply such a non-violent approach to the role of the ruling authorities of nations. As cited above in Romans 13:1-8, such leaders are given the authority to "wield the sword" by none other than God, from whom all power and authority are derived.

For this reason, the very next sentence from the Moderator not only appears to be in conflict with scripture but with historical reality and common sense as well: "I would suggest that nothing could be more naïve than the continued insistence that a war on terrorism has made us safer, or that it has any potential to do so in the future."

As individuals, especially within the context of the Christian community, we are not permitted to return evil for evil, or an eye for an eye. We are called to love even our enemy and to pray that they might be transformed by grace, working through faith, to become the Holy Spirit-filled person that God created them to be.

I would never criticize any follower of Jesus who would stand before Osama bin Laden, speaking the truth in love and, like Jesus, being willing to be led like a lamb to the slaughter as a living witness to the higher and eternal truth of God's will for us all.

I would, however, quickly condemn any national leader who suggested that our country stand before those who would destroy us in a similar manner.

Perhaps this particular war on terrorism is *not* making us any safer. That is a reasonable position to debate. But it is *not* reasonable to conclude that there is no possibility that a war on terror will ever make us any safer.

Israel is a lot safer with a wall and a vigilant military protecting it from those who would take pleasure in murdering their women and children along with anyone else who might be identified as a Jew.

It is also worth noting that our own national independence and the unprecedented guarantees of freedom that we enjoy were gained through the sacrifice, death and destruction of war.

"Four score and seven years later," would our Moderator suggest that the "Northern States" should have allowed the "Southern States" to secede, thereby preserving the institution of slavery, weakening the Union and sowing the seeds for its future disintegration. "What if" 200,000 non-violent abolitionists had gone to Atlanta, New Orleans and Richmond after the attack on Fort Sumter? Would that have resolved what was inherently unresolvable?

I want our Moderator to be assured that I do not equate his speculative musings "with being a traitor to one's country," as he fears some may do.

On the contrary, I respect and admire his desire for some new paradigm "that will help us to become unstuck." I also share that same desire and pray that we might someday soon be given the grace to discern it clearly.

In the meantime, however, I shall choose to stay the course with the fundamental character of our Reformed Faith left intact, including Calvin's "two-kingdom" understanding of the distinct divine anointings of Church and State. The first, for the proclamation and demonstration of the good news of Jesus Christ and God's coming kingdom; and the second, to protect and preserve the righteous freedom of God's people from "the rulers of the darkness of this world" even if, by God's concession to our hardness of heart, it leads nations to war.

"Maranatha! Come, Lord Jesus!"

SATURDAY, JANUARY 15, 2005

Seeing Long Distance

I was able to see my daughter in Seattle today. No, I didn't go there and she didn't come here. But I saw her nonetheless. We even smiled and waved at each other.

For Christmas I gave my two youngest daughters a pair of web cams and the software to go with them. I know this is very old technology but it is new for me to be able to have it in my home and use it to see my far-away daughter. The two sisters not only looked at each other today but talked to each other on their cell phones while they looked at each other. Not only that but they also played a game of internet cribbage at the same time.

I reminded me of my youth back in 1960 when I watched with wonder as the television networks broadcast the first "live" pictures beamed from Europe to America by satellite. The satellite was the Echo I and the pictures they showed on the TV were of Big Ben in London and the Eiffel Tower in Paris. I could see cars and trucks moving on the streets and people walking in the distance...in "real time." It was a magical and marvelous moment. It was a moment that changed the world.

Today we see live images of tsunami ravaged coastlines and rescue efforts at the site of a Southern California mudslide. Videophones connect us to live scenes in places where no regular cameras can broadcast. I am captivated by it all.

Especially when it gives me a chance to not only see my daughter in Seattle but to wave at her, too!

SUNDAY, JANUARY 16, 2005

Gospel Choir

Sometimes a photo captures something you were not able to see when you took it. This is one of those. At the end of September 2004 I took my middle daughter to Seattle Pacific University where she moved into her dorm and went through orientation for her first quarter of classes as an incoming Freshman. SPU gives the royal treatment for incoming students and their parents. The first evening we were welcomed with a program in the gymnasium that included a musical selection from the university's Gospel Choir. I took the photo from across the gym. From that distance the choir formed only a small group in the center of the picture. Later, when I downloaded it onto my computer, I zoomed in to see what details might show up. To my pleasant surprise I discovered amazing detail, expressive faces and a sepia-like graininess that reminded me of a cross between Rembrandt and

Norman Rockwell. With a little cutting and trimming I came up with these beautiful compositions, unretouched and just the way it was when they were too far away for me to see! I hope you enjoy them. Be sure to click on them to get the full effect.

MONDAY, JANUARY 17, 2005

The Rev. Dr. Martin Luther King, Jr.

Today is Martin Luther King, Jr. Day. It is a good time to reflect on why we have such a day set aside to remember Dr. King and, more importantly, the great and noble cause for which he gave his life.

I grew up during the Civil Rights struggle. Even as a child in Northern California, far from the drama where our nation's destiny was being reshaped, I sensed that something historic was taking place; something the likes of which I might never see again.

Slavery in the Western Hemisphere began almost as soon as Columbus landed somewhere in the Bahamas (most likely Plana Cays) back in 1492. As Spanish, and later, French, English and Portuguese, began settling into the New World they needed laborers to tame the "wilderness." Unfortunately for them, most of the indigenous people had the audacity to die off, victims of diseases previously unknown to them. Yet labor had to be found; and found it was, in the form of the West African slave trade.

The slave trade was not a new thing in Africa. Stronger tribes had from time beyond time enslaved their weaker neighbors and traded people for goods and wealth as needed. Islam also found its own niche, primarily in East Africa. But the New World provided an unprecedented market for slave labor. Soon, tens of thousands of Africans were sold by Africans to Europeans. By the time the slave trade was effectively ended in the mid 1800's those figures had risen into the millions.

The United States was among the last of the Western Nations to end the practice of slavery. Abolitionists tried to stop it through legislation and vigilantes like John Brown tried to change national opinion through violence. Both failed as did middle-ground approaches like the Missouri Compromise.

Slavery led to the bloodiest war ever fought by American troops. When the Confederate States of America lost the war it not only lost its declared independence but its right to slavery as well.

Reconstruction brought carpetbaggers to fill the political void left in the South. Corruption and greed filled the vacuum left by the absence of Abraham Lincoln and his moral firmness and clarity. While the white citizens of the South were crushed into economic submission those who had formerly been slaves fared even worse. Prejudice, bitterness, poverty and misplaced pride created a culture of oppression for every Negro in the South. Although guaranteed equality under the law by the Fourteenth Amendment to the Constitution, state and local laws were enacted and often brutally enforced that kept the former slaves and their descendents from competing with anyone else for economic wealth, education or full participation in the political process.

For over seventy-five years, from the collapse of reconstruction in the 1870's to the mid 1950's, little changed. Local white terrorist groups like the Ku Klux Klan "culled the herd" of any Blacks that were deemed to be too uppity or assertive of anything resembling equality. Threats were backed up by lynchings of hundreds of (mostly young) Black males.

In spite of this cultural and legal oppression, Black Americans developed a thriving counter-culture of their own. Within their own segregated communities they taught their own children and serviced their own needs with professionals who had been trained and educated in a small group of elite Colleges existing soley for Black students.

This uneasy social equilibrium began to unravel following World War II. Too many men had served as the military grew increasingly integrated during the conflict. Too many men had seen that the blood that was shed by each race was indistinguishable, one from another. Social taboos began to weaken. Black men who had fought and died for a common cause among white men began to question the status quo. Men like Jackie Robinson (1947 Brooklyn Dodgers)began to integrate professional sports and the increasing mobility of people from North to South and South to North made the old ways of segregation increasingly intolerable.

Finally, on December 1, 1955, a tired Black woman named Rosa Parks sat down on a Montgomery, Alabama, bus and refused to give it up to a white man. She was arrested. A Black boycott of Montgomery's bus system lasted 381 days, even beyond a Supreme Court ruling in November 1956 that declared segregation on public transportation to be unconstitutional.

With Rosa Parks, the media and the nation had a face and a person to represent the long history of racial abuse. In the person of the Rev. Dr. Martin Luther King, Jr., at the time a pastor at Montgomery's Dexter Avenue Baptist Church, the nation found an eloquent voice that raised the issue of racism to that of a moral imperative. Institutional racism, forced segregation and the quasi-legal contortions that justified it were vigorously decried as hateful distortions of the founding documents of our nation, especially the ringing words of the Declaration of Independence:

> *We hold these truths to be self evident, that all men are created equal , that they are endowed by their Creator with certain unalienable Rights, that among these are life, liberty and the pursuit of happiness...*

The violent reaction to attempts to integrate schools in Little Rock, Arkansas, in 1957, three years after the Supreme Court had ruled that segregated schools were "inherently unequal," revealed to America the bitter hatred towards Negroes and the lengths some would go to resist the tide of change.

Both White and Black folks from the North began to head South to stand alongside those Blacks who were calmly, yet firmly, defying segregationist laws in lunch counters, public drinking fountains, and voting registration. Such people were termed "Freedom Riders" and their effect on the growing Civil Rights movement were crucial to its eventual success.

The Southern White resistance to the inevitable produced vicious assaults on non-violent demonstrators and marchers and a number of brutal murders. The majority of Americans were shamed, embarrassed and humiliated by the film footage shown on the nightly television news. Slowly, but with an air of progress stirring amidst the chaos, the critical mass of public opinion turned. In 1962, then-Attorney General Robert Kennedy, sent National Guard troops into Southern states to enforce federal anti-discrimination law and allow James Merideth to enroll at the previously all-white University of Mississippi.

On August 28, 1963, 200,000 people "marched" on Washington D.C. to demonstrate their demands for an end to legalized segregation. The closing speech of the day was delivered by Dr. King. It's repeated refrain, "I have a dream..." stirred the nation and elevated him as the foremost spokesperson for the Civil Rights movement.

In response, President Kennedy was emboldened to submit his "Civil Rights" bill to the congress, over a year earlier than he had planned. Following his assassination on November 22, 1963, Lyndon Johnson, a Texas Southerner and new President, continued to support and endorse it.

This comprehensive legislation passed in 1964 and follow-up law, the Voting Rights Act, was passed in 1965.

On April 4, 1968, while I was a Junior in high school, Martin Luther King, Jr. was assassinated in Memphis, Tennessee. Two months later, Robert Kennedy met the same fate at the hands of a gunman in Los Angeles.

All of this I remember because I saw the drama unfold. I saw the moral rightness in the Civil Rights struggle and I was inspired to assimilate its lessons through the powerful rhetoric of a man who "spoke the truth with love" to the people of America, and articulated a vision of the way things should one day be.

Today, as we take a day off from work, it is good to remember our national past, both good and bad, as personified in the Rev. Dr. Martin Luther King, Jr. Just as any of us, Dr. King was flawed and imperfect. But the banner of freedom he helped raise for his people and for all of us still rallys us to the high ideal of equality for all.

Following his death, a friend and I took city buses across San Francisco to attend a massive memorial service at Grace Cathedral. Following the service, we joined the religious and civil leaders in a procession through the great Ghiberti Doors and around the top of Nob Hill. When we returned to the Cathedral I was astonished to see people still streaming out of the church, just beginning their memorial march. There were so many people, the strains of "We shall overcome" echoed off the surrounding buildings as it was being sung simultaneously yet not in unison by tens of thousands.

I remember that moment as though it were yesterday. That moment galvinized my determination to never flinch from defending the civil rights of any and all who would ever be judged on the basis of the color of their skin rather than "the content of their character."

Is there more to be done? Yes, of course, although I believe it is less than many would like us to believe. Slowly, slowly I have watched as Dr. King's dream has begun to be turned into reality. The freedom is now there for the taking. The opportunities have been unleashed. These freedoms came through a struggle that was by no means easy. We should not expect that the struggle to implement them be any easier.

TUESDAY, JANUARY 18, 2005

Bible Ad Rejected by :"Rolling Stone"

Apparently the Bible is no longer the innocuous, dust-gathering, family heirloom sitting unused on the shelf of millions of American homes. It seems that the largest-selling book since the invention of the printing press has, for the first time, become controversial and unacceptable; at least to the editor and publisher of Rolling Stone magazine.

USA Today printed a story today relating how an ad, promoting the "Today's New International Version" (TNIV) translation of the Bible published by Zondervan, was rejected by the aging counter-culture's flagship publication.
Here is the ad, copied from the on-line USA Today feature. It is poor quality and essentially unreadable. I will put up a clearer one as soon as I can find it.

According to USA Today, "the rejected ad shows a serious young man, apparently pondering the problems of modern life. The text touts the TNIV as a source for "real truth" in a world of "endless media noise and political spin." A blue Bible peeks up from the corner of the ad." The ad also carries the ad campaign's slogan: "Timeless truth; Today's language."
Kent Brownridge, general manager of Wenner Media, parent company of Rolling Stone, was quoted as having said that "(the ad) doesn't quite feel right in the magazine." He then added, "The copy is a little more than an ad for the Bible. It's a religious message that I personally don't disagree with." But, he said, "we are not in the business of publishing advertising for religious messages."

I wonder if an ad for the Koran, the "Wisdom of the Buddha" or the Kama Sutra would have violated this unwritten and previously unknown "policy?" Are we seeing a genuine concern for those who subscribe to Rolling Stone? Is there a fear that the sight of an ad encouraging them to read the Bible as a source of "truth" might cause dizziness, nausea and intellectual disorientation among readers notoriously noted for their advocacy of diversity and inclusion of all points of view?

What is it about the Bible that has suddenly caused it to become a *cause celebre*? More to the point, what is it about today's liberal culture that has made the Bible *persona non grata*?
It seems that anything related to the Christian or Jewish faith (except for Madonna and the Cabala, of course) sends shivers of discomfort and antipathy among the more radical of the blue state liberals.

Jesus said that he did not come to bring peace, but a sword. More pointedly he said, "For I have come to turn 'a man against his father, a daughter against her mother, a daughter-in-law against her mother-in-law' a man's enemies will be the members of his own household.'" (Matthew 10:34-36)

Jesus knew that he would cause scandal. If he is the Lord he claimed to be then those who flaunt their independence from God are under his judgment. No one likes to be judged, of course. Especially by someone who doesn't seem to agree with you on nearly everything that you believe to be important.

The Bible stands as a judgment and a threat to the liberal left, especially those still stuck in the late 1960's "down with authority...don't trust anyone over 30" mentality (most of whom are now, of course, untrustworthy!).

It appears that for some people a crucifix in a jar of urine is OK but the Bible isn't. I fear for the day that such people find themselves in positions of power to legislate and impose their bigotry and hate-filled philosophies on what was once proclaimed to be the "land of the free and the home of the brave."

Perhaps I'm making too much out of a little misunderstanding between a magazine and an ad agency. On the other hand, could it be, perhaps, that this little episode represents just the tip of an ever-emerging iceberg?

Will we see more attempts to marginalize and discredit the Bible, Christians and the faith they confess? Will we one day deem public prayer to be offensive? Will we one day see the word "God" stricken from public discourse and public education? Will we live long enough to see public displays of the Ten Commandments or a Christmas nativity scene be declared unconstitutional? Will people be labeled as narrow-minded, homophobic, sexist, dangerous threats to America and the world simply because they go to church and worship God on a Sunday morning?

Honestly, I haven't read Rolling Stone for over 30 years. I didn't even know they carried ads at all, being so anti-capitalist and all that. Still, I'll give them credit for turning down paid advertising to uphold the integrity of their corporate principles. This they have the right to do. But I bet that more than a few of their younger readers will some day soon pick up a copy of the TNIV and discover, to the surprise of both themselves and the editors of Rolling Stone, that there is, indeed, "timeless truth" in it.

This is because truth is like styrofoam in a bucket of water. You can stuff it down; you can drop heavy weights on it; you can try to break it up into pieces; but sooner or later it will rise to the top in spite of every effort to sink it to the bottom. Don't forget. There was a time when people thought that Jesus was dead and buried, too!

WEDNESDAY, JANUARY 19, 2005

Hey, Dude! Where's My Newspaper?

This week the Honolulu Advertiser daily newspaper stopped the afternoon edition that I have subscribed to for the past five years. Now I get the morning edition. Except today, when I went out front to get it, it wasn't on the driveway, or in the bushes or near the front door. Nuts! Only three days into the new delivery time and they already mess it up!

My wife had already left to drop off Daughter #3 at the High School before heading off to work and, when I finished my breakfast, I went into the garage, opened the garage door, backed out my car, closed the garage door with the remote and drove to the church. In the afternoon, when I picked up my daughter from school, she mentioned that I had left the garage door open when I came home last night. My wife had closed it when she left the house this morning.

This evening, after dinner, I drove my daughter back to the High School for presentation and sign up for Advanced Placement (AP) classes for her Junior year beginning next Fall (she has decided to take AP English). As we backed out of the driveway she said, "Oh, look. There's the newspaper. It was in the garage under your car!"

She was right, of course. The newspaper delivery person had thrown the paper through the open garage door and under the car. By the time I came out to look for it my wife had already closed the door.

I guess there is a lesson in this somewhere. Maybe something about people in glass houses or taking out the beam in your own eye or judge not lest ye be judged or ....well, you get the idea. And so did I.

THURSDAY, JANUARY 20, 2005

More Bodies More Money?

At dinner tonight my daughter mentioned that one of her high school teachers had suggested the idea that the number of dead from the South Asia tsunami might be intentionally inflated to increase the amount of emergency relief money that has been pouring in.

My immediate response was, the money is not coming in to help the dead people but to help the ones who are alive. And no one needs to inflate the numbers of displaced and decimated individuals and families in Indonesia, Sri Lanka and Thailand.

An informative article on today's FoxNews provides insight into the confusing and contradictory numbers of dead being released by various agencies even within the same country. I find it cynical for anyone to suggest that these numbers are being artificially inflated for whatever reason. I suppose we are living in a cynical society but it's sad to think that my daughter and other high school students are being taught to think cynically about relief aid to victims of a tsunami.

Bush Inauguration: Who Is That Standing Behind the President?

I love looking at photos of famous people mixing with the public. What I like best is not the famous people but the regular folks who are pictured standing in the background. I like them because nobody ever notices them. They are anonymous witnesses to an event that was worth photographing. Each of them has their own tale to tell. They are faces of mystery, waiting to be solved.

There were plenty of mystery people populating the photos of today's second inauguration of George W. Bush as President of the United States. Of course he and Laura look great...they are both naturally photogenic. But so are some of the shadowy figures lurking in the background. These generic and obscure people must be known and loved by someone, somewhere. If you know or can identify any of them please let me know.

Introducing.........**INAUGURAL MYSTERY PEOPLE PHOTO GALLERY**

Any luck?

FRIDAY, JANUARY 21, 2005

Too Much God In Bush's Inaugural Address?

George Bush cited the word "God" three times in his inaugural address yesterday. The words "Jesus," "Lord," "Christ," "religion," "church," "Providence," "scripture," "Bible," "Koran," "Christianity," "Islam" and many other "god-type words" were not mentioned at all!

Yes, I admit that he did mention that each person is valuable "because they bear the image of the maker of heaven and earth." And, yes, he did make a reference to "the author of liberty." But I cannot, for the life of me, understand why someone of such rhetorical and political skill as Peggy Noonan can summarize Bush's speech as simply, "Way Too Much God."
The president's speech seemed rather heavenish. She writes. *It was a God-drenched speech. This president, who has been accused of giving too much attention to religious imagery and religious thought, has not let the criticism enter him. God was invoked relentlessly. 'The Author of Liberty." "God moves and chooses as He wills. We have confidence because freedom is the permanent hope of mankind . . . the longing of the soul."*
Yes, I do believe I *did* sniff a whiff of "heaven" in this speech. But, before I go on, let me go back to the three times the word "God" was cited.

The first time the word "God" appears is in a quote from Abraham Lincoln:
"Those who deny freedom to others deserve it not for themselves: and, under the rule of a just God, cannot long retain it."
These words were spoken by Lincoln in a speech delivered before the first Republican State Convention of Illinois, held at Bloomington, on May 29, 1856. (It is interesting to note that Lincoln used the word "God" eight times in this stridently anti-slavery speech.) I suppose Ms. Noonan would prefer that, from henceforth, American presidents only publicly quote passages from Lincoln where the word "God" does *not* appear.

The second time the word "God" appears it shows up as part of a theological assertion, *"Not because we consider ourselves a chosen nation; God moves and chooses as He wills."* Although it has a sort of timeless sound to it, this phrase appears to be original with this speech. It's parallel cannot be found on Google or any other search engine. It does, however, reflect an unequivocal Biblical/Christian understanding of God's providence.

In the context of the speech it could be more simply written as follows, "It is not for us to decide whether we are a nation 'chosen' by God or not. God does whatever God wants to do. And, in any case, that is not the reason we have 'confidence in the eventual triumph of freedom.'" That's all. Rather than claiming that God has somehow "chosen" the United States for this purpose, Bush says that we cannot determine whether we have been chosen or not. Such a claim is not necessary in any case, for our hope for universal freedom transcends any notion of "manifest destiny" or having received some sort of "divine favor" as a nation.

The third time the word "God" is used it appears in his closing sentence, *"May God bless you, and may He watch over the United States of America."*

Is this "Way Too Much God?"

But what about the phrase, "author of liberty." Has Ms. Noonan never sung the hymn, "My Country 'Tis of Thee?" The fourth, and final, verse begins, "My father's God, to Thee, Author of liberty, to Thee I sing." These words were written by Samuel F. Smith in 1832 with the final verse being a prayer asking for God's blessing on our country.

This unattributed citation supports the Bush thesis that human freedom is not a right granted by government or created and sustained by a national constitution. If this were the case then liberty and freedom, being conceived, created and granted by human hands, could just as easily be taken away by them. Freedom, with humanity as its foundation, is hardly a universal right. Every tyrant, every culture, every nation would be free to affirm human liberty or not. The idea of freedom itself would be reduced to that of an opinion.

Bush refuses to buy into this humanistic approach to human liberty and freedom. Instead, taking his place alongside the writers of our nation's Declaration of Independence, Articles of Confederation and the U.S. Constitution, he affirms that, "We hold these truths to be self-evident; that we are endowed by our Creator with certain unalienable rights; that among these rights are life, liberty and the pursuit of happiness."

Bush asserts that freedom is a right granted to every human being by God. As such it is both universal and irrevocable. It is good, it is right and, furthermore, being God's will, it will one day triumph.

Ms. Noonan somehow thinks that human freedom can be affirmed as a universal right without citing "God," "providence," "Divine Law," or even "the author of liberty." She is wrong. And, being an intelligent person, she should know she is wrong. The logic is simple and clear.

What she, and others, mean when they say that Bush uses too much "God-speak" is that they do not believe that liberty is a universal right. They believe that liberty is merely a choice, or an option that was chosen as the founding principal of our nation. Other nations, apparently, are free(!) to make different choices. Such alternative choices should not be judged as being better or worse, good or evil. Such judgment on our part must be seen as forcing American values and culture onto other, equally valid cultures with their own, equally valid, set of values.

What we have here are people dancing around the fundamental issue of whether our human freedom is granted by God or created by human invention and chosen as one equally valid option among many.

Personally, I feel much more comfortable with George W. Bush on this one. With his philosophy of freedom he would not be able to take it away from me even if he wanted to! Ms. Noonan and her ilk, however, cause me to break out into a cold sweat. If, as they imply, freedom is granted by a human hand, then it follows that, by a human hand it can be taken away.

Are they so blind as to not see this? Do they not see that they undermine the very values they pretend to hold?

"Way Too Much God," Ms. Noonan? Not by a long shot!

SATURDAY, JANUARY 22, 2005

FBI List Female Suspect As a Man

One of the people sought by the FBI in connection with a tip that Chinese nationals had entered the United States illegally with the intent of committing terrorism in Boston is Mei Xia Dong. Dong was listed in the January 20 FBI alert as being, "male, possible DOB 11/21/77 and Chinese passport #G08386268."

Today, in an update, the FBI announced that,

> *Mei Xia Dong, Chinese/female(originally thought to be male), was located upon being identified as one of 14 subjects allegedly involved in a Boston terror plot. Mei Xia Dong was located in a U.S. Customs and Border Protection detention facility in the San Diego , CA , area. She was arrested for an immigration violation by U.S. Customs and Border Protection Agents on November 11, 2004 , and had remained in custody since that time.*

I find it curious that the FBI was able to identify Mei Xia Dong's Chinese Passport number and her date of birth but did not know that he was a she! A number of possible scenarios came to mind...

--Perhaps mainland China has seen a recent upsurge in sex-change operations?

--Perhaps some low-level FBI geek wrote in the wrong thing in the blank space after the word "Sex." Perhaps he had intended to write Yes" and, thinking better of it, got confused and entered "Male" instead of "Female?"

--Perhaps there has been a high-level coverup involving Max Factor and foundation make-up?
or
--Perhaps we have inadvertently stumbled upon an historic moment...the first time since the sixth day of creation where a woman has been pulled out of a man!

On the other hand, I suppose we can all benefit from a good ribbing once in a while!

SUNDAY, JANUARY 23, 2005

Johnny I Hardly Knew Ye

1925-1005

Johnny Carson died this morning. The news caught me by surprise. I did not even know he was in poor health. Only yesterday I heard a radio commentator say that Carson was still submitting jokes to David Letterman from time to time and that Letterman occasionally added them to his monologue.

Carson and the Tonight Show are inseparable from my adolescence and progress into adulthood. When he began hosting the show in 1961 I was too young to stay up to watch him. When he retired, I was often too tired to stay up to watch him!

For me he was the closest thing to my generation's Will Rogers. He was likeable, politically androgynous, naturally shy, genuinely interested in other people and possessing a wry and cutting humor that was never demeaning. Somehow, when Johnny had finished his monologue I always felt that the high places had been brought low and the low places raised up just enough to make the world seem like a happier and better place than it had seemed just a few minutes before.

Carnac the Magnificent

Carson put "beautiful downtown Burbank" on the map for every American, whether they actually knew or cared where Burbank was or even if it existed in reality at all. With Carnac the Magnificent and all his other alter-egos Carson drew us out of our depressing preoccupations with the civil rights riots, the tragedies of political assassinations and the angry cultural clashes spawned by the Vietnam War. Hippies and the "Summer of Love," Neil Armstrong walking on the moon & the rise and demise of the Beatles were covered, each in their turn, during his tenure.

One night in Winnemucca, Nevada, my wife and I had the strange experience of watching the Tonight Show at 10:00 pm, being broadcast from Utah's Rocky Mountain Standard time which always broadcast his show simultaneously with Central Standard Time (which, in Utah, meant 11:00 pm each night).

To be honest he was just as witty and funny at that earlier hour as he was two hours later someplace else!

It has been said that the popularity of his show caused a significant decline in conceptions and births in the American population. People were more interested in watching Carson than, well....in other things!

It was hard to believe that, when Carson finally retired in 1992, he would, by choice, disappear into his own private world of personal friendships, tennis and a few appearances at selective charity events. The spotlight he reflected so well for so many years had no lasting ownership on his life. He valued and preferred privacy to the adoration of an admiring public and, to its credit, the media loved him enough to respect his wishes to be left alone. It was by his choice that we must say, "Johnny, I Hardly Knew Thee."

Ed McMahon

By contrast, Carson's sidekick, Ed McMahon ("Heeerrrrrrrreeeeee's Johnny!") stepped out of the Tonight Show and has since inundated us with TV ads offering us the possibility of being Sweepstakes Winners or talking to us about retirement health benefits. While Carson will be remembered warmly and well, I suspect that McMahon will always be more likely to be associated with junk mail than with anything he accomplished as America's nightly straight man.

Like Will Rogers before him, Johnny Carson's life was forged in the values of the American mid-West "heartland." Like Will Rogers Carson found his popular legacy in entertainment and settled for life in Southern California. Both men were shy but enjoyed making others laugh. The laughter each of them shared was not contrived but genuine. The laughter came from hearts that were full of optimism, full of a love for America and committed to the ideal that "all people are created equal." And if someone needed to be brought down a notch in order to become equal with everyone else, they were both the first in line to do the job.

Will Rogers

In the spirit of Will Rogers I can honestly say that "I never met a Tonight Show with Johnny Carson that I didn't like." For me, every weekday night was the "Best of Carson."

Good-night, Johnny

MONDAY, JANUARY 24, 2005

A "Vox Blogoli" Response to Jonathan Rauch and the Atlantic Monthly

His Royal Blogness, Hugh Hewitt, has decreed a new "Vox Blogoli" in response to a selected paragraph from a new article in the *Atlantic Monthly* magazine written by Jonathan Rauch. I have taken the liberty of cutting and pasting the excerpt from Hugh's site to mine. Here it is:

"On balance it is probably healthier if religious conservatives are inside the political system than if they operate as insurgents and provocateurs on the outside. Better they should write anti-abortion planks into the Republican platform than bomb abortion clinics. The same is true of the left. The clashes over civil rights and Vietnam turned into street warfare partly because activists were locked out of their own party establishments and had to fight, literally, to be heard. When Michael Moore receives a hero's welcome at the Democratic National Convention, we moderates grumble; but if the parties engage fierce activists while marginalizing tame centrists, that is probably better for the social peace than the other way around."

I like to think of myself as a "religious conservative" of the mainline Christian denominational variety. I do not consider Democrats to be particularly evil and sometimes I even vote for them! My congregation, while probably having more flavors of Republicans, is diverse enough politically to force us to depend more on Jesus Christ for our unity than our political viewpoints.

Clearly I have more in common with my Evangelical friends than I do with my liberal Christian friends (who have now claimed the title, "Progressive Christians" in place of the old term, "liberal"). Even so, I consider members of both groups to be my friends...and more than that, my brothers and sisters in Christ!

Having said this, I am puzzled to see Mr. Rauch parallel "religious conservatives" with "insurgents and provocateurs" who "bomb abortion clinics" and are, to the right, what Michael Moore is to the left. In point of fact, I have always identified more with the Rev. Dr. Martin Luther King, Jrs. of the world than with the "fierce activists" I am associated with in this article.

Of course, being merely mortal and vain, there are times when I dream of actually "provoking" my congregation on a Sunday morning! Generally speaking, however, I am more than content when I am able to keep them from dozing off during our 9:00 am worship! And never, ever have I planted an IED beneath their chairs to regain their attention! An insurgent I am not. In fact I am not ashamed or embarrassed to say that I have never bombed a single abortion clinic in my life. And, of the hundreds and even thousands of evangelical and conservative Christian leaders and believers that I have met and known, I cannot think of a single one who would consider such behavior to be a logical outgrowth of their faith.

I can only wonder if Jonathan Rauch has any friends who consider themselves to be "conservative Christians?" I can only wonder if he has ever met or ever even spoken with a "conservative Christian?" And I wonder if he has ever attended a worship service at a "conservative Christian" church?

From where I sit, "conservative Christians" are the foundational center of American culture and its citizenry. Where Mr. Rauch appears to consider himself to be a moderate Democrat in contrast to the extreme *left* wingers, most evangelical and conservative Christians would similarly, more often than not, consider themselves to be moderate Republicans in contrast to the extreme *right* wingers!

Michael Moore clearly represents a marginalized fringe of the Democratic party (taken as as a whole) whereas conservative Christians are the moral *center* of the Republican party. Those who push the limits of propriety and grace in the Republican party, such as a David Duke or a Patrick Buchanan, usually find themselves shuffled out of the party into the realms of political purgatory until, repenting of their sin, they can be forgiven and restored.

The right wing equivalent of a Michael Moore would be shunned by the Republican party. The vast majority of party members would be embarrassed by the presence of such excess, such bitterness, such dripping vitriol and egotistical self-promotion.

That is not to say that Republicans do not have their share of loonies running around. Each political party lives in a big tent that is filled with a wide range of diverse characters. Loony constituencies in both parties elect loony politicos to City, County, State and Federal offices and the parties have to live with them and, insofar as it might be necessary, work with them.

But such nut-cases are not cheered, praised and encouraged by the "religious conservatives" in the Republican party. Most certainly they are not given the seat of honor next to a former Republican President during a nationally televised national convention.

In short, there is no real parallel between the Democratic and Republican parties at all, except for the fact that both are political parties!

The culture of the Democrats and their widely diverse and conflicting Constituencies bear little or no structural resemblance to the culture of the Republicans. Whereas the Democrats consist of a fragmented constellation of special interest groups each seeking to promote their particular agenda, the Republicans, "religious conservatives" included, consist of individuals and groups who share a common consensus as regards their core moral, ethical and cultural values.

The consequence of all this is that, at its heart, the Democrats tend to focus on political programs while the Republicans tend to focus on political principles.

As someone who once, in my teens, supported the presidential candidacies of Bobby Kennedy and ">Clean Gene" McCarthy, I have the perspective of having been on both sides of the political divide. I wonder if Jonathan Rauch has ever been a Republican? or a "religious conservative?"

I have long since been inoculated against feelings of disgust when I see myself and millions of other Americans being unfairly and predjudicially caricatured as over-the-top, gun-waving, freedom stifling, ignorant, narrow-minded, bigoted Red-necked, White-skinned and Blue-nosed crazies simply because we go to church on Sundays and believe the Good News of God's saving love in Jesus Christ.

Jonathan Rauch's radical mis-read on "conservative Christians" reminds of a man who once served as Campus Pastor at Whitworth College in Eastern Washington. One day, he said, a student came into his office expressing his disgust and his determination not to believe in a God who takes pleasure in letting babies be born deformed, who causes planes to fall out of the sky, who sends earthquakes and floods to destroy entire cities, who calls his chosen few together and sends everyone else to hell and requires his followers to believe and do irrational and illogical things in order to be "saved."

"What do you have to say to that!" the student demanded.

The ("religiously conservative") Chaplain quietly replied, "I agree with you completely! I don't believe in a God like that either! If you have a few minutes I'd be happy to tell you about the God I *do* believe in!"

I would truly enjoy the opportunity of having Mr. Rauch join my Central Oahu congregation for worship on a Sunday morning. I have no doubt that, if his eyes and ears are closed to the reality of the experience, he will find it dull, boring and a waste of an otherwise perfectly good Sunday morning. I doubt very much that he would find myself or my congregation to be in any way a threat to his liberty or in any way reminiscent of Michael Moore.

If, on the other hand, Mr. Rauch's eyes and ears are open to the reality of the experience, I strongly suspect that his heart might just soften a little bit and maybe, perhaps, potentially, theoretically, discover that "religious conservatives" can be more normal than he might have first believed.

And, I would add, if he was open enough for God's Holy Spirit to get inside him even for a moment, he might find that he had a few spare minutes to let someone explain to him what they really *do* believe!

TUESDAY, JANUARY 25, 2005

"Vox Blogoli" Revisited--Updated Thoughts on Jonathan Rauch, Hugh Hewitt & the Blogoshere

In light of Jonathan Rauch's appearance on Hugh Hewitt's radio program today, and in light of the *Atlantic Monthly*'s agreement with Mr. Rauch to allow the entire text of his article to be posted on Hugh's website, updated thoughts are being solicited for yesterday's "Vox Blogoli." So, here are my updated thoughts.

Hip, hip hooray for Jonathan Rauch! You did a beautiful, gracious, mature and very unusual thing. You listened to your critics with open ears and respected their written responses to the excerpt from your article that Hugh posted on his website yesterday.

After reading Rauch's entire article this evening I can easily see that same gracious and mature character reflected in his prose (and even a successfully intentional attempt to be "fair and balanced").

I suppose it would be easy to take a cheap shot at Hugh for lifting that one particular section of text out of the context of the entire article, and such a shot might well be justified.

On the other hand, the disputed section of text was written without enough objectivity to recognize that its implied comparisons would be patently offensive to millions of Americans, in particular, those who might identify themselves as "religious conservatives".

The fact that this "mis-intended" paragraph was pentultimate in the article only served to exaggerate its impression on those who read it, including most certainly, Hugh Hewitt.

To his credit and to my relief, Jonathan Rauch admitted that he had mangled his intended thought with inappropriately juxtaposed imagery. He also apologized for it. He made no excuse for it. He blamed no one else; and suggested that if the rest of the article were to be considered it would show that this particular section was not at all consistent with either the tone or thesis of the whole.

I have read the whole article and I must concur with Mr. Rauch's own assessment. In light of this I am willing to believe that he may, in fact, actually have friends who are "religious conservatives" and is more likely than not respectful of and not un-informed concerning their values and beliefs!

As Hugh has pointed out, the entire exercise was a valuable proof of how quickly the blogosphere can respond to even the smallest and least malicious misstep in grammar and syntax in the MSM.

While clearly a wonderful improvement for accountability and self-correction in the media the use of the blogosphere in such a way as was done by Hugh raises certain concerns.

We who blog must be extremely careful not to allow ourselves to be manipulated by those who we admire and trust. It is tempting to write our "Vox Blogoli" responses in a way designed to "please" Mr. Hewitt or conform to what we think might be his own thoughts and opinions.

It would be sad, indeed, if the blogosphere divided itself into the sort of political party divisions so carefully parsed by Mr. Rauch in his article. It is far better for each of us to craft and hone our own voice rather than attempt to "clone" it after someone higher up in the ecosystem. It is not healthy, either, for good men like Hugh to feel too empowered in his opinions and commentary by allowing him to think that we praise and rejoice at his every utterance.

Hugh, I promise to do all I can to keep you humble! Don't let your growing following go to your head lest you begin to think more highly of yourself than you ought to think.

Indeed, although it might cost you some of your listenership, perhaps you should take a point of caution from Jonathan Rauch's article. Just like the Washington D.C. politicos, your status is maintained by being provocative and divisive. I suggest that you would be even more believable and authentic if you occasionally represented some of the unity of thought amongst the middle-majority of Americans, and chastise those in both political parties who seek to divide us as Americans for their own political gain.

For example, your concern over whether Arlen Specter was right-wing-pure enough to be allowed chairmanship of the Judiciary Committee or not. Is it now impossible to be a "mixed-blessing" such as are exemplified by such folks as John McCain and Arlen Specter on the Republican side and Joe Lieberman and Zell Miller among the Democrats? Must political positions always be adversarial and polarizing in order to be legitimate and respected?

Do you hear me, bloggers? Keep your independence! Don't become anyone's toady! Speak the truth as *you* understand it...but always in love...and with a level of dignity and respect all too lacking in the political arena today.

WEDNESDAY, JANUARY 26, 2005

Meteorite Suspect Held In Cambodia

Actual photograph of the suspected meteorite

According to **AFP News** a "Suspected Meteorite" fell from the sky in the highlands of northwestern Cambodia early today.

Now I don't know much about this sort of thing but it appears reasonable to me that something that weighs over 10 pounds, looks like a rock, is found buried 16 inches into the ground where it was still warm to the touch, in the exact spot that something fell from the sky with a sound like "a bomb," and set fires that destroyed several hundred hectares of rice fields, should be considered a prime suspect as being a meteorite.

Although the rock was recovered and is being held by police it is not yet clear what charges will be brought against it. The rock's lawyers refused comment except to say that their client is innocent of everything and was only a simple, honest rock that had never been suspected of being a meteorite until today. "It will all be explained in court," one lawyer said as they left the police station this afternoon.

In the spirit of justice and fair play it is, I feel, important to remind my readers that everyone, even a rock, has the right to be considered innocent until proven guilty. Until then, we can only speculate and wonder whether, with all this publicity, the rock will be able to receive a fair trial in Cambodia. The same lawyer quoted above hinted that a request for a change of venue to Modesto, California, would likely be made in the next several days.

THURSDAY, JANUARY 27, 2005

I Didn't Know That!

Did you know that the mother of former Monkee Michael Nesmith was the inventor of Liquid Paper? Neither did I. At least not until daughter Number Three told me all about it a few minutes ago.

And did you know that the same General Santa Anna who won at the Alamo, lost Texas to Sam Houston and was eventually exiled from Mexico is credited with being the co-inventor of modern chewing gum?

It seems my wonderful wife has subscribed to a nifty magazine called, "Mental Floss." This magazine is an assortment of oddball trivia focusing on a different subject each issue. It is totally useless for almost anything that is important to me or anybody else which is why, of course, I will have to read every word of it when my daughter is done with it.

Oh, and by the way, did you know that the guy who invented your car's Cruise Control was.......blind? (I'm not sure I really want to think about that one too much!)

FRIDAY, JANUARY 28, 2005

Tears In Paradise

"Semper Fi"

Two days ago a Marine helicopter went down in a sandstorm in Western Iraq. Thirty-one Marines and one Seaman were killed; all who were aboard. Twenty-seven of those men (they were all male) were deployed from Marine Base Kaneohe, on the Windward side of Oahu, about a 45 minute drive from where I live.

Although none of them (so far as I know) were originally from Hawaii, their spouses and children live here, attend school here and work here. Many U.S. and Hawaii State flags have been lowered to half-staff. Counselors are visiting schools helping staff learn how to deal with the deaths of a child's parent or friend's parent. I expect that some of the Marines may have attended a church somewhere on the island or may have coached little league or a soccer team nearby.

A retired Marine officer commented that a helicopter crash such as this can happen any time in any place. It could just as likely have happened at Camp Pendleton or some other mainland Marine base as in Iraq.

This does not bring me any solace; nor will it make any surviving family or friends feel any better, either. They are gone. All of them. In a moment. In a twinkling of an eye. Like Icarus we have attempted to tame the heavens and, like Icarus, our frail mortality has humbled us; bringing us back down to earth in more ways than one.

Yet the One who made the heavens and the earth is still Lord over all...including these fallen soldiers. We can do little more than trust them to the care and mercy of Almighty God and, for those who have faith in Jesus Christ, claim the certain hope of life beyond life and the resurrection to eternal life.

Ladysmith Black Mambazo

Ladysmith Black Mambazo

Last night my wonderful wife and I had the privilege of seeing Ladysmith Black Mambazo in concert at the Leeward Community College theater.

LBM came into being in 1961 when founder, Joseph Shabalala, brought friends and family members together in singing an a cappella singing style derived from traditional South African *isicathamiya* music. After winning every song contest available they became an icon for the Zulu communities in South Africa where they suffered under the oppression of Apartheid. In 1986 they gained world-wide recognition by way of their collaboration with Paul Simon on his historic "Graceland" album. In many ways they became a cultural symbol for Black African pride, hope and determination to gain freedom and justice in their native land.

Now, celebrating the 11th anniversary of the dismantling of Apartheid, Ladysmith Black Mambazo is on a world tour, sharing their considerable talent, humor and culture while, at the same time, promoting their latest albums, "Raise Your Spirits High" (nominated for a 2004 Grammy) and their just-released "No boundaries" (where they are accompanied by the classical strings of the English Chamber Orchestra).

The *isicathamiya* vocal style was not strange to our ears, partly because of the Paul Simon album and the resulting (but short-lived) popularity of such music in America. More to the point, the "call-response" style of music grounded with a repetitive choral background counterpointed by a solo voice adding lyric melodic and rhythmic variations reflects a traditional African vocal style first brought to the Americas in the hearts and minds of slaves.

Jazz and Gospel are two of the modern reincarnations of this type of music which can be heard in almost any African-American Christian congregation on any given Sunday morning. This reality, I think, is at the crux of Mambazo's influence and popularity in South Africa. They are a symbol of the strength and enduring power of traditional African culture. Whereas the Boer/Afrikaaner culture has largely collapsed into oblivion, the very culture that the Afrikaaners had tried to suppress and destroy has survived.

As a Christian I must believe that truth is ultimately stronger than falsehood and that freedom is stronger than oppression. The mere existence of Ladysmith Black Mambazo and the triumph of their world tour is, I think, evidence that my faith is well-founded.

The performance was sold out and they received two standing ovations. This is how it should be. They have not only earned it, but they deserved it.

SATURDAY, JANUARY 29, 2005

Just Wondering.......

Why is it that every time I wash my t-shirts they come out of the washing machine inside-out? Today it was 8 out of 11 that emerged this way. Is there an engineer or a physicist somewhere who could explain this to me?

Just in case you were wondering, yes, I have tried turning them inside-out *before* putting them in the washing machine. The results are the same!

Just wondering.....

SUNDAY, JANUARY 30, 2005

Iraq Votes: Profiles In Courage

A Day Like the Fall of the Berlin Wall

Today the Iraqi people voted for freedom. I will remember today much as I remember the day that the Berlin Wall came down...demolished from both the inside and the outside. It is a day that many felt would never come. It is a day that many did not want to come. But today it came. Freedom, autonomy and giant step towards genuine independence.

Iraqis vote!

London Herald

BERLIN WALL TUMBLES

The American and coalition troops represented the "outside" of the wall and the Iraqis themselves the "inside." Today, those "inside," with the help and support of those living in "outside" freedom, began the official and authentic demolition of the wall of oppression, tyranny and despotism which has confined them to hopelessness for the past 50 years.For more pictures of the day's voting in Iraq check out Adam Keiper's slide show. Awesome!

Remembering American & Coalition Sacrifices

Much has been sacrificed to bring forth this great, wonderful and historic day. Over 1,000 American men and women, both military and civilian, coalition troops, too, and many other international civilians who had flocked to help build a new Iraq, hoping either for personal gain or simply to participate in creating history, have lost their lives fighting for someone else's hope for a better tomorrow. They have fought to protect their own countries' security as well, knowing that the more stable and free the world is, the more safe it is for everyone else!

Remembering Iraqi Sacrifices Under Sadaam

Not to be forgotten, of course, are the Iraqis whose lives have been lost in this struggle to be free. Over 1,000,000 Shi'ites in the south, either slaughtered as a lesson to others or mass murdered as reprisals for their revolt against Sadaam Hussein following the first "Gulf War" back in 1991. Hundreds of thousands of Kurds. slaughtered, some by poison gas, perhaps as a "Sadaastic" experiment to see how effective chemical weapons can be. The million plus Iraqis and Iranians who died in their own war, instigated by Sadaam in the 1980's might also be seen as sacrificial victims to a tyrant's twisted delusions of grandeur. And their are the Kuwaitis who were killed or who forever disappeared when they were invaded by order of Sadaam.

We must also, today, remember the women and children, tortured, raped, beaten, imprisoned and threatened daily as reprisals for a wrong word or a perceived act of defiance by a husband, father, or other family member.

Remembering Iraqi Civilian Casualties

And we must not forget the actual-count estimates of 15-18,000 civilians who have died as a direct result of the American/coalition invasion and occupation. While many of these deaths have been at the hand of the terrorist/resistance, it is clear that the large majority have been what has been euphemistically referred to as "collateral casualties." Their lives were tragically sacrificed by those who did not have any intention of causing them harm. Yet we must repent and mourn their loss and number them among the martyrs for freedom.

The uniformed troops loyal to Sadaam who died in combat must also be acknowledged with respect as so many of them fought honorably in defense of their country.

Forgetting the Terrorists

Those who resort to the extreme acts of terror, hiding among civilians and dealing random and indiscriminate death to foreigner and Iraqi alike, whose goal is only to destroy rather than to build up, who in no legitimate way represent the Iraqi people, these who who commit barbarous acts of videotaped beheadings, disembowlings and acts of indecency and desecration on the bodies of their victims, these shall forever be numbered among the citizens of hell, forgotten by both God and humanity. Damned by their own hatred and consumed by their misplaced passion. Never will any nation erect a monument to their memory. Indeed their only monument will be the rise of a free nation above their unmarked and forgotten graves, a monument to their ultimate irrelevance; lives wasted, thrown away; for nothing. Those who seek death will find it. It shall be their inheritance forever.

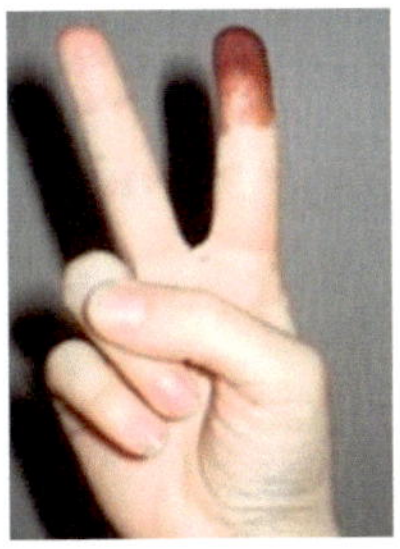

Purple Fingers

Tomorrow I shall color my right index finger blue as an act of solidarity with the people who voted in Iraq today. This suggestion came from someone who wrote the idea on Andrew Sullivan's blogpage earlier today. It would be nice if many others did the same. No doubt it will be a good conversation starter during the coming week! Speaking of colored fingers, Diary from Baghdad, a blog kept by an Iraqi civil engineer named Rose, had a very brief entry today. It read simply,

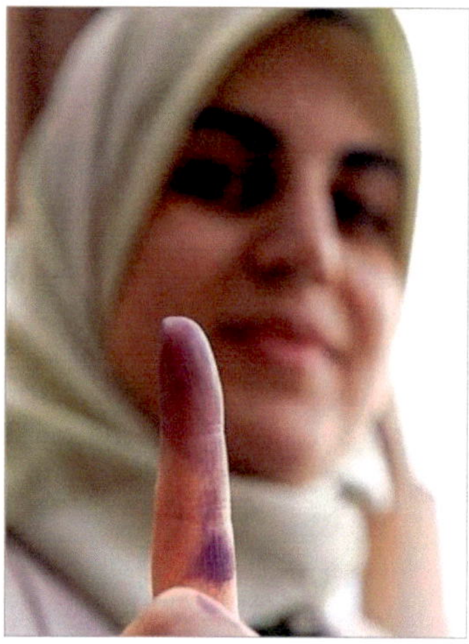

"I did it, I voted YES,YES, I did it. I have the courage to do it." And with these words was this picture:

Choices: Theirs and Ours

The journey is not yet done. There are many more miles to go and many more decisions that must be made. But today the Iraqi people came to a crossroads. They considered the risks, the dangers, the uncertainties and the possibilities. And they voted their decision for all the world to see. Every nation that has a shred of decency and honor, every individual who has the love of neighbor in their heart, can do nothing less than to offer their full and enthusiastic support to the people of Iraq. To travel the rest of the journey alongside them will be a privilege!

MONDAY, JANUARY 31, 2005

Being a Pastor is...Never Dull!

Today I led my weekly Bible Study through two more chapters of Job and shared prayer with those who attended.

Today I wrote one final article for our monthly church newsletter and reformatted the page that had already been made print-ready by our newsletter editor. I had to sort of squeeze it in at the last minute. Learning word processing skills has come with the job!

Today I spent some free time finishing up some music I wrote and performed as a wedding gift a year ago but never put in shape to present on a CD.

Today I listened and counseled with someone trying to improve a stressful relationship.

Today I listened to a man in my congregation who, after a long life of searching, had finally given his life over to God and accepted the Christian faith. What a story! It reminded me of C.S. Lewis' "Surprised By Joy!"

Today I met with our church New Building Team and made a final decision on who the architect will be for our upcoming $1 million expansion/remodeling project.

Today I sent an email to a new family in our congregation letting them know that they had given me their home and email addresses but not their phone number. I hope to visit them this week!

Today I consulted with the host of one of our upcoming Lenten Small Groups, confirming that I will be providing the scripture texts that I will be using in my sermon series so they can study them ahead of time each week.

Today I rested from yesterday morning when I led worship, preached, chatted with several new visiting families, engaged in some impromptu emergency counseling during our fellowship time and then subbed as teacher for our Senior High Sunday School Class.

Today was the sort of day that keeps me from becoming stuck in a rut. Today was the sort of day the keeps me filled with joy! Today was the sort of day that keeps me humble before the Lord. Today, like almost every day, I had the opportunity to use a variety of spiritual gifts and natural talents to further the Gospel in my congregation. Today I spent intimate, personal time with good people, sharing difficult times and wonderful times all mixed together! What a privilege to be a pastor! What an adventure!

I can hardly wait to see what tomorrow will bring! Praise the Lord!

TUESDAY, FEBRUARY 1, 2005

Honolulu Advertiser Registers One Hit and Two Misses.

First, the Hit

Radical Muslim Literature Found in American Mosques

Today's Sunday Honolulu Advertiser, to its credit, published some of the findings released last week concerning Islamic booklets and other materials published by the Saudi Arabian government found in numerous Muslim mosques scattered around the United States. The writings reflect some of the more radical interpretations of the Qur'an as understood by the fundamental wahhabi sect which is preeminent in Saudi Arabia. The radical interpretations of the Qur'an as practiced by Osama bin Laden and his peers are, for the most part, derived from this Islamic sect/tradition.

Among other things the literature declares that it is lawful to shed the blood of adulterers and others even when living in a nation whose own laws forbid it. Muslims are encouraged not to demonstrate any respect towards unbelievers, even if they are the holders of high office. They are also discouraged from engaging in any activity that sustains or furthers the agendas of unbelievers, whether in business or in government. Imams who were interviewed denied that they personally supported or taught these things in their mosques. Some denied even knowing they were sitting on their literature racks and tables.

I find it hard to believe anything that the Imams say, especially since they are not bound by this interpretation of Islamic law to speak honestly with "infidels." For Muslims of this persuasion it is counted as honorable to boldly lie about anything for any reason to someone outside of their faith. For example, there is no doubt in anyone's mind that Yassir Arafat was constantly lying to the Israelis, the United States, the United Nations and to just about every non-Muslim nation or agency that he ever worked with. The Palestinians, however, viewed such lies as a demonstration of his cleverness and his faithfulness to Qur'anic law. Such lying both strengthened respect for his leadership and, for the Palestinian and Arab people, demonstrated what fools and suckers the Israelis and Americans are.

This culture of dissemblance is epidemic in the Middle East. We should not be surprised to find it spreading like a cancer throughout the Muslim communities in the United States. Although still a minority view of American Muslims, the ideas are spreading rapidly, especially since many if not most of mosques built in recent years have been built and "staffed" with Saudi Arabian money (both private and governmental) to promote the particular wahhabi brand of Islam in our country.

I commend the Advertiser for the courage to print a short summary of this study. From what I have read on the internet, very few major media outlets have felt comfortable enough to share this information with the American public.

Now the First Miss

Ward Churchill Scandal Info Out of Date

Today's Advertiser printed an article discussing the current scandal at Colorado State University over tenured professor Ward Churchill. Although the article, originating with the Washington Post, covers the story fairly well it completely omits the revelations of the past week declaring that he is not a member of the Keetoowah Tribe of Oklahoma (as he has claimed, using a "associate member" card once available to anyone, whether Indian or not) and **statements** by Dennis Banks and the American Indian Movement (AIM) asserting that Churchill "*has fraudulently represented himself as an Indian, and a member of the American Indian Movement*" and "*has been masquerading as an Indian for years behind his dark glasses and beaded headband.*"

The Advertiser should have known of this information and should have included it as part of the article. It is sloppy and lazy to print outdated news that could easily have been brought current with a simple internet search.

The Second Miss

Truth About Terrorism Conference Not Revealed

The Advertiser's report on the self-styled "International Conference on International Terrorism" currently taking place in Riyadh under the sponsorship of the Saudi Arabian government failed to mention that Israel, without doubt the greatest target of international terrorism, was not invited to attend or participate.

In a recent email correspondence with the Saudi embassy regarding this conference a man by the name of Thomas Wuthrich wrote:
What kind of monstrous joke is your country trying to perpetrate in issuing an invitation to its "anti-terror" conference to the world's foremost sponsor of terror, Iran, while shunning one of the foremost victims of terror, Israel?
It should come as no surprise to you when polls show that Saudi Arabia is among the

countries least trusted by Americans.

And, no, I am not a Jew. I am merely someone who sees clearly.
Mr. Wuthrich received an unsigned response from the Saudi embassy information office:
Thank you Mr. Wuthrich. One of the foremost victims of terror??? I think not. Please keep in mind Israel is in violation of more United Nations resolutions than all other countries of the world combined. Iran is not in violation of any United Nations resolutions. Image is different than reality.

Is this the sort of "International" conference we should be supporting? Evil Israel is a pariah while Iran is squeaky clean? If "image is different than reality" then I must be living in a completely different "reality" than the Saudi writer of this paragraph. Actually, now that I think about it, I am convinced that I am living in a completely different reality!

The Honolulu Advertiser does the public a great disservice by presenting this conference and "International" or legitimate by any objective terms. The continued lack of recognition of Israel as a nation by Saudi Arabia and other Middle Eastern nations is a travesty that must be resolved before any real progress on international terrorism can be made. If such nations are our nation's friends, then the United States must certainly be Israel's greatest enemy!

I pray that this is not so. But I fear that once again our country is being played for a fool...and the radical Islamists are laughing at us. To our disgrace, they are right to do so.

MONDAY, FEBRUARY 7, 2005

"The Terrorists Are These Jews and Christians"

The following "interview" with a Wahhabi cleric in Saudi Arabia is taken from Little Green Footballs. The subject closely parallels and supplements my previous posts here and here (scroll down to "First, the Hit" & then "The Second Miss"). I'm sorry to say that there is nothing in this interview that surprises me. From the perspective of the speaker, what he says is completely rational and makes perfect sense. It is important for every Christian and every American to realize that some people do not see the world in the same way that we do. We must learn to think as they do in order to understand their justification for what we (rightly) call evil. Once again, as I have said before, do not think that all or even most Muslims agree with Al-Qarni. There are as many different opinions within Islam as there are in Christianity. The main difference is, however, that Christians do not blow up women and children simply because they are not Christian.

"The Terrorists are These Jews and Christians"

("Little Green Footballs" says:) Even as the (*government*) of Saudi Arabia promote(*s*) their absurd sham conference on counter-terrorism (which the US, to our disgrace, attended), their television stations and mosques continue to pump out a steady stream of jihad rhetoric and hatred of Jews and Christians. MEMRI has excerpts of a February 3, 2005 IQRA TV program with Saudi cleric Musa Al-Qarni:

"<u>The Jews and Christians are Allah's Enemies...</u>We Ask Allah to Strengthen the Jihad Fighters in Iraq."

Al-Qarni: The uproar and the chaos that we see today in the human race; the killing, the acts of aggression, the rape, the robbery, and the disgrace of honor; what causes this is that the banners which are hoisted high are those of the Jews, the Christians, and other religions and faiths, and not the banner of "There is no God but Allah and Muhammad is Allah's Messenger." Let's have a look at what is written in the Koran. What position must we adopt towards Allah's enemies? Is it the position we have adopted? First of all, we must be aware of the fact that at present we see that [the West] doesn't want us even to say the words "Allah's enemies." They don't want us to say that the Jews and the Christians are Allah's enemies. They don't want us to say that the Jews and the Christians are the enemies of the Muslims and the enemies of Islam. This is fixed and established in the Koran and in the tradition... If this is so, if this is something fixed, how is it that we find in the things that we say, among our children, our own flesh and blood, among Muslims, people who are in denial of these things, who deny that there is a great enmity between Muslims and non-Muslims? It is true that we say that Islam's fundamental approach is that of mercy, and that the fundamental principle of Islam is [that it is a] mercy for human beings. But [it is for] he who submits to Allah's religion and extends his hand to allow Allah's religion to spread all over the earth and to make Allah's word supreme; it is toward him that religion is merciful. However, whoever fights against Allah's religion, and fights those who love Allah, distorts the image of Islam and the Muslims and does so much to weaken Islam...

Let's take a real-life example. Today, the Jews are occupying the Muslim lands, raping their women, killing their children, and destroying their houses; are these acts being perpetrated by the Muslims or by the Jews?

Interviewer*: By the Jews, as anyone with eyes can see. This is clear to the entire world... The Terrorists are These Jews and Christians*

Interviewer: You shouldn't blame them for this. We are the ones to blame if we agree to change the Koran and the tradition to suit them.

Al-Qarni*: The terrorists are these Jews and Christians who implement these policies through the use of force, repression, and tyranny, and to this end make use of planes, tanks, and all manner of deadly weapons.*

Interviewer*: Aisha's second question [is about whether] Islam spread by the sword. They always say that Islam spread by the sword. How should we respond to them?*
Al-Qarni*: First of all, we ask by what means is the freedom that the U.S. wants spread? The freedom that it wants now to market?*

Interviewer*: Through missiles and bombs...*

Al-Qarni*: Through B-50s, bombs that the international community has forbidden, hundred of thousands of armed soldier; this is how freedom has spread.*

Interviewer*: And we don't see any freedom. All we see afterwards is subjugation...*

Al-Qarni: *At any rate, if we return to our discussion of the heart of the matter... First of all, we must realize that Allah obligated us to disseminate this religion all over the globe. And first, it sould be spread through outreach and calling people to Allah's word, through pleasing words, gently, and through good deeds. Through letting people hear Allah's words and showing them Islam. However, if we run up against someone who opposes this path and attempts to obstruct the spread of the upright religion and the light, and to obstruct their reaching others; in this case it is a duty to fight such a person. And Allah said: "Fight them until there is no more strife and Allah's religion reigns supreme." We don't agree with those who disavow this completely and say that the religion [of Islam] doesn't use the sword. No. Islam uses the sword when there is no other alternative. Therefore wisdom, as the religious authorities say, consists in utilizing each thing in its proper place. If there is need for the sword, then it is wise to use the sword, and if the occasion requires kind words and outreach, then it is wise to utilize them. We ask Allah to strengthen the spirits of the Jihad fighters in Iraq, and to help them against their enemies, the Jews and the Christians. Likewise, I emphasize that the Jihad that the Muslims are fighting in Iraq in order to repel the enemy aggressor, the Jews and the Christians, who are attacking land and honor. I emphasize that this Jihad is legitimate Jihad, Jihad for Allah's sake, and it is considered defense of Muslim countries, their lands and their honor. The doubts that are raised against this Jihad are not correct and are out of place.*

TUESDAY, FEBRUARY 8, 2005

13,000-17,000 "Insurgents" Estimated In Iraq--Whoop-de-Doo!

In a late-breaking news report today a senior American military official released estimates that there are 13,000 to 17-000 insurgents present in Iraq. Of these, 5,000-7,000 are "committed fighters" who are mostly former Ba'ath Party members, many others are "fence-sitting" ex-criminals who provide support and materiel for the terrorists, 1,000 work with al-Zarqawi's network and 500 are non-Iraqis.

Let's see, with a total population of 25,374,691 people that would come out to be about .063% of the population.

Come to think of it, if only 17,000 showed up at Aloha Stadium for a University of Hawaii football game it would be a really big disappointment.

If someone organized a national march on Washington D.C. and only 17,000 showed up, the news media would consider it to be a failure.

The same official estimated that somewhere between 10,000 and 15,000 insurgents were killed in Iraq during the past year. Many of these were replaced by others, he said, so it is hard to keep even approximate statistics on these things.

To my way of thinking, if that many were taken out last year during a time of political and social chaos, without Iraqi troops or guardsmen and without a unifying central government, then the year 2005 should provide even more success at rooting them out. Even more so if the vast majority of Iraqi people come to the conclusion that they can and must take charge of getting rid of them themselves and begin sharing intelligence information with Iraqi authorities and refuse to shelter them in their homes and neighborhoods any longer.

The fact that terrorists have taken to kidnapping the mentally retarded **to** do their suicide-bombing dirty work for them demonstrates how short the self-destructive line of eager volunteers is getting.

I sincerely doubt that Mr. al-Zaqawi will be strapping on body explosives any time soon. His *modus operandi* is to get the other flunky to blow himself up. We can only wonder what will happen when the few remaining terrorists run out of flunkies!

Iraq today is like a chess game where White has moved in such a way that mate is assured in four more moves. Black can still take White's pieces, of course, but in a futile cause. After last week's elections it should be clear to the Iraqi people and to the world that the insurgent's cause is now officially futile.

WEDNESDAY, FEBRUARY 9, 2005

A "Real World" Wake-Up Call

Daughter #2 attending college on the mainland found a job on campus that fits her schedule, will add hours as they become available and be flexible when her class schedule changes each quarter. Six hours on Sunday afternoon and evening. What could be better? The perfect job! Except....

Last Sunday, in the middle of the Super Bowl game she had to leave the Super Bowl party and go to work. Just like millions of other Americans. She felt cheated, of course, and I would have felt cheated, too! But I suspect that her feeling of being cheated was not that of a child missing out on something because their parents were taking them somewhere else or because were grounded for something they had done. Instead, I believe that what my daughter felt was an adult feeling, where it was her own decisions and her own commitments that required her to miss something else she wanted to do.

One of the hardest things to learn as an adult is how to live with conflicts of all kinds. Every choice an adult makes, whether when to go shopping, what degree to work for in college, where to seek employment or whether to get married or have children, involves saying "No" to something else. In real life there are consequences to the choices we make. We must learn that we can't have it all and embrace the need to make sacrifices in life.

Those who do not learn this generally do not fare very well in life. They either squander what they have or become paralyzed and unable to make any real decisions, sacrifices or commitments at all.

My daughter is learning a great many things at college, and, as I had predicted, the most important lessons are not those she is learning in the classroom.

Eason Jordan Eason Jordan Eason Jordan Eason Jordan Eason Jordan

It seems that everyone in the Conservative blogosphere is snapping their jaws at CNN News Director, Eason Jordan, these days. Mr. Jordan reputedly made statements at a recent international conference in Davos, Switzerland, either implying or actually accusing the US

Military, either officially or by individual soldiers, of targeting journalists in Iraq.

These comments, made in the presence of several hundred people, including US Rep. Barney Frank, US Sen. Chris Dodd and David Gergen. There is some confusion as to what was actually said, in what context, in what order and whether or not or how much and in what way Mr. Jordan attempted to clarify or back-track on his initial comments.

The entire thing is recorded on a Davos videotape but they are refusing to release it due to a "rule" that precludes identifying specific speakers at certain informal session.

If, indeed, Mr. Jordan is guilty of the more serious attributions he should either back them up with hard evidence, resign or be fired from his position. It would not do CNN's reputation any good to have their News Editor accusing the US military of such atrocities without any proof to back it up. Is CNN "fair and unbiased?" Do they present the news and "let the viewer decide?" Oh, I forgot, that's Fox News....

Ash Wednesday

This evening my congregation hosted the local Lutheran congregation for our annual combined Ash Wednesday worship. Today, however, we also included the Korean congregation that "nests" in our church facilities. The Korean pastor, after 40 years of pastoral ministry in the United States and missionary service in Korea (he is an American citizen born it what is now North Korea) had never participated in an Ash Wednesday service. Neither, according to him, had any of the members of his present congregation.

So, three pastors sharing the lead in worship (which was all in English, by the way) and one of them giving and receiving ashes on the forehead for the first time, along with members of his congregation. Our midweek children's "Kid's for Christ" program also attended the service. Half of the children do not attend our church on Sunday. I doubt that any of them had attended an Ash Wednesday service before, either.

But the children, along with the adults, carefully confessed their sins in writing on a small piece of paper and then came forward with the adults to drop their confession into a bowl where they were consumed by fire. (This burning parallels the Old Testament image of a "burnt offering" but, more importantly, represents the offering of our prayer to God in the rising flame and smoke, and also the visual impact of seeing that our sins, when offered to God with a repentant heart, are consumed and forgiven....gone forever).

The children could not take their eyes off of this mini-bonfire in the middle of our worship center. Unlike the adults, who dropped in their piece of paper and returned to their seats, the children dropped their papers in and then stood, immobile and transfixed by the flames. Adults had to squeeze past them to get to the bowl but no one pushed or complained. After several minutes I gently asked the children to return to their seats. I did not want that incredible moment of wonder to end too soon!

A few minutes later those same children came forward and received the mark of ashes on their foreheads (ashes not from the burned confessions but from the Lutheran's tradition of using ashes from the previous year's Palm Sunday palm fronds). Along with the ashes came the words, "Remember you are dust; and to dust you shall return." I have no idea what this enigmatic reference to our human mortality meant to those children. They are so young and full of life. I'm not sure if most of them have ever even thought about aging, sickness or death. For them there is only "eternal and abundant life!" In their innocence they represent to us adults what we long for....life free from the fear of death. And, in their innocence, they represent to us adults something of the new life and salvation we have experienced and received from our once dead and now risen Lord and Savior, Jesus Christ.

As if this were not enough, we then celebrated the Sacrament of the Lord's Supper. For this, most of the children had left, being picked up by parents who knew they had to get some sleep before school tomorrow morning. But those who remained, who had parents with them, came forward for the third time this evening; this time to receive the body and blood of Jesus. Although they once again did not "understand" what was taking place I have no doubt that they experienced awe and wonder and curiosity over the cups of juice and wine (with Lutherans we have to have wine!) and the pieces of pita bread that were dipped into the cup before being eaten, bread and juice together (which is called "intinction," by the way).

My guess is that those children and those Korean Christians experienced God in the most significant way tonight, for they were experiencing things that were new and full of symbol and poetry, things that radiated heat, light and the smell of smoke and ash; the odor of wine and the transformation of paper into charred blackness. And there was also, of course, the experience of someone marking your forehead with a small cross made from ashes and hearing someone tell you that one day you will be just like that ash.

It was a good service. I felt refreshed and renewed. I felt grateful to God for his love and forgiveness; and for the journey to sacrifice his Son made for my salvation.

Forty days of Lent. I do not think that forty *lifetimes* would be enough to even begin to digest the mystery and Spirit of tonight's Ash Wednesday worship. Perhaps that is why God created us to live forever and why God so lovingly provided for us to recover that life once again after we had lost it through our sin. Perhaps it is only in the span of eternity that we will really begin to understand what took place this evening. Or, instead I suppose, we could ask one of the children. Although they might not have the vocabulary to express themselves with much precision, I expect that they understood better than us adults. Who would'a guessed!

THURSDAY, FEBRUARY 10, 2005

If You Can't Trust Government Who Can You Trust?

In a recent survey taken among U.S. Department of Fish and Wildlife scientists, the Union of Concerned Scientists and Public Employees for Environmental Responsibility determined that it was not unusual for Bush Administration officials to request that scientific data be changed in ways that would make it support the environmental policies of the President.

This is not the first time the Union of Concerned Scientists has raised this issue with the Bush administration. Nearly a year ago the administration wrote a detailed rebuttal to such charges for submission to the U.S. Congress.

Although not everybody thinks that the Union of Concerned Scientists is reputable, politically neutral group (see here and here) the survey results do raise important questions.

--Is this "fact twisting" unique to the Bush administration or has it been more or less "the way things are" under administrations in the past?

--Is it possible that the political leanings of a significant number of scientists in the U.S. Department of Fish & Wildlife result in their own skewing of data to produce the "environmentally correct" conclusions they want to find?

--Is this sort of "data manipulation" taking place in other Federal agencies such as the Department of Transportation and Safety? The Atomic Energy Commission? The Food and Drug Administration?

--Are the Federal Agencies so corrupted (both within and without) by political bias that we must turn to "Good Housekeeping" and "Consumer Reports" to get the real scoop on honest information?

Call me a cynic, but my trust in honest government is at a low ebb this afternoon. Don't think that I am disparaging the character or integrity of any individual Federal employee. Those I know personally I would trust completely. Yet, human nature being what it is, far too many people find too many ways to justify tweaking research data to not only conform to their particular bias, but also to maintain the cash flow in grant funding on which their livelihood depends.

This new report does not surprise me and I suppose that this is what makes me feel so bad. I don't know who to be angry at! The Bush administration? The Federally employed scientists? The Union of Concerned Scientists?

As always, I find some consolation that a just and merciful God will bring his judgment to bear on this matter and will not allow any distortion of the truth to derail his good and righteous plan for either human history or creation.

FRIDAY, FEBRUARY 11, 2005

Eason Jordan Resigns

After two weeks of growing criticism over remarks made at the recent World Economic Summit in Davos, Switzerland, CNN Chief News Executive Eason Jordan announced his resignation this evening. (see my previous post for information about the content of his remarks)

His resignation statement and the CNN article which accompanies it still leave the central question unanswered, "What, exactly, did Mr. Jordan say and what transpired after he said it." Although the answers are most likely to be found in the videotape of the session neither Jordan nor CNN have publicly asked for it to be released. I cannot imagine them not agressively seeking such evidence had the story not revolved around one of thier own. This smacks of hypocracy of the highest and meanest sort.

In the end it is not Eason Jordan's comments that have damaged CNN's already embattled reputation but how the news network has stonewalled and deflected all efforts from bloggers and other news agencies to "come clean" and present the truth in as honest and straightforward manner as possible.

Even in their resignation announcement CNN had the gall to write the following description of the controversy:

> *The Davos organizers have said the session, like most at the forum, was off-the-record, and they have refused to release a transcript to preserve their commitment.*
>
> *At the heart of the dispute is what Jordan said about the deaths of journalists in Iraq. Several participants said he told the audience that U.S. forces had deliberately targeted some journalists.*
>
> *But Jordan strongly denied that he had made such a suggestion and said he did not believe journalists had been deliberately targeted.*

The first paragraph fails to mention that CNN has refused to publically call for the release of this tape, effectively burying whatever truth there is to be found. Would they have done this if the evidence on the tape had been anything other than damning?

The second paragraph fails to mention that the "several participants" referred to include a U.S. Senator (Chris Dodd, D-Conn), a U.S. Representative (Barney Frank, D-Mass) and the nationally respected editor, Harvard professor and political commentator David Gergen, each of which expressed shock, disbelief and even disgust over what they claim to have heard Mr. Jordan say at the Davos session. Is this good reporting? or more evidence of obfuscation of the truth at CNN?

The third paragraph represents Jordan's denial of having said the things he has been accused of saying. With CNN failing to seek out and report the facts Jordan is allowed to retain the status of persecuted martyr, being unjustly forced to step down as a personal sacrifice for the rest of the CNN team.

CNN would like us to think that, in the end, it is Jordan's word against most everyone else who were in the room and who heard what he really said. They would like us to think that the whole controversy simply revolves around a badly parsed sentence or two and a near universal misunderstanding of what he was really trying to say.

Although it is not *juris prudence* in the American legal system to do so, I am sore tempted to declare that the shameful behavior of CNN and the lack of evidence to the contrary leaves me no choice but to declare Jordan Eason guilty until proven innocent.

I am still open and hopeful of having this personal verdict overturned as a result of some good investigative reporting or from the actual public release of the videotape. If, however, such evidence should ever surface I strongly doubt that CNN will have had anything to do with it.

Good links on this story can be found at Powerline, Instapundit, Hugh Hewitt, Sisyphean Musings & Michelle Malkin.

SATURDAY, FEBRUARY 12, 2005

Driver Ed Teacher Run Over By Student

Oops! According to **this story** from AP a Driver Ed teacher in Stone Mountain, Georgia, was run over and pinned beneath a car by one of his students. It took firemen 15 minutes to extracate him, along with his broken leg, broken ribs and a shoulder injury. The story does not say whether the student received a passing grade.

Parent's Challenge School's Bible Class Time

Since 1929, public schools in Staunton, Virginia, have made sure the students in grades 1-3 get to know their Bible. Until 1948 the 30-minute study segments were part of the school curriculum. After the Supreme Court declared it illegal the schools and the children's parents agreed to what is, in most places, called a "release time" program. In "release time" students are offered a short "elective" during the school day. The "Bible Class" is one elective and, since the school cannot teach it, the students are released to local churches for their study each day. Students who do not opt into the "elective" remain at school and do homework or some other supervised activity.

No one really questions whether or not this is legal or not. Similar programs in other places have been upheld by courts as long as other faith groups or other community programs have similar access to interested students during school hours. In most places, including Utah, which once had the nation's largest "release time" program, the administrative headaches in meeting legal compliance have forced the termination of such programs.

In Staunton, and a few other small, rural Bible Belt" communities, the tradition has continued because of strong community and parental support.

Now, Staunton is being forced to face up to the issue by some parents who have recently moved into the community from places where the concept of "release time" seems like something created by fundamentalist, lunatic fringe fanatics still living in the Middle Ages. This is far from the truth, of course, but this quaint tradition, based on strong, historic community values based on the Word of God, has now been challenged. More than a few local parents, emboldened, perhaps, by the newcomers, have also expressed their desire to do away with the program.

Way back in 1846 James Lowell wrote a poem protesting America's war with Mexico. This poem is now a well known and popular Christian hymn, "Once to Every Man and Nation." In the third verse are these words, perhaps applicable to the present dilemma facing the parents and school board in Staunton:

New occasions teach new duties, time makes ancient good uncouth,
They must upward still and onward, who would keep abreast of truth.

Or, in the more contemporaneous words of Bob Dylan,

The line it is drawn The curse it is cast
The slow one now Will later be fast
As the present now Will later be past
The order is Rapidly fadin'.
And the first one now Will later be last
For the times they are a-changin'.

SUNDAY, FEBRUARY 13, 2005

Quote of the Day

From the November 8, 2004 United Nations report on the sexual abuse, pedophilia, pornography rings and prostitution engaged in by U.N. Peacemaking troops and officials in various places including the Congo, committed against the very refugee people they had been sent to protect. The official U.N. position on such behavior was promoted as being "zero tolerance." The report, however, declared that,

"'The situation appears to be one of 'zero-compliance' with 'zero-tolerance.'"

And these are the people who throw stones at America?

Photo of the Day

According to the Associated Press, this photo shows an Iraqi man celebrating today's announcement of the 48% plurality vote for al-Sistani's Shi'ite party. Amazing. A happy Iraqi? Celebrating the results of a free and democratic popular electoral vote? In my lifetime? How in the world did this happen? Could it be....?

Quote of the Day #2

Christian writer Barbara Johnson says the most profound things with a wink and a smile. Joni shared this quote from her book, "God's Most Precious Jewels Are crystallized Tears," at our Stephan Ministry meeting tonight:

We talk about grief and hardship as time spent in "the valley." But later, looking back from the hilltop, we see that it was there, in that valley, that we became better persons, selfless servants, stronger Christians. As my daughter-in-love, Shannon, says, we grow when we're down in the valley, because that's where the fertilizer is!

MONDAY, FEBRUARY 14, 2005

Bret Stephens & Eason Jordan: Conflict of Interest?

Blogs such as Captain's Quarters, Hugh Hewitt and many others have commented on the apparent conflict of interest between Wall Street Journal Editor, Bret Stephens, and his reporting on the "Eason Jordan" incident at the recent meeting of the World Economic Forum in Davos, Switzerland.

A summary of the "conflict of interest charges" are concisely summed up in today's posting by Captain Ed. His response is to today's unsigned WSJ editorial (on-line by subscription only) which declared the whole "Jordan" incident to be over and the conflict of interest matter concerning Bret Stephens to be laughable. (Note: It has since been revealed that Mr. Stephens was himself the one who wrote the editorial belittling the charges of his conflict of interest).

CORRECTION: *Hugh Hewitt has posted a correction today stating that he was in error yesterday when he identified Mr. Stephens as the writer of this editorial. I add my apology for repeating his error.* 2/15/05. The Captain's summary is as follows:

I assume that the OJ (e.g. "OpinionJournal" a publication of the WSJ), editors read my objection or that of the Dinocrat, and they have mischaracterized the conflict in any case. Stephens belongs to the Forum of Young Global Leaders, which has exactly 1,111 members and is closely affiliated with the World Economic Forum, which means Stephens has an interest to protect with the WEF that he did not disclose. The YGL forum appears to fall under the purview of none other than Eason Jordan, whose bio describes him as a member of the WEF's Global Leaders of Tomorrow programme.
Whether or not that influenced Stephens' reporting is only known by Stephens, but that connection should have been disclosed to WSJ/OJ readers, and the OJ's defense of his silence speaks volumes about their editorial standards. (They also made my mistake of calling Jordan a "board member" of WEF, which I retracted here, so
I'm fairly sure that the OJ has my blog in mind.)

What has captured my own imagination in this matter is the fine print of Bret Stephens' "contract" agreement which enables him to serve on that Forum of Young Global Leaders for the next three years. On page 8 of the official brochure promoting the "FofYGL" are a short list of "rights" and "responsibilities." The first of three "responsibilities" is of particular interest as it requires the member to:

Respect diversity of opinion within the group but likewise support the consensus behind its public statements.

Normally this would not pose a problem. But, for Mr. Stephens (who was attending both as a "member" participant of the conference and as a correspondent for the WSJ) the Eason Jordan affair placed him between a rock and a hard place.

First, he is required by his membership commitment to "respect diversity of opinion within the group." I can only assume that this would include even the most outrageous comments that might be offered, including those of Mr. Jordan. For Mr. Stephens to express criticism of Mr. Jordan's comments would be "disrespectful," would it not? The additional fact that Mr. Jordan sits on the Board of Directors that oversees the Fof YGL only serves to compound the problem for Mr. Stephens.

Second, he is required by his membership commitment to "likewise support the consensus behind its public statements." Does this limit Mr. Stephen's options in commenting on the WEF's declaration that it would not release the video or transcripts of the session in question? For Mr. Stephens to request or demand the release of the video would be to "withhold support" from "the consensus behind its public statements" would it not?

Should a journalist be required to promise that they will not express dissent or criticism of an international organization as a condition of membership? Should a journalist who has made such a promise then proceed to pretend that they are free to be completely objective in their new reporting on that organization?

I join with Captain Ed, Hugh Hewitt and all the others in asserting that this does, in fact, constitute a conflict of interest on the part of Bret Stephens. Mr. Stephens should have disclosed this matter or, with honor, have asked to be excused from reporting on the controversy completely.

TUESDAY, FEBRUARY 15, 2005

Parents Reunited With "Baby 81"

Murugupillai Jeyarajah and his wife, Jenita, welcomed their baby son, Abhilash, back into their family today. "Baby 81," given that name because he was the 81st survivor admitted to the local Sri Lankan hospital in the aftermath of last December's tsunami, had been claimed by numerous grieving families.

The confusion of emotions and hopes from desparate and desolate parents brought to mind the so-called "judgement of Solomon" when the biblical King of Israel was presented with two mothers and two babies, one dead, one living. Each mother claimed the living child as their own and appeared before Solomon to seek a resolution of their conflicting claims.

According to I Kings 3:16-28, Solomon decreed that the living child be cut in two with each woman being given half. One woman fell on her knees and begged the King to spare the child and give it to the other woman. Seeing her love for the child revealed, Solomon declared that she was the child's true mother.

In Sri Lanka, however, there was no King Solomon. But, after much effort and scraping for funds, DNA tests were conducted that verified the claims of the baby's true parents.

According to one radio news broadcast, the child's parents indicated that "***the family will break coconuts, scatter rice and slaughter a rooster to give thanks***" for their son's safe return back into their arms.

Now I know what Sri Lankans do when they are feeling thankful! Next November I think that, instead of turkey, I'll just send our friends into the back yard to break some coconuts and slaughter a rooster! Oh....it's a cultural thing? Well, maybe we could still scatter the rice...would that be OK?

WEDNESDAY, FEBRUARY 16, 2005

BBC Reports Plutonium "Missing" at English Power Plant

A BBC report today citing The Times as its source, claims an annual audit due to be published later will show that 30kg of plutonium is classified as "material unaccounted for" during 2004. The report indicates that this would be enough plutonium to manufacture seven nuclear bombs.

The Department of Trade and Industry said the audit "does not represent any material going missing," adding that, "It's not unusual for the accounting process to indicate material unaccounted for....Again, it's not an indication of any missing material." Last year the audit showed that there were 19kg of plutonium "missing" on the balance sheet.

The plant in question, Sellafield, processes thousands of tons of nuclear material every year.

I can understand how difficult it must be to tally up all that plutonium day after day and have it all balance out neatly at the end. On the other hand, I would be both encouraged and more likely to believe them if, every couple of years or so, the tally would indicate that they ended up with *more* plutonium than they should!

Churchof England General Synod to Make Decision on Gay & Lesbian Priest Issue

Last year's consecration of an openly homosexual American Bishop created an international split within the Anglican communion. The so-called "Windsor Report" made recommendations late last year. Now, the Primates of the Anglican Communion will meet to discuss the issue later this month and try to decide what the Church of England's response will be. The divisive issue will be discussed on the third day of the synod's first session of 2005.

According to a BBC report,

> *"The general secretary of the Lesbian and Gay Christian Movement, the Reverend Richard Kirker, has called for a change in the Church of England's stance. He said the Church would be able to 'sort this problem out' if it connected with the "basic Christian principle that everybody is equal in the sight of God". Mr Kirker added: "The longer there is a delay on officially permitting the ordination of gay people as priests or bishops... the more marginalised the Church will become."*

Most non-North American Anglicans would be more inclined to agree with only the final part of that final sentence, that by "officially permitting the ordination of gay people as priests or bishops... the more marginalised the Church will become."

For the vast majority of Anglicans in the Third World and, perhaps, even a majority of American Episcopalians, the Episcopal Church of the United States has already become marginalized and irrelevent insofar as it no longer represents an historic or biblical expression of the Christian faith.

Look for a "lose-lose" situation for American Episcopalians. If the General Synod refuses to accept Bishop Robinson's consecration and demands that it be revoked, expect the American Bishops to adopt a stance of defiance that could lead to their dismissal from the Anglican Communion. On the other hand, if the General Synod allows the consecration to stand, expect the American Episcopal Church to divide, decline and disintegrate.

With those two alternatives in view, the more likely scenario is for the General Synod to hem and haw and hedge and prevaricate and beat around the bush and platitudinize and more or less pray fervently that with lots and lots of talking the whole mess will just sort of evaporate and go away.

I have read that ostriches do not really stick their heads in the ground to avoid things that frighten them. I pray that the Bishops and the others meeting in General Synod in England later this month will prove to be real "ostriches" and not the mythical variety.

THURSDAY, FEBRUARY 17, 2005

A Wallet Returned

This evening I lost my wallet. I left it on the roof of my car (like an idiot) when I stopped by the Tesoro Station for a fillup. Five minutes later, when I got home, I remembered what I had done. So, back to the gas station. No, it had not been returned at the station store. It was not anywhere to be seen sitting on the road, either.

The lady at the station store had said to kiss the wallet good-bye. "No one's going to return it," she said. I disagreed saying, "Most people would return it. I expect to get it back."

I did get it back even sooner than I had expected. When I returned home again my daughter #3 was standing outside with her cell phone. A man named "Donald" had called just a few minutes after I had left saying he had found my wallet. When I talked to him on the phone he was just two minutes away at a nearby McDonald's. So, two minutes later, less than 30 minutes after losing my wallet, Donald handed it back to me.

He would not take any money in return but did accept my thanks. "Years ago," he said, "I lost my wallet and someone returned it to me. I have always said that if I ever found someone else's wallet I would do the same thing." And today he did just that.

Thank you, Donald. I'm glad you found my wallet. I'm glad you were able to "do unto me as someone once did unto you!" And I'm glad you proved me to be right about most people being honest.

Last, but not least, "Thank you, God!" Whew!

FRIDAY, FEBRUARY 18, 2005

Terri Schindler-Schiavo: Why Do People Want To Kill Her?

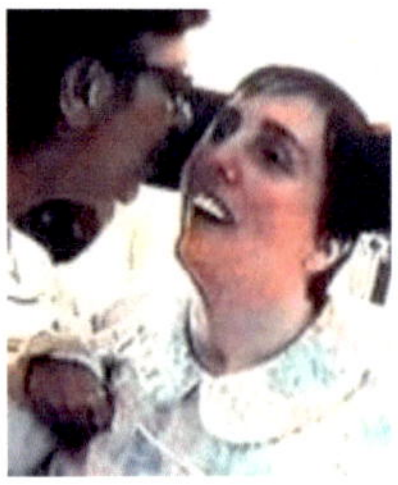

Why do so many people want Terri Schindler-Schiavo dead? What has she done to deserve this bitter legal battle over the right to kill her as soon as possible?

As a result of recent court rulings Terri's feeding tube could be removed as early as next Tuesday, resulting in her death from dehydration and starvation in 10 to 14 days.

Until today I thought I could understand some measure of rational arguement on the part of her husband, Michael. But, after reading a legal offer from Terri's family to her husband, publically released just over a week ago, I am baffled.

In this legally-binding offer, which can be read in full at Terri's website, the Schindler family says that they will take full responsibility for Terri's care, require no financial support from her husband, grant him full possession of any inheritance, insurance or malpractice money, allow him to divorce or dissolve his marriage to Terri (and, if he wishes, be married to the woman he now lives with and with whom he has had two children of his own) with assurance that they will waive any right they might have to take legal action against him in the future.

I do not understand how any otherwise sane human being would choose to reject this offer in favor of asserting their "right" to kill their wife.

By all accounts Terri is not only alive but able to respond to simple verbal directions, express emotion and respond to visual stimuli. Aside from a "brain freeze" caused by a still-unexplained collapse in her home in 1990, her body continues to function normally and well. Other than general hygene, her only external dependence for life is her need to be fed through a feeding tube. In this sense, she is not unlike tens of thousands of Americans who suffer from Parkinson's, quadrapelegia, stroke or other disabilities and diseases.

The care that she requires can easily be provided at home by minimally-trained family members and friends. She might also respond to various forms of physical and psychological therapies, all of which have been denied her by her husband since 1991.

I just don't get it! How can constitutional law refuse to affirm her unalienable right to life? What crime has she committed that requires her to be executed by court order? What precedent will this set, allowing future courts, medical panels or others to subjectively determine whether a living human being will live or die? (see a previous posting on this subject here)

Relevent laws written both before and after her collapse; laws written with the explicit intent of protecting people just like Terri, have been repeatedly set aside by the court. For example:

1. Alhough an advanced directive is required in Florida prior to removing nutrition, Terri never had one.

2 Florida Law defines Persistent Vegetative State as a complete lack of awareness and a complete inability to interact. In spite of clear evidence to the contrary, the court has insisted on declaring that Terri is in a Persistent Vegetative State.

Christian quadrapelegiac Joni Eareckson Tada has said this about Terri's situation:

"This is deplorable. What's happening here is just a part of a larger effort to class persons with severe cognitive disabilities as non-persons."

Please pray for Terri. Pray for her family. Pray that our country will be spared the doom of an ever-expanding culture of death.

Terri is every bit alive as you and I. She is every bit as alive as a living baby in the womb or a living baby nearly completely out of the womb!

In the end, I still cannot figure out why so many people want Terri dead when the clear option of life is readily available. Lord have mercy upon us.

Ward Churchill & Lawrence H. Summers: Two Very Different Men Reveal Academia At Its Worst

Well, well. Our dearly-beloved University of Hawaii has found enough academic libertarians to muster **an invitation** for Professor Ward Churchill, the noted Indian rights agitator who cannot tell the difference between Adolf Eichmann and a stock broker, to speak on campus this coming Tuesday, at 7 pm in the UH Art Auditorium. The invitation was extended by the

American Studies Department and others not as yet named. The theme of Mr. Churchill's lecture will be, "Speaking Truth to Power: Academic Freedom in the Age of Terror."

I wonder who's tax dollars are being spent to fund and host this visit?
Update: Today's newspaper indicates that little, if any, tax money is involved and that Mr. Churchill will not receive a speaking fee. 1/19

Meanwhile, back at Eastern Washington University there are apparently some students and faculty who would like to re-invite Churchill to their campus. It's apparently a matter of "free speech" to pay him $x so he can talk.

Hmmmm. New thought: If "free" speech is free then why do colleges have to pay people to speak? Maybe the solution for all of this is to let Mr. Churchill pay his own way to say what he wants to say!

On the other hand we have poor President Lawrence H. Summers of Harvard University. Whereas Mr. Churchill has a BA and an MA from an experimental state college in Indiana that was later shut down because of its failure to succeed, Dr. Summers is a bona fide academic by any stretch of the imagination. His mini-biography in Wickopedia is worth reproducing here:
Lawrence H. Summers 1954, U.S. economist and government official, b. New Haven, Conn. Educated at the Massachusetts Institute of Technology (MIT) and Harvard, he taught at MIT and in 1983 became the youngest tenured professor in Harvard's history. He served on the President's Council of Economic Advisors in 1982-83 during the Reagan administration, edited the Quarterly Journal of Economics in 1984-90, and in 1991-93 was chief economist of the World Bank. He left Harvard in 1993 to become under secretary for international affairs in the Treasury Dept. He was deputy secretary under Robert Rubin from 1995 until 1999, when he succeeded Rubin as secretary (1999-2001). Summers became president of Harvard in 2001.
It seems that Dr. Summers provoked the ire of the political correctness secret police when, after being specifically requested to be provocative at an academic seminar, he challenged the participants with a number of research theories related to the differences between men and women and their respective natural abilities to excel in various academic disciplines. One question he raised was something along the lines of, Are women less able to rise to the highest positions of the sciences because of gender-related predispositions?

Well, ever since that discussion question was asked, students and faculty of various institutions have been out to cut him down to size. It is quite possible that he will even lose his position as President of Harvard because of this so-called controversy. (Note: The complete transcript of Dr. Summers' comments may be found **here**. Context is everything...particularly in this instance.)

How ironic that university faculty and students are demanding that Mr. Churchill be granted the right of free speech to spew forth his hateful, unscholarly and unresearched opinions at any time and any place of anyone's choosing; while, on the other hand, university faculty and students are demanding that Dr. Summers apologize, recant and not repeat his comments because they have been deemed offensive by some.

Am I missing some modicum of logic here? Has an informed attitude of respect for excellence been replaced by the gut-level emotion of subjectivism?

From what I have read, Mr. Churchill is not worthy to untie the shoes on Dr. Summers' feet.

Lawrence Summers then it must be official: The world has turned upside-down and rational discourse and the exchange of ideas in academia are now officially dead on arrival.

Note: For an earlier posting on Ward Churchill see here.

SATURDAY, FEBRUARY 19, 2005

University of Hawaii Equivalency Test Results: Ward Churchill=Bill O'Reilly

Today's Honolulu Advertiser carries a remarkable quote from University of Hawaii American Studies professor David Stannard. Stannard (whose department is co-sponsoring next week's lecture by besieged University of Colorado professor Ward Churchill) defended the invitation, saying,
"If we invited a right-wing political commentator like Bill O'Reilly, we'd defend him the same way we defend Churchill."

Response #1: Ok, Dr. Stannard. I dare you to invite and sponsor Bill O'Reilly to lecture on the UH campus during the next 12 months. I would like to see you back up your rhetoric by defending his right to speak freely.

Response #2: Mr. O'Reilly was one of those responsible for bringing Ward Churchill and his writings to national attention. Everyone (except for Bill O'Reilly) knows that he is more than a little inclined to lean towards the conservative side of the political spectrum. However, ***using O'Reilly as a "right-wing" equivalent to the "left-wing" Ward Churchill is nothing short of an outrageous slander of the Democratic Party.***

Few people accuse Bill O'Reilly of being overly far from the center of current Republican ideology. Although his "shtick" is to produce outrageous commentary he in no way represents the far-out-in-right-wing-field folks who, for the most part, are considered to be an embarrassment and a liability to the Republican Party as a whole.

If, however, Ward Churchill is a "left-wing" equivalent of Bill O'Reilly then I must assume that Dr. Stannard must consider Prof. Churchill to be a relatively "mainstream" Democrat. Can this be true? Is Ward Churchill (and his rabid and bitter hatred towards the American political establishment and any and all who, through honest labor, undergird our nation's strength and power) representative of the ideology of the Democratic Party? Are his opinions welcomed to the table when drafting a national platform? Are all the "little Eichmanns" engaged in commerce, trade and industry who vote Democratic listening to him with nods of approval?

If the answers to any of these questions is true then the Democratic Party has sailed off the edge of a flat earth. If the answers to any of these questions is *not* true, then Dr. Stannard owes the Democratic Party a sincere and humble apology.

Response #3: If Dr. Stannard does not believe that Ward Churchill is an acceptable representative of mainstream Democratic political thought then he also owes Bill O'Reilly a public apology for citing him as an analogous equivalent.

Response #4: Memo to Dr. Stannard: In my opinion, the "right-wing" equivalent of Ward Churchill would have to be someone of the stature of David Duke. Perhaps Dr. Stannard would like to invite Bill O'Reilly *and* Mr. Duke at the same time. Then we could see how "far right" Mr. O'Reilly really is! Plus, as a bonus, we would all get to see Dr. Stannard defending David Duke's right to speak freely on the UH campus as well.

SUNDAY, FEBRUARY 20, 2005

Growing Churches: A Good Point

The quote is from The Pen and the Sword and the comment is from Jolly Blogger. Worth reading and thinking about, I think....

Reality check: The fastest growing faiths on the American continent are Islam, Mormonism, and Catholicism. Islam is growing by promoting a disciplined lifestyle and a sense of religious identity. Mormonism is growing with their own two-wheeled propogation of their message...young, handsome, clean-cut men on bikes going door to door and talking with people. Catholicism is growing because
a huge number of Baptists and other thinking believers are getting increasingly disgusted with the nonsense that masquerades as authentic Christian witness.

Hmm . . . there's nothing very seeker sensitive or even culturally sensitive about the three groups he mentions, they apparently aren't accomodating their message and methods to the culture nor are they trying to redefine or reframe their messages for a "postmodern" generation (at least as far as I know). So tell me again why I need to re-think and repackage my faith to win "today's generation."

Unintended Laughter In Worship

Folks laughed in worship this morning but it wasn't because I had told a particularly hilarious joke (Note to reader: They never laugh at my jokes). Instead, it happened during sharing joys and concerns for prayer. Each Sunday, prayer request cards are passed forward to be shared with the congregation. A slip of my tongue accidently rephrased one request as follows:

For our good friends in San Diego who just had a baby girl, Morgan, who was born 3 months pregnant....

The correct word was, of course, "premature." I'm sure that some people are still laughing. I know I am!

"Oh, Be Careful Little Mouth, What You Say..."

I take heading for this post from a verse of a Christian children's song. The next line reads, "For the Father up above is looking down in love, so be careful little mouth, what you say."

Unfortunately, it appears that God isn't the only one listening in on our private conversations. It seems that an **old friend** of President Bush initiated a series of private conversations while "W" was Governor of Texas. What he didn't tell his friend was that he had a tape recorder running while they were talking. As part of publicity for his book release he has allowed at least some of these recordings to be "leaked" to media outlets, in particular the **New York Times**.

What is revealed in these tapes should be of interest only to what the Bible calls, rumour-mongers, back-biters and gossips, all of whom are roundly condemned by scripture. The irony is that the man (who I will not dignify by printing his name) is, according to Fox News, a former Assembly of God preacher. Ed Morrisey at **Captain's Quarters** has described the man as a "Judas Preacher" and a "disgusting piece of human slime." I don't know as if I want to join in the name-calling game, but this sort of "betrayal" does remind me of a man who once kissed his friend on the cheek in a garden. I can do without "signs of affection" like these.

As one blogger has commented, the content of the tapes are not necessarily a bad thing for the President. *"It seems that what the President says in private tracks with what he says in public for the most part. Bush, unlike (name omitted), is a good trustworthy man."*

It is always good to be careful about what we say, both in public and in private. But as for me, it is more than enough to know that God is up above, listening down in love.

MONDAY, FEBRUARY 21, 2005

An Obituary Swarm?

One week ago it was Arthur Miller. Today it is Hunter Thompson, John Raitt and Sandra Dee. Over the years these folks brought humor, tragedy, outrage, drama and inspiration into my life.

Although I cannot commend them all as models for the Christian life I can, and do, appreciate them for raising questions I might not have otherwise asked, for providing the simple pleasure of big screen silliness and for sharing a voice and a smile that raised us all nearly to the level of the angels.

A Muslim Response to the Freedom House Investigation of Radical Islam in America

A web site called, Free Muslims Against Terrorism, has published a response to the recent investigative report that discovered radical Wahhabi-inspired literature, published in and by Saudi Arabia, being displayed and distributed in a number of major mosques across the United States (see my previous posts on this matter here and here).

In spite of the fact that the MSM has virtually ignored the report the writer of this response takes aim at those who have tried to write it off as one more example of "Muslim bashing." Read the following excerpts and then click the link and read the whole thing.

Muslim-bashing. That's the accusation many of my fellow Muslims now hurl at the various news outlets for their news stories about a Freedom House investigation that found extremist Islamic literature in some leading American mosques. This name-calling is unfortunate.

Since 1980, the Muslim world has experienced an enormous growth of religious fanaticism and extremism the likes of which Islam has not experienced in its 1,400 years. This movement continues to grow because of the spread of who've Islam; a sect that used to number no more than one percent of all Muslims, but because of money and technology, has spread to more areas around the world.

Extremism is also growing because of an ideology called political Islam. The basis of political Islam is the rejection of secularism and the belief that the mosque and the state should be completely intertwined. Unfortunately, history has shown that when politics and religion are completely intertwined, disaster results.

Most importantly, extremism in the Muslim world continues to grow because most Muslims are unwilling to admit that we have a problem with extremism and support for terrorism. The response by Muslims to the Freedom House report is not the first time that the Muslim community resorted to denial and accusations of Muslim-bashing when presented with evidence of Muslim culpability.

"Bird of Paradise" Worth Bucks!

I just discovered that an outfit called BlogShares has just listed me as a potential "site for sale." The information on their site is as follows:

URL http://tbirdofparadise.blogspot.com/
News feed Syndic8.com
Valuation B$3,303.43
Added 19:11 20 Nov 2004
Last Updated 00:19 21 Feb 2005
Status Available to Trade.
Industries None[Vote for which Industry this blog belongs to][Who voted this blog's industries]

They also post all sorts of other data regarding my site. I wonder where they get it from? Hugh Hewitt? BlogRolling? SiteMeter? TTLB? I guess blogging is sorta like George "W" in my previous post...except for the blogger, you KNOW you are being taped!

Oh...and by the way, if anyone has $3,303.43 they want to throw away just let me know!

"BS" as a Christian Concept

Somehow the website Inside Higher Ed was repeatedly referred to "Bird of Paradise" last night and today. After checking it out I discovered a review of two small semi-serious philosophical tomes (printed by Princeton University Press & MIT Press) on the subject of "b---s---."

After reading the review I (very reluctantly) must confess that most of what I read struck me as being true. In responding to the review I would add, however, that the proliferation of this subject is not limited to advertising, industry, commerce, editorials, Congress, the White House, academicians, North Korea or bloggers. Sadly, I must also include many publishers and manufacturers of so-called "Christian" books and products. While not naming names I would simply like to offer my belief that each year, Christian publishers, etc., get together and plan out what gimmick they want to use to exploit their very naive, innocent and trusting customers in the coming months.

Let's see, one year it was "angels." Another year it was anything to do with "Veggie Tales." Then, of course, there has been the "Left Behind" fictional fantasies (that reveal more about Tim LaHaye than about the Christian faith, the Word of God or the "end times"). The "Prayer of Jabaz" and sequels have served the industry well the past few years as has the "Purpose Driven Life" and the never-ending parade of new translations of the Bible and their various incarnations, such as the "Cat-Lover's Bible" and the like.

Don't get me wrong. When I associate these sorts of things with the "BS" word I am not necessarily referring to either their content or their real or imagined edification of God's adopted children. Rather, I mean the crass, craven and manipulative marketing that attempts to persuade us into believing that we really, really need these things and without them our lives would be....well....would be left empty of meaning, void of understanding and essentially ignorant of "the things that pertain to God."

Scripture teaches us that one of the spiritual gifts is that of "discernment." A book like Rick Warren's, "The Purpose Driven Life," would have become a big seller even without the hype. Indeed, to its credit, this particular book seems to me to have been one of the leased-hyped and least exploited quality Christian products to have come along in a very long time. Most Christians, when left to themselves, can "discern" what is "good and true" and what is not. In my own congregation we have used and continue to use this book in many different and fruitful ways.

Nonetheless, as followers of Jesus we must be always on the lookout for those who would, like Simon Magus, seek to use the power of the name of Jesus for their own personal or corporate profit. I have seen far too much advertising money spent on promoting so-called "Christian" books, CDs, etc, that are not worth the paper or plastic they are printed on. The theology (I use the word very loosely) of all too much of this merchandise, is so vaguely sentimental, emotional and popularized as to render it not only unBiblical but more than capable of leading many otherwise good-hearted souls astray.

I do not use the word "BS" in conversation nor is it even in my very limited vocabulary of angry epithets. But, insofar as it represents an academically acceptable concept, it can not only be colorful, but it can also accurately describe far more things than I think God would like.

TUESDAY, FEBRUARY 22, 2005

Help Free Two Bloggers In Iran

The **Committee to Protect Bloggers** has asked us to post the following:

FREE MOJTABA AND ARASH DAY -- WESTERN HEMISPHERE
From Honolulu to Eugene, from Tegucigalpa to Toronto, it is Tuesday, February 22.Today is Free Mojtaba and Arash Day in honor of the two Iranian bloggers currently incarcerated by the

Iranian government.Read about Arash and Mojtaba.Here is what you can do. With additional contact information.Banners are available at various locations on this blog.We have already had a tremendous response, including encouragement and thanks from bloggers in Iran. Let's make a difference today. Freedom of speech is not a partisan issue, not an issue of culture or ethnicity, it is a bloggers' issue and a human issue.

Happy Birthday George Who????

A poll taken at the 10th oldest college in the United States and the first chartered after our independence recently commissioned a poll. The results were compiled from the responses of 800 adults from across America.

Asked who was the greatest president, 20 percent of those polled chose Lincoln. Reagan was picked by 15 percent, Franklin D. Roosevelt by 12 percent, John F. Kennedy by 11 percent, Bill Clinton by 10 percent and George W. Bush by 8 percent. Washington was picked by 6 percent. (see article here).

So, George Washington, the Father of our Country and generally recognized by virtually every historian for over 200 years as the-one-without-whom-we-would-never-have-become-the-nation-we-are-today ranks only 7th, below the likes of Bill Clinton, JFK and George W.

What have we become when most of those polled acknowledged that they really knew very little about George Washington and had not been taught anything about him since elementary school?

The poll is all the more disturbing when you discover that it was taken at the request of Washington College, which is, according to their website,

. . . a private, independent college of liberal arts and sciences located in historic Chestertown on Maryland's Eastern Shore—was founded in 1782 and is the only institution of higher learning that the first president (who himself never attended college) patronized during his lifetime. Washington donated 50 Guineas to the newly founded school, gave his consent for it to be named in his honor, served on its Board of Visitors and Governors, and received an honorary degree in 1789.

Happy Birthday, George! And thank you!

Caution! Marines At Work Ahead

I came across this photo this evening. I have no idea where the picture was taken but my guess is, "somewhere in Iraq." Hat Tip to The 50th Star

WEDNESDAY, FEBRUARY 23, 2005

Ward Churchill Admits He Is Not An Indian...I Think?

Popular Honolulu radio hosts, Perry & Price (KSSK), aired some interesting information about Ward Churchill on their morning commute show. According to them, two local reporter/journalists cornered Churchill following his "lecture" last night at the University of Hawaii. After dodging repeated questions about his status as a Native American **he finally responded to a question asking "Are you a Native American?" by saying, "No."** Unfortunately I have not yet found any outside source to confirm this report but will keep probing. This unconfirmed admission was not reported in either Honolulu paper this morning nor is it posted on any of the TV News.

Somehow, this anecdote sounds a little suspicious to me, but here in Hawaii, if Perry and Price say it's true then it must be true! In the meantime I am holding my breath.

In a related matter, the Honolulu Star-Bulletin printed a blunt and straightforward editorial roundly criticizing those who invited him to speak in Hawaii. The editorial, which is entitled, "Churchill Invitation Is Embarrassment for University," can be found here.

Another Temporary Reprieve for Terri Schindler-Schiavo

Today a Florida Circuit Court judge granted a temporary stay in proceedings that were designed to bring about a final determination as to whether brain-damaged, but otherwise alive and healthy, Terri Schindler-Schiavo's feeding tube can be removed so that she can starve to death as her "husband" desires.

The website maintained by Terri's sister and parents on her behalf received so much traffic that it had to be temporarily taken down today. A statement of thanks from the family to all those who have been supporting Terri is all that is posted at the moment.

The judge is taking time to consider a request by the family that Terri receive new and improved medical examinations to determine the condition of her brain. An attempt by a representative of the Florida Department of Children and Families to speak in court was denied by the judge, who called it politically motivated and "an affront to the court."

Please continue to pray for Terri, her family and the judge, so that she might be spared the unnecessary taking of her life and so, under the care of her family that loves her, she can receive the rehabilitation treatments that have been denied to her by her husband for the past 13 years.

Ward Churchill DOES Admit He Is NOT a Native American Indian

The allegation made in my earlier post has been confirmed. This morning's Honolulu Star-Bulletin does indeed quote Ward Churchill as having defiantly confirmed that he is **NOT** a Native American. According to the newspaper,
Churchill did address the issue of his ethnicity, admitting that he is not Native American.

"Is he an Indian? Do we really care?" he said, quoting those he called his "white Republican" critics.

"Let's cut to the chase; I am not," he said.

His pedigree is "not important," Churchill said: "The issue is the substance of what is said."

He went on to explain that the issue of whether he is Native American has been blown up by sloppy reporting and reporters quoting other reporters.

In spite of his confession to have perpetuated a fraud for many years and, as a consequence, having used that fraud to be hired as faculty, granted tenure and made the department head for Ethnic Studies at the University of Colorado, Churchill offered no apologies.

Although local student and community Republicans organized a protest outside the building where he spoke, many others, more than twice as many as could fit in the auditorium, eagerly listened to his "lecture." Some students were there because they had been assigned to attend by their professors.

What a celebrity!

A Sinner Repents

From Hugh Hewitt comes a link to a story that shows that God can change a hardened heart. A few days ago **I** posted my thoughts on the man who had taped his conversations with then-Texas-Governor George W. Bush. In advance of an upcoming book release he had recently shared some of the tape with several media outlets. After scathing criticism from all quarters, the man, who I can now name as Doug Wead, has cancelled talk show appointments and has asked his lawyers to determine the best way to turn the tapes over to President Bush. Profits from his book, he says, will also be turned over....not to "W" but to charity. Praise God and thank you Mr. Wead!

THURSDAY, FEBRUARY 24, 2005

Christians: Beware of Wolves In Christ's Clothing

Cheat Seeking Missile**s** and Evangelical Outpost draw attention to an amazing story.

Liberal (very liberal?) blogger The Rude Pundit has advised his readers to keep the recent Jeff Gannon story alive (Gannon is the White House journalist who was recently "outed" by Democrats for 1. being a homosexual and, 2. having been a male prostitute years ago). Liberal media has made a big deal about it but are disappointed that the conservative (especially Christian) folks didn't seem to show much insterest).

The Rude Pundit's strategy is for his readers to: Pretend they are a conservative Christians and email swarm-conservative-Christian bloggers, expressing outrage over 1. Gannon's homosexuality or 2. His former prostitution.

Read his actual post here.

I cannot imaging a Christian blogger of any influence proposing such a deceitful, dishonorable, stupid and lame idea. The Bible says that "God cannot be mocked." Jesus says,

"At that time if anyone says to you, 'Look, here is the Christ!' or, 'Look, there he is!' do not believe it. For false Christs and false prophets will appear and perform signs and miracles to deceive the elect–if that were possible. So be on your guard; I have told you everything ahead of time."

Yes, Virginia....there is an "anti"christ!

Temporary Withdrawal Requested by Anglican Bishops

The Senior Bishops of the various Anglican Churches from around the world have finished their meeting in Northern Ireland with a consensus request. According to the BBC,

In a key passage, the communique says: "... We request that the Episcopal Church (USA) and the Anglican Church of Canada voluntarily withdraw their members from the Anglican Consultative Council for the period leading up to the next Lambeth Conference" [the ten-yearly meeting of all Anglican bishops, due next in 2008].
The ACC is a liaison body, with members drawn from each province or member church. To step down would mean a church was no longer a full member of the Anglican family. . .
What brought that simmering row to a head was the decision by US Anglicans to appoint an openly gay priest, Gene Robinson, as a bishop, and the Canadian agreement to bless same-sex unions.

I do not see either body backing down or retreating from the path they have taken. I also cannot see conservative, traditionalist members waiting until 2008 to see which way the wind will be blowing. If the American and Canadian Bishops do not "repent" and submit to the will of the Anglican Communion as a whole, I believe we will see an increase in membership migration both to other denominations as well as to "independent" congregations forming new alliances or linking up with Anglican communions in other countries.

As the BBC News puts it, "Out of (*these*) polar opposites, even Solomon himself would find it hard to forge a united church."
For background read my previous post here.

No News Is Good News?

The CNN home page at the moment looks different somehow (9:49 pm HST). Why? After looking it over several times it dawned on me that there was not a single story on either Iraq, Afghanistan, Iran or North Korea.

The nearest thing on the site concerned Bush's meeting with Putin and their agreement to halt the spread of nuclear weapons. Oddly enough, there was also no story listed for the Lebenese/Syrian situation, Koffi Anin's ultimatum and Assad's apparent decision to withdraw gracefully. Perhaps that was posted earlier. News gets old very fast, I guess.

There was news of today's bombing in Iraq at the World site, of course, but I wonder when the last timie the CNN Home Page has been "terrorist-" "Iraqi-" and "Afghani-free." Is this a sign of progress? Hmmm. . . .

FRIDAY, FEBRUARY 25, 2005

Hugh Hewitt & Vox Blogoli 2.2

Response to Hugh Hewitt
The question is:

Whether the Senate majority Republicans should continue to allow the minority Democrats to continue to fillabuster President Bush's judicial nominees (as they have been doing for the past four years)

or

Whether they should use their majority status to end the obstructionism by changing the Senate Rules to strictly accord with the U.S. Constitution which states that a simiple majority shall prevail in such nominations (this is, according to some pundits, referred to as the "nuclear option").

My answer is both "Yes" and "No."

1. **One** judicial nominee should be presented to the Senate for confirmation (I prefer one nominee over a slate of nominees so as to reduce the legitimacy of the fillabuster).

2. Allow the Democrats begin their fillabuster and allow it to go on for several days, allowing the press to cover the obstructionism and make the Constitutional provisions clear to the public.

3. Call for a vote to change the Senate rules, allowing both Democrat and Republican Senators to speak for and against (these on-the-record statements will provide a gold mine of quotes for mid-term elections.) The key pro-change arguement should be "undermining the Constitution" and "abuse of tradition."

4. Vote the change in the rules and proceed.

5. As is proper, allow Senate members to advise as they speak for or against each nominee as presented. I do not like presenting candidates en masse as a "slate" Such an approach gives the appearance of railroading.

6. Vote each nominee up or down. It may be somewhat time-consuming this way but will, in the end, appear to the public as "fair and balanced."

In short, let a retreating McClellen draw them in and then rout them on the flank with Grant.

Three Weeks Left to Live

A Florida judge ruled today that he has granted a stay of execution (oops) I mean a stay of his order to remove the feeding tube from Terri Schiavo until March 18th. This will, he says, provide Terri's family enough time to file any final appeals in the case.

Terri's father says that he is grateful for whatever time they might have left to try and save her life. Terri's mother added that, as a Roman Catholic, Terri would never approve of euthanasia. Apparently the judge has not been convinced and did not respond to the family's request for a more technologically modern series of tests to update the ones done over 10 years ago.

It is hard to believe but...the judge has never allowed Terri Schiavo to be present in court and has never visited her. As far as the judge and the law is concerned she is a non-person in a vegetative state with no rights to be protected except that of her so-called husband who, as her legal "guardian," has fought for over ten years to have her killed.

It is interesting to see the media bias in the linked CNN report where twice she is described as being on "life support." This is a lie. A feeding tube is not considered "life support." The feeding tube can be removed and she will not die. She is no more artificially being kept alive than you or me! Take away my food and water, deprive me of nourishment and I will die, too. So will you.

Continue to pray for Terri and her family. Pray that some way out might be found to spare her life and return her to the care of those who love her. Terri's new web page is still under construction but will soon be found here.

My previous posts on Terri can be found here and here.

SATURDAY, FEBRUARY 26, 2005

A Truly Well-Placed Public Service Announcement

Fox News On-Line has posted a story today on the current status of Terri Schiavo (who now has until March 18 until the judge allows her to be killed).

In the middle of the story (literally and physically) the following public service ad appears:

Perhaps the ads rotate? I can't imagine that they changed it on purpose!

SUNDAY, FEBRUARY 27, 2005

Sharon = Saddam??

This afternoon I attended an interfaith presentation sponsored by the Roman Catholic Chamanade University in Honolulu. The speaker was a Muslim man who I have spoken with and have had in a church adult class to represent the Muslim faith. He is gracious, intelligent, active in the small Muslim community in Hawaii, has a wonderful sense of humor and is in the process of becoming an American citizen. He is not a trained Islamic scholar and did not claim to possess any authority as a spokesman for his faith.

He spoke on "Islam and Peace." I know him to be a man who represents those who would like to see major reform in Islamic countries, including representative democracy. He was openly critical of Muslims to allow cultural values and traditions to supersede the imperatives clearly articulated in the Qur'an. All in all an honest presentation but not altogether convincing...far too much of Qur'an's approach to infidels and those who resist or threaten Islam was ignored, especially in the later revelations of the Prophet.

In the midst of affirming that all religious seek to raise human beings to their highest and best, he made a slip and, for a moment, stepped out of "religious" content and into the political.

In a short aside on good and bad people, his list of "bad" people included folks like Hitler. The final two names in his list were "Sharon" and "Saddam Hussein."

In the Q & A which followed the presentation, one woman, who identified herself as being Jewish, challenged the comment that appeared to equate Sharon and Saddam as equally evil.

The response revealed a way of looking at things that I found myself completely unable to understand (something that does not happen often). The speaker defended his comment and did not back away from it. There was clearly deep passion and emotion in his feelings about Sharon and he spoke far longer in response than he should have, given the nature of the gathering.

After he had spoken, the Moderator of the event (who is also a Muslim and the designated lay leader for the Honolulu mosque) added that the only difference between Sharon and Saddam was that Saddam murdered people in his own country whereas Sharon murdered people outside of his country.

I have spent much of the past three years trying to read and study Islam to the point where I can, in some small way, see the world through their eyes. The deeper I have gone, the more troubled I have become, even with this fine man today, who reflects personal support for a non-violent form of his faith.

In the Arab Muslim world, and by extension, the rest of the Muslim world as well, the existence of the state of Israel represents a deep and continuing affront, insult and injustice to the Palestinian people as well as to the Muslim faith.

Yes, we can all agree that Israel's current President, Ariel Sharon, has a more or less deserved reputation of having been a strong and sometimes unmerciful military commander whose role in what some call the massacre of Palestinian civilians is still hotly debated. His support of West Bank settlements and his brutal and often devastating response to the second intifada have, among most Muslims, raised him to the status of a war criminal and has become the personification of all that is hateful about Israel.

But, for Muslims, Saddam Hussein was their demon. He was their tyrant. He was a Muslim fighting and oppressing other Muslims. He was an embarrassment to some and a hero to others...because he was "strong" and stood up against America. I have experienced the same ambivalent hate/admiration dichotomy in the old Soviet Union regarding Josef Stalin. "He did some terrible things," Russians have told me. "But he was a strong leader and led us to victory against the Nazis in the Great War."

In a similar way, Saddam's perceived strengths more or less excused his excesses.

For Sharon, however, there are no redeeming virtues. He kills Palestinian women and children. He seizes and divides their land. He builds a wall to shut them both out and in. He is not to be trusted. He is evil.

There is a cold, hard logic here that I think I would need to be a Palestinian, an Arab or a Muslim to either understand or emotionally react to with the passion that I saw this afternoon.

Personally, I do not see the moral equivalent between Saddam Hussein and Ariel Sharon. The one was essentially a tyrant and an aggressor. The other is a freely elected representative of a more or less free people determined to, at all costs, preserve, protect and defend his people from those who desire to have them swept into the Mediterranean Sea.

The situation in Israel/Palestine has been disgustingly brutal during the past four years. I am not hopeful for any settlement that will ensure any lasting "peaceful coexistence" as part of a "two nation" agreement.

But I am hopeful the the level of violence can be reduced to pre-second inifada levels and that the terrorist wings of Hamas, Islamic Jihad and Fatah can be marginalized by a growing measure of political stabilization and rule of law in the West Bank and Gaza.

But, as I discovered this afternoon, the passion does run deep. One can only hope for the best and develop friendships that can somehow transcend our many and varied differences. As for me, I intend to continue my friendship with this and with any and all anti-terrorist Muslims. I will do so because I believe that friendship is always the first step towards peace. I will also do it because I believe it is what Christ Jesus would want me to do.

MONDAY, FEBRUARY 28, 2005

All You Evil Right-Wing Pastors......

The Democratic National Committee has elected former Presidential candidate and former Governor of Vermont John Dean as its Chairman. Many political conservatives thought that his appointment would be self-destructive for the Democratic Party, feeling that Dean was too far "left" to be representative of the Democratic center. I appears that they were right.

Last Friday, on his first foray into Democratic fundraising and morale-building, Dean spoke to enthusiastic crowds in Lawrence, Kansas. Among his comments was this:

"The issue is not abortion," Dean told the closed-door fund-raiser. "The issue is whether women can make up their own mind instead of some right-wing pastor, some right-wing politician telling them what to do."

Huh? Dean is afraid that women will only do what right-wing pastors tell them to do? Does Dean feel that woman are so brain-dead that they will, like robots, allow themselves to be programmed by their pastors? What an insult to women...and to pastors, too. Has it crossed his mind that maybe there are millions of women who agree with what their pastors are saying? That they have the ability to read the Bible on their own and consider the value God has placed in human life, especially the weak and defenseless? Are "right-wing" pastors some sort of demons, like the boogie men that hide under children's beds? Who are these "right-wing" pastors, anyway? Pastors like me? Like Billy Graham? Like Pope John Paul II?

A bit later, Dean added this comment:

"Moderate Republicans can't stand these people (conservatives), because they're intolerant. They don't think tolerance is a virtue," Dean said, adding: "I'm not going to have these right-wingers throw away our right to be tolerant."

Now that's a tolerant attitude! Sort of like, "I have the right to be tolerant and I will destroy anyone who disagrees with me!" Is this the level of rational discourse to be found at the highest levels of the Democratic Party today? Whatever happened to the eloquence of men like the much admired (by Republicans as well as Democrats) Adlai Stevenson? Or the intellectual idealism of a John F. Kennedy? Or the charismatic vision of a Bobby Kennedy? Or even the down-to-earth, folksiness of a Hubert Humphrey? Why has the party of the blue collar worker morphed into a parody of the worst stereotype of ivory-tower, intellectual elitists? Does Dean really believe that his unintelligible rants will win over a single "moderate Republican?"

At the end of a busy day in Lawrence, while speaking at private rally in a supporter's backyard, Dean added (according to the Lawrence Journal-World) this observation:

*And concluding his backyard speech with a litany of Democratic values, he added: **"This is a struggle of good and evil. And we're the good."***

Oh, oh. Republicans are now evil, to be listed in the same class as the tyannical Iranian Ayatollahs and Kim Jong Il of North Korea. Everyone who voted for George W. Bush is now to be viewed by the Democratic party as "**little Eichmanns**," perhaps? Or Saddam Husseins? Or Osama bin Ladens? Has the word "evil" any objective meaning at all for John Dean? Or is it merely rhetoric without meaning at all? Simply mindless emotions expressed through meaningless words? It is as if Shakespeare anticipated John Dean and carefully described him when he wrote the famous soliloquy for Macbeth, which ends with these words:

"...a poor player/ That struts and frets his hour upon the stage/ And then is heard no more: it is a tale/ Told by an idiot, full of sound and fury,/ Signifying nothing."

Little glamour at the Oscars

I only caught the presentation of the first Academy Award before leaving for a church meeting this evening. I returned in time to see the presentation of the awards for Best Director and Best Movie.

Unfortunately I also saw Chris Rock trying to pretend that he belonged on stage as the evening's MC. He failed to convince many people. He was loud. He was abrasive and he wasn't funny. His repeated comments regarding Jude Law reminded me of David Letterman's disastrous attempts at trying to milk a laugh from "Uma & Oprah." When the cameras panned the audience they appeared to be smiling for the sake of decorum only. The only thing that could have possibly helped Mr. Rock tonight would have been a prompter holding up signs letting the audience know when to laugh. Maybe a laugh track might be considered in the future to at least give the illusion that something funny is taking place.

The glitz and glamour of Hollywood has always been a carefully-crafted yet fragile public relations illusion. Why the "Academy" would want to risk dismantling its aura of pseudo-intelligence, beauty and class is beyond me. Then again, perhaps Chris Rock IS what the Hollywood elite are all about these days.

THURSDAY, MARCH 10, 2005

Darfur: Thoughts On Why Nothing Is Being Done To Stop the Killing

*What follows is a **very long** post on Sudan and Darfur. It reflects my understanding of this tragic situation as well as the competing international interests that have essentially neutralized all attempts by the United States to impose a decisive solution or a significant intervention that might end the violence. The post was written as a response to a letter containing several articles on Darfur mailed to me by a member of my congregation. (Note that I have not attempted to document my data with links or footnotes although there are some helpful links listed at the post's end).*

I have been closely watching and following the situation in Sudan since 1980 when my wife and I met two Christian missionaries who had been working in South Sudan with irrigation assistance but had been forced to leave (along with most other Westerners) because of growing violence against Christian and animist Africans by Arab Muslim military attacks from the north. The major explosion of the so-called "civil war" came two years later which meant that our friends could not return to continue their work there or to visit the people they had worked with. Eventually, many fled southern Sudan into Kenya which is where our friends eventually returned to missionary service (later moving to Pakistan after which they retired to Minnesota).

This "civil war" was always not so much a civil war as it was a systematic slaughter of civilians in the south by government forces and government-backed militias. The *modus operandi* was exactly the same as that now being used in Darfur. Government planes bomb and strafe a village followed by the swift arrival of armed troops (primarity Arab Muslims). Men are frequently rounded up and shot, women raped, the village looted and burned and older children sent to the Arab north and sold into slavery.

In many cases a person's life or liberty could be "purchased" by becoming a Muslim. Tens of thousands of African Christians have endured execution or slavery rather than confess Allah and Mohammed as his Prophet.

Because of the Christian population in south Sudan and the historic presence of missionary agencies who worked in that area for decades the American Evangelical Christian community tried desperately to get media attention and political pressure to be brought against Sudan to stop the killing. The situation was made more difficult with a small minority of the south Sudanese taking up arms and fighting back against the Khartoum government, partially in self-defense and partly in an attempt to gain independence from the north (which had legislated and adopted *sharia* law, based on the Koran, for all Sudanese, whether Muslim or not).

American efforts to confront Sudan over the issue of the killings in the south and its tacit approval of the slave trade were led primarily by several Christian U.S. Representatives (virtually all Republican) backed by Christian evangelical mission and relief organizations. Many international human rights organizations also began speaking up, especially on the slavery issue.

To his credit, President Clinton imposed sanctions and restrictions on American oil companies who wanted to get in on the ground floor with recently-discovered massive oil reserves in Sudan. European countries did not join in supporting the U.S. on this issue, preferring to pursue their own self-interests. France, especially, took advantage of the American absence in engrandizing itself to the Sudanese government in return for taking the lead in oil exploration and the development of the Sudanese oil industry. France is still the biggest business partner with Sudan along with China, whose growing need for oil and lack of concern for anything remotely connected to human rights makes Sudan a good place to go shopping.

As the New Yorker article explains, the pressure exerted by Clinton and a few other cooperative countries (Canada not among them, by the way) led the Sudanese government to start a process of negotiation with the south. Under President Bush's continuation of the policy (with much restraint and minimal criticism in order to facilitate the peace process) a cease fire and nearly-completed truce agreement has been worked out between Khartoum and the southern rebel forces.

Unfortunately, this truce freed up government troops who soon were being used to control a growing resistance movement in the Darfur region of western Sudan. The Darfur rebels hoped to make a deal similar to that being negotiated with the south. Unfortunately for them, Darfur has been found to possess a large share of Sudan's oil. It was not in Khartoum's national interests to allow anyone but themselves control of that resource.

Virtually all the population in Darfur is Muslim. But Khartoum used the cultural divide between north Darfur Arabs and southern Darfur Africans to split the resistance and gain the Arab leadership as proxy allies to "cleanse" the area of the majority African (non-nomadic) population.

This began several years ago and has been fairly well covered by major media such as the Washington Post, New York Times and the Wall Street Journal as well as international human rights groups and Christian relief organizations.

Throughout this entire Sudanese series of internal killing and destroying, the United Nations and most of Western Europe, have either mouthed toothless threats, hoped that the neighboring African countries would step in to help or allowed the United States to spend generously on human relief programs while they continued doing their lucrative business deals with Khartoum.

Both Clinton and Bush have made aggressive and very public appeals to the international community to join with the United States in forcing Sudan to back down. As is obvious, the basic response has been for the United Nations to continue to mouth platitudes and for France and China to, essentially, tell the U.S. to go to hell.

Interestingly enough, Iraq was similarly being used by France as a major source of its oil and economic investments. This was, of course, taking place while, on paper at least, France was a signatory with the sanctions imposed by the United Nations.

France and other European nations had little objection to the invasion of Afghanistan (because they had virtually no economic interests there) and even provided at least token troops and support.

With Iraq, however, these nations (including Russia) fought tooth and nail to keep the United States from invading one of their "cash cows." In my opinion, it has not been President Bush's "unilateralism" that has caused France and Germany and a few other nations to give the United States a cold shoulder. Rather, the issues are more fundamentally centered on a conflict between European security interests (which might have some sympathy for the invasion of Iraq) and economic interests (which clearly favored the status quo).

In some ways the "Old Europe" has been placing itself in opposition to the United States and our foreign policy priorities long before President Bush took office and invaded Iraq. Repeatedly, especially as regards the Middle East, America's long-term economic and security interests have come into conflict with the short-term interests of France and Germany.

Part of this is economic. The United States has a strong and robust economy that can outlast an international crisis and eventually rebound. France and Germany (as well as most of the Scandinavian countries) are plagued with few natural resources, weak economies and a declining workforce. With lowered productivity they are increasingly unable to maintain the socialized societies that have evolved over the past 50 years. The huge numbers of unskilled East Germans who became part of the unified Germany has almost bankrupted the entire economy. Both France and Germany have increasingly relied on immigrant labor, largely from the Arab and other Muslim Middle East countries. It is estimated that Sweden may well have a majority Muslim population by as soon as 2025.

While the United States economy can absorb a disruption of oil production and economic investment in places like Iraq, Iran and Sudan, most of "Old Europe" cannot (or will not). Increasingly, China is also becoming more and more dependent on the status quo in promoting its own economic growth and stability.

What this means concerning Sudan and Darfur is that the United States is unable to bring the necessary pressure to bear on Sudan without seriously threatening the economic and political stability of France, Germany and, to a lesser extant, China.

In Iraq, the United States, for its own long-term interests, weighed the matter of competing interests and, in the end, refused to let France, Germany and Russia determine our foreign policy.

Sudan, however, is not as high a priority for these long-term U.S. interests as is Iraq. Iran, Syria/Lebanon, Palestine and Israel are of more immediate concern. The United States cannot afford to further alienate and damage our political and economic responsibilities to France, Germany and China over Sudan. There is, however, strong mutual interest in freeing Lebanon from Syrian control and containing Iran's nuclear weapons program. In addition, American insistence that China be a full partner in negotiating with North Korea means that we cannot afford to confront them over Sudan at this time either. Until these matters are resolved I am afraid that, short of a change of heart in France and China, there is little that the United States can do except provide aid for the refugees and continue to shame the United Nations and the leading nations on the Security Council (which include the permanent membership of France, Germany and Russia and China....Japan is largely supportive of the United States position) into doing something more substantial than posturing with verbal clichés and symbolic wringing of hands.

Thus far, Europe and Africa appear to be both unwilling and unable to assert the sort of economic, political and military pressure on Sudan to halt the "cleansing" of Darfur.

It is no small thing to note that only the United States has (unofficially) labeled the purging of the Darfur African population as genocide. In addition, the United States, both through government aid and private, charitable giving, is providing the vast majority of relief to the people of Darfur.

One positive note is that the American outrage over Darfur is a bi-partisan outrage. It has transcended the divide between Democrats and Republicans, especially in the House of Representatives.

In a just world, the Sudanese government would be squeezed out of existence by a united international community. But the world is not just. And today the people of Darfur are the victims.

I have no doubt that, if the spread of governmental reform continues its success in Iraq and Afghanistan and, if that spirit of reform begins to move in places like Iran, Syria, Palestine, Saudi Arabia and Egypt, then Sudan will become not only a pariah in the eyes of the United States, but a pariah amongst its awakening neighbors, as well.

By God's grace, peace and justice will one day come to the people of Darfur. Until that day comes we must not allow them to be forgotten or abandoned. And we should remember them with our pocketbook as well as with our prayers.

By the way, a wonderful internet site on the Darfur situation with many links to photographs is http://www.savedarfur.org/go.php?q=/100Hours/PhotosOfDarfur.htm (be sure to click on "Latest News" at the bottom of the page for daily updates on matters related to Darfur). Other photographs can be found at
http://www.hrw.org/photos/2004/darfur1/index1.htm
and http://www.nytimes.com/2005/02/23/opinion/23kristof.html?ex=1266901200&en=d9bc5fbe39eed505&ei=5090&partner=rssuserland
(which contains a very disturbing report on the atrocities).
Lastly, Little Green Footballs (which is a pro-Israel, conservative website), has some links to many matters concerning Darfur at
http://littlegreenfootballs.com/weblog/?entry=14554

Please forgive me for getting carried away in this matter. Your information inspired me to take time to think and rethink this matter through. As you might gather from my thoughts I do not think that the international inaction concerning Sudan is either racist or representative of a devaluing of the lives of Africans over others. Nor do I think that American military intervention (without the full support and participation by our European and African allies) is a good idea at this time. We must, however, continue to support the government of Chad which is presently bearing the burden of the Sudanese refugees.

FRIDAY, MARCH 11, 2005

Tie--Dies: Judge Calls Terri Schiavo "Out"

When I was younger and played softball it was a rule of thumb that "tie base goes to the runner." The idea is that it's harder to get a hit than to make an out so the more difficult of the two gets the nod.

With Terri Schiavo, however, the judge handling her case seems to feel that a "tied case goes to the grave." As I ponder the evidence in this case it is not clear whether Terri is conscious or not. **Tie**. It is not clear whether she expressed a desire to not be subject to life support. **Tie**. It is not clear whether she would have been able to respond to rehab treatment. **Tie**. It is not clear that she is subject to life termination under the law. **Tie**. And, it is not clear whether her brain damage was from a natural cause or from a physical assault (ie. choking). **Tie**.

So far as I can see there is no overwhelming case for either side...especially when so many of the questions cannot be answered because normal and acceptable medical care has not been provided for Terri by her husband.

So it is up to the umpire--oops, I mean judge--to make the call. He can choose to either let her live or to allow her to be killed. The husband wants her dead and her family wants her to live. Which results in another **Tie**.

It seems not only reasonable but compulsory under these circumstances for the judge to rule for life. It is easy to kill someone. It is more difficult to give them life. Life, once taken, cannot be restored. Life, once given, can still be taken at a later time if circumstances become clearer in the future.

If it was not very clear that the overwhelming evidence in a capital murder conviction proved the defendant guilty would a judge issue a death penalty? Certainly not. Conviction by a jury requires "beyond a reasonable doubt" and a sentence of death normally must exceed even that requirement.

Terri Schiavo's circumstance does not qualify for even the simplest level of "beyond a reasonable doubt."

The saddest part of all this is that the judge has never seen the "play" and has refused to even review it. Although urged to go by Terri's family, he has never gone to visit Terri and see for himself what her condition is, nor has he ever allowed her to be present in the courtroom where he is passing judgment on whether she will live or die.

I feel as if the judge was making his calls from a different rule book than everyone else.

When a baseball game is over the losing coach can raise a protest flag so that the reason for the protest can be reviewed.

When Terri's feeding tube is pulled next Wednesday millions of her supporters will join her family in raising the protest flag one last time. But this time, when it comes time for the review, the game will be over for Terri.

In the Olympics, when a competition ends in a tie, both participants are declared to have won and each receives a gold medal. It does not look as though Terri will be getting a gold medal from the judge next week.

SATURDAY, MARCH 12, 2005

Isn't God Wonderful! A Brief Testimony of God's Providence

Every once in a while someone will express their thanks to me for something I've done as a pastor by giving me some money. Depending on the circumstances sometimes I accept the gift and keep it. More often, however, I simply turn and give the same amount of money as an anonymous gift to the church.

Yesterday, someone with a legitimate financial need dropped by the church to see if I could help them. The church has given me a small discretionary fund that I can draw on as I see a need but sometimes I simply give (not loan) them something from my own wallet. This is what I chose to do yesterday. At the time I could not figure out why I felt so good about being so generous to this person but somehow it just seemed the right thing to do. The person wept with gratitude. The church they attended (not in my town) had said they couldn't help and there was a strong feeling of hopelessness and despair. My gift reaffirmed the person's faith in God and I was asked to pray with them before they left. In any case, I told them that the gift was not from me, but from God.

I had also told the person that often I do say "no" to people when they ask for money. I could not, however, explain why I felt so compelled to say "yes" to them on this particular occasion.

This morning, while thinking about this, I suddenly understood. In the past two weeks I had received "thank you" gifts from two different people/churches for things I had done for them. I considered whether to give the money to the church or keep it. For some reason (that made me uncomfortable at the time), almost on impulse, I decided to keep the money. Now I know why. The amount of the two gifts was *exactly* what the person had needed yesterday and was the exact amount of money I had given them. The money had turned out to be God's after all!

God is good...all the time! All the time...God is good! Amen!

WEDNESDAY, MARCH 16, 2005

A Trip to California for Presbytery

I just returned today from a 2 1/2 day swing through California. Although I had a quick visit to see my sister and mother in the San Francisco area the real reason for my trip was a Presbytery meeting in Los Angeles.

The meeting was held at the Beverly Hills Presbyterian Church located at the rather tony address of Santa Monica Blvd. and Rodeo Drive. The congregation were great hosts providing a wonderful meal and warm hospitality.

The meeting was also better then average. The business of the evening was divided up within the overarching structure of a Sunday morning worship service. Whenever the tedium of administrative business got to the breaking point we would suddenly be refreshed with readings from the Bible, 5-part renaissance motets by the wonderful church choir, unison prayers of confession, the singing of great hymns (Low in the grave he lay, Jesus my savior.....). I tell you, Presbyterian ministers love to sing. Even the Elders joined in with more gusto than they normally would have on a Sunday morning!

The high point for me came in several extended discussions concerning how to encourage, empower and integrate Reformed Protestant immigrant churches into our Presbytery. Throughout the Los Angeles basin are hundreds of small congregations rising spontaneously within a wide variety of immigrant communities. In earlier years we saw it with Japanese, Chinese and Welsh groups. More recently we have seen it with Korean, Filipino, Latin American, Iranian, Sudanese, Ethiopian, Vietnamese, Taiwanese and many others.

Presbyterian and other Reformed churches have had a tremendous influence in overseas missions over the past two centuries. Their are many nations that have independent national "Presbyterian" type denominations. When members of these churches immigrate to America they seek out other immigrants with similar Christian backgrounds to worship with in the context of their native language and cultural identity.

Some of these churches either "nest" or integrate with an "American" congregation. Most, however, remain both autonomous and isolated from the wider Body of Christ. There is often a yearning to become more "connected" to American churches.

Many attempts are now being made across the United States by PCUSA Presbyteries to extend friendship and support to these immigrant churches. Offering leadership training and linking them to the larger Church through welcoming them in some way into a presbytery are among these attempts. Two overtures from last year's General Assembly concerning these matters were presented, discussed, debated and voted on. One approach was narrowly rejected by our presbytery while the other was narrowly approved.

What was apparent in all of this discussion was the genuine desire to encourage and support as many of these groups as possible with the aim of helping them grow in strength and in numbers as part of our PCUSA denomination.

Although we may be divided on the particular "means" to the "end" there appeared to be near unanimity on the value of the "ends."

In my own congregation here in Hawaii we "nest" a Korean congregation (PCUSA), a Samoan (independent congregational) church and a Micronesian (primarily from Chuuk...formerly known as Truk) fellowship. Whether Reformed Protestant or not, it is a joy to be able to provide a place for these expatriate Christians to gather together for worship and fellowship each week. They are grateful for our prayers and support (they use our facilities gratis) and we, in turn, are grateful to be able to count them as our friends and family in Jesus.

Sure, of course I would like to build up and increase our denomination by by "making" them Presbyterian. But I am more interested in simply building up the Body of Christ in any way possible.

Jesus did not come to create denominations, but to call faithful followers who know the voice of their Shepherd and claim him as their Lord and Savior. Being Presbyterian is a very good thing. But, if you are not a Christian first, it doesn't really matter, does it!

Why I Am Not Qualified To Be a Pastor

Throughout my 26 years of ordained ministry in the Presbyterian Church (USA) I have often felt that I was not connecting with my congregation...that my words and leadership somehow were missing the mark. Tonight I discovered where I have gone wrong all these years.

Andy and Theresa (and toddler daughter Makayla) came over for dinner and dessert tonight. Andy's mother is also a Presbyterian pastor (in Pennsylvania) but, for her, it is a second career.

Andy explained that he felt his mother's first career had greatly helped her to become an effective minister and pastor to her congregregation. What was her secret? ***She had been a 1st grade public school teacher!***

I wonder if my congregation will give me a sabbatic leave to get my elementary school teaching credential? Maybe then they would be able to understand what I am talking about on a Sunday morning!

Thanks, Andy, for the tip!

FRIDAY, MARCH 18, 2005

Presdent Bush Comments on Terri Schiavo

STATEMENT BY THE PRESIDENT

The case of Terri Schiavo raises complex issues. Yet in instances like this one, where there are serious questions and substantial doubts, our society, our laws, and our courts should have a presumption in favor of life. Those who live at the mercy of others deserve our special care and concern. It should be our goal as a nation to build a culture of life, where all Americans are valued, welcomed, and protected and that culture of life must extend to individuals with disabilities.

D-Day for Terri Schiavo

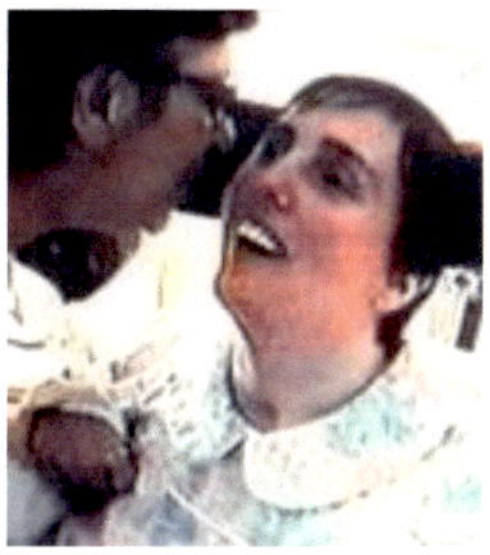

Today is the day that Terri Schiavo's so-called "husband" finally gets his chance to do what he has been waiting for over 10 years to do....starve his wife to death.

Unless the Florida or Federal legislators pass the bills that have been submitted to prevent it, a person innocent of any crime except to be unwanted by one person, will be executed by the "cruel and unusual" method of starvation.

Without food and water Terri will live nine days, perhaps ten, before withering away to a lifeless corpse. I wonder if someone will be allowed to place ice chips in her mouth to relieve the pain of cracked lips and swollen tongue. Probably not. After all, that might delay the humane act of putting her out of her misery. I'm sure that, when her husband claims she asked not to be kept alive by artificial means, she was hoping and praying for this.

As I have written of Terri before. (here, here, here and here) I have also stated that feeding tubes are not considered either "artificial" or "life support" on medical or ethical grounds. This not a removal of life support. It is not mercy killing. It is simply killing.

This will be the third time that a judge has allowed her feeding tube to be removed. Twice before that ruling has been recinded by some other legal action.
The hardest part of this for me is the uncertainty of knowing whether or not she is in a "permanent vegetative state" or not. Scores of the top neurologists in the country have stated that Terri has never been given even any of the most credible diagnostic tests to determine her true condition. Both her husband and the judge have refused to allow them. A recent article summarizing the tragic and incomprehensible extent of Terri's medical neglect can be found **here**. Other information is available at "terrisfight" the site maintained by Terri's own family.

I don't know whether Terri will be glad to finally die. I don't know whether the medical diagnoses endorsed by the judge are correct or not. I don't know whether Terri said to her husband what he says she told him. I don't know for sure. And nobody else knows either.

No one on trial for a crime would be convicted on the basis of such conflicted and unverifiable evidence. Certainly, no one would be sentenced to the death penalty under the cloud of such "reasonable doubt."

That is what is so chilling. That our society and our legal system is so willing and eager to choose death over life. And for no real, tangeable reason except that her husband very, very much wants her to die.

Apparently, in the future, no one will need to murder someone they consider to be an inconvenience. They will simply be able to have the government do it for them.

As a Christian pastor I must remember the example of my Lord, Jesus, who never killed anyone or caused anyone to die. His touch brought only healing and life. He is never once recorded as having said, "Let them die."

It is God who says, "You have profaned me among my people for a few handfuls of barley and scraps of bread. By lying to my people, who listen to lies, you have killed those who should not have died..." (Ezekiel 13:19)

It is God who declares, "This day I call heaven and earth as witnesses against you that I have set before you life and death, blessings and curses. Now choose life, so that you and your children may live ." (Deuteronomy 30:19)

For Terri's sake. For our sake. For my sake. For God's sake. Let us choose life.

Argentine Bishop Dismissed by Government for Citing the Bible

A Roman Catholic Bishop appointed by Rome and approved by the Argentine government to oversee military chaplains has been removed by the government. Here is a key quote, the full article from BBC is here:
Health Minister Gines Gonzalez Garcia recently said he was in favour of legalising abortion. Bishop Baseotto replied that the minister's stance made him an apologist for murder

Quoting a passage from the New Testament, he said Mr Gonzalez Garcia deserved to have a millstone hung around his neck and should be "thrown into the sea".

But the government has said the statement evoked Argentina's controversial past. During the military regime that ruled the country from 1976-1983, political opponents were thrown into the sea during the so-called "death flights".

The bishop says his comments were taken out of context, but BBC Buenos Aires correspondent Elliott Gotkine says his position now appears untenable.

Unfortunately the article does not explain why Mr. Gotkine feels the bishop's "position now appears untenable."

And what was it, exactly, that the bishop quoted:

Jesus said to his disciples:

Things that cause people to sin are bound to come, but woe to that person through whom they come. It would be better for him to be thrown into the sea with a millstone tied around his neck than for him to cause one of these little ones to sin. So watch yourselves.

"If your brother sins, rebuke him, and if he repents, forgive him.(Luke 17:1-3)

In rebuking the Health Minister it would appear that the bishop was only doing his job!

I believe that it is reasonable to believe that the bishop considered the possiblility that someone might associate the words of Jesus with those infamous "death flights". Even so, the words he quoted were eminently appropriate to his point.

Whether the citation and resulting "association" were intentional or not, it most certainly appears that, in Argentina at least, quoting Jesus can get you in a heap of trouble!

SATURDAY, MARCH 19, 2005

Birds and Their Nests

Every spring the mynah birds try to build their nests on the top of the pillars that support our Worship Center roof. They leave massive amounts of debris on the ground and it takes a lot of work to keep it cleaned up

.

No matter what we do the birds come back for more. I have tried moth balls, rags soaked in bleach, rubber snakes, furniture polish spray (lemon scented...yuch!) and more.

Today, after cleaning up on our monthly work day, Charlie produced some light netting material. It took him 30 minutes to arrange it around one half of one pillar. After looking it over he now figures that the birds will probably find a way to get inside and enjoy the privacy!

Jesus said, "Even the birds have nests but the Son of Man has no place to lay his head."

In our case we wish it was the other way around!

Jessica Lunsford's "Remains" Found

Note: So many have visited this post but few have left a comment. Please let me know why Jessica's story is of interest to you, personally. Thanks, BofP

UPDATE: You can find a more recent post on Jessica here and a poem here.

The "remains" of a 9 year old Florida girl, kidnapped and murdered by a convicted child molester, were found early this morning by investigators in the exact location described by the chief suspect who has confessed to the crime.

The story's headline got me to thinking about the word "remains" and what the word really means. "Remains" are what are left after something is gone; wood shavings on the work room floor; food left on the plate after dinner; ruined, rotting wood and stone, lying on the ground where a house once stood.

The world sees human "remains" as what is left when a person dies. Like a fallen tree dies and decays, Jessica Lundsford, too is dead. Her remains are all that is left; left overs from what once was but is now gone forever.

"From dust thou art and to dust thou shalt return." At the beginning of the season of Lent these were the words we spoke on Ash Wednesday as we placed the mark of the cross on our foreheads with the ashes of grief and repentence.

But Lent ends with Easter, and Easter gives us a new understanding of life...and death.

"She is not here," the angels say. "She is risen!"

On Easter the tomb of Jesus was empty. Well, not completely empty. There were remains: the winding strips of his burial cloth was scattered around and the linen cloth that covered his head was neatly folded in a corner. With Jessica, too, there are remains. But in light of Easter we no longer view those remains as the remains of a fallen ruin. They are, for us, more like the shed skin of a lizard; the broken, empty pieces of a cocoon; wood shavings on the work room floor; discarded, unneeded left overs of a new creation.

In a Christian funeral we lay the remains in a place of remembrance and say words similar to these, "We commit her *body* to the grave" and "We commit her *soul* to the care and mercy of Almighty God in the sure and certain hope of resurrection to eternal life."

We believe that God created Jessica, gave her life and sent his Son to redeem her and prepare a place for her in eternity.

According to the news article,

Jessica's distraught father said earlier Saturday that his daughter is "home now," but made no reference to the discovery of her remains.

"Everyone heard me say time after time that she would be home," said Mark Lunsford, choking back tears. "Well, she's home now. It's over...She's right here with me."

I will not argue with Jessica's father. I cannot say whether she is with him or not. I do know that her precious remains have been found and will soon be returned home to her family. Jessica, however, is at home with God.

SUNDAY, MARCH 20, 2005

UPI Headliine Bias?

A March 17 UPI article on new Homeland Security Secretary Michael Chertoff's first public speech is entitled, "*Analysis: Homeland Security Fumbling Threat Assessment*."

The article, by UPI Homeland & National Security Editor Shaun Waterman, presents itself as an objective news story (which, in all fairness, it seems to be). ***What is mystifying is the article's misleading and prejudicial headline***. The article contains no analysis that I can discern, and negative opinions on various national security issues are balanced with positive ones. Nor does the word "fumbling" (or any remotely-related synomyn) appear anywhere within the article.

It is well-known that headlines convey stronger impressions to the casual reader than the articles themselves. Why is UPI seemingly trying to misrepresent and spin an article in a manner that reflects badly on the Bush administration?

Can anyone out there help me on this?

Be Careful Where You Park Your Scooter

Reuters shares the story of Heidi Brown, a British woman who went to the motor vehicle department to get license plates for her new moped/scooter. Someone told her it would be all right to park it against a nearby fence for the requisite inspection.

While waiting her turn inside, nearby shop owners reported the scooter to police as a possible bomb waiting to go off. Police, finding no license or registration on the scooter (which had been chained to the fence) evacuated nearby buildings and sealed off three roads and then.....blew up the scooter!

The article did not say whether or not police have apologized to Ms. Brown.

Sudanese Troops To Be Deployed As Peacekeepers In Somalia ("Sudanese Peacekeepers?")

The Somalian parliament has rejected the proposal that peacekeeping troops serving in their country be drawn from the neighboring countries of Kenya, Ethiopia and Djibouti.

According to the BBC, "The Ugandan foreign Minister said the decision was made out of respect for the sensitivities of the Somalis, (especially) Somali warlords (who) have said they will attack troops from neighboring states - especially from rival Ethiopia - if they form part of a peacekeeping force."

More acceptable were troops from Sudan and Uganda (yes I'm serious, I'm not making this up).

The article added that, "Somalia's government and parliament are currently based in Kenya because the Somali capital, Mogadishu, is considered too dangerous."

(***Warning***: *Incoming sarcasm alert*): I'm sure that the Sudanese troops, who are currently busy slaughtering black Africans in their own country's Darfur region, will go a long way towards bringing stability to Somalia.
Please read the article for yourself. It is even more surreal than Salvador Dali.

MONDAY, MARCH 21, 2005

Terri Schiavo and the U.S. Congress : Washington Post Columnist Just Doesn't Get It

In today's Washington Post, columnist Richard Cohen mocks congressional Republicans for passing legislation that permits a federal court to review the legal aspects of the Terri Schiavo case. In an article dripping with sarcasm, Cohen, at one point, sums up his view of the Republican rationale as follows,
Frist and his (mostly) GOP colleagues were operating under such pressure that they sometimes did not know which subterfuge to adopt. ***After all, it should not matter -- it must not matter -- if Schiavo is in a vegetative state or not****. What should matter -- under right-to-life reasoning -- is that she is alive. In many respects, she is as alive as a zygote the moment after fertilization or a fetus that will die shortly after birth -- or any other manifestation of life as it either exists or is proclaimed to exist. Life is life, Frist. Get with the program.* (emphasis mine).
I believe that Cohen has got it wrong here. Very wrong. Completely backwards, in fact.

The central concern of virtually everyone who is fighting for Terri's life (including myself and her family) is that it **does** matter whether Schiavo is in a vegetative state or not.

While there are clearly other important issues involved in this morally and legally tangled drama/tragedy, the one thing that sets this particular case apart from many others is the fact that **it is not clear whether Terri Schiavo is or is not in a persistent vegetative state**.

Her family and others who have visited with her over the past 15 years claim that she is conscious, aware of and interactive with her environment and able to express emotion in response to stimuli.

Every attempt to have a non-biased medical assessment made of Terri using the standard and usual diagnostic tests which determine whether or not a person is in a persistent vegetative state, has been denied by both Terri's "husband," Michael, and the presiding judge. The judge has gone so far as to refuse to even visit Terri to see for himself whether the testimony he has received from persons personally selected by Michael is accurate or true.

Most people would like to have a "second opinion" before having major surgery. Judge has not even allowed Terri a to get a "second opinion" concerning her condition before sentencing her to death by starvation (note that Terri is NOT on life-support).

Terri's family has repeatedly offered to take her home with them and care for her themselves. Since this offer has also been rejected repeatedly, they have simply asked for that second opinion.

That is all. That is the whole issue. Everything else; all other issues, both moral and medical; follow from this one, simple question as to whether Terri is "brain dead" or not.

For many of us, this uncertainly (supported by the manipulative and inconsistent behavior and testimony of Michael Schiavo) leaves us with the fear that a conscious, cognizant human being, unable to express herself due to a major physical disability, is being denied her God-given and Constitutionally-supported right to both life and liberty by being starved to death at the insistence of her husband.

At its core this is not a "pro-choice" or a "pro-life" issue. At its core it is not (or should not) be a "great political issue" either. Nor should it surprise us when a matter of law and the interpretation of law also becomes a matter of interest and concern amongst those who have been elected to legislate those laws in the first place!

Mr. Cohen's column today clearly demonstrates that yelling loudly and showering sarcasm on those with whom one disagrees does not show very much respect for the life or death issues involved in this debate. Good men and women have taken responsible and informed positions on both sides of this situation. Unfortunately, Mr. Cohen is not one of them.

Minnesota School Deaths Leave Me Speechless

Note: You can read a related poem **here**.

A teacher, a security guard, five high school students were shot to death at school yesterday by another high school student who, having previously killed his two grandparents, then shot and killed himself (see the article here).

The Chippewa Red Lake Indian Reservation, the nearby town of Red Lake, Minnesota, and Red Lake High School are reeling in shock and disbelief today. So am I.

A tsunami I can handle (see here & here), even with nearly 200,000 human deaths. The amoral power of nature is to be both respected and feared, of course, but there is no conscious intent to harm, there is no malice aforethought or even a question of right and wrong in such a tragedy.

But the senseless, intentional, malicious and deadly actions of a student named "Jeff" that took away the lives of nine other living, breathing human beings in their home and in their high school classroom, leaves me numb.

As a Pastor of reasonable intelligence and knowledge of the Word of God I can rattle off all the biblical and theological truths about sin, evil, spiritual warfare, and the forgiving, redeeming, sacrificing love of God until I'm blue in the face but it will be a long time, if ever, before I will be able to come to any measure of "peace" about what happened in Red Lake.

For those who were killed I feel a profound sense of sadness and grief, almost as though they were my own children, my sister or my brother. The unfairness and injustice of it all appalls me. Even if I had "all knowledge and faith to remove mountains" it would still be incomprehensible to me. I have the same feeling I had in the cemetery in Leningrad (now St. Petersburg) where 1,000,000 victims of the German siege of that city are buried, the vast majority of whom were civilians.

Along with Job in his suffering, I cry out "Why?" to God even though, unlike Job, I already know the unanswerable answer to that question. Six million Jews murdered. Nine native Americans murdered. I feel a sense of horror as though reality and the whole of creation have been twisted out of shape. I can hardly recognize the world as being the same one that I woke up to just 16 hours ago, when those ten people in Red Lake were still living and their future was still open to a different outcome.

As for "Jeff," I have little or no feeling at all. You see, I can relate to those who were killed. I can imagine and even feel the confusion, the fear and the terror that must have overtaken them in their last, fleeting moments of life.

But as for "Jeff," I cannot imagine. I cannot feel. Yet I weep for him, but not in the same way that I weep for those who he killed. I weep for "Jeff" because he became, or allowed himself to become, so badly fallen from the image of God that I can no longer relate to him as one human being to another. At least not now. Not today.

I am in no position to either ask for or to offer forgiveness to "Jeff." Others will have to grapple with this matter, and that struggle will sear their souls until it leads them either to an eternal hardening of their heart or leads them to their knees as they confess and repent to God of their own weakness and sin.

Psalm 51:17 tells us that "the only sacrifice acceptable to God is a broken spirit. A broken and contrite heart God will not despise." No doubt there are many broken spirits and many broken hearts in Red Lake tonight. In time, by God's grace, there will be contrite hearts as well.

As for myself, all I can do is pray. I pray for the victims of this terrible crime. In prayer I entrust them to the care and mercy of Almighty God. And I pray for their friends and families. I pray for them what Jesus taught in his "Sermon on the Mount" when he said, "Blessed are they who mourn; for they will be comforted."

And, yes, I pray for "Jeff." Although I am not inclined to pray for "Jeff" my Savior and Lord compels and commands me to pray for him. I am not quite sure what it is that I ought to pray for, but I shall entrust him, also, to the care and mercy of Almighty God. For I know that God is merciful, but also just. God can be trusted to sort this all out with a measure of perfect righteousness that, at present, completely eludes me.

And I pray for "Jeff's" family, who have lost three loved ones today. The grief, suffering and guilt they must be experiencing must surely test the limits of their physical, emotional and spiritual endurance.

Somehow, for the moment at least, Easter seems to be very far, far away.

May God have mercy on us all.

TUESDAY, MARCH 22, 2005

Should She Be Kept Alive? or Should She Be Allowed To Die"

She is unable to eat by herself. All nutrition and liquids are administered to her by others. Without it, she will die. She lies in a bed, able to move her arms and legs, but unable to walk or stand. Even sitting in a chair requires her to be strapped up. Otherwise her body will slump in a heap to the floor.

She is unable to communicate her thoughts. Indeed, it is not really clear that she even has thoughts at all. Her brain clearly does not function the way a normal adult brain functions. There is little or no hand-eye coordination, either. She drools and, on occasion, must be suctioned to prevent her from suffocating from throat and nasal congestion.

She must be diapered and requires around the clock, 24-hour, 7 day a week care. She cannot bathe herself. Her eyes frequently appear to stare blankly into space. She cannot read or write or even respond to the simplest direction. It is not even clear whether or not she can distinguish between colors or differentiate between one person's voice and another.

She is not ill, or diseased and is in relatively good health. There is no reason to believe that she will not live out her full adult life. Neither Social Security nor Medicare are able to cover the ongoing costs of her long-term extended care requirements.

Some say that she should be allowed the right to die, even if it means withholding the food and water that keeps her alive. Her parents are more than willing to bear the full cost of her care and have repeatedly offered to take her home.

But, because of a myriad of legal complications, she has been declared a ward of the court. And now the judge who oversees her case has determined that there is compelling evidence to order that all food and liquid be withheld from her until she dies of starvation and dehydration. The judge, by the way, has never visited her in person, but has relied only on information provided to him by the ones who feel she should be allowed to die.

Her parents have filed appeals seeking a second medical examination of her condition or a new legal review by another judge or a different judicial venue. All such requests have been turned down repeatedly.

Somewhere in Florida, a young woman named Terri Schiavo is dying. But this is not the person I have been describing in this essay. Instead, I have been describing a scenario involving a perfectly healthy 3-month old infant girl.

But the law's the law. "If the law supposes that," said Mr. Bumble, "the law is a ass, a idiot."

WEDNESDAY, MARCH 23, 2005

Schiavo Case Setting a Precedent?

The American legal system has now set a remarkable precedent. From henceforth (and even forevermore?) there will be a new set of case law that permits the courts to approve that which, without their approval, would otherwise be illegal.

For example, if I were to allow my old granny to die peacefully and painlessly by withholding food and water from her I would be arrested and thrown in jail.

But, if I had a court of law allow me to withhold food and water from my old granny that would be just fine and dandy.

Perhaps this new concept can be expanded.

For example, if I were to cut down my neighbor's tree without his permission I would be charged with trespassing and destruction of personal property.

But, if I had a court of law allow me to cut down my neighbor's tree without his permission that would be ok.

It appears to me that we have at last reached the place in our history where the law has become whatever the courts feel the law ought to be at any given time. Since we have now progressed as a national culture to the point where right and wrong, good and evil, truth and fiction are relative, it only makes sense that this concept be extended to legal and illegal as well.

Is it wrong to murder your wife? Well, if you are a white, middle-class Christian it probably is. But, if you are an immigrant Arab Muslim male asserting your right to avenge a perceived slight to your honor, then..... well..... who are we to criticize or judge someone based on standards that are foreign to them. It would be culturally insensitive to punish them for something they do not view as being "wrong."

So, let's look forward to the day when we will have no more need of codified law at all. If there is a conflict or disagreement over some trivial matter (such as my taking your car from your garage without you knowing anything about it and driving it to work because mine was broken down and I really, really, really had to get to work on time...) then we can just go over to Judge Judy's and let her figure it out any way she wants to. (Hmmm, maybe one of those "eight ball" answer thingies would work, too!)

Things That Do Not Make Sense

The starving to death of Terri Schiavo does not make sense to me. But, apparently, there are lots of other things that do not seem to make sense, either. Here are thirteen things (mostly astrophysics and "medicine") that, so far at least, do not make sense to anybody.

THURSDAY, MARCH 24, 2005

Maundy Thursday

The word,"Maundy," comes from the Latin word, *maundanum*, which means, "command" (as in "mandate"). It was on that final night with his disciples that Jesus said, "A new command (*maundanum*) I give to you, that you love one another as I have loved you." (click picture to enlarge) Tonight at our worship we will remember Jesus' betrayal, the washing of his disciples feet (I will do the washing), the breaking of bread, the pouring of the cup and the singing of a hymn before they went out to the Mt. of Olives.

There will be some special music, of course, and two other hymns will be sung. But the service will be short and simple. As Pastor I will say very little. A narrator will provide most of the spoken word via a script. One of the children will ask me a series of questions about the Lord's Supper (a la the questions asked by children at the Jewish Seder meal) and I will respond with the words of institution from I Corinthians 11:23-26.

Maundy Thursday is always both happy and sad for me. There is so much to be sad about, of course. But the joy of friends sharing a meal together at such a momentous moment deeply moves me. If I were ever to be required to eat a final meal I, too, would wish that it could be shared with friends.

Tonight, we will share the meal with the crucified and risen Lord. We will not forget that it was also on this night that he declared, "No longer do I call you servants....but I call you friends..." And so we are.

That, my friends, is what makes me happy.

FRIDAY, MARCH 25, 2005

Good Friday, Terri Schiavo & Jetseta Gage

Today is Good Friday when Christians remember the execution of Jesus Christ with permission from the Roman Governor, Pontius Pilate. Pilate found him innocent of the charge of sedition but, for political reasons, allowed him to be crucified under threat of a riot led by members of the Jewish high council (Sanhedrin) in Jerusalem.

"Crucifixion" by Giotto (click to enlarge)

Most people in Jerusalem that day (with more than 10 times the normal population gathered for the celebration of Passover) undoubtedly felt that Jesus' death was unjust and unfair. But the Jewish leaders had a point. They had found Jesus guilty of blasphemy for having claimed to be equal to God. In one sense they were right to make this charge. The only way they could have been wrong was if Jesus *was* equal to God. Easter morning proved them wrong.

Jesus' crucifixion proved the limitation of human justice. Both Rome and the Jewish leaders got the law wrong or else ignored it and twisted it around for some other purpose.

Things have not changed since that first Good Friday.

Today we have once again discovered, in the starving of **Terri Schiavo**, the limitation of human justice. It appears to me that both federal and state courts have, this past week, either got the law wrong or else ignored it and twisted it around for some other purpose.

Jesus was not the first innocent person to be "legally" killed and Terri Schiavo will not be the last.

For Jesus, we have the upcoming celebration of the good news of his resurrection from the dead.

For Terri, we have the upcoming celebration of the good news of his resurrection from the dead.

I pray that this good news will bring some measure of comfort to Terri's family and friends. It does not assuage my anger and disappointment in the circumstances surrounding her impending death, but it does bring me some measure of comfort and peace knowing that God is just in a way that we can never be; knowing that Jesus' death has brought forgiveness, salvation and eternal, resurrection life to those who receive it by faith; even Terri; even me; even you.

Today we mark the death of still another innocent life. The body of 10-year old **Jetseta Gage** was found today near her home in Iowa. It is suspected that a family friend, a convicted sex offender, took her from her home in plain view of her family. What happened between then and the discovery of her body can only be imagined...if we even dare to imagine.

Because of the first Good Friday...and because of Easter...I have hope for Jetseta and for Terri. Their innocence will be vindicated and, with God, they will rediscover the love and (even greater) life that others have denied them here.

The Bible tells us that Jesus took the pain and suffering upon himself that we deserved. No doubt, members of Terri's family and Jetseta's family would have done the same for the one they love if they had been given the chance.

That is how much Jesus loves us. That is how much God loves you.
For God so loved the world that he gave his only-begotten son, that whoever believes in him shall not perish, but have everlasting life. (John 3:16)
When my oldest daughter was around the same age as Jetseta, she memorized this verse but unknowingly switched one word for another. In her version the verse read: "shall not perish, but have ever*living* life." It may not be technically correct, but I like my daughter's version the best.

Media Continues To Slander Christians

As Hugh Hewitt and Powerline have already noted, such writers as Professor Juan Cole of the University of Michigan and syndicated columnist Maureen Dowd have begun making explicit comparisons between "radical Islamic fascists" (such as the Taliban) and "conservative Christians."

Unless these writers for some reason admire and respect the Islamic fascists (which does not seem likely) then I must assume that the comparison is intended both to alert the Americans to the irrational and threatening presence of Christians in our midst and to label conservative Christians as totalitarian terrorists intent on imposing their faith and values onto everyone else...or else!

Today, a third columnist, Trudy Rubin of the Philadelphia Inquirer, has added her voice to the anti-Christian media madness.

In a column entitled, "Religion Out Abroad/In At Home" Ms. Rubin states her fear that, "The Middle East - and the Afghanistan of the Taliban - offer frightening lessons about what can happen when that barrier between church and state is shattered."

Now I should make it clear that she is not, apparently, concerned that radical Islamist fascists might find its place is American politics. No, what seems to terrify her is the possibility that Christian beliefs and values might actually inform the way in which some elected officials make moral and legal decisions.

Rubin implies that, should Christianity "take over" the United States we would become at least as bad as Afghanistan under the Taliban.

Trudy Rubin is out of her mind and frightens me to death! Are there really people in positions of influence in our country who feel justified in presenting such foul, hateful, vindictive slander against an entire religion; indeed the very religion that birthed the concept of "freedom under law" in the first place?

Elsewhere in her article Rubin presents these examples as proof of the horrors of conservative Christians:

Some wealthy conservatives who fund Christian lobbying groups have views that sound not so different from Islamists in the Middle East. Examples: Christian philanthropist Howard Ahmanson Jr. says he seeks "the total integration of biblical law into our lives," and the grant-giving Maclellan Foundation endorses "the infallibility of the Scripture."
Does Ms. Rubin realize that she has just lumped every Presbyterian and virtually every other Christian in America in the same category as Middle East Isalmists? I cannot believe that she is as ignorant of basic Christian faith and doctrine as this comment represents. Or is she? Like Professor Cole and Maureen Dowd she appears to have descended into the realm of ideological fantasy. Nothing she writes in this column appears to bear any semblance to reality.

My God! What might happen if people who believe in the infallibility of scripture should assert themselves? Ms. Rubin speculates on this possibility by saying,
"(Although) we do not yet face the full challenge of fundamentalists who murder their opponents...we've seen a hint of this in the murders of doctors who perform abortions--and in the threats faced by Florida Judge George W. Greer in the Schiavo case."
Personally, I have read comments on white supremacist web sites that were more rational than this...and not as frightening!

To add to the surreal fantasy of her article Rubin also cites as evidence of this looming threat the recent "memo" supposedly distributed to Republican members of Congress last week. Either she is ignorant of or has chosen to ignore ABCs backtracking on their "bombshell" story and the rising evidence that the memo was seen being distributed on the House floor by Democratic staffers.

Although she blames conservative, fundamentalist Christians for pressuring the U.S. Congress into interfering in the Terri Schiavo case she omits to point out that the "Sciavo" bill passed the House by a vote of 203 to 58 with almost as many Democrats voting *for* the bill as voted *against* it (47-53).

As a Christian I am beginning to worry about the growing conflict between radical secularists and people of faith (particularly Christians) in America. After reading opinions like the ones cited above I am beginning to believe that there are people out there who truly and sincerely want to lock me in and shut me up in the best interests of our country. How ironic that these same people proclaim that Christians are the ones who are the true threats to freedom.

The truth is right in front of them. All they need to do is look into a mirror.

Chocolate Crosses, Good Friday & Easter

I heard a news story this morning concerning whether chocolate crosses are appropriate or inappropriate. Several persons, including a clergyman, were interviewed. Chocolate crosses? To be honest I had never thought about chocolate crosses before today. Is it something like the joke that says, "Whatever you do, *do not think* about blue elephants!"

I'm afraid that seminary did not prepare me for this particular theological dilemma, nor have I found any relevent scripture verses to buttress one viewpoint over another. Let's consider the subject......

First, there is the basic cross. That's all it is, just a chocolate cross with a small bunch of flowers (roses?) in the middle. This, I suppose, would make a nice "thank you" gift to your Sunday School teacher or, if you attend one, your teacher at a Christian School.

Then there are the "bite sized" crosses (foil wrapped so they will not melt together into a blob, I suspect). These are for the nibbler in the family. Perhaps the woman of the house who likes to think that, because they are small, they won't add much of anything to their calorie count and their carb-free diet. After all, if one small cross doesn't mean anything, then neither would two of them....or three....well, you get the idea. A perfect gift for Mom (husbands give this at your peril).

Then there is the big chocolate cross that actually stands up with its own chocolate pedestal. This could be used as a center piece for an Easter luncheon; perhaps surrounded by some colored cellophane "grass" (pink, yellow and green are my favorite colors) and a chocolate bunny, egg and chick as reminders of what this special day is all about.

Last, there is the elegant, carefully sculpted and detailed chocolate Celtic Cross. This is, of course, a wonderful gift for your pastor; especially if he or she is a member of a Reformed Protestant congregation.

Lutherans might be somewhat skeptical of such a gift, wondering if it contains some sort of hidden Calvinist message, so be careful with the Lutherans.

Congregationalists and Methodists do not seem to possess strong feelings on much of anything so any of the above crosses would do equally well the them.

I looked but couldn't find a Baptist chocolate cross. It would, of course, be plain and simple, perhaps even a bit rough around the edges to remind them of the hymn, "The Old Rugged Cross."

Catholics would require their chocolate cross to be a crucifix. This might seem to create a special difficulty for the average consumer/customer/church attender. But not to worry, the true body and blood of Christ are present only in the bread and wine, consecrated during the Mass. Since the chocolate image of Christ would represent merely a "remembrance" of Christ or, possibly his "spiritual" presence, it would then become equal to the Protestant "body of Christ" which is only bread and the Protestant "blood of Christ" which is only grape juice or wine (Epicopalians and Lutherans would from time to time be exempted from this judgement depending on who was Pope and what the most recent Vatican Council or Ecumenical Statement had to say). In any case, since the chocolate crucifix is simply the equivilent of plain bread and grape juice, Catholics should be able to enjoy it with a clear conscience.

Personally, as a Presbyterian pastor, I am partial to the chocolate Celtic Cross. But there is something about all of this that makes me feel uncomfortable. Perhaps it is the commercialization or the trivialization of the central symbol of our Christian faith that these chocolate crosses seem to represent.

No, sir. No chocolate cross for me on Easter this year. But, of course, I hope to enjoy some of those wonderful "hot-cross buns!"

SATURDAY, MARCH 26, 2005

Did You Know About Kaliningrad? I Didn't

Did you know that there is still one part of Germany that Russia (and the former U.S.S.R.) has never relinquished since World War II? Even after all of Eastern Europe has become free and independent and aligned with the EU, NATO and the West, a poor little patch of land, surrounded by Poland, Lithuania and the Baltic Sea, remains in Russian hands.

The central city of this isolated "chip off the old bloc" is Kaliningrad. Before the Soviets took it over after the defeat of Hitler, the city was known as Koenigsberg. It was the birthplace of Emmanuel Kant (who everyone considers to have been German..not Russian, by the way). The Soviets systematically purged as many native German people from the area as they could, replacing them with Russians.

Today, Kaliningrad and the territory it administrates, is going through an identity crisis. Everyone around them is prospering under Western-style politics and economics. They, however, for all practical purposes have been abandoned by their Russian "homeland." Russia, for its part, does not want to lose the territory due to its "warm water port" access to the Baltic Sea. On the other hand, there is little or no political reason to invest any money to clean up the pollution, rebuild the infrastructure or stimulate the economy there.

It is said that one beach area is unfrequented by locals because the skeletons of WW II soldiers have never been removed from where they fell in battle nearly 60 years ago. More of they younger members of the population have traveled to Western countries than have ever been to Russia itself.

Someday I expect that the people will get fed up with their situation and either demand either independence, self-rule or to become part of Poland or Lithuania. Mr. Putin, or his successor, will not be pleased. Watch this spot for future developments. I know I will!

(You can read more about Kaliningrad in this BBC article **here**)

Easter Poem 2005

Red Lake is weeping and Terri is dying;
Jetseta, Jessica lie in their graves.
Easter is here but the women keep crying.
How are able to claim, "Jesus saves?"

Iraq, Afghanistan, Sudan, Korea.
People are dying who yearn to breathe free.
"Jesus has risen!" Is that the idea?
Why then do people keep ceasing to be?

Innocent people whose lives have been taken;
Justice denied and the wicked rejoice.
Why are the children and helpless forsaken?
Where is the Savior who'll lift up his voice?

One tomb is empty while others keep filling.
Blood that was shed for poor sinners has dried.
Where is the mercy amidst all the killing?
Where is the hope for all those who have died?

Somewhere near Bethany, Jesus is standing.
"Golden Jerusalem" spreads out below.
Why is he weeping instead of commanding
That "Peace and Goodwill" unite both friend and foe?

Love is the answer for love is the reason
God lets us choose what our future will be.

Choices confront us whatever the season.
Loving? or Hating? The choice must be free.

God's love is perfect but ours is not nearly.
We choose the wrong way more often than not.
Sin is what comes when we fail to see clearly
What we should do. We deserve what we've got.

Easter does not mean that sin is deleted.
Sin still runs free though it's future is sure.
Easter reveals that sin's pow'r is defeated.
Death has been slain and Christ's blood is the cure.

Jetseta, Jessica, death will not hold you.
Easter's a victory Jesus will share.
With him you'll rise; in his arms he'll enfold you.
All of your sins and your griefs he will bear.

Those up in Red Lake and poor, starving Terri;
Jesus has risen! The dead, too, will rise!
In him is Life—it is death you will bury!
God's love in heav'n you will see with your eyes!

Innocent people will die as I'm writing.
Still God is ruling in heaven on high.
We who remain here in faith must keep fighting.
Love is our weapon, and vict'ry's our cry!

One day our Lord will return. We will greet him.
Those who are dead will arise like the Son.
We who are living will rise up to meet him.
Heaven and earth will at last become one.

Hallelujah! Amen!

SUNDAY, MARCH 27, 2005

Terri Schiavo Developments: Cheers & Jeers

Today's news carried a variety of stories related to Terri Schiavo. Some were positive. Others...well...were less than helpful. Here is how I see it.

Cheers: As the Schindler family entered seclusion, having failed in the last of their legal options, they asked protesters in front of Terri's hospice to go home and spend Easter with their families. There is a time for a protest vigil on behalf of Terri and there is a time for worship and celebration of God's victory over sin and death. Clearly, the focus today should be on the latter. After all, it is the primary source of comfort and hope for the former! The family added that the protestors would be welcomed back on Monday.

Jeers: Michael Schiavo's lawyer, George Felos, described Terri (who has been denied food and water for the past nine days) in this way, "She looked beautiful. In all the years I've seen Mrs. Schiavo, I have never seen such a look of peace and beauty upon her." That should go a long way towards encouraging bulimic and anorexic women in their pursuit of "beauty." Oh...by the way...isn't that what Felos and Michael have claimed led to Terri's heart stoppage in the first place? How ironic!

Cheers: Apparently Michael permitted a Catholic priest to give Terri communion today. When the priest reported this to those outside the hospice the news was greeted with cheers. I join them. He said he was able to put a drop of communion wine on her tongue but that her mouth was too dry to be able to receive the bread/wafer. I wonder if that was the first drop of moisture she has enjoyed in over a week...

Jeers: The **LA Times** continues its embarrassing attempts to be clever. In an article by Walter Roche Jr. and Sam Verhovek today, a pathetic attempt was made to equate the 1988 decision of Tom DeLay's family to remove life-support (IVs, ventilator, etc.) from his father, critically injured in an unspecified at-home accident. After a long buildup, creating the appearance of possible hypocrisy in the congressman's positions, the article continues, "*DeLay has denounced Schiavo's husband, as well as judges, for committing what he calls 'an act of barbarism' in removing the tube. In 1988, however, there was no such rhetoric as the congressman joined the family consensus to let his father die.*"

The article then proceeds to disprove their entire thesis by quoting Dan Allen, Rep. DeLay's aide, as saying, "*The situation faced by the congressman's family was entirely different than Terri Schiavo's. The only thing keeping her alive is the food and water we all need to survive. (DeLay's) father was on a ventilator and other machines to sustain him.*"

DeLay's 81-year-old mother added that "*she believes there might be hope for Terri Shiavo's recovery. That's what makes her family's experience different*," she says. "*Charles DeLay had no hope.*"

I can find hypocrisy in this article but it is not with Tom DeLay.

Cheers: For Florida governor Jeb Bush for respecting the rule of law even when it "**is a ass**." "I cannot violate a court order," he said. "I don't have powers from the United States Constitution or, for that matter, from the Florida Constitution, that would allow me to intervene after a decision has been made."

In being steadfast in his personal opposition to the starving of Terri and yet refusing to scandalize and cruelly interfere with the inevitable conclusion of this drama by making a mockery of the law, Jeb Bush has set a good example for the rest of us to follow. As Kenny Rogers puts it, "You gotta know when to hold 'em; know when to fold 'em..."

Others have already made a mockery of the law by ordering death by starvation of a living, breathing human being without giving her the opportunity to have a second medical opinion concerning whether she is in a "persistent (or permanent) vegetative state" or not.

Jeers: For all those zealots who have made death threats on Michael Schiavo and Judge Greer. They are despicable people who have lost both their minds and their morality. As if "life is so precious that I'm going to kill you if you don't let Terri live!" Yeah, right. I'm convinced. Not! Put them in jail where they won't hurt anybody.

Cheers: For those protestors, including ministers and children, who have been arrested or turned away in front of the hospice during the past few days for attempting to bring water or Communion to Terri. This is exactly the type of non-violent, symbolic protest that is more than just an effective media trick. It clearly and persuasively communicates compassion for someone who is very much in need of a "cold cup of water."

Jeers: For the Hospice of the Florida Suncoast for violating two of the most fundamental tenets of the philosophy of hospice care:

1. Admitting someone (Terri Schiavo) who is not terminally ill (normal admission standards for hospice care require a person to be terminally ill with an estimated life expectancy of six months or less--the Hospice's own website states that they "Provide dignified, quality comfort care that enhances the lives of dying people and their families"); and,

2. Withholding food and water from a non-dying patient. (hospice protocol permits the withholding of food and water from a terminally ill patient in the final stages of dying only--even then the Hospice's own website quotes the following standards:

Will the person nearing death who does not receive artificial food and fluids be thirsty?
-Usually, the person does not experience thirst or hunger.
-If a person has thirst, it will only last a day or so and ice chips or small sips of fluid with good oral care should relieve this symptom.

What can be done to provide comfort?
-If the person is awake it may be comforting to offer ice chips if they can be tolerated.
-The person will also benefit from frequent oral care with a soft brush or sponge to relieve any dryness in the mouth. A saline spray to the mouth may also be comforting.
-Moisten the person's eyes, or use a warm, damp cloth over them a few times each day.
-Moisten the person's lips, and use lip balm to prevent dryness.

-Use lotion without alcohol added to maintain skin comfort.

Back in the early days of the hospice movement in the United States (1970's) I was privileged to co-found the Hospice of Cache Valley in Logan, Utah. I served as its President for five years. It is now a functioning program of the Logan Regional Hospital. I mention this to indicate that I know what I'm talking about.

Final Jeer: The revelation that Michael Schiavo's lawyer, George Felos, served as Chairman of the Board of Directors for Hospice of the Florida Sunshine Coast from at least 1997 to 2001. Is there a conflict of interest here? Has the Hospice been receiving payment for Terri's care in violation of their charter/incorporation papers? It is no wonder that the families of other patients in the facility have complained about the media circus revolving around the Terri Schiavo case. She has no business being there in the first place. Pathetic.

MONDAY, MARCH 28, 2005

Easter: The Day After

The day after the first Easter in Jerusalem must have been a strange time for Jesus' disciples. Jesus is alive. But what does it mean. Is he back for good? Are they going to go back to the same life and ministry they had before? I'm sure that they are more than a little afraid of Jesus, too. Afraid to touch him. Afraid to get too close to him. Unsure who, exactly, he is. At least these are the feelings I imagine I would have. It took forty days with the risen Jesus, ten more days of prayer and fasting and the inspiration and power of the Holy Spirit before they were willing and able to put their experience into words full of meaning.

Today is *also* the day after Easter. I am neither afraid, confused or uncertain of very much about Jesus (although aware of the limitations of what I do know). But I do know one thing that Jesus' disciples did not know the day after his resurrection. I know that tomorrow I will not be going back to doing things the same way as in the past. Every Easter marks a New Birth of New Hope founded on the good news of God saving love revealed to the world on that first Easter.

Today I am still addressing the same issues of ministry that I faced two days ago. But I have been renewed and refreshed by Easter. My hope and confidence in the work of the Church have been confirmed and reaffirmed. My Lord overcame death, for heaven's sakes! How can I allow myself to be discouraged or uninspired when given the opportunity to challenge old obstacles in new, improved ways!

Easter is my personal New Year. The old has passed away. Behold, the new has come! I haven't made any resolutions. I have no doubt that God will take care of the details.

Another Child Abduction In Florida

A twelve-year-old girl was apparently abducted by two men on Easter Day in Port Orange, Florida. The State has issued an Amber Alert for Nicole Horton. Please keep her and her family in your prayers. Pray also that her abductors will have a change of heart and release her.

P.S. Are we experiencing an increase in these incidents or are they just being reported nationally more than they usually are? Anybody out there know?

Terri Schiavo: Another Cheer & Jeer

Cheers: Micahel Schiavo has announced that **he will permit an autopsy** for Terri after all.

Jeers: For Randall Terry and other protest leaders who have pushed the pro-Terri demonstrations beyond what the Schiavo family wants. Terri's brother, overheard arguing with one demonstrator, **reportedly said**, "You're not speaking for our family." Captain's Quarters has a good commentary on this **here**.

Finally...Something To Smile About

Daughter #3 came home from theater practice (she's Stage Manager in a production of "Annie") this evening and mentioned that some of the theater crew wnet to A & W for lunch and were told that they were out of root beer! Isn't that like Kentucky Fried Chicken running out of chicken? They might as well close up the store and go home for the day. Why else would anyone want to eat at A & W?

TUESDAY, MARCH 29, 2005

UN=Kofi Annan?

Paul Volcker's second investigative report on the United Nations Oil for Food scandal has been released. Kofi Annan was let off the hook insofar as he was not found directly culpable for any of the criminal behavior covered in this part of the scandal. He was, however, found lacking in securing a proper internal investigation of the matter when the issue was first brought to the public's attention.

The investigation ordered by Annan was completed in one day and, of course, found nothing to worry about.

Could it be that Mr. Annan knew that his son, Kojo, was in deep trouble for his role as an "advisor" to the chief contracting company dealing with Iraq on this matter? Was this a lame attempt at a coverup?

The new report apparently doesn't say (I haven't yet read it, or even seen a full summary of its findings).

Today, when asked if he was considering resigning from his position as Secretary General of the United Nations, Kofi Annan reportedly replied, "Hell no!"

Apparently Mr. Annan feels that the United Nations cannot function without him. Either that or else he feels that he IS the United Nations.

As a Christian pastor of a congregation, I could not imagine staying in my position under such a cloud of suspicion and inept oversight of my ministry. I would offer to step down until the matter was resolved one way or the other. My church, Christ's Church, the reputation of the Gospel, are far too important for me to in any way place myself or my own self-interests ahead of them.

I serve the church. The church does not serve me. I do not have any "rights" to my position at all. I serve on behalf of others and for their own best interests. As John the Baptist once said of Jesus, "I must decrease so he may increase."

If my holding on to the position of pastor caused division and discredit to my church my heart would be broken. I don't really care whether I am successful or not personally. I only care that the Good News of the Gospel is effectively proclaimed and encouraged within the congregation that I serve and that this same Gospel is equally well presented to the local community in as unstained a manner as possible. And I would feel exactly the same about this whether any charges brought against me were true or not.

Kofi Anna is sending exactly the wrong signal to the world of nations. He is putting himself above criticism and above the higher priority of preserving the integrity of the organization he serves. He is acting like an elected leader who refuses to step down from power when the time for them to resign is far overdue. Unfortunately, the United Nations does not have any "citizens" to demonstrate or riot in the streets to demand his removal from office. The only "citizens" of the UN are the cozy swarm of ambassadors and their staffs whose own self interests preclude them from holding one of their own's feet to the fire.

I'm sure that Mr. Annan is proving to be an inspiring example of leadership for such people as Egypt's Mubarak and Syria's Bashar Assad. There is an irony in this occurring just as democracy and government of the people, by the people and for the people is breaking out everywhere else in the world.

Perhaps someone could give him a copy of Rick Warren's book, "The Purpose Driven Life." The first sentence on the first page might give him something to think about: "**It's not about you**."

Terri Schiavo Gains Some New Friends

Terri, at this late and grave hour, has discovered that she has more friends than she thought she had; and from some unexpected places.

The Rev. Jesse Jackson arrived in Florida and has been lobbying Florida State legislators who voted against the law that would have prevented the removal of her feeding tube to change their votes.

Writer Nat Hentoff, writing for the Village Voice, expressed his repugnance for the legal maneuvering that has allowed an American court to sanction starving someone to death, calling it "judicial murder."

Captain Ed at Captain's Quarters wonders if commentators on the left such as Paul Krugman of the New York Times will be including Jesse and Nat in their characterizations of Terri's supporters being "Right-Wing Bible Thumpers!"

This episode in the Schiavo drama reminds me of the epic poem, "The Song of Roland." Roland, realizing that he and his men are about to be defeated by the Muslim forces (who are invading France at the time), blows on his horn for help. Charlemagne hears the alarm but arrives too late. All are dead.

I am glad, of course, for this public support from such high-profile, liberal Democrats. In this particular case, however, "better late than never" will bring small consolation to Terri's family. Just ask Roland.

More Journalistic Disengenuity in Schivo Case

More media spin of the same ilk as the bogus LA Times story on Tom DeLay's father:

A recent Columbia Journalism Review article compared a Texas law that allowed the discontinuance of life support (against family wishes) for Sun Hudson and Spiro Nikolouzos (a statute signed into law by then-Governor Bush) with the now President Bush's outspoken support of Terri Schiavo and his statement that, "When in doubt...err on the side of life." The article appears to posit a contradiction if not a hypocracy in this comparison. Frankly, I don't see it.

Hudson and Nikolouzos (also spelled Nikolous in the article) were both on life support ventilators which were doing all of their breathing for them. Their bodies, due to injury and birth defects, were unable to breathe on their own and their was a clear medical consensus that neither would ever be able to do so. When the decision to discontinue this life support was made, their respective families were given 10 days to locate another facility that would concur with their wishes and continue them on life support (a fact omitted in the CJR article, by the way). No facility could be found that would provide this care for them in their condition. So, even against the families' wishes, their life support was removed. Both died very quickly.

Although there are many ethical and moral issues involved in these cases they are light years removed from Terri Schiavo's situation.

Terri is not on any form of life support (a feeding tube is not ordinarily considered to be life support...only at the end stages of a terminal illness is it considered to be life support and hence, appropriate to be discontinued).

Terri's body is physically functioning normally (she even has her monthly "period" which requires pain medication...although it has been said that she is not able to experience pain? Hmmmm....).

There is no medical consensus on her mental status (ie. whether she is in a permanent vegetative condition, a persistent vegetative condition or something even less than that. Note that the fact that her mental status has been legally determined by a court ruling does not necessarily prove the existence of a definitive medical diagnosis).

Lastly, there are dozens if not hundreds of medical facilities which would be willing to continue to provide care for Terri. Not only that, but her parents and family have offered to provide care for her in their own home...something routinely done in thousands of homes across our country every day.

With the two people in Texas, when their ventilators were disconnected they died, because they were not able to live without it.

With Terri, her life relies only on the same food and water that you and I require to sustain our own lives. If food and water were to be withheld from you and me, we would die. The same is true for Terri. She is not terminally ill. She is not dying. The only way to get her to die is to kill her in some way or other. The method of choice requested by her husband and approved by Judge Greer is starvation. Without intervention, Terri would live. With the Texas pair, without intervention they died.

To compare these cases as being comparable is to stretch logic well past the breaking point. Certainly there is grief and death and controversy in each of these situations. But that does not make them morally, ethically, medically or legally comparable.

I conclude by quoting the Columbia Journalism Review where it admits, "The cases are different..."

For anyone to suggest or imply that they are not different is both misleading and dishonest.

WEDNESDAY, MARCH 30, 2005

Seething Sino- Suit-Seeker Slays Sinister Cyber-Saber Seller

According to Reuters, Qiu Chengwei, a Shanghai online game player, took the law into his hands when he stabbed Zhu Caoyuan to death earlier this week.

It seems that Qiu had won a powerful "dragon saber" while playing "Mir 3" and, being, by nature, a nice guy (apparently), he "loaned" the saber to Zhu. Zhu then turned around and sold the saber (which only exists in the world of the online game) to another player for the equivalent of $870 US.

Qiu sued to either get the saber back or to collect the money from Zhu but became impatient when the wheels of justice moved too slow.

Legal experts in China are still debating whether an item existing only in cyber-space can actually be considered legal property subject to existing law or whether such property is only illusory and of no real value under the law.

Personally, although I believe that a fanciful imagination is a good gift from God, I also believe that, when we allow our fantasy to trump the real world of God's creation and replace God with gods created by a computer programmer, we have committed a significant sin....the sin of idolatry.

Jesus said, "What does it profit us if we gain the world but lose our soul?"

Qiu and Zhu lost both a life and a soul without even caring about the world at all...at least the real one. It was literally a fight over "nothing."

"Abducted" Girl Found In Florida

Jacksonville, Florida, TV News4JAX reports today that **Nicole Horton**, who had been reported missing and likely abducted by two men in Port Orange on Easter Sunday, has been found.

According to the news report, "*The Florida Department of Law Enforcement provided no information, other than the girl was found and the case has been resolved.*"

No matter what actually happened Nicole has been found. This must be considered to be good news.

THURSDAY, MARCH 31, 2005

Terri Schivo: Rest In Peace

Terrisfight has posted this simple statement today:

Terri's struggle for life has ended this morning.
December 3, 1963 - March 31, 2005

"Now cracks a noble heart. Good-night, sweet Terri, And flights of angels sing thee to thy rest!"
(Hamlet Act V Scene II Line 304)

Stealing Classified Goverment Documents No Big Deal

Former Clinton National Security Advisor, Sandy Berger, will plead guilty to illegally taking classified documents from the Library of Congress back in the summer of 2004.

Not only did Mr. Berger take documents but he has failed to account for several of them that have never been returned. According to Fox News, among the missing documents is a sensitive "after-action report on the Clinton administration's handling of Al Qaeda terror threats during the December 1999 millennium celebration."

If I had done something like this I should have expected to be at least charged with a felony leading to some serious jail time. After all, such behavior ought to be deterred. Right? Wrong.

Apparently (Fox News again),
"The charge of unauthorized removal and retention of classified material is a misdemeanor that carries a maximum sentence of a year in prison and up to a $100,000 fine."
A misdemeanor? A *maximum* sentence of one year in prison? You've got to be kidding?

I could get a year in jail by spray painting the word "love" on a federal building!

Burning a draft card used to carry a penalty of up to five years in prison. After all, a draft card was federal property (sort of). But so were the documents that Berger did not return. Isn't that the same as burning them? Perhpas he sold them for financial gain? Does anyone know?

In any case, shameful as it is, the outcome of this whole mess is not surprising.

Way back on July 23, 2004, La Shawn Barber predicted this outcome,

Berger is not going to jail because the old boy network has too much to lose if he does.

Republicans and Democrats do this stuff, probably more than we all realize. Berger took the files to withhold information that makes Clinton look bad and used information that makes Kerry look good (to the unfortunate souls voting for him). That's my assessment.
If Berger goes down for this, he's taking a lot of people with him. That *is why he's not going to jail.*

I think she got it spot on.

WEDNESDAY, APRIL 13, 2005

A Divided Country--Coke? Soda? Pop? or ???

Politickal Animal directs me to a site that displays the regional word of preference for a generic carbonated beverage. Before you ***click on the map*** below, what do *you* call it: Soda? Coke? Pop? or something else?

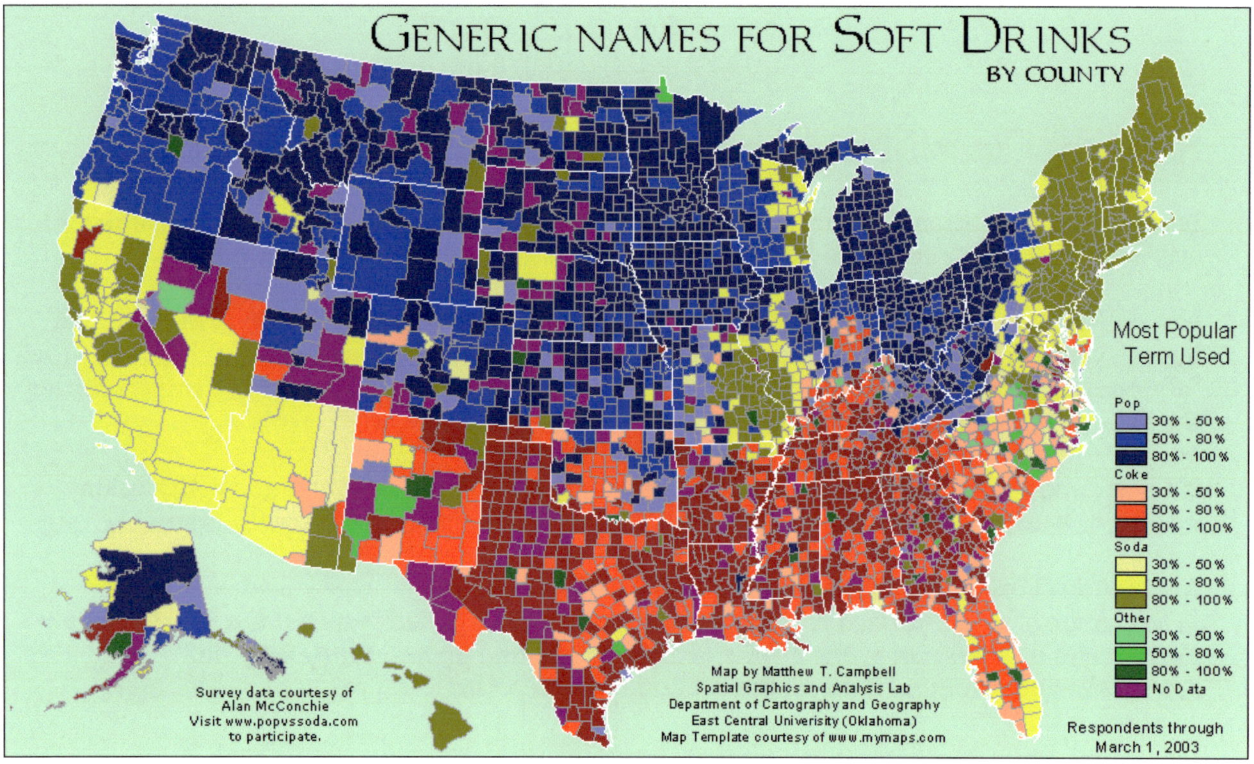

Two More Girls Reported Missing--Are We Seeing a Pattern Here?

Fox News is reporting that two teenage girls in unrelated circumstances have been reported missing, one in Florida and the other in California.

The California case involves 14-year old Ashleigh Markley who disappeared while visiting her grandmother in Lincoln, California on March 29. Ashleigh, who lives in Citrus Heights, near Sacramento, is believed by police to be with 29-year old Lindsay Jones (aka Lindsay Rehders) who she met at her grandmother's home at Easter.

In Florida, police are searching for 13-year old Sarah Lunde of Ruskin. Sarah has run away before but there are concerns that this time she might have been picked up by a local sexual predator. According to the Fox News report, sheriff Deputies are "checking on ***24 registered sexual predators or offenders*** who live near the family's mobile home." (my emphasis)

Twenty-four registered predators or offenders living in the same neighborhood? What is this all about? Do they attend probation meetings together? Is there some sort of local 12-step program that they are members of? And why do these things always seem to happen around Florida trailer park areas? (Less than two months ago Jessica Lunsford was kidnapped from her Florida trailer home, sexually assaulted, murdered and buried under another nearby trailer, home to the registered sexual predator/offender who lived there--see **here** and **here**).

I pray with all my heart that these two girls will be found safe and sound or at least phone home and tell their families that they are all right.

It is hard for teenagers to understand, but one of the primary roles of the family is to provide protection and shelter from a very cruel, morally unbalanced and dangerous world that exists all around us.....sometimes even in the trailer next door.

TUESDAY, APRIL 19, 2005

The Flying Sausage & the Virgin Mary

Here's a little quiz. One of the following stories is ***not*** true. The other six ***are*** true. Can you find the fake one?

1. Court Brief Attempts to Strip "T"s

The ACLU has filed a lawsuit in a Washington D.C. district court accusing the Federal Government of violating the establishment clause of the first amendment. The reason? Because the letter "t" (which resembles a cross) appears on virtually all government documents.

"The Christian faith is clearly promoted by the use of this particular symbol. No other religion has the symbol of its faith presented in the same manner," ACLU lawyer Jacob Jernigan said.

Tonight Show host Jay Leno added during his nightly monologue that, "It sounds like dotting your 'i's and crossing your 't's could wind up landing you in jail! Who knows, minding your 'p's and 'q's could be next!"

2. Beware of flying frozen sausages

An Englishman learned that the hard way Monday afternoon, according to British wire services

"He was driving his car when the offending item came through his open window and hit him on the nose," an ambulance-service spokesman told reporters.

The unnamed man, 46, had left work and was heading home to South Woodham Ferrers, Essex east of London, when the meat missile entered his vehicle.

Despite having broken his nose, and losing a lot of blood, the driver declined to be taken to the hospital.

"It must have been an incredibly lucky, or unlucky, shot to get the sausage through a moving car window," commented the spokesman. "I have never seen or heard of anything like this before."

Police said they were looking into the incident.

3. Empty Beer Trucks' a Bummer for Bandits

The last of three stolen beer trucks has been found at the bottom of the Snake River Canyon near the Hansen Bridge.

It was one of three empty Budweiser trucks stolen from a Twin Falls, Idaho, distributor sometime after it closed on April 8.

Two of the trucks were found the next day. One was dangling over the Salmon Falls Creek Reservoir canyon rim. A second truck was on its side nearby.

Evidence suggests that disappointment may have motivated the thieves to attempt driving the trucks over the canyon edge after discovering they were empty.

Watkins Distributing is offering $5,000 for information that leads to the arrests of people involved.

4. And You Thought the *Bathrooms* Smelled Funny

A Fresno, California, High School substitute teacher charged with smoking marijuana with students has apologized for his actions.

Chris Bochin wrote a letter to The Fresno Bee saying he set a terrible example for students. He says that five years of pot smoking made him "mentally powerless."

He was arrested last month after smoking marijuana with five ninth-graders in a science class. The students were suspended for five days.

Bochin has pleaded innocent to charges of giving marijuana to minors and contributing to their delinquency. His case is scheduled to be heard next month in Fresno Superior Court.

His lawyer says Bochin is receiving drug counseling

5. Great Great Grandma Guns Down Grocery Gunman

A man accused of bursting into a Jacksonville, Florida, convenience store demanding money was in the hospital Friday, shot, authorities said, by the great-great-grandmother working behind the counter.

"I think he thought I was an old woman and would just give him the money," Grammer, 64, said Friday. "My life was at stake. I thought he was going to kill me."
So she pulled a pistol out from under the cash register and fired once, hitting the man in the chest.

He fell to the ground, dropped his gun and then fled, leaving a trail of blood. Grammer fired two more shots as he was running away.

The sheriff's report said a man fitting the suspect's description and injury went to a hospital a short time later. He told doctors he shot himself.

Grammer, who has 10 children, 32 grandchildren, three great grandchildren and three great-great-grandchildren, said she worried she had killed the man.

"All I could think about was his poor parents," Grammer said.

6. The Devil Is In the Details

An Oakley, California, man has asked the federal government to rename Mount Diablo, saying the current name, which means devil in Spanish, is offensive to his religious sensibilities.

"Words have power, and when you start mentioning words that come from the dark side, evil thrives," Art Mijares told the Contra Costa Times. "When I take boys camping on the mountain, I don't even like to say its name."

To make the change, Mijares would need to persuade federal, state and local governments that it's necessary.

It's been called Mount Diablo for at least 164 years. Changing its name would also mean changing its name on tens of thousands of maps, books and historical documents.

7. Our Lady of the Underpass

"When you come down here -- that's why I wanted to come down here and see for myself -- when you come down here and you see it, it's real," said Joanne Grablik, of Inverness. "It is beautiful."

State police said what the people are seeing is a salt stain from the Kennedy overpass.

Obdulia Delgado, of Chicago, said she was driving home along Fullerton Avenue on April 10 after getting off work at St. Elizabeth Hospital when she saw what she believes to be the Virgin Mary on the wall. She quickly pulled over and examined the form, and then began praying.

"Monday through Friday I go to school and Saturday and Sunday I work, so since I haven't been able to go to church, I asked her, 'Please help me with school because I'm having my finals,' but I felt like she was like, 'If you can come to me, I'm going to go to you,'" Delgado said.
Delgado said she rushed home and told her husband, Fidel, what she saw.

Fidel Delgado said he was skeptical of his wife's claim until the two went to the site.

"I was just stunned," Fidel Delgado said at the underpass Monday morning.

There was some discussion early Monday about the city coming in and either painting over the image or power washing the image off due to the traffic congestion it has been causing. However, the area is under the jurisdiction of the Illinois Department of Transportation and officials there said that there are no plans to remove the image.

"Everybody's amazed. It's hard to begin to believe, but when you see it, it changed something in you. You believe in the faith," Snezna DiLorenz said.

"It's a miracle. It's an image of something ... you can't describe it," Jose Recinos said.

"We're here because the Virgin Mary is on the wall, and she's inside the wall, and we were just curious, but at the same time we're scared, wondering why she's there and what the meaning is of her being there," Annette Byrd said.

Police were at the scene Monday to keep an eye on the crowd.

Answer to Quiz: (scroll down a bit)

.
.
.
.
.
.
.
.
.
.
.

Number 1 is the fake. Radio talk-show host Dennis Prager made up the story tonight to use as an example showing just how low the reputation of the ACLU has fallen.

People who phoned in expressing their concern seemed to have no problem believing that the ACLU was fully capable of doing something as stupid as this.

Numbers 2-6 are taken almost verbatim from FoxNews and Number 7 was gleaned from Chicago's NBC5 On-Line. What a weird world we live in!

Even the names are almost too good to be true!

WEDNESDAY, APRIL 20, 2005

Burma Accused of Using Chemical Weapons

BBC News reports that Australian physician Dr Martin Panter, president of Christian Solidarity Worldwide, has accused Burma of using chemical agents to attack Karen rebels along its border with Thailand.

According to Panter (who personally claims to have performed medical examinations on affected rebels) yellow gas was observed spreading from exploding shells causing many of the rebels to throw up blood and grow too weak to walk. Some developed blisters, acute diarrhoea which led to the death of several of the rebels.

The good news is that reported use of chemical weapons is very rare. It does not matter whether the "good guys" use it or the "bad guys." As "**Another Mother for Peace**" might say, "Chemical weapons are not good for children and other living things."

The bad news is that too many nations still possess too many arsenals of chemical weapons. Nations that produce, sell, buy and/or use such weapons should receive stiff international sanctions that really hurt.

It is only if the world of nations (including the United States) agrees to such penalties that any progress can be made. If the report is true, Burma should be sent back ten spaces and lose the next two turns.....at least!

Massechusetts Version of Maximum Security: Drunk Prisoners Take Over Cell Block at Cedar Junction Prison

The Boston Globe began **this article** with this very amusing paragraph:

OFFICIALS PROBE DISTURBANCE AT CEDAR JUNCTION PRISON

(Boston Globe Archives, 2005-04-20)

> *Prison authorities are investigating how eight inmates, believed to be intoxicated on homemade brew, took control of their cell block in the state's maximum security prison, MCI-Cedar Junction, for several hours Monday night, officials said.*

The rest of the article is a rambling attempt to say, *"We had everything under control the entire time....**nothing to worry about**....although we have absolutely no idea how it happened....**don't worry, be happy**...."*

Quote of the Day

"Poultry are one of the most badly treated animals in the modern world. It has been shown that they have high levels of both cognition and feelings and as a result there has been a recent trend of promoting poultry welfare. There is also a tradition of keeping poultry as pets in some parts of the world. However in modern cities and societies it is often difficult to maintain contact with pets, particularly for office workers. We propose and describe a novel cybernetics system to use mobile and Internet technology to improve human-to-pet interaction."
-- Mission statement of The Poultry Internet

ht: SiliconValley.com > > > > PETA has more here.

Viet Nam Vet Spits Chewing tobacco On Jane Fonda

A Viet Nam veteran stood patiently in line at a Jane Fonda book signing in Kansas City, Missouri, this morning. When he reached the front of the line he spat his mouthful of tobacco juice in her face.

"She's a traitor," the 54-year old man said. "I consider it a debt of honor. She spit in our faces for 37 years," he said.

I will not dignify the man by mentioning his name. Although he might be genuinely angry at Ms. Fonda that does not give him any right to spit in her face. Nor should anyone who shares his feelings express any sympathy or solidarity with this man or what he did.

I see little difference between spitting tobacco juice in Jane Fonda's face and throwing a pie in Bill Kristol's face or dumping salad dressing on Pat Buchanan's head (see my thoughts on these matters here). Such attacks, although non-lethal, push us over the line from civility to barbarism.

Although the Kristol, Buchanan, and other, similar, attacks brought big outcries from conservative bloggers, I find it interesting that they are all silent concerning today's attack on Ms. Fonda. These same people demand that Muslims denounce Muslim terrorists lest their silence be interpreted as assent, but fail to see that they must do the same with conservatives who "cross the line" of either civility or the law. Their silence today clearly sends an unfortunate message out into cyberspace.

Personally, I wish that each of these people targeted would press charges against their attackers to the full extent of the law. Then, I would like them to file civil charges against them as well, squeezing them out of every dime that they might possess and then turning it all over to a non-partisan charity. Letting these social embarrassments off the hook only encourages them. Such behavior must not be tolerated. The law exists, in part, to restrain such people. When the law is not prosecuted its power to restrain is forfeited.

Jesus said, "Love your enemies and pray for those who persecute you." This is not to be interpreted as Jesus' contribution to national security policy, but it must certainly be understood to apply to tobacco spitters, pie throwers and salad dressing squeezers.

It is also worth noting that, in Romans 12:20 the Apostle Paul quoted a similar thought from Proverbs 25:21-22, which concludes, "and you will heap burning coals upon their heads."

I encourage Bill Frist, Tom DeLay, and every other conservative to love their enemies and not throw stuff at them. Simply looking their "enemies" in the eye and "speaking the truth to them in love" will (if it is indeed the truth that they speak) serve to scorch every God-numbered hair on their heads.

It is a far, far better thing to stand for civility than to fall as a barbarian.

THURSDAY, APRIL 21, 2005

"Death to Israel" 'tres chic' at UCLA

The pro-Palestinian Al Awda ("Right of Return") convention held at UCLA this past weekend, April 15-17, was not a big affair but the fact that it was allowed at all makes it so and the fact that it generated so little controversy or opposition makes it frightening.

It is currently "politically correct" to support the "Palestinian Cause." One look at the materials being sold and displayed at this mini-event, however, shows that the only "justice" being sought is the total destruction of the nation of Israel and its return to the Palestinian (read "non-Jewish") people. The fate of Israeli Jews is implied by this banner....

The destruction of Israel as a Jewish state is also clear in this button....=

and t-shirt...

Even more frightening is the determination to continue the violent struggle to kill Israeli Jews in whatever manner possible until the objective is accomplished. Even if it takes generations, as this button so eloquently represents...

How can those who support such determined haters and murderers pretend to be advocates of peace? Such people are either ignorant dupes or else something far worse.

It does not take a rocket scientist to observe that there is much unjust suffering among the Palestinian people in the West Bank and Gaza. Yes, much of their suffering has come at the hands of the Israeli military (usually either in pursuit of terrorists or in retribution for attacks on Israelis). Yes, the building of the "wall" is creating an unprecedented hardship on tens of thousands of people who are not eager to hurt anybody. And, Yes, Israeli settlement policies have incited much understandable bitterness and anger.

But it must also be asserted that Israel as a country and Israeli Jews as a people, have never professed to pursue or put into practice a policy designed to lead to the systematic murder of every Palestinian and their complete removal from the West Bank, Gaza or even Israel!

And yet those participating in and supporting this Al Awda convention at UCLA are clearly expressing their determination to reclaim all of Israel and destroy it as a Jewish state and all the Israeli Jews with it.

In the end either Israel goes or Al Awda (and their ilk) goes.

When the day comes when Israeli/Jewish groups begin holding conventions on college and university campuses displaying banners, buttons and t-shirts like these, perhaps then I will reconsider.

Until then, however, I will continue to support the right of Israel to exist as a free and independent Jewish state along with the Israeli's right to protect and defend themselves against those (like Al Awda) who are invading and blowing up women and children in an attempt to kill them all and destroy thier country.

If there will ever be peace, it will be up to the Palestinians to ask for it. When they do, and when the Al Awdas, Hizbollahs and the Al-Aqsa Martyrs' Brigades are crushed into irrelevence, then, and only then, will there be peace in Palestine and peace in Israel. Shalom and Salaam.

ht:**lgf** for passing on the story and the photos

The Most Popular Protestant Pope Ever

Calvin and Knox must be turning over in their graves. It was, after all, Knox who declared that, "the Papists have perniciously taught and damnably believed" the doctrine of *transubstantiation* (Scot's Confession, Chapter 21).

I cannot imagine either of them losing any sleep over the death of any Pope who reigned during their lifetimes.

Yet, here we are, 450 years later, witnessing Calvinists, Lutherans, Methodists and even Baptists (for heaven's sakes....Baptists!) giving thanks to God for the life and steadfast witness of Pope John Paul II to.......uh......what?.....the Christian faith? ....or...... uh.....oh, yes......the good, conservative, traditional, historic, Biblical, moral teachings of the Church.

I suppose that there are those, such as James Lileks and myself, who still think that John Knox and Martin Luther were more correct than not about their rejection of the doctrine of transubstantiation. And then there is the matter of the veneration of Mary, the intercession of the Saints and all those extra-biblical books crammed into the otherwise empty, narrow space that separates the Old Testament from the New. Plus, of course, there is the fact that some of us agree with the Swiss Reformer Heinrich Bullinger, who declared (in the Second Helvetic Confession) that,

we do not approve of the doctrine of the Roman clergy, who make their Pope at Rome the universal shepherd and supreme head of the Church Militant here on earth, and so the very vicar of Jesus Christ, who has (as they say) all fullness of power and sovereign authority in the Church.

In reality, I suppose we look at the new Pope Benedict XVI as sort of the head of a really, really, really big denomination!

In spite of all the differences, the remarkable thing is that the Protestant world, for the most part, has begun to affirm that the Pope-the-Bishop-of-Rome is, at heart, one of us.....a brother in Christ.

Although Pope Paul VI was respected by non-Catholic Christians, he was still viewed as representative of the "We" versus "Them" ideology spawned by the acrimonious divisions of the Western Church during the Protestant Reformation.

One of the great miracles of Pope John Paul II, and one of the things that will one day give reason to either bless him or curse him, was his effectiveness in gently lowering the walls that had separated Protestants and Roman Catholics for all these years.

--He accomplished this not by spurious, unrealistic or insincere petitions for ecumenical unity, but by simply being a faithful witness to the saving Lordship of Jesus Christ who is King of kings and Lord of lords, triumphant and eternal in his love, mercy, justice and truth.

--He accomplished this by steadfastly setting Jesus Christ and the Christian Gospel alongside Nazi-ism, Communism and every other "ism" and declaring them, in comparison, to be morally and spiritually bankrupt and opposed to all that is good and right as God has revealed such things to us.

--He accomplished this by embracing the poor and suffering of the world, not with promises of "liberation" or "revolution" but by holding the rulers of all nations accountable for both causing and allowing such poverty and suffering to exist.

--He accomplished this by simply being a Christian....a Roman Catholic Christian, of course .....but a Pope who chose not to be crowned with the elaborate **triple tiara** and who preferred to be buried in his leather walking sandals than the traditional red shoes of the fisherman.

--He accomplished this by following the spirit of the Apostle Paul in emphasizing the unity of our Christian faith rather than constantly elaborating on those things that divide us (see **Ephesians 4:1-6**).

Because of Pope John Paul II, Roman Catholics and Protestants have been able to move from "Cold War" to "Detente" to the outer edges of "Reconciliation."

This has been a historical "paradigm shift" of the highest order. At present, it is more apparent in the "First World" nations than it is in the "Third" and it will take all the Spirit-filled wisdom imaginable for Benedict XVI to continue this historic and healthy narrowing of the unholy divisions in the visible Body of Christ.

The irony of all this, of course, is that those in the liberal churches who were most eager to cast aside all differences for the sake of ecumenical unity turned out to be the ones most alienated by the steadfast conservatism of John Paul II. Those Protestants who have held their ground on matters of both the Biblical purity of their faith and the Biblical purity of their lives have, on the other hand, experienced a growing sense of spiritual kinship with Rome while, at the same time, refusing to compromise on any of those things that still separate them.

Pope Benedict XVI will, I have no doubt, experience, appreciate and build upon that sense of kinship with many of the conservative, evangelical Protestant and Reformed churches. He will also find many willing and able allies among us as we work with common cause to be salt, light and leaven to a world that is all too bland, dark and flat in the things that really matter.

Three cheers for the Pope! By God's grace may he be blessed as well as be a blessing for a world that desperately needs a blessing.

ht:Politickal Animal for the Lileks link

SATURDAY, APRIL 23, 2005

Senator Kerry, Faith & Politics

Hugh Hewitt recently made an unlikely comparison between John Kerry and Stan Laurel. Frankly, I don't get it.

John Kerry is intelligent, smart, calculating and cold.

Stan Laurel is simple, simple, simple and lovable.

John Kerry is a man of many words.

Stan Laurel is a man of few words.

John Kerry isn't funny.

Stan Laurel is funny.

John Kerry has a wife named Teresa.

Stan Laurel has a friend named Ollie.

John Kerry has spent his life running.

Stan Laurel has never been seen running.

I will certainly grant Hugh the one point that both men are famous for their whining, but beyond that I still don't get it.

If I were to correlate John Kerry with an entertainment figure I would probably choose Wile E. Coyote.

Both have long, narrow faces.

Both are determined.
Both run and run but never get what they want.
Both never seem to give up and quit.
Both have great ideas that usually manage to backfire.
Plus, it's hard not to feel sorry for both of them.

It is true that Wile E. Coyote says very little if anything except for holding up a sign that says "Help" every once in a while. This is in contrast to John Kerry who often says more than he should and, so far as I know, has never held up a sign that says "Help." For that matter, I am not aware that John Kerry has ever fallen off a cliff, landing with a puff of dust on the canyon floor below, either.
Nonetheless, I am much more comfortable with this analogy for one other reason: The Acme Company and the Democratic National Committee have been equally valuable in helping their particular client to succeed....that is to say, to succeed in running flat out into rock walls painted with illusory train tunnels and soaring high into the sky with rockets tied onto their backs where they subsequently implode.

John Kerry's speech on the Senate floor yesterday was just as much an attempt to "catch and eat" the Republican majority as Wile E.'s rock catapults are used in his attempt to "catch and eat" Roadrunner. And just as successful.
Kerry seems to have a problem with Republicans seeking support from people of faith. He seems to have a problem with Republicans using "faith" as a platform by which to communicate their political agenda.

This is ironic since Kerry has never seemed to have had a problem seeking support from people of faith himself. Nor has Kerry ever seemed to have had a problem using "faith" as a platform from which to communicate his own political agenda.

It's odd that I can never recall John Kerry speaking to a white congregation, only African-American ones. It will be interesting to see what color the "people of faith" will be when they appear with Senator Frist this coming Sunday evening.

I wonder if Black faith does not really count as "faith" for Kerry. And why does he believe that it is only Republicans who "appeal to religious division?"

In 2004, John Kerry, spoke "at a predominantly black church with veterans of the (civil rights) movement."

> *Kerry sprinkled his remarks with scriptural references calling for matching faith with deeds.*
> *"We need to remember those words as we march forward against a sorry politics where too often words suffice, where deeds aren't demanded," said Kerry, ridiculing promises Bush made during the last election.*

Let's see, this sounds suspiciously as if Kerry was saying, "My scripture and faith move us forward while the scripture and faith of my opponents produce 'ridiculous promises,' 'sorry politics' and 'words without deeds.'"

The news article that described Kerry's Sunday church presentation also stated that,

Taking his campaign to the heart of the deep South, Sen. John Kerry said Sunday he faces the same "politics of last resort" that confronted marchers seeking equality in the civil rights movement.

This sort of sounds like he is implying that the people who worship at George W. Bush's church are no different than "Bull" Conner, George Wallace (who was a Democrat, by the way) or the KKK (of which Democratic Senator Robert Byrd was once a member).

Just one year after this church "sermon" the same John Kerry, now standing on the Senate floor, has the nerve to state,

Forces outside the mainstream now seem to effortlessly push Republican leaders toward conduct that the American people really don't want in their elected leaders, inserting the government into our private lives, injecting religion into debates about public policy where it doesn't apply.

Dear me, no! We wouldn't want to "inject religion into debates about public policy" would we? Except, of course when injecting religion into debates about public policy "*does* apply?" And when is that, Mr. Kerry? When *you* speak during Sunday morning worship services in African-American churches, quoting scripture and suggesting that Republicans in general, and President Bush in particular, are attempting "to divide the nation along racial lines?"

Is that injecting religion into a debate about public policy where it *does*? or *does not* apply?

It seems that it is permissible for Senator Kerry to rally African-Americans from their church pews to rise up against the empty promises of Republicans but it is not permissible for Senator Frist to rally 1,000 Christians from many different denominations, races and economic backgrounds to rise up and protest the Senate minority's blocking of the nomination of conservative judges to U.S. Appeals Courts.

Please, Mr. Kerry, people of faith can be led by that faith to arrive at different conclusions about political policy. It is disingenuous indeed to suggest that it is improper to take a political stand based, either in part or in whole, on one's faith.

I have never heard a Republican leader say that "my faith is better than" someone else's. What they do say is what I believe you would wholeheartedly agree with, that "my faith has led me to affirm certain core values in relation to life, liberty and the pursuit of happiness that appear to be different than yours."

In the end the issue at hand is not really one of religious faith at all. It is not religious belief that determines American law and policy but those who are elected to office by a majority vote and those who are nominated by them to appointed office. If that majority happens to include a large group of voters who share common values drawn from similar religious beliefs, it is both unconscionable and unconstitutional to state that the public expression of that faith is somehow "crossing a line" that should not be crossed or somehow corrupting the political system.

It is not wrong for Christians, Buddhists, Muslims, Jews or anyone of any other faith (or no faith at all) to vote their conscience ***as*** a Christian, Buddhist, Muslim or Jew. Nor is it wrong for a politician to honestly do the same.

John Kerry has neither spoken nor acted like a Stan Laurel. He has acted like a cocky coyote who has plunged, with confidence, into a situation that is too deep, too complex and too fast for him to fully understand. As always, there will be consequences. Just ask Wiley E.

Those watching the show will get a big laugh out of it. "Beep. Beep."

Humor On the Left

I am conservative, politically, but, every so often, I do enjoy a good laugh from a well-aimed poke-in-the-eye from a clever liberal pundit.

The past election cycle and the current rhetoric in the U.S. Congress affirms, I think, that there is more mean-spiritedness (as well as outright hate) among liberals than conservatives these days. I also sense more of a willingness for conservatives to laugh at themselves.

I can remember the recently-elected President George W. Bush speaking to what I seem to remember as a public high school in Texas. "I am living proof," he said (or something like it), "that anyone can become President of the United States. Even those of you with a C-average!"

I cannot picture John Kerry or Teddy Kennedy laughing at themselves in such a light-hearted manner. The closest thing to an exception is John Dean, who recently, successfully and unintentionally, achieved self-parody by mimicking a drug-snorting Rush Limbaugh. After the Minnesota crowd finished laughing, Dean added, "I'm not very dignified but I'm not running for president anymore!" At least he is honest concerning his character!
In all fairness ("warning-*sarcasm alert*") , after typing in "liberal humor" on Alta Vista "search" I discovered such amusing sites as Evil GOP Bastards, Michael Moore.com, and Democratic Underground (with its evolving list of the "Top 10 Conservative Idiots").

The one thing liberals have over conservatives when it comes to humor, however, is their inherent bent towards satire. While leafing through our local, "Green Party-leaning" free throwaway newspaper, "Honolulu Weekly," I came across these two comics (clicking on them will enlarge them).

This first one is "This Modern World" by Tom Tomorrow. In the second panel I had to smile at the double-reflective parody on the conservative attitudes towards "Fahrenheit 911" and those who thought it worth watching. The final panel takes a well-deserved shot at the incessant conservative whining over liberal bias in the mainstream media.

While I consider this bias to have been well-documented there are times (such as this, couched in Kos' usual "colorful" vitriolics) when the bias appears to have popped up in the opposite direction.

The second comic is "Troubletown" by Lloyd Dangle. It's not a bad "over the top" parody of many actual attitudes swirling around in some "fundamentalist" Christian circles. Some of us have rolled our theological and spiritual eyes more than once when approached by some well-meaning soul-winner with a handful of Jack Chick tracts.

I do take offense at the mocking and unnecessarily anti-Christian tone of the third panel, however. That which is sacred and holy to others should never be mocked. It may be discussed, it may be debated, it may even be declared to be foolish and wrong-headed. But it is bad form and bad humor to satirize, parody, mock and belittle the core religious beliefs of others. Even so, given the inherently "irreverent" nature of satire and parody, I am willing to forgive one panel out of 16.

Humor and laughter are good for the soul and good for the intellect, too. A well-aimed barb can deflate many an inflated ego. If pompous asses must be "de-pomped" then I will vote for humor as the most effective cure every time.

Both liberals and conservatives need to relearn the art of true and genuine humor. The laughter that comes from such genuine mirth comes from deep in the soul, and not at the price of the dehumanization of others.

As Abraham Lincoln knew so well, a good sense of humor is most useful when it enables your enemies to not only see your point, but to laugh along with you as well. "Good" humor turns enemies into friends. "Bad" humor drives them farther away.

I would welcome the day when liberals and conservatives can once again be genuine friends affirming their common humanity and love of America....even while passionately debated the merits of their respective political agendas. I would welcome the day when jokes told on the the Senate floor by a Democrat bring laughter from the other side of the aisle, and vice versa.

"A house divided against itself will fall." A family that laughs together can and will stand together. Even in politics!

Sara Lunde Buried Today

Note: An earlier post on Sara can be found here. Please leave a comment. I would like to know how you have been touched by Sara's death. Thank you, BofP

A church funeral service drew 100 mourners for Sara Lunde in Ruskin, Kentucky, today. According to FoxNews the Apostolic Church of Jesus Christ was filled with friends, family, law enforcement officials and the father of Jessica Lunsford who suffered a similar fate at the murderous hands of a convicted sex offended less than two months ago.

Sara was buried later in the afternoon at a local cemetary.

Her Uncle is quoted as saying, "Sara is certainly in a much better place now."

Personally, I share that belief. But I doubt that Sara was eager to leave this world for that "better place" so soon.

It seems somehow trite and empty to try and find comfort in a sentiment that, loosly translated, could mean, "Her torturous and murderous death was all for the best."

The Apostle Paul, faced with the possiblity of martyrdom, once **wrote**, "I desire to depart (die) and be with Christ which is better by far..." But Paul was an adult, facing the consequences of his own freely-chosen beliefs and actions. He had set his priorities in life and was willing to live and, if necessary, die for them. His eyes and his heart were fixed on Christ and his heavenly kingdom. The world had worn him down.....his body was tired.....his body chained to the stone wall of a jail cell. Death would mean not only victory but rest from his weariness. He would have finished the race set before him and he would receive the crown of life.

Sara's death was not the consequence of her freely-chosen faith or actions. Her life was just beginning, not nearing an apparent end. She had not yet set her priorities for life or for death. Her heart, while seeking to know and serve Jesus Christ as her Lord and Savior, was not yet yearning to cash in her salvation for a seat at table in the Kingdom of God.

Her life was not poured out; it was not given; it was taken.

While I am glad to know the truth of the Gospel, the saving love of God in Jesus Christ and the sure and certain hope for resurrection to eternal life, I would much prefer to have Sara back with her family and friends in Kentucky.

But maybe I'm just being selfish. Maybe I am still in shock and denial of this tragedy.

Perhaps we would all be better served by claiming the promise found in Romans 8:28, "We know that in all things God works for the good of those who love him, who have been called according to his purpose."

For those of us who "love God," as Sara reportedly did, we should be keeping our eyes open to see what opportunities for "good" will come out of this tragedy. Sara's death was not "good" by any means. But, by God's grace, good may yet sprout, green and beautiful, from the ashes of her life, watered by the tears of her death.

From the very beginning God has declared that human life and love is "very good." For Sara's sake we must live and love so that the world might begin to look more and more like John's vision of the coming day when,

(God) will wipe every tear from their eyes. There will be no more death or mourning or crying or pain, for the old order of things has passed away."

He who was seated on the throne said, "I am making everything new!" Then he said, "Write this down, for these words are trustworthy and true.

Lord have mercy. Christ have mercy. Lord have mercy.

Come, Lord Jesus! Amen.

SUNDAY, APRIL 24, 2005

"It's Time" for Pope Benedict XVI

First, here is a photograph taken when the newly-elected Pope Benedict XVI made his first balcony appearance to the gathered people in St. Peter's Square. Second, here is the photo that appeared on the front page of the Honolulu Advertiser this morning (scanned)

Can you see what caught my eye in both pictures? This.... !

It looks to me like a watch. It is not a digital watch but the old-fashioned kind with the watch hands twirling about that I prefer to wear myself. If anyone can identify the brand please leave me a comment!

My question is, "Why does the Pope need a watch?" Is he going to cut short his comments if the

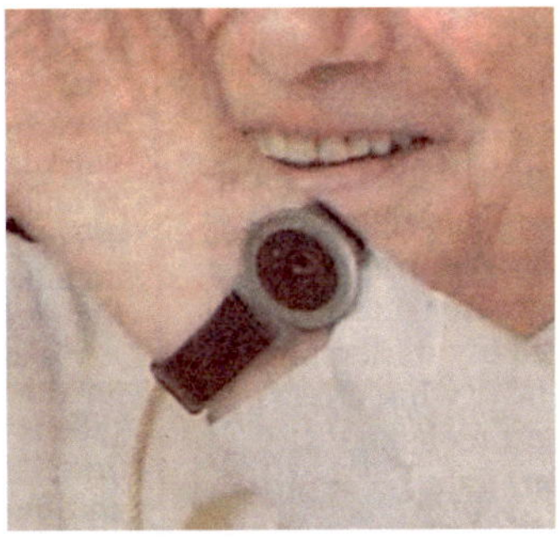

Sunday homily is going overtime? Will he ever need to leave a committee meeting early to get to a doctor appointment on time? Does he have to keep track of time so he will remember that it's time to feed the dog? or take the car down to the shop for a tune-up? What's with the watch?

Isn't his day laid out minute by minute for him by his personal secretaries? Don't others tell him when to stand up and sit down and when to say "Amen?"

What does it say to someone who, having waited for many days to have an audience with the Pope, sees him glance at his watch just as they approach him for a blessing and exchange of greetings?

I always have read that Rome was the "timeless city." Apparently Pope Benedict XVI doesn't see it that way.

For some reason, with all the elegant trappings of the papacy wrapped around him with the same sort of care that goes into dressing up one of the Swiss Guards, the watch seems somehow out of place.

Especially when his hands are raised in front of his face as he give a sign of greeting or of blessing.

Even as a Presbyterian pastor I have always associated the Pope as being a sort of eternity personified, the representative of the Roman Church as a bearer and caretaker of the eternal Gospel, a sort of Beginning and End all wrapped up together, a reflection, so to speak, of the ***Alpha*** and ***Omega***.

The watch, on the other hand, symbolizes mortality, the sand flowing inexorably downward through the timer.

Perhaps the new Pope already is aware of this and sees this as a reminder that he, too, is human just like the rest of us. Amidst the power and the glory, that watch looks to me like a small nod to humility and to the transitory nature of temporal wealth and power. In that sense I suppose that it serves a greater purpose than simply reminding Benedict XVI that it is time to take his blood pressure medication.

Now, all I need to figure out is why Queen Elizabeth needs to carry around a purse? And what in the world does she keep in it?

Oh! It just came to me! I bet the Pope wears ***this*** kind of watch! It would make sense, yes?

MONDAY, APRIL 25, 2005

Peruvian Model Changes Her Mind: Refuses to Sell Her Virginity for $1.5 Million

According to BBC News, an 18-year old girl living in the dusty outskirts of Lima, Peru, recently stunned the country by putting her virginity up for sale to the highest bidder.

Gracia-No Longer for Sale

Gracia (last name not available) earns $60 (US) or so each month from modelling and acting but says that it is not enough to support her ailing mother and younger brother.

Her innovative idea to raise money caused many critics to declare her to be nothing less than a prostitute. Others, however, expressed admiration for her creativity and good sense to get something from what most girls "give away for free" to their boyfriends in public parks after dark.

According to Gracia, a Canadian man offered her $1.5 million because, "He said he'd prefer I didn't do it, but if I was going to do it with anyone, it should be with someone who treated me right and I think he knew his bid wasn't going to be topped.

"He was really happy when I said No."

Now that Gracia has changed her mind some are calling the whole thing a publicity stunt.

Gracia, however, expresses disappointment on the lack of compassion her desparate offer generated.

"They don't bother asking what's going on in my life, what I am like and what has forced me to take this decision. They only judge me and point their fingers at me.

"I came out and said publicly what my situation was and nobody, nobody has been capable of saying, thank you, I'll help you with something," she said.

"And there are people who have loads of money, loads of jobs."

I remember American Christian teacher/writer Tony Campolo describing the time in Haiti when he ran into a 10-year old girl on the street selling her body for money. Campolo took her up to his hotel room, ordered ice cream and spent the afternoon watching Disney cartoons with her on the television.

Campolo still wonders if that might have been the first time that girl had ever been treated as someone special for her own sake rather than for what she could offer to someone else.

While Gracia's offer and subsequent retraction might provide the plot for a good movie (sort of a mirror image of "Indecent Proposal") it also served to publically expose the plight of hundreds of thousands of Peru's poor.

If I was part of a charitable organization in Lima attempting ease the burden of poverty, I think I would stop by Gracia's place and invite her out for a cup of coffee. Then I would offer her a job as a spokesperson for others who consider themselves fortunate to survive just one day at a time.

Gracia could then become a positive "model" for others, showing that choosing personal moral integrity (in a manner reminiscent of the biblical Ruth) can help lead even the poorest girl away from the shackles of poverty; from despair to hope; from hope to freedom.

This story has touched me deeply. Perhaps it's because my daughter #2 is just about the same age. Perhaps because, as Gracia says, there are plenty of people around with plenty of money. Perhaps it's because far too many of those people love their money more than they love people like Gracia. Or perhaps it's because those rich people look a lot like me.

Osteoarthritis & Heberden's Nodes

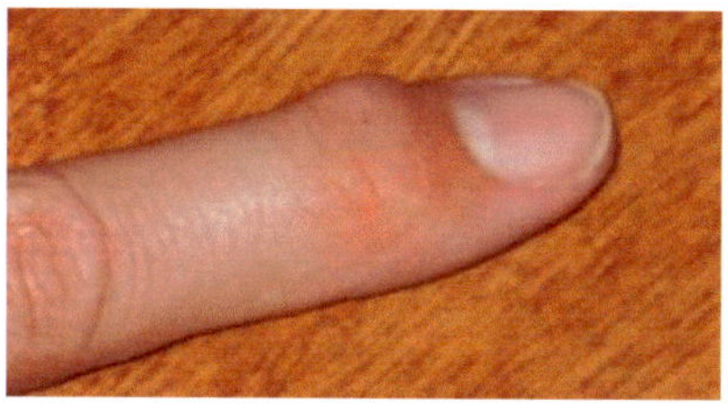

No, I do not have sinus congestion (as in, "I hab a code in my nodes"). But I do have nodes. The kind that come with arthritic fingers.

When such swelling appears on the *mid*-finger joint (commonly called the "proximal interphalangeal" joint, or "PID") it is called ***rheumatoid*** arthritis and, when the joint swells, the swellings are called "**Bouchard's Nodes**."

When such swelling appears on the *terminal* finger joint (commonly called the "distal interphalangeal" joint, or "DIP") it is called ***osteo***arthritis and, when the joint swells, the swellings are called "**Heberden's Nodes**." That's the kind that I have on my two index fingers.

I have had such a node on my right hand index finger for well over 20 years. At times it aches and pains miserably. Although I have had tenderness and pain in my left hand index finger for over five years, the node more or less "erupted" in great swelling (and real hurting!) while attending a local Christian Conference in Honolulu earlier this month.

Tonight, having nothing better to do, I did a little internet research and discovered, as mentioned above, that these swellings actually have nodal names! And don't you find it strange that arthritis in the top joint of a finger is called osteoarthritis while arthritis in the the middle joint of a finger is called rheumatoid arthritis? Why the difference?

You can read a really good, simple explaination of this at the Van Denmark Orthopedic info site here. That's where I got the info.

By the way, have you heard this one?

Person #1: Today I met a man with a wooden leg named Smith.

Person #2: Oh, really? What was the name of his other leg?

I think I shall call my two nodes ***Mr. & Mrs. Heberden*** from now on!

TUESDAY, APRIL 26, 2005

Healing Prayer: The Miracle & Mystery

Two Sunday's ago, following worship, 15 or so church members and Elders gathered with me in my office to lay hands on and pray for two young women in our congregation.

One woman, the mother of two small children, had had a small cancerous abdominal tumor removed a year ago and, at her first-anniversary check-up, a second, new lump had been discovered. Surgery to remove the as-yet undiagnosed lump was scheduled for the following morning. She is a new Christian, having studied and prayed about her faith for some years. I had the privilege of baptizing her several months ago.

The other woman had been suffering from terrible headaches and, in recent weeks, her left eye had begun to be visibly pushed forward from behind. A CAT scan had detected what appeared to be a fairly large tumor behind that eye, located in a place difficult to access for either surgery or biopsy. A MRI (Magnetic Resonant Imaging) test had been scheduled for the following Thursday to help determine a more precise measurement and analysis of whatever it was that had appeared in the CAT scan. This woman, too, is a Christian, although of an uncertain and searching faith.

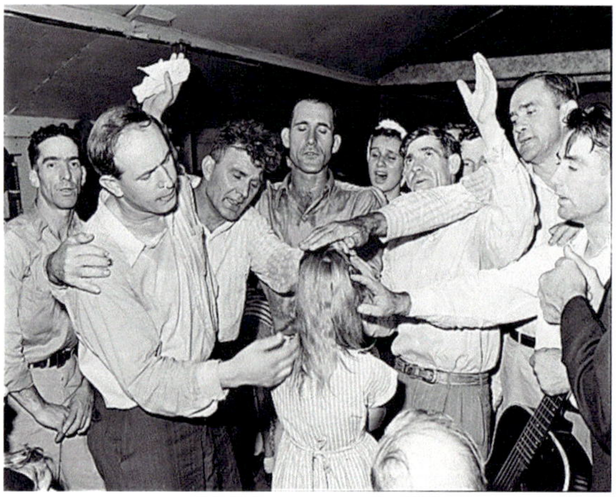

In any case, the prayer was intense for each of these women. No one spoke in tongues nor were there any other dramatic manifestations of the Holy Spirit, simply profound prayers for healing, offered to God in faith.

And what, you might ask, was the outcome of these prayers? The answer to that question lands somewhere between puzzlement and wonder.

During surgery the following morning the surgeon discovered that the cancer had not only recurred but had spread throughout a large area of her abdomen. The two-hour surgery that was planned stretched into a seven-hour surgery as the doctor attempted to remove as much of the malignancy as possible.

After she heals from the surgery she will be undergoing an extensive regimen of chemotherapy. Her faith and trust in God, however, remains strong. She radiates joy and is searching for ways in which "God can work for good" in this situation that she, herself, described to me as "tragic." A description that I completely agreed with.

On Thursday, the second woman had her MRI. On Friday I spoke with her and she explained how the experience had helped her reprioritize her life. So much that she had taken for granted had suddenly become central and precious to her. Although she did not yet know the results of her test she said she was at peace with whatever would be found. Her trust in God's love and her faith in his goodness had been profoundly reaffirmed in her heart. She even spoke of her desire to offer a testimony of her experience during worship some Sunday.

In any case, she received a phone call on Friday night giving her the results of her MRI test. She did not, however, tell anyone else the results until she phoned one of our Elders who had accompanied her when she had the test. To put it simply, the MRI could not locate any evidence of a tumor at all. None. Zip. A dye had been injected to heighten whatever image that might have existed. Even a small cyst filled with water would have shown up clearly. But there was nothing there. Whatever had been pushing on her eye, whatever had been causing those headaches, whatever had been clearly seen on the CAT scan.....was gone.

Prayer is, for me, the greatest mystery of my Christian faith.

I can handle the Trinity, the incarnation, the atonement and even the Genesis creation stories without losing much sleep. But prayer.......prayer is another thing altogether. How it "works?" Why God asks it from us? Why or why not it makes a difference? I don't really know. Scripture gives many helpful hints and tips on prayer. But, more important, scripture tells us that prayer, when offered in faith in a manner consistent with the will of God, can unleash a power that.....that......well.....according to Jesus, can move mountains!

Two Sundays ago we prayed identical, passionate prayers of faith for two women who we love equally. For one, the mountain was lifted up and cast into the sea. A mystery of healing and prayer answered just as it was asked.

For the other, it was as if the mountain had been lifted up only to fall heavily upon her, crushing her under its unfathomable weight. A mystery of prayer asked, but unanswered. At least not answered according to our impassioned pleas.

This is not the first time I have participated in healing prayer that resulted in what, by all objective evidence, can honestly be described as a miracle.

Strangely enough, however, it is not the answered prayers, the miracles of healing that surprise me. In a spiritual sense, such results seem almost normative to me....the way it is supposed to be. Although I rejoice and stand before the Lord in complete humility and awe, I do not find myself puzzling over the miracle.

The unanswered prayer, however, leaves me pondering an even greater mystery than the answered prayer. For in the unanswered prayer will come suffering, pain and, quite possibly, death.

To find meaning and purpose in life is not a great challenge to most of us. But to find meaning and purpose in suffering, pain and death is quite another matter. I am led to sit at the feet of Job. I am led to stand at the foot of the cross where I watch the suffering, pain and death of the eternal Son of God, fully and inseparably incarnate in the person of Jesus Christ who is my Lord and the Savior of the world.

In the suffering, pain and death of Jesus, however, I can discern something unique and very surprising. I discern, in that bleak darkness, the un-snuffed light of hope. The light of life that will rise again and never be challenged by darkness again. Ever.

For Jesus died. And Jesus rose from the dead.

Jesus was dead. Yet now he is alive forevermore!

In the healing, God is praised.

In the suffering, God is found.

It is a wonder....and a puzzlement.

British Open Cracks Door for Hawaii Golfer Michelle Wie

Michelle Wie, our own favorite 15-year old golfer from Hawaii, has entered the men's pro golf tour's John Deere Open. According to a new rule, the highest placing player not presently eligible for the British Open in July will invited to play in that auldest Major of all.

This means, of course, that should Michelle actually accomplish this feat, she would become the first woman golfer to ever play in the British Open....or any of the Major golf tournaments, for that matter.

Personally, if a woman is able to compete with a man on their own terms I believe that it would be wrong to deny them that opportunity. Women, being the "weaker sex" would, of course, only invite male atheletes 60 years old and older to enter their events.

It is virtually impossible for Michelle to reach her goal this year. But even so, the very fact that the world press is talking about it shows just how much of an impact this talented, amateur Oahu teen has already made in the world of pro sports.

Good luck to ye, lassie!

Mein Gott! The Toads are Exploding!

According to BBC News,

Toads in an area of northern Germany are being killed off by a mysterious disease - they are exploding.

Thousands of the amphibians have died in recent days in a pond in Hamburg's Altona district, with their bodies swelling to bursting point. The toads' entrails are propelled for up to a metre (3.2ft), in scenes that have been likened to science fiction.

Scientists are baffled.

Besides being outrageously bizarre and, at least in the cartoon-like images flitting about in my imagination, hilariously funny, this story provides one other happy thought....For some reason I am absolutely delighted to read those three words, "Scientists are baffled." I find them strangely comforting, somehow. Hmmm........

BOOM!

.

WEDNESDAY, APRIL 27, 2005

Police Shoot Dead Man Who Held Son Hostage

Yes, the headline above is correct: " Police Shoot Dead Man Who Held Son Hostage." At least that's what the news teaser said today on FoxNews online. I actually looked up the story, wondering, 1. How a dead man could hold his son hostage?; and, 2. Why the police had to shoot him if he was already dead?

Either one of FoxNews' copy editors has a sense of humor or else he/she needs to be sent back for a course in remedial English. One can only hope that it is the former. Either way, he/she made me smile!

Zimbabwe Elected to UN Human Rights Commission (Really!)

Under the objections of the United States, Canada and Australia, Zimbabwe was elected as a new member of the United Nations Human Rights Commission.

According to BBC News, the U.S. representative, "accused Zimbabwe of maintaining repressive controls on political assembly and the media. He asked how they could expect Zimbabwe to support international human rights at the commission while it disregarded the rights of its own people."

Not only has Zimbabwe violated "human rights" but Mugabe has allowed his cronies to seize "white-owned" wildlife parks and sanctuaries, including the world-famous "Sikumi Tree Lodge."

The lodge was once a showpiece of eco-tourism and was where the Queen had lunch during the Commonwealth Heads of Government meeting in 1991. Now it plays host to those willing to pay to shoot rare game.

Back at the UN, Zimbabwe's ambassador to the UN, Boniface Chidyausiku, said that **when it came to human rights no country was beyond reproach**.

Perhaps so, Mr. Ambassador. But some, including you, live in more fragile glass houses than the rest of us. Clear out the beam in your own eye, Mr. Chidyausiku, before you start pointing out the specks in everyone else's.

THURSDAY, APRIL 28, 2005

Darwin's Theory of Evolution Proved! New (sort of) Species of Ivory-Billed Woodpecker Appears

Darwin's theory of macro-evolution has long been attacked and rejected by fundamentalist Christians and even a few scientists with, at least on paper, brains.

This week, however, the argument that there is absolutely not one shred of physical evidence that illustrates this theory conclusively has at last been put to rest. The evidence was recently discovered in an isolated back-country forest in Arkansas.
It seems that, after 60 years of extinction, the Ivory-Billed Woodpecker has re-created itself, either from nothing or as a genetic mutation of (perhaps) the smaller Pilated Woodpecker. So, it seems that Darwin was right all along and the young-earth creationists and Intelligent-Design folks will have to throw in their towels, burn their Bibles and scrape those fish things off or their cars.....you know, the big fish with "Jesus" or "IXTHUS" on the side and wide-open mouths about to gobble up the little fish with the tiny legs poking out underneath.

Of course it is inevitable that some right-wing-fundamentalist-religious-wing-nut will try to push some absurd theory that the scientists were wrong all along and that the Ivory-Billed Woodpecker was never extinct to begin with! Do these people think that Darwinists are just a bunch of idiots? Everybody who's anybody knows that the most self-evident explaination is never the real one! That would be too simple and obvious, not to mention possibly putting many Darwinists out of a job.

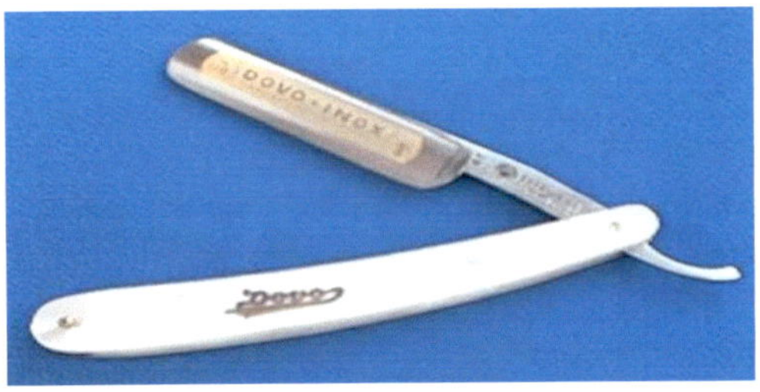

In any case, Darwinists would much rather shave with a sharpened piece of flint than to use that old-fashioned Occam's Razor!

President Bush Speaks on Energy & Social Security

I enjoyed listening to Dubya take on the press this evening. He seems to almost enjoy the opportunity to speak straight out what he thinks and answer the tough and often "gotcha" style questions.

My three responses:

Energy: Didn't Jimmy Carter, or Gerald Ford, or Ronald Reagan, or somebody present these same ideas before? Where's the beef?

Social Security: Although I was born in 1951 and will fall into the "New and Improved" Social Security proposal; and although it sounds like I may lose some of my anticipated retirement benefits in order to shore up the greater needs of the lower-income retirees; in spite of all this, I think I like what the President says. It's really a tax increase in disguise, especially for the higher wage earners, since their contributions stay the same but their benefits are reduced. But, nonetheless, I like the private account idea. Bush talks as if he believes that the American people are smart enough to make decisions about such things. The Democrats talk as though the American people (or at least the poor and minority ones) are not smart or reliable enough to be entrusted with their own money...as if "Big Brother will all the thinking for you!" I think Bush is right, that most Americans *are* smart enough to like his idea....and that most Americans are far more intelligent than the Democrats would like to think!

Bonus: When "Hutch" asked the final question of the press conference, in referring to the proposed lowering of Social Security income returns for wealthy retirees, he added, "like Dick Cheney."

Without a blink, Bush immediately shot back, "Now let's not get personal, here. That was a cheap shot!"

Undoubtedly many of the more radical Democrats felt that Bush & Cheney got "nailed" with that remark, virtually everyone else in the nation will probably agree with Bush that the comment was tacky, inappropriate and mean spirited. I believe that the President hit a home run with his quick retort.

Pentagon to Release Military Casket Photos

After nearly two years of wrangling over the public release of Pentagon photos of slain American soldiers' remains being returned to the United States in flag-draped caskets, the government has at last (under the possible threat of an impending court order), to release over 300 of the pictures.

To this I say, "Amen!" Let the press and the wackos do whatever they want with these pictures. Mainstream and otherwise sane Americans will view them with a mixture of pride and sorrow. Our military treats its fallen soldiers with the respect due to heroes who who have laid down their lives for their country and for the higher aspirations of other countries abroad.

Let their stories be told. From beginning to end. They would not be embarrassed or ashamed for their sacrifice to be seen. These pictures will not increase the grief of their families.

We are a nation that both exists and thrives and prospers in the full light of truth. Anyone who uses these photos in a dishonorable manner will reap the whirlwind of public opinion.

For those who have returned home, leaving their life-blood behind in the sand and clay of foreign soil, "Thank you."

FRIDAY, APRIL 29, 2005

Bizarre 3rd Grade Needle-Sticking Story Doesn't Make Sense

A CNN story about a 3rd grade girl in Pennsylvania sticking 19 students with her mother's diabetes blood-testing needle "this week" is riddled with contradicions.

Issue I: The article says she stuck students during breakfast, at lunch and in the classroom. That would appear to be over a 3 to 4-hour period of time. Didn't anyone say, "Outch" and tell a teacher or adult staff? If so, why didn't the school confront the girl immediately?

Issue II: The article says that one of the students "stuck" subequently tested positive for HIV. This raises several problems:

Problem #1: According to Wikopedia, "The window period is the time from infection until a test can detect any change. The average window period with antibody tests is 22 days. Antigen testing cuts the window period to approximately 16 days and NAT further reduces this period to 12 days. (FDA 2001)" Yet, accordiing to the article, this test resulted in a "positive" within a matter of days?

Problem #2: "Health officials said the virus could not have been contracted from the needle stick." Yet, further down in the same article, "According to the Centers for Disease Control and Prevention, the risk of HIV infection after a needle stick is low, with an average of one in 300 cases leading to infection."

Which is it? Impossible? or Unlikely? or just Unlucky? If I was the parent of the infected child the difference between "impossible" and "maybe" would make a very big difference.

Problem #3: Has anyone considered the possibility that the child who tested positive for HIV already had the infection before being stuck? If so, whoever was stuck with the needle after them would be at a much higher risk, no?

Problem #4: Is the diabetic mother who owned the needle HIV positive? Was she tested? Is her right to "privacy" trumped by the health implications for the children? Is this a legal matter of concern? It is certainly a medical and a moral matter.
Issue III: According to the article, the girld "was suspended and will probably be moved to another school," said Paul Vallas, the school district's chief executive. Huh? Moved to another school? Whatever happened with the concept of being expelled? Would I want my child sitting next to this girl in class or in the lunchroom for the next 3 or 4 years of elementary school? Is the school district requiring psychological testing? Is their criminal or civil liability with the girl's mother? Is there a police investigation taking place?

Conclusion A: My uninformed hope is that this is simply a matter of very, very poor news writing and that the matter is presently in the hands for good people making good decisions, etc.

Conclusion B: My even greater hope is that this whole story, which reads like an urban legend, is a complete fabrication.

CBS On the Prowl for New Evening News Anchor

With Dan Rather enjoying early retirement, CBS continues to ponder how to repackage their news programming in a way that will help them rise up from the non-cable news cellar. The man or woman they choose as chief anchor and news director will play a major role in whether the new news format will succeed or fail.

Tonight, **Hugh Hewitt** has challenged the blogosphere to suggest names of people who might be a good pick to represent the new-and-hopefully-improved public image of CBS News.

After reading Hugh's request my thoughts moved as follows:

1. CBS's major problem is integrity and trust. Until that is restored it doesn't matter what sort of bells and whistles they produce.

2. Integrity and trust must be restored immediately by someone already regarded as established and reliable. This would rule out a young, up-and-coming man or woman who, over a span of years might create such trust but would not generate any buzz or confidence at the outset.

3. The person must be immediately recognizable by a large number of Americans, both within and outside of the corridors of power.

4. The person must have well-established and respected relationships with both political leaders and the world news media, including press, radio and television.

5. It should not particularly matter whether the person's personal biases are considered to be "liberal," "conservative," "middle-of-the-road" or "neutral" so long as the personal bias is open and honest, the person is not considered "radical" and does not come with a track record of having had active leadership in a major partisan political campaign or is strongly associated with public service to one particular political party.

6. The person's primary character values must demonstrably be known and shown to include "fairness."

7. While personal experience in the area of "blogging" would not be necessary, a healthy respect and understanding of the dynamics and culture of the growing assimilation, digestion, regurgitation, repackaging and dissemination of news and information on the internet would be both vital and mandatory.

8. As mentioned above, the immediate need for CBS is to regain its reputation for integrity, trustworthiness and fairness. An older, experienced person could bring that image back quickly without necessarily remaining in that role forever. As soon as the reputation of the network has been redeemed that person could then step down, either completely or into the "special reporter" or "commentator" role, allowing one or more newer faces to enter the position and carry the momentum along for possibly an entire generation of new viewers.

9. Curiously, there are a number of good people who could fit this description quite well. But the one that immediately popped into my mind is the one I will run with.

I propose that CBS contract and sign Bob Woodward from the *Washington Post*, to serve as CBS News Director and Evening News Anchor during this period of rebuilding and restructuring.

Bob Woodward has a proven record of keeping up with the cultural and technological trends of the day so would be able to endorse and understand the necessary innovations that CBS will have to consider to be a cutting edge news source once again.

Bob Woodward, despite having a clear liberal bias, is widely viewed to be "fair" by a broad spectrum of political leaders on both sides of the aisle.

Although not necessarily the most reliable source on the web, **Wikipedia**'s article on Bob Woodward does offer this interesting, insightful and relevant paragraph.

> *Woodward is widely regarded as one of the top reporters of the last half-century, and has earned trust and accolades from government officials and journalists of all political persuasions. In 2003, Al Hunt of The Wall Street Journal called Woodward "the most celebrated journalist of our age." The Weekly Standard called him "the best pure reporter of his generation, perhaps ever." And in 2004 Bob Schieffer of CBS News said "Woodward has established himself as the best reporter of our time. He may be the best reporter of all time."*

Woodward presents a confident, photogenic on-screen image and is well-spoken both in prepared presentations as well as in impromptu conversation. He is also known to seek out the hard, central truth of a story without bending or twisting the results to conform to some predetermined reality.

I could go on with many other positive points but will assert some self-control and stop. While there are also many negatives (the largest of which is his personal inseparability from the Watergate matter) I cannot imagine another journalist of his caliber who could accomplish the goals I have listed above.

In any case, I sincerely hope and pray that CBS chooses well. The more honest, fair and balanced news sources we have, the better off we will be.

Mice With Human Brains? Stuart Little Could Become a Reality Show!

Researchers, working within ethical guidelines established by the National Academies, have begun mixing human liver, blood and brain cells with those of lower animals. Pigs have been created that have human blood, and some experimental sheep in Nevada have livers that are part human.

Of particular interest are mice which, at an early stage of development, have had human brain cells injected into their own brains.

Many scientists have discovered that their own fantasies about what might come from such research are so frightening that they serve as an independent check on what they will allow themselves to do.

According to a CNN on-line report,

Particularly worrisome to some scientists are the nightmare scenarios that could arise from the mixing of brain cells: What if a human mind somehow got trapped inside a sheep's head?

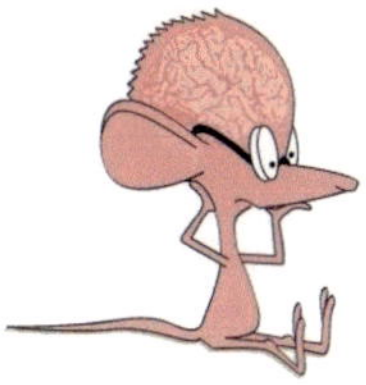

This past January, an unofficial ethics committee supported a proposal to create mice with brains nearly completely composed of human brain cells.

Stanford law professor Hank Greely, who chaired the ethics committee, said the board was satisfied that the size and shape of the mouse brain would prevent the human cells from creating any traits of humanity.

Could there actually come a time in the future when we could encounter a real, honest-to-goodness Stuart Little? Not if they have anything to do with it, says Greely,

Just in case, he said, the committee recommended closely monitoring the mice's behavior and immediately killing any that display human-like behavior.

"Human-like behavior?" Like walking on two legs? Eating with a knife and fork?
Would such a mouse be morally responsible for the choices it makes and for their consequences? Could it develop delusions of grandeur?

Is it possible that the mouse could experience self-awareness? An awareness of God?...Like those childrens' stories which have mice kneeling at the manger in praise and worship of the new-born baby Jesus in the Bethlehem stable?

Are human beings, which the Bible says were created in the "image of God," now on the verge of creating animals in the "image of Man?"

Personally, I am well aware of both the potential benefits and the potential horrors which could result from this, and other, forms of genetic research and development. But his should not be surprising. Every human creation has, from the beginning, resulted in a mixed blessing. The work of our hands has always brought both blessings and cursings upon us.
While I am not against this sort of research *per se*, I do sense the presence of some of the same motivations that (Biblically) brought about the Fall of Satan, the Sin of Adam (& Eve), the Great Flood and the Tower of Babel: namely, our desire to become like God...immortal and omnipotent.

Any endeavor spawned by such motives will inevitably turn out badly. Although God will not long tolerate such arrogance, such has, in the past, been tolerated long enough for those who have sown the wind to, in the end, reap the whirlwind.

When mice begin to display "human-like behavior" it will, sad to say, become necessary to kill them.

Hmmmm......I seem to remember that when Jesus began to display true and authentic "human-like behavior" (the first time such behavior had been seen since "The Fall") those in charge of things decided that it had, sad to say, become necessary to kill him, too!

SATURDAY, APRIL 30, 2005

Christian Faith, Judicial Court Appointments & Janice Rogers Brown

In recent months many liberal Democrats have begun to disparage those who profess the Christian faith (especially Roman Catholics) and who affirm that their faith shapes their politics and world-view. It has been claimed, for example, that if a person's personal faith leads them to believe unlimited abortion is morally wrong, they should be disqualified from serving as a Federal judge. National Christian leaders who have spoken out publicly on these matters have been called "anti-Christ" "un-Christian" "fascist" and "far right-wing fundamentalists" seeking to impose a "theocracy" or (a new term to me) "Dominionists."

This rhetoric has been hard to reconcile with the fact that over half of all Americans attend a house of worship each month and that 90% of Americans believe in God most of whom are Christians. When offered the chance to vote on social issues, state voters have, for example, averaged nearly 70% against the legalization of "same-sex marriage." Similar high percentages of Americans polled consistently oppose unrestricted access to abortion at any stage of pregnancy or for any reason.

One of the Federal Circuit Court nominees receiving the most brazen opposition and explicit discrimination based on her faith is California Supreme Court Judge Janice Rogers Brown. Her legal qualifications are impeccable and, even in notoriously liberal California, voters recently returned her to her State Supreme Court position by a whopping 76% of the vote (contrast this with Bush's 45%). Democratic opposition to her appointment has centered almost exclusively on her being a Roman Catholic who actually takes her faith seriously. (Didn't this issue get taken care of with Democratic presidential nominee John F. Kennedy back in 1960?)

Perhaps the issue would be simpler if Judge Brown were not also African-American. This, of course, poses yet another threat to the Democrat's illusory mantra that minorities are oppressed, weak and desperately clinging to the Democratic Party to save them.....from who? People like Judge Janice Brown?

Despite having her nomination filibustered for months and months, Judge Brown has refused to either back down or to dodge the issue of her faith. In a recent speech she blasted those who suggest that a person's Christian faith should cast a pall upon their qualifications for public service as a Judge or in any other area.

Captain Ed at Captain's Quarters provides a good recap and analysis of Judge Brown's comments. Everyone who, as a (conservative) Christian, has been offended for being categorized as an "out-of-the-mainstream extreme right wing religious nut job" or similar implied bigoted comment from the Democratic leadership in the US Senate, should read this post and be very, very grateful for people like Judge Janice Rogers Brown.

Other posts on Janice Brown and/or anti-Christian comments from Democrats can be found here, here, here, here and here.

Veiled Egyptian Women Shoot Up Cairo Tourist Bus & Then Shoot Themselves

In Cairo today, two veiled women shot at a tourist bus and missed everyone. As nearby security personnel closed in one of the women shot and killed the other and then shot and wounded herself. You can read the story **here**.

The article does not explain the women's motivation for their attack. To help fill in that missing detail, I have written a dialogue between the women, speculating on what they might have been thinking about.

Note: This is not intended as an insult to Islam or to Muslims.
It is, however, intended as an insult to those who support or who participate in terrorism.

Woman #1: *Well, today's the day we glorify Allah and show the infidels what we think of their.....uh.....what is it that we think?*

Woman #2: *We show the infidels what we think about their....their infidelity! You idiot!*

Woman #1: *Oh, yes. Sorry. I guess I'm just a little nervous.*

Woman #2: *Nervous? About what? Oh, I see. You're nervous about shooting and killing innocent people on a tourist bus this morning? What's the big deal? There are probably mostly women and children on the bus. What are they going to do, shoot back at you or something?*

#1: *Well, no. You drew the long straw so you get to do that for them, right?*

#2: *Right. So what do you have to be nervous about?*

#1: *Nothing, I guess. I feel like such a wimp.*

#2: *We are not wimps! Our husbands have commanded us to do this so we're going to do it. Is that a problem for you?*

#1: *Well, I suppose that being chosen for this honor is a real testimony to the love and passion my husband has for me. I've never really been so honored in my life....as a woman, I mean.*

#2: *That's more like it. After all, you've been practicing your shooting skills for almost a week. I bet you've hit that target with Britney Spear's picture on it more times than anyone else! And Richard Gere? Right between the eyes!*

#1: Yes, I know. But I thought he was on our side?

#2: No. He's an infidel trying to be a different infidel while pretending to be a friend of folks like us. What a joke. As if one infidel is any better than another! Besides, the odds are that he won't be on that bus today anyway.

#1: But, now that you mention it, what if their are Muslims on the bus. They aren't infidels, so why should we be shooting at them?

#2: Because we will be sending those false believers who make their living by sucking up to those imperialist, fascist mothers of occupiers straight to hell where they belong. In any case, if we kill a good Muslim by mistake, we are doing them a favor by making them a martyr for jihad. And, when they get their 27 virgins in heaven, they will be very grateful to us.

#1: Let me get this straight. If a good Muslim man is martyred for jihad, he goes straight to paradise and receives 27 virgins as a reward. Right?

#2: Right.

#1: When we, who are good Muslim women, are martyred for jihad, we go straight bo paradise and receive what?

#2: We each get to be one of those 27 virgins, of course!

#1: But I'm not a virgin....and neither are you!

#2: I know it doesn't make a shred of sense, but my husband told me that that's what the Imam said in his sermon last Friday so it must be true.

#1: But I've read the Holy Koran over and over again and I have never seen anything about blessings for women in paradise. How does the Imam know this?

#2: Just hush your mouth and don't go bad-mouthing the Imam or the Prophet (blessed be his name). We must be simple, faithful women and do what we can to defend Islam against the infidel invaders.

#1: But.....

#2: Why don't you just......! Oh, alright, speak your peace and be done with it.

#1: But is this what all Muslims think? I mean, is what we are going to do have the blessing of all Muslims everywhere? Or are we just being set up by some radical fringe Muslim sect?

#2: Maybe yes, maybe no. It doesn't really matter, now, does it? There are no divisions in Islam. We are all one faith and one people. There is unity in our faith and, like all true sisters and brothers, we will stand up for each other at all times as a matter of family honor and pride. ......except for those creepy Shi'ites, of course.....and those Sufis.....and all those other non-Wahabbi's who follow the false paths of Islam.

***#1:** But that's nearly 95% of the world's Muslims!*

***#2:** Yes, and that just makes our responsibility that much greater.*

***#1:** Thanks, I feel a lot better now. By the way, could I ask you a favor?*

***#2:** Sure. Go ahead.*

***#1:** After we shoot up the bus and it's time for you to kill me, would you pretend that I'm Barry Manilow? Down at the target range, you've never missed him yet!*

SATURDAY, MAY 07, 2005

"Kingdom Of Heaven" Is a Movie Worth Seeing

Well, I've gone and done it. I just returned from watching the movie, "**Kingdom of Heaven**." I haven't had the time to mull it over very long, but I would like to record my first impressions (my anticipatory post of the movie can be found **here** and, as you will see, my reaction is far more positive than that earlier post).

Cinematic quality--consistently excellent.

Special effects--Good enough to carry the drama (although the exploding fireballs were a bit much. What did they have in them, plastic explosives?)

Story line--Mostly good to very good.

The young "knight," Sir Balian, played by Orlando Bloom, never really seems to mature in either age or wisdom throughout the film, however.

And, how a village blacksmith came to possess such a knowledge of the knightly skills of personal combat and a mastery of the era's most technologically advanced methods of warfare (not to mention the capability to command the defense of a besieged city against an army of over 200,000 men) is never explained. This, among other things, forced me to suspend logic and lessened the "believability" of the movie somewhat.

Also, although as a leader of men he seemed a "sincere" enough , I did not sense the presence of enough *gravitas* to have motivated me into following him into the "jaws of death."

The other roles, especially that of Sibylla, "Queen of Jerusalem", (played by Iva Green) demonstrated far more complex and believable character development.

Entertainment Value--Extremely High. I never lost interest in the movie once.

Historical Accuracy--Fairly good, so far as I am able to grasp it.
The world of Medieval Jerusalem seemed dusty and dirty enough. The geography of Jerusalem was laughingly naive (but, then again, so was the Jerusalem of Mel Gibson's "The Passion of the Christ").

The complex diversity of personal motives, philosophies and beliefs seemed to reflect reality as I know it.

The siege scenes and other battles seemed to reflect medieval warfare fairly well (although I expect the real thing would have been far more bloody and ghastly than shown in the movie....the battle of the breached wall of Jerusalem, if in fact there was such a thing, would have left a pile of dead soldiers 5-10 deep with rivers of blood making the fight a slippery mess, indeed).

The role of the Knights Templar in seeking to destroy the infidel "Saracens" by whatever means possible (serving under the direct will and authority of the Roman papacy) also seems reasonable enough...although such men would not necessarily have been as corrupt and wicked as those shown in the movie.

The desire of men to have peace with one another (while maintaining control over the other) also seemed to be reflective of a true part of human nature.

I cannot believe, however, that such a belief was widespread or even a significant motivation for those in power and authority in those times. Moral and Religious nuance is not a great motivator for those who must fight and kill one another.

The themes of moral "black and white," "good vs. evil" and "religious absolutes" on both sides were played down almost to the point where they were unrecognizable (except, of course, for the really, really bad guys!

Theology--Accurate enough for a Hollywood epic film. Much better than, for example, "The Ten Commandments," "The Robe" or "The Last Temptation of Christ!"

One big omission was the absence of any religious leadership on the Muslim side. Was Saladin the Imam as well as the "King" and "General?" What was the religious motivation and Koranic imperative that drove the Muslims to retake Jerusalem at all costs? Maybe that is asking too much for an action movie. But, seeing that the Christian side was shown to have had spiritual leadership (although generally shown to be either cowardly, corrupt, wimpy or hateful) where were their Muslim counterparts?

It seems that it is still OK to insult Christian spiritual leadership while it is politically incorrect (and possible life-threatening) to cast any aspersions on Islamic spiritual leaders....even if they lived 1000 years
ago!

There is a curious fatalism throughout the movie, on the Christian side as well as the Muslim. God is ultimately in command of history....both of nations and of individuals. All things ultimately exist to serve God's good and perfect will. Yet, as Saladin slyly demonstrates, it took good military sense and planning on Saladin's part before Allah started winning battles for the Muslims! Thus free will is also affirmed. As a Christian I found this paradoxical matter to have been handled well. The fact that it was dealt with at all is a credit to the film.

In many ways the movie seemed to focus on the enigmatic saying of Jesus, "**The Kingdom of God is within you**." The main characters pointed to the head and to the heart as the location of this Kingdom, in contradistinction from the physical city of Jerusalem which was and still serves as a symbol for that Kingdom whose day is coming.....but not yet!

As a good protestant, I have to agree with the film's thesis that forgiveness and reconciliation with God does not come through a physical pilgrimage to a sacred spot (such as Golgotha, where Sir Balian had hoped to find both God and salvation for himself and for his dead wife). Although such a pilgrimage, as an expression of faith, may help prepare a person's spirit for true repentance, it is, of course, God's saving love in Jesus Christ, received by faith as a free gift of God's mercy, that ultimately reconciles us to God.

The film, however, seems to locate redemption in the purity of one's heart. Yet no matter how pure we may try to be we will always fall short. Sir Balian not only commits murder early in the film but, even while professing to gallantly and heroically uphold the knightly virtues of honesty and purity, commits adultery as well. His willingness, later, to sacrifice his own status and desires for the sake of others, while noble and pleasing to God, cannot atone for his earlier sins. Only Jesus can do that.

Before the siege of Jerusalem, the "Bishop" sarcastically commented that making every man a "knight" does not make them a better fighter. Sir Balian disagrees, saying simply, "Yes, it does."

The medieval Christian ideal of the "purity of the heart" is well displayed in this scene and those which follow. This nobility, later satirized and glorified by Cervantes in "Don Quixote," still remains one of the lasting gifts to us from this otherwise savage and grim age.

Along with more than a few excellent films from the past two or three years ("The Passion of the Christ," "Bruce Almighty" etc.), this movie provides a wonderful opportunity for people to consider both the trivialities and profundities of faith and religious conviction as well as their impact on history, both then and now. I hope that Christian pastors will use this opportunity wisely, and not miss it by nit-picking the movie to death over historical and doctrinal *minutiae.*

FRIDAY, MAY 13, 2005

Newsweek's "Koran Desecration" Story Creates "Practical" Considerations In Kabul

In its May 6th issue, Newsweek magazine reported on a recent unconfirmed story alleging that a US soldier at Guantanamo reportedly may have possibly have flushed a Koran down a toilet....or maybe not....

In response, Muslims in Afghanistan have been rioting. At least 16 people have died in the violence and more than 100 have been injured. Angry, but peaceful, protests have also taken place in Pakistan, Indonesia and Gaza.

At least one Afghani college student has thoughtfully considered the various alternatives open to him in his quest to find the most satisfying way to express his outrage over this insult to Islam. Finally, after much soul-searching, he has announced what he considers to be the "most practical" response.

> *"Demonstrations serve no purpose, we should do something practical. I am ready to blow myself up for the sake of my religion to embrace martyrdom," said Mohammad Ghafoor, 18, a student protesting in Peshawar, Pakistan.*

Yep...when you are feeling frustrated, powerless, angry and wanting to do something practical why not just go someplace and blow yourself up? On the practical side, you will not have to deal with your feelings any more.

On the ironic side, General Meyers, Chairman of the Joint Chiefs of Staff, shed some interesting light on the situation yesterday:

> *"They have looked through the logs, the interrogation logs, and they cannot confirm yet that there was ever the case of the toilet incident," the General said. "He did note a log entry, which they still have to confirm,* ***where a detainee was reported by a guard to be ripping pages out of a Quran and putting them in a toilet to stop it up as a protest.*** *But not where the US did it."*

Let's follow the logic....Newsweek prints an unconfirmed rumor.....teenagers in Afghanistan begin killing each other and blowing themselves up .....and some holy warrior sits in his cell tearing pages out of his Koran and stuffing them down his toilet.

Is it just me, or does this sound like a wonderful plot line for a novel by Camus?

ht:lgf

SATURDAY, MAY 14, 2005

Nick Berg's Sister Speaks Her Mind

Remember **Nicholas Berg** who Zarqawi personally beheaded last year? Remember how Nick's father blamed the death of his son on President Bush" Well, now Nick Berg's sister, Sara, has written a letter to the **Philadelphia Inquirer** to express her feelings about her brother's death and the American media's response to it.

Some things are unforgivable. What Abu Musab al-Zarqawi and his many accomplices did to my brother Nick is unforgivable. It was not an act of war; it was a cold-blooded, premeditated heinous crime. To call it anything else suggests that it is an acceptable act of war, an acceptable response to America's military action. It is not.The world would be a better place if al-Zarqawi was no longer in it. He is pure evil. I don't think someone like him is capable of any human feeling anymore. The only way to keep people like him from harming thousands of other people is to eliminate them.Before this happened, I did not comprehend the magnitude of his evil and of people likehim. But to experience the heinousness of what he did to someone as good and as innocent as my brother has totally changed my perspective. I don't know how to respond in a humane way to such inhumane acts. I don't think a humane response is necessary.What the media did to my family is also unforgivable. They made the worst week of my life infinitely worse. Decision-makers in the media need to make more humane decisions about what is a story and how they get it. Someone should have thought of a shocked, astounded and grieving family when they made those decisions. They spoke of their sympathy for us, but not once did they think the sympathetic thing to do would be to stop harassing us and allow us to grieve in peace.
Sara BergVirginia Beach, Va

Thank you, Sara, for sharing your heart and mind with us. We join you in the grief that came with his violent death. We also join with you in the desire for justice and peace for Iraq....and the world. A peace that can never come until either folks like Zarqawi are removed from our midst or the Lord returns (which will bring the only true peace we will ever know!)

ht:Environmental Republican

SUNDAY, MAY 15, 2005

Newsweek to Apologize for Koran Story....Sort Of......

Newsweek is backing down on its May 9 story of investigations into a US soldier at Guantanamo Bay flushing a Qur'an down a toilet. Newsweek Editor Mark Whitaker has written an explanatory account explaining how they may have erred. Among other things he states,

Top administration officials have promised to continue looking into the charges, and so will we. But we regret that we got any part of our story wrong, and extend our sympathies to victims of the violence and to the U.S. soldiers caught in its midst.
Meanwhile, in the upcoming issue of Newsweek, assistant managing editor Evan Thomas (quoted at **Powerline**) has written an even longer and more detailed explanation of what went wrong with their reporting. Unfortunately, instead of throwing water on the firestorm of rioting, demonstrations and death in several Islamic countries, Thomas ends up by tossing gasoline instead. Using an even more unreliable source Thomas describes more unsubstantiated and unconfirmed "reports" of Koran desecration:

In the meantime, as part of his ongoing reporting on the detainee-abuse story, Isikoff had contacted a New York defense lawyer, Marc Falkoff, who is representing 13 Yemeni detainees at Guantánamo. According to Falkoff's declassified notes, a mass-suicide attempt, when 23 detainees tried to hang or strangle themselves in August 2003, was triggered by a guard's dropping a Qur'an and stomping on it. One of Falkoff's clients told him, "Another detainee tried to kill himself after the guard took his Qur'an and threw it in the toilet." A U.S. military spokesman, Army Col. Brad Blackner, dismissed the claims as unbelievable. "If you read the Al Qaeda training manual, they are trained to make allegations against the infidels," he said.
Oh, and by the way, in case he hasn't poured enough gasoline on the fire Thomas adds a few more pieces of firewood to keep it burning:

More allegations, credible or not, are sure to come. Bader Zaman Bader, a 35-year-old former editor of a fundamentalist English-language magazine in Peshawar, was released from more than two years' lockup in Guantánamo seven months ago. Arrested by Pakistani security as a suspected Qaeda militant in November 2001, he was handed over to the U.S. military and held at a tent at the Kandahar airfield. One day, Bader claims, as the inmates' latrines were being emptied, a U.S. soldier threw in a Qur'an. After the inmates screamed and protested, a U.S. commander apologized. Bader says he still has nightmares about the incident.

Such stories may spark more trouble...

Such stories ***may*** spark more trouble? How can Newsweek continue to justify the printing of such inflammatory innuendo and rumor?

When told that the anonymous "reliable" source who provided the original story has also now backed away from it, Pentagon Spokesman Lawrence DeRita exploded, "People are dead because of what this son of a bitch said. How could he be credible now?"

Shakespeare quoted **Lady Macbeth** as she looked at her hands, metaphorically stained with the blood of the murdered King Duncan, *"Out damned spot....who would have thought the old man to have had so much blood in him?....Here's the smell of the blood still: all the perfumes of Arabia will not sweeten this little hand. O, O, O!"*

Substitute "Newsweek" for "Lady Macbeth", "Muslims" for "old man" and "them" for "him" and you will get a fairly good literary description of what is taking place. **Fifteen+ dead**.....and still counting.......

Note: Captain Ed, Mudville Gazette and others have much to say about this...
Update May 16: LaShawn Barber compiles many more blogger posts

TUESDAY, MAY 17, 2005

PETA Says Researchers "Punched" Monkeys

This story on CNN claims that PETA has forwarded documentation of animal abuse at "Covance", a Princeton, New Jersey-based research company. A video bearing visual proof was also enclosed.

I don't approve of punching out monkeys. If the charges are true, Covance needs to clean up its act, pronto!

On the other hand, I have a problem about the video. Who took it? Covance employees? Why would they take a video of themselves mistreating monkeys? Are they as stupid as the Abu Ghraib reservists?

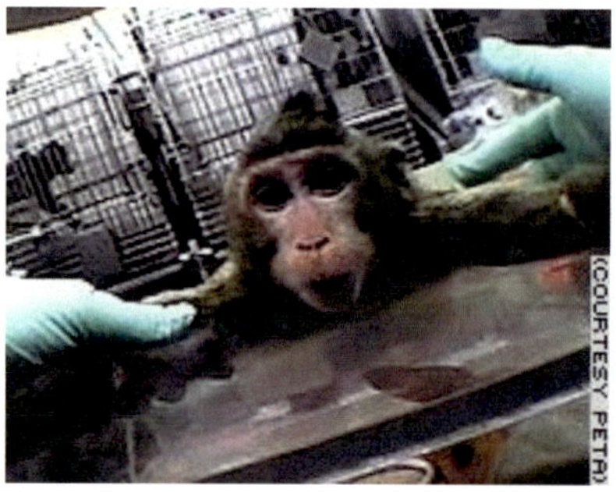

The photo in the article, supposedly taken off of the video, shows the camera right in the face of a monkey, held or tied down on a table. I don't get it. Why take a video of that? With the camera that close it is obvious that the picture was not taken serruptitiously. Everybody in the room would have known the video was there.

And, by the way, how did PETA get ahold of this damning video?

Is it possible that PETA somehow set the whole thing up? Including arranging for the monkeys to be punched out for their video?

Something doesn't seem to add up very well here. Maybe there will be a follow-up story. On the plus side, PETA has not yet burned Covance to the ground.

Accused Terrorist Luis Posada Carriles Arrested In Miami

Cuban ex-patriot Luis Posada Carriles, arrested by Federal agents near Miami today, has spent his life fighting. With the CIA he helped plan the failed Bay of Pigs invasion. He supposedly left the CIA in 1968 and went on to become a major suspect in the blowing up of a Cuban airliner in 1976 that killed 73 people and blowing up a hotel in Havana in 1998 that killed an Italian tourist.

He spent nine years in a Venezuelan jail before escaping in 1985 without ever having been convicted. Soon after, he reportedly helped the United States run arms to the anti-Sandanista rebels in Guatamala.

In 2000, during a visit to Panama, was convicted of plotting with three Cuban exiles to kill Castro and sent to jail. Later he received a presidential pardon.

More recently, Posada claims he was smuggled over the Mexican border into Texas and came by bus to South Florida where he had been seeking asylum. Both Cuba and Venezeula have demanded his extradition in connection with the 1976 airplane bombing, a charge the Posada continues to claim as untrue.

The question is, what to do with him? I say, send him back to Venezuela. If he starts talking about his US spook contacts, too bad. It is not a good thing to harbor suspected terrorists wanted in other countries, even if those countries are not our friends. Sure, some Cuban-Americans will be angry at the Bush Administration. But that could not be any worse than demonstrating our national hypocracy to the world in regards to terrorists and terrorism.

As a frightening side note, if Posada is indeed a terrorist as claimed, then shouldn't we be a little concered about how easily he crossed the Mexican border into Texas?

Countdown to Senate Filibuster Showdown

Tomorrow, Senate debate on Presidential Circuit Court Judge nominee Owens and Brown will begin. Early next week, a motion will be made to end the debate and call for a vote, yea or nay on the appointment.

If the Democrats respond with a filibuster then it will become High Noon in Tombstone. The Republicans will then have to decide whether to stand their ground and draw their guns for a final shoot-out at the Capitol Corral.

Blood, as well as guns, will be drawn and it is likely that both parties will suffer non-fatal wounds in the exchange.

My bet is on the Republicans to draw quickly and shoot straight, leaving the Democrats reeling about and shooting wildly in all directions. The ensuing melee will end quickly with the filubuster rules for Judicial nominees lying dead in the street. Both nominees will be voted into office and both parties will limp around blaming each other for the pseudo-carnage.

Once again, the Democrats will be shown to be losers. Their anger and hatred for President Bush and the Republican Congress will grow to even greater self-destructive levels than those recently reached by Senator Reid (calling Bush a "loser") and John Dean (too many quotes to choose from).

Right-wing Republicans will cheer and rejoice at the defeat of the "bad guys." More moderate Republicans, like myself, will find it hard to smile as we contemplate how painfully divided and disfunctional our Senate has become.

Such bitter and irrational division is never the best plot-line for a story with a happy ending.

This is not "good guys" vs. "bad guys." This is Americans vs. Americans; Americans who have come to a point where their differences are virtually irreconcilable with each other.

Ultimately, it will be the American voters who will sort this whole thing out. As time passes, one vision for American will ascend and the other will descend in popularity. The historically beneficial balance between our two-party system will begin to break down. Power and influence will grow disproportionately large for one party or the other. In the end, we may all be the losers.

I pray that the Democratic party will come to its senses as soon as possible. There is nothing to be gained by this High Noon showdown. Surrender graciously to the inevitiblity of the majority rule of law. Let the judicial nominees be voted on for their merits or lack of merits. If the choices are bad, the American people will notice and will be more than willing to pour out their dissatisfaction on the Republicans.

I think that what frightens the Democrats more than anything else, however, is the thought that the American people will, when all is said and done, be happy with these judges. Once again the Democrats will have reached for the gold ring and missed it. As their party continues to grow smaller and smaller, that gold ring will move further and further away.

Once in a while, nightmares do come true.

WEDNESDAY, MAY 18, 2005

NBA? Who Cares?

I like sports. I like watching good competition on TV. Most of what pretends to be good competition on TV isn't. So...when the NHL struck out last season I didn't even miss the assorted playoff games I might have watched.

Today, on the FoxNews web page, I copied off the following stories being promoted:

Amazon Deforestation Worsened in 2004
Flood Cuts Off, Cripples Alaska Town
NBA Labor Talks Collapse
Kansas Cops: Bank Robbery Suspect Shot
Another Charge for Wendy's Finger Finder
Dad Charged With Beating Softball Coach
Iran VP: We Won't Nix Nuke Program
Report: U.S. Must Change Tack in Arab World
Pregnant Student Defies Graduation Ban
Woman Claims Koran Desecration
Trump: Twin Towers Should Be Rebuilt
Cops: Boy Killed Parents, Went to Prom
Pit Bull Kills Toddler in West Virginia
Study: Champions Usually Wear Red
Fifth Grader Takes Gun From Pre-Schooler
Israel, Palestinians Trade Attacks

[Uzbek Rebel Leader Wants Islamic State](#)
[Apologetic GI Gets 6 Months for Iraq Abuse](#)
[FBI: Grenade at Bush Rally Could've Exploded](#)

Somehow, the "***NBA Labor Talks Collapse***" story looked really out of place among the other stories. That and the "Study: Champions Usually Wear Red." Does anybody really care? People killing each other, spreading hatred, carrying guns to school, criminal convictions, attempted assassination of the president....and the NBA? You've got to be kidding!

The NBA is all about big, athletic men and rich owners making lots of money.

The other stories tell of life and death.

It's good that most newspapers still keep the sports on a separate section or else they would look out of place there, too!

Sadaam & Bush--Old Fake Photos Still Phunny

In the months before the US invasion of Iraq there were lots of parodies on Sadaam Hussein. Some of ones in picture form are still floating around the internet. I ran across these today and thought they were still funny:

I like the first two best....but Dick Cheney in shorts (#4) is worth a double-take! Also, in photo #5, is it just me or does Bush look way too much like Mel Brooks?

Note: I found the first photo at Sugar and the other five at Cody Renshaw.

THURSDAY, MAY 19, 2005

Memo to Conservative Bloggers and Internet Pundits: Give Indra Nooyi a Break!

Much anger has been spewing forth from the blogosphere against PepsiCo President Indra Nooyi's speech at the Columbia Business School MBA recognition ceremony last Sunday (see Powerline here & here, Hugh Hewitt & others).

I say, give Ms. Indra a break.

First of all, she did not lie about anything.

Second, she did not lie about anything that maligned our soldiers or our military as did CNN's Eason Jordan, Newsweek's Michael Isikoff or, more recently, Linda Foley, president of the 35,000-member Newspaper Guild, who recently asserted (*a la* Eason) that U.S. troops deliberately are killing journalists in Iraq.

Third, she did not say anything that put anyone else in danger of their lives.

Fourth, she did not speak in a nation-wide venue. She spoke locally to a specific group of people at Columbia.

Fifth, she is not someone who carries a great deal of influence in American public foriegn policy (although PepsiCo's international marketing, etc., makes them a significant player in international economics and trade).

I have read the text of her speech and have come to these conclusions:

1. Her illustrative use of the five fingers on the hand was a result of a major brain malfunction. There is absolutely no way "in the world" (pun intended) that her meaning could be misconstrued.

2. On the other hand, it is my opinion that she was not so much expressing her personal opinion about the United States being the extended "middle finger" of the world as she was attempting to illustrate the way much of the world *perceives* the United States to be.

It is not a bad idea to tell graduating business students that the rest of the world does not necessarily look at us in the same way that we look at ourselves. No doubt Ms. Indra has learned this bit of *realpolitik* from first hand experience in the trenches of international trade competition.

3. She did not leave that "extended middle finger" as the closing image of her metaphor. She specifically used that it as an image to be avoided as these new graduating students begin to enter the international business community as representatives of this country. "When you extend your hand in a gesture of greeting to a foreign trader," she seemed to be saying, " be sure that you present yourself as being a member of the world community instead of as a big bully projecting your national identity with a "do it my way or the 'highway'" attitude."

Is there anyone out there in the 'sphere who would contest Ms. Indra's thesis that much of the world (rightly or wrongly) views American political and economic policies as arrogant? Is there anyone out there who would not agree with her desire for business graduate students to be sensitive to the feelings, needs and viewpoints of other nations? Is there anyone out there who does not believe that there is much needed to be done to improve our country's image around the world? Is there anyone out there who would not consider this advice to be excellent "Adam-Smith-Free-Market-based" advice that is good for both the producer and the consumer?

4. Within the tex of her speech, Ms. Indra clearly and unequivocably affirms her love of America, her apprciation of its essential goodness and the priviledge she feels in being able to live and work here.

Are all of you calling her a liar? On what grounds? Does she have a long track record of other "America-bashing" comments?

Is there not one of you who will extend to her the benefit of the doubt that maybe, just maybe, her intentions were honest and sincere? That she might have simply gotten so caught up in what she thought was a clever metaphor that she lost sight of how it could be easily perceived to mean something far different that she had meant it to mean?

5. There is no reasonable way to justify granting this incident the status of being national news. It is worthy of neither the attention nor the amount of jump-on-the-bandwagon criticism being leveled on her by the conservative new media.

The incident is local, folks. It is between Ms. Indra, those who were present when she spoke, PepsiCo and Columbia University. Not every "molehill" needs to be granted the status of "mountain." Let the parties directly involved sort the matter out themselves, with dignity and some measure of privacy. Ms. Indra has absolutely no reason to apologize to you or me, to the American puplic or, for that matter, to the world.

As I surf through the web I sense the same sort of "blood-in-the-water" mob mentality that we normally associate with such things as the Salem Witch Trials.

I am embarrassed and ashamed that we would treat this woman in this way. It is neither fair to her, to PepsiCo or to the world of international opinion who will think even less of our country as a result of this irresponsible response to her words at Columbia.

We have rightly and correctly been complaining for months and years about the "other side's" vicious, exaggerated and substance-less attacks on President Bush's judicial nominees.

Today, in light of the attacks on Indra Nooyi, I am wondering if there is really any difference between Democrats and Republicans.

Media Continues to Distort Army Detainee Abuse

Let's see how creative the news media is these days.

After a lawsuit by the ACLU under the Freedom of Information Act, the US Army was required to turn over 2,500 pages of documents. CNN News read through it all and came up with this headline today:

Army: Soldiers did mock executions
Newly released documents show Iraqi detainee abuse

Then comes the news story itself:

More than 2,500 pages of documents just released by the Army reveal instances of detainee abuse, including mock executions, by U.S. soldiers in Iraq.

The Army released the documents this week as part of a Freedom of Information Act request by the ACLU. The same request resulted in the release of several thousand pages of similar documents earlier this year.
Wow! 2,500 pages of detainee abuse! What a scandal! Really? Naw, just kidding!

Buried down in the fourth paragraph we find this previously hidden fact:

At least three soldiers were investigated and reprimanded for handling detainees outside of authorized military parameters, according to the documents.
Golly gee! Three, count 'em, three soldiers reprimanded in over 2,500 pages of documents?

Oh, excuse me, Mike Mount of the CNN Washington Bureau (whose byline heads the article) wants to make sure we do not underestimate the extent of this abuse by our servicemen in Iraq. So of course he says, "At ***least*** three soldiers..." Perhaps there were four? or 200? What's your guess? My guess is.....three! Why? Because that's what the documents tell us.

Apparently disappointed at the absence of a juicy story of any significance whatsoever, it became necessary to conjure one out of thin air.

First: The dramatic, eye-catching and damning headline.

Second: The subtitle, spelling out the story's source and expanding on the nature of the atrocities committed by the US Army.

Then comes the lead paragraph, leading the reader to imagine that the US Army has committed hundreds or even thousands of acts of "detainee abuse."

Finally comes the truth. There is virtually no story at all. Three incidents. No one died. No one was even injured. At least one incident took place after a tense and traumatic attack on a US Army vehicle when emotions were high. All incidents were reported by other soldiers. Those found guilty of violating military code of conduct were punished. End of story.

Since "three incidents" are not enough to justify a story at all, the writer's imagination ponders the fact that, although his material only mentions three incidents, there must be other incidents not recorded in these documents. Therefore, why not use that unsupported assumption to pump up the story a little by writing, "at least three incidents."

Hey, most people don't read beyond the headlines and the first two or three paragraphs of a story anyway. In any case, if they come away with a distorted impression of what actually was contained in those documents, well.......that's their problem, isn't it?

My guess is that journalism schools have added a new prerequisite to their curriculum lately: ***Obfuscation 101***.

Mike Mount must have gotten an A+.

FRIDAY, MAY 20, 2005

Dissent Among the Conservative Elite is Considered to Be SPAM

I just submitted this comment on **Huffington's Toast** which then brought up the following immediate response. Does it sound like "spam" to you?

Shame on everyone bashing Indra Nooyi. As a conservative Republican blogger (one of Hugh Hewitt's "progeny") I am embarassed by the undeserved bile being dumped on this woman. Enough is enough or, in this case, too much already! Even Hugh has "lost it" on this one. I have laid down my thoughts on this matter on a post entitled "Memo to Conservative Bloggers and Pundits: Give Indra Nooyi a Break." Please read it and prove me wrong. Sincerely, Bird of Paradise

"Sorry, but your comment has been flagged as spam by the beta version of the spam filter running on this blog: this might be an error, in which case all apologies. Your comment will be presented to the blog admin who will be able to restore it immediately."

SATURDAY, MAY 21, 2005

Cocaine Prevents Diaper Rash--Aussie Research Breakthrough!

Here's an "Ooops" for you. After five months of training in Melbourne, Australia, the team of drug sniffer dogs was supposed to have been trained to identify cocaine.

Unfortunately, when the final test was given, it was discovered that the training bag, that was supposed to have contained cocaine, was filled with talcum powder, instead.

Anyone now passing through the Melbourne Airport carrying an infant with diaper rash will not only be caught and arrested, but prosecuted to the full extent of the law.

Police are not sure whether the dogs can be retrained. They are also trying to figure out whether the bag had been mislabeled or whether someone took the cocaine and replaced it with the talcum poweder.

Ah, yes. The Whizz-ard of OZ!

Archimedes, the Crusades, Palimpsests & the Bible

The manuscript as it appears to the eye

The oldest known manuscript of Archimedes (287-212 BC) was discovered in 1906. The 10th century Greek text of a previously missing treatise had been scraped off of the vellum and over-written by a Latin devotional text 200 years afterwards. This type of over-written text is called a palimpsest and is not unusual in ancient manuscripts where quality writing materials were often scarce.

A CNN News story today explained how particle accelerator technology is being used to decipher the final 20% of the document.

A web page dedicated to this manuscript presents a historical context that is every bit as good as an Indiana Jones movie.

"THERE GOES ARCHIMEDES WITH HIS CONFOUNDED LEVER AGAIN"

It is believed that the manuscript was copied in Constantinople, which was then called Byzantium, the capital of the shrinking remnant of the Eastern Roman Empire.

In 1240, the Fourth Crusade, not strong or foolish enough to engage the vastly superior Muslim military firmly entrenched in Jerusalem and the Holy Land, turned its eyes on the Christian Orthodox bastion of Constantinople instead.

The upshot of the story is that, in defense of the city, defenders set fires that destroyed much of the city and many of the treasures it contained, including its vast library of manuscripts. After the city's fall, the crusaders pillaged the city resulting in a fire that consumed even more of the city than had the first.

Somehow, this manuscript of Archimedes survived all of that. Singe marks still mar the document but whether or not they came from that siege of Constantinople is difficult to tell.

Hagia Sophia

(Later, after being restored to the Byzantine leaders, Constantinople remained a Christian city until the **Ottomans captured it in 1453** and converted it into the Muslim capital of the Ottoman Empire. It was at this time, by the way, that the great Christian Cathedral, Hagia Sophia, was converted into a mosque.)

Meanwhile, it is believed that the manuscript found its way to the Mar Saba Monastery, located between Bethlehem and the Dead Sea, and then, eventually, to the Greek Patriarchate in Jerusalem.

Next it showed up back in Constantinople where, in 1846, its existence was first noted but its identity and value were not recognized. In 1906, it was finally identified as a copy of Archimedes' "Method of Mechanical Theorems."

It then disappeared once again only to reappear in a private collection in Paris. In 1989 it was sold to its present owner for $2 million.

Text from Gospel of John 16 dated 130 AD

Closing Note: As with so many other ancient writers, this oldest and unique Archimedes document dates nearly 1200 years after it was first written. This is also true of Plato, Aristotle and everyone else you could possibly think of. The exception to this rule is the Bible. The earliest New Testament manuscript is a papyrus fragment from the Gospel of John dated less than 100 years after the Gospel was written. Thousands of other fragments and complete New and Old Testaments are also extant from the years that immediately followed. Scholars assume that the Greek texts of Archimedes and Aristotle are essentially correct even with only one manuscript copy with over a thousand years separating it from its origin. Why, then, do so many people question the authenticity of the New Testament?

SUNDAY, MAY 22, 2005

Atheists Planning Evangelism Strategy

The following article appeared on the Honolulu Advertiser Saturday Religious Page on May 21st. I can't identify its origin but......well, I'll just let it speak for itself:

Atheists to study plan of action

Atheists are gathering in San Francisco this weekend to discuss ways to organize and make godlessness more palatable to others. It's the first "All Atheist Weekend," a gathering of five San FranciscoBay Area chapters of nonbelievers.

We feel very threatened by what's goiong on in this country, but we realize that we can't just sit here in a corner by oursleves," san Jim Heldberg of San Francisco Atheists. "If we do, the religious right is just going to run us over."

Several studies have shown that a growing number of people don't consider themselves affiliated with any religion. But the number joining atheist groups hasn't increased much over the years.

Yep. They've finally caught on to the the religious right's sinister secret strategy: "To run over the atheists."

Actually, the Bible already has something to say about all of this in Psalm 14:1.

"The fool says in his heart, 'There is no god.'"

Newsweek Magazine Dumps America In the Trash

Newsweek, already in hot water for publishing, retracting and the apologizing for an unconfirmed report that a Koran had been flushed down a toilet by an American soldier at Guantanamo Bay, is in more hot water than previously thought.

A sharp-eyed expatriate American blogger overseas (Riding Sun)has passed on this copy of the Japan edition Newsweek for February 2nd:

The headine reads, "The day America died." As you can see, the American flag in soiled and tossed into a trash can with the staff broken. What a shameful thing for an American-owned magazine to do! Disgusting, in fact. If the American edition published a cover picture with the Japanese flag depicted in the same manner do you think that the Japanese press would take notice and object....just a little?

Little Green Footballs, Instapundit, Captain's Quarters and Lileks (who is having trouble actually believing such a thing is true) have all caught on to this new development.

I do believe that Newsweek's Editor, Fareed Zakaria, is going to be taking a lot of flack from the blogosphere in the coming days. What a shame that the MSM will hide their eyes from the entire fiasco.

It is one thing to see Palestinian militants and Al Qaeda-type terrorist groups burning the American flag or having people walk on it (as al-Sadr had his followers do last week), but to see "mainstream" American publishers doing the exact same equivalent thing on the cover of their magazines is outrageous.

I'm almost tempted to suggest that Mr. Zakaria be required to have an American flag tatooed onto his forehead as a punishment. If America is in the garbage can then I am too. And Mr. Zakaria should be given priority accommodations somewhere down in the bottom of the can along with his magazine.

MONDAY, MAY 23, 2005

Bear In Heat Cools Off In Swimming Pool

When a 140 pound black bear wandered into her sububan San Fernando Valley back yard, Maryam Salahael grabbed her children from the swimming pool and raced into the house to call for help.

The bear eventually took a short dip in the pool (see story here) before California Fish & Game officers arrived. After tranquilizing the bear they took her into the Santa Susanna Mountains where she was released.

Officer Cindy Wood is quoted as saying, "It looks like it's possibly in heat. She probably just made a wrong turn and ended up in a neighborhood."

Gee, you'd think it would be the ***male*** bear who wouldn't think to stop to ask for directions!

Senate Filibuster Deal Will Be a Test of Integrity

Today's Senate deal, hatched by enough Republicans and Democrats to preclude a Republican majority to reject it, has put the pressure on both parties to deliver on what the deal commits them to do.

The Dems will have to allow an up or down vote on Federal Circuit Court nominees Owens, Brown and Pryor. Nominess considered after their vote can be filibustered for "good cause."

Republicans, on the other hand, agree that they will not vote to rescind the filibuster rule for judicial nominees unless the Democrats act in "bad faith."

The Plus Side: The Democrats save face and the Republicans don't have to vote in a rules change that could come back to haunt them should they ever lose the Senate majority.

Also, should both parties toe the line on the deal, virtually every nominee will eventually be voted on by the whole Senate. Apparently the filibuster will be considered "in order" when objecting to moral or ethical concerns about a nominee's character but not for objections over their idiology or judicial philosophy.

The Negative Side: Seven Republican Senators, acting independently from their party leadership, cut a deal that effectively sold out their party's majority to the Democrats on this issue. This action, in my opinion, ends Bill Frist's role as the Senate majority leader. He should be asked to step down and be replaced by one of the 48 Republican Senators who did not sign on to today's agreement.

The seven Republicans who compromised are: Lincoln Chafee (Rhode Island), Susan Collins (Maine), Mike DeWine (Ohio), Lindsey Graham (South Carolina), John McCain (Arizona), John Warner (Virginia) & Olympia Snowe (Maine).

The MSM is already heralding these Republican dissidents as if they had somehow saved democracy and the Constitution from the power-crazed idiologues in their own party. This alone should make most conservatives worry.

Republican John McCain and Democrat Robert Byrd lead the cheerleading when the deal was announced. It seemed as if these two men could not stop saying enough nice things about each other.

Byrd: "We have lifted ourselves above politics, and we have signed this document in the interests of the United States Senate, in the interest of freedom of speech, freedom of debate and freedom to dissent in the United States Senate....Thank God for this moment and for these colleagues of mine."

McCain applauded Warner and Byrd for bringing both sides together to forge an agreement based on Senate principles: "trust, respect and a mutual desire to see the institution of the Senate function in ways that protect the rights of the minority."

Those Republican Party volunteers who worked so hard to acheive a Senate majority will most certainly be disappointed, if not appalled, at this turn of events.

Personally, the hug-fest between McCain, Byrd and Warner gives me the creeps. I do not trust Senator Byrd to say anything honest ever and I wonder what sort of mutual backscratching has been going on behind the scenes. We can expect to see some very significant pork coming home to roost in Arizona and South Carolina in the coming months. I also doubt very much whether there will be any military base closings in the states represented by these seven Senators from each party (think Snowe....think Maine). I suspect we have had more than one deal cut today.

The unity and effective control of the US Senate by the Republican party has been sold out for a "mess of pottage." Having tasted blood in the water I do not believe for minute that Dem Senators like Kennedy, Reid and Kerry are going to feel any reason to play by rules set up by others.

When the time comes for them to come in for the kill they will do so. And they will face a splintered and leaderless Republican party when they do.

Just wait for the first US Supreme Court nominee!

(As always, I hope I am wrong).

Update: Having written my comments first I am in the ego-inflating position to say that Captain Ed (see his final two paragraphs and compare) agrees with me!

TUESDAY, MAY 24, 2005

In Zimbabwe Successful Black Farmer Feels Threatened

Apparently in Zimbabwe these days, being white farmer means you have to turn over your land, even if your family has owned the home and property since 1921.

But being a black farmer doesn't make you immune from suspicion and threats, either. Especially when you are good at it.

Just ask "Lewis," the focus of a **BBC News** article today.

Although he loans his tractor to his neighbors, sometimes plows their fields and spends time trying to teach them the practical and economic principles of farming, Lewis thinks some of his neighbours want to bring him down.

"It's just pure jealousy," he sighs. "They see what I have on the farm and wonder why I have it and they don't."

Grant Ferriett, who wrote the article, comments,

> *When I first interviewed him more than five years ago, (we sat on the veranda of his large farmhouse as) he explained how he hoped to set an example for other would-be farmers.*
>
> *This time he preferred to meet in the anonymity of a parked car in the suburbs of Harare.*

A few displaced white farmers remain in Zimbabwe hoping to recoup their losses in other entrepenural business activities. Many more have opted to immigrate elsewhere.

One family, a former neighbor of Lewis now living in Australia, had this to say about their decision to leave Zimbabwe,

> *"When you see what we've got here and the friends we've made, there's no way I'd go back to that nonsense in Zimbabwe," says Rob.*
>
> *His wife, Anna, agrees.*
>
> *"It was just the uncertainty of not knowing what was going to happen next. Here the biggest worry is whether the washing will be dry."*

And that, my friends, is how to destroy a nation and its economy in one easy lesson.

What's the Big Deal About Embryonic Stem Cells?

With the House of Representatives passing legislation authorizing Federal money for embryonic stem cell research the Senate and then the President will have some tough decisions to make. If the final bill gets to the President in its present form he will veto it. If there are enough votes to overrule the veto it will become law.

Why is this such a big deal? Two issues are at work.

First: A moral issue. Many Americans find the idea of creating human embryonic life and then destroying it for medical research to be ethically untenable. The idea of killing innocent life to possibly save another's life is simply not acceptable. President Bush argues that he does not believe that it is appropriate for the Federal government to take people's money to fund research programs that a large number of citizens believe to be immoral.

It is worth noting that Bush does not believe in enforcing any ban on private industry to either fund or participate in such research. At least not with existing embryonic cell lines.

Since the vast majority of Americans who have such moral objections are also political supporters of President Bush, his decision is not only based on a reasonable respect for moral diversity but on political reality as well. It would be, however, both cynical and unfair to claim that the political issues form Bush's primary motivation on this matter. It appears that he personally considers himself to be one of those who has moral and ethical reservations on such research and development.

His opponents, however, neither believe such research to be morally or ethically wrong nor support Bush politically. It is to their political advantage to defeat him on this issue. Morally, however, I believe that their argument comes up short.

While Bush does not believe that people should be forced to pay taxes in support of unnecessary programs that they believe to be morally objectionable, those on the other side believe that they should. Which side is more tolerant of diversity? Which side imposes its will on those who disagree and makes them pay for it with their own money?

I believe that President Bush's position represents a more defensible moral position than those who argue against him. I also believe that Bush's position represents a greater toleration and respect for diversity of opinion. Point #1 goes to Bush.

Second: Economics. If there is so much potential for amazing medical breakthroughs in human embryonic stem cell research then one would think that private investors would be standing in line to funnel capital funds to support such research. If it's such a sure thing then there ought to be real incentive for folks to try and make a lot of money out of it.

Why, then, is there such a need for the Federal government to subsidize this research? Can't researchers "sell their product" to the capital market on the basis of its own merits? Why aren't people like John Kerry or Teddy Kennedy shoving wheelbarrows of investment capital into the research if they think it is so promising and important?

My guess is because they, and many, many other investors, do not believe that it is going to ever make them any richer than they already are. In short, they want the research to be paid for out of the taxpayer's pockets. That way, if it turns out well, then they will take the credit for its success and the research companies will not have to repay any of their profits to those who provided the capital...ie. you and me.

If people are unwilling or unable to be motivated by either altruism or greed to support something, it makes no sense for the Federal government to step in and force them to support it. This should be left up to the private sector to sort out.

California passed an initiative to spend many millions of its tax dollars for this sort of research. I think that this decision was certainly foolish from an economic standpoint and, also, probably far inside the gray areas of being unconstitutional. But at least the people spoke their mind and their will....imposing the majority's desires onto the dissenting minority.

I think that Bush wins the economic argument on this matter also. If people smell success in research there will be no end of people willing to invest their money into it. The demand for the Federal government to foot the bill strikes me as evidence that the research smells like a loser and that the battle in the Congress is far more about political power than it is about medical research.

At least that's how **I** see it!

WEDNESDAY, MAY 25, 2005

UN Troops Leave a Legacy of Bastards In Liberia

I use the word "bastard" hesitantly. It is not a politically correct term these days. But the shocking legacy of sexual misbehavior by UN troops (particularly in Africa) requires a shocking vocabulary to describe it. Ironically this (mis)behavior gives a new meaning to the UNICEF symbol .

Recent revelations of UN misbehavior in Congo forced UN Secretary General Kofi Anan to declare a "zero tolerance" policy on such matters (as if this was a new and surprising bit of news). The reality is damning to the UN. Consider this excerpt from a recent story in the Economist concerning a unique school in Liberia:

THE UNECO children's centre looks like any other Liberian school. Its pupils wear smartish uniforms and are eager, after 14 years of civil war and not much schooling, to learn. What is unusual is that every child at UNECO has been fathered by a foreign peacekeeper and then abandoned. The centre was founded by Dr Abraham Cole, a local teacher, "to show our gratitude to peacekeepers by taking care of their children."

Despite its name, the school receives no UN support besides food from the World Food Programme. Most of the 136 children at UNECO and a similar centre further north were conceived during the 1990s, when both the UN and Liberia's West African neighbours sent troops to Liberia. The number of abandoned babies is now set to surge, however. For the past 18 months, Liberia has hosted one of the largest and most successful UN peacekeeping missions, whose 15,000 blue helmets have now been around long enough to make more babies. A UN staffer said he expected 1,500 UN babies by the end of next year.
Two phrases from these two paragraphs stand out for me:

First: That this school was built "*to show our gratitude to peacekeepers by taking care of their children.*" Huh? Thank you for preserving the peace while you raped, seduced and impregnated our young women and then abandoned them and your own children when you returned home to your "real" families?"

How come UN troops are honored for such behavior? If American troops commited such things they would be reviled by the world....and rightly so. And for Mr. Anan to act as though this was a "new thing?" Shameful! What does this say about the moral standards of the nations providing troops for the UN peacekeeping missions? Why in the world would we want American troops serving under the UN to be placed under the command of military leaders from such nations? Bah, humbug! Call me a Scrooge!

Second: "*Despite its name, the school receives no UN support besides food from the World Food Programme.*" When I was in Jr High I first heard the phrase, "Slam. Bam. Thank you ma'am" and a related phrase, "Hit and run." I had no idea at the time that these phrases were describing the behavior of UN troops around the world!

I'm reminded of the man who came to rid a house of mice. After totally destroying the home he stood in the middle of the rubble holding two mice by their tails. To the homeowner he said, "There, I'm done. That will be $200 please."

Can't you just feel the love?

Denmark Tries to Tax Sperm Donors

According to BBC News, the Danish government, always seeking new sources of revenue, wants to begin taxing sperm donors. The nation's main sperm bank has countered by saying that being required to release the names of donors so they can be taxed would force them to close their doors.

In a letter to Taxation Minister Kristian Jensen, the compan defended the donors' right not to pay tax, saying: "It is a special kind of work and the fees paid cannot be compared to normal working income."

I can see the job resumes... Previous employment: "Sperm donor." I wonder what that work experience qualifies someone for? If the sperm bank shut down would that make the donors eligible for unemployment benefits?

Best of all is the BBC News' teaser line for this article: "Sperm bank fears donors may dry up under new Danish tax." You've gotta love those Brits!

THURSDAY, MAY 26, 2005

Senate Democrats Thumb Their Noses at John Bolton and Taunt Their Republican Colleagues

Back when I was in elementary school I remember the mean kids sneering at the smaller kids and mocking them with the infamous thumbs-in-the-ear, the finger wiggle and a "nya-na-na-na-na--na!"

I was reminded of that behavior today when the the Senate Democrats filibustered the Republican's attempt to present UN Ambassador nominee John Bolton for an Up or Down confirmation vote.

"Ha, ha, ha!" they seemed to be saying. "We dare you to use the "nuclear option" for an Ambassadorial nomination!"

Senator Majority Leader Bill Frist, who proved earlier in the week that he has lost control of his party membership proved once again that he does not have "the right stuff" to do the job.

It was Frist who insisted on presenting Bolton for confirmation before presenting Circuit Court nominees Janice Brown and William Pryor, who were already guaranteed a final vote by the infamous compromise by the "fallen fourteen."

Now he may have to wait out the Bolton filibuster until the upcoming Senate recess, thereby missing the chance to get the Circuit Court nominees off of the "on-deck circle" where they have been squatting for the past several years.

I keep on telling myself that "he must have plan....he's got to have a plan....he can't be this incompetent....can he?" Well....it's looking more and more each day like he is disintegrating into "Bozo-hood" before our very eyes.

How long can the Republican majority allow the punk kid Democrats to kick sand in their faces? A bully will remain a bully until someone bigger and stronger smacks him down and puts him in his place. I'm not suggesting violence, of course, but if the Republicans do not feel that they are strong enough to call the opposition's bluff, then they do not deserve to be the majority at all.

It now appears that the Democrats set out the compromise over Circuit Court nominees (allowing three to get through but making no further promises for the next two nor regarding any upcoming Supreme Court nominations) with the full intention of flaunting and abusing the filibuster rule on all other non-judicial appointments.

And Frist and the Republicans stand around as if they are "Shocked! Shocked!" by all of this! Those who should be in command of the situation look like a bunch of amateurs.

When are they going to publically declare the Senate Democrats to be "obstructionist?" When are they going to begin to leverage negative publicity against the Democrats for their outrageous and unprecidented behavior?

I've been waiting for five months to see what plan the Republicans have concocted. After the events of the past week I am becoming convinced that there is no plan....only indecision and confusion.

When I take our dog for a walk she likes to stop at nearly every tree to either sniff or to pee. Senate Republicans are looking a lot like trees lately.

FRIDAY, MAY 27, 2005

Tom Delay Writes a Nice Letter to NBC

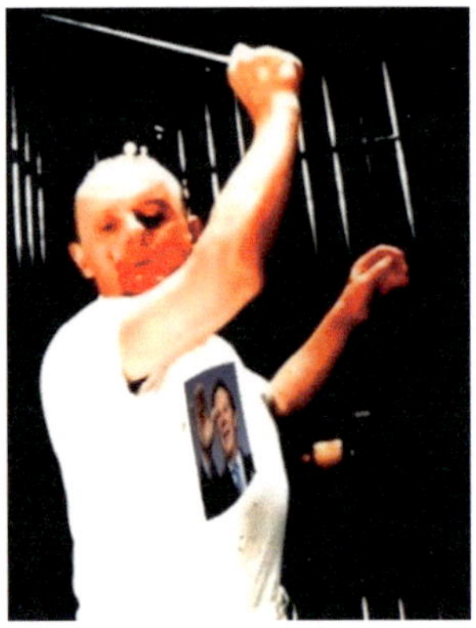

After being told that last night's episode of NBC "Law & Order: Criminal Intent" contained a less than flattering reference to his name, House Speaker Tom Delay sat down and wrote a restrained but substantive and biting letter to the broadcast network.

What Delay objected to was this line of dialogue, in the context of searching for a murderer of a Federal judge:
"Put out an APB for somebody in a Tom DeLay t-shirt."

You can read Delay's letter here.

Saudi King Fahd Is "Well"...Unless, Of Course, He's "Dead." So's Zarqawi...and Elvis, too!

CNN tells me that King Fahd is "well" (thank you very much).

The Washington Times tells me that King Fahd is "dead" (thank you very much).

I suppose they could both be correct but I'm not exactly sure how....

CNN tells me that Zarqawi is "well" (thank you very much).

An Italian news site tells me that Zarqawi is "possibly dead" (thank you very much).

I suppose that he could possibly be one or the other but possibly not both.....

I suppose that Elvis Presley could be "possibly dead," too. But then again, he could possibly be "well."

Might it be possible that Elvis Presley, King Fahd and Zarqawi are all the same person? Hmmmm........it's possible........there is a bit of a resemblance.......

SATURDAY, MAY 28, 2005

LA Times' Tom Rutten's Boilerplate Baloney

I know the difference between sitting down and writing off the top of my head (as I am doing now) and taking time to carefully outline, research and document my thoughts. Tom Rutten's *LA Times* piece today entitled, "Newsweek erred. So has U.S.," strikes me as a prime example of the former.

The first several paragraphs set up the idea of the "fog of war" and how human beings are differentiated from other animals in being able to make "rational distinctions" between....well, he never really says what we are able to make rational distinctions between!

In any case, "*sane societies are prudent about the demands they place on their young men and women under arms and set them bright lines of conduct to follow when such demands are made.*"

He proceeds to opine that the critical reaction to ***Newsweek***'s mis-reporting of the Koran-in-the-toilet urban legend as fact, was "*mostly nonsensical* ." As evidence he states:

> *According to a U.S. military inquiry undertaken in response to the* ***Newsweek*** *item, five of 13 alleged incidents in which the Koran was somehow abused by guards or interrogators at Guantanamo turned out to be true. "No credible evidence" was found that an Islamic holy book was flushed down a toilet, which one supposes should be some sort of comfort. The military's investigation, however, is incomplete, and who knows what yet may emerge from this Cuban cesspool.*

What a mess of obfuscation. First, he credits Newsweek for forcing the military to initiate an investigation. Nonesense. The docmentation was presexisting and massive; over 10,000 pages of it. Nothing in all of that data had ever raised a red flag for anyone responsible for oversight at Guantanamo. Why? Because there wasn't any! What the military did in response to the Newsweek article was to "re-re-review" what had already been reviewed many times up the chain of command.

Second, by implying that finding "five" incidents of Koran abuse somehow exhonerates Newsweek, Rutten fails to mention that the five incidents include such horrific acts as twice placing (a) Koran(s) on top of a TV set (what are the Guantanamo prisoners doing with TV sets, anyway?), and the accidental, incidental touching of a Koran by a female guard. Wow! (Rutten's biography mentions that he is the father of two children. I wonder if the equivilent of such flagrant, insensitive and intolerant behavior by his children would be subject to public outrage and international review?)

Third, his objective credibility is flushed down the toilet when he refers to Guantanamo as a "Cuban cesspool." I'm sure that he could explain what this means, but why bother when everyone already knows, right? (wink wink).

His next paragraph rightly places the blame for the international Muslim response to the Newsweek story on the Imams and radical Islamists who "*do not require provocation to violence or hatred of the United States*."

Unfortunately he then blames the resulting deaths on American-supported "government troops" although not one such death has ever been documented, not one name of those supposedly killed has been uncovered and not one description of how, when, where or by whom those deaths occured has been published. Until such specific evidence arises, Rutten has once again fearlessly dipped into the pool of urban legend (which, by the way, I did also at first.....but at least I keep up with the news and have learned better by now. Why hasn't Rutten?).

Now comes the zinger: "*The problem here is not desecration of the Koran, but of our own fundamental values.*" According to Ruttn, the desecration of our American values are exemplified by the following:

Ever since the invasion of Afghanistan, the Bush administration has been running a secret prison system in which people are tortured — some to death — and fundamental legal and human rights are ignored with impunity. That is true in Guantanamo, as it was true in Abu Ghraib in Iraq and Bagram in Afghanistan. It may be true in other places, as well, but we don't know that. We may never know that.

As with most propaganda-style journalism he begins with a true statement but then follows it up with a lie. The truth is that we *do* have a semi-secret prison system (although international observers have been permitted to visit, observe conditions and comment, and that the existance, location, purpose and command structure of these facilities are public record, as well as tens of thousands of records released as a result of legal action by the media and human rights groups).

It is also true that there have been beatings and one or more deaths (as a result of either beatings or of natural causes) at both Bagram and Abu Ghraib. Rutten's implication that there have been beating deaths at Guantanamo is a blatent misrepresentation of reality, of course....otherwise known as a lie.

The BIG lie is, of course, where he states so blithely that detainees' "*fundamental legal and human rights are ignored with impunity*." There is not one shred of evidence to support this accusation.

In every case, it has been members of the military that reported the abuses, it has been the military that has brought charges against those who acted improperly and it has been the military that has discharged, demoted, court-martialed and imprisoned those who have been found guilty. In not one single case has anyone associated with the media uncovered any incident of abuse that had not already been identified and was under investigation by the military. Even the Abu Ghraib abuse photos were released to the press by the military, which had possessed them for months (with public acknowledgement, by the way....secrecy? The press didn't care until they had photos!) while agressively investigating and prosecuting the case.

After rightfully chastising Amnesty International for inappropriately referring to these prisons as a "gulag," he shows, at least, that Americans are looking into these charges. But, with another lie, he blasts the investigations as being "tentative" and "hesitant" and the prosecutions as being "circumscribed."

Every piece of evidence suggests exactly the opposite of this. The military has pursued these investigations "aggressively" and "assertively." As for prosecutions, they have indeed been "circumspect" (as well they should be, since one definition of the word is to be "*Heedful of circumstances and potential consequences; prudent*."). But they have also been blunt and honest, even to the point of disciplining high ranking officers who were, by any stretch of the imagination, neither aware of the abuse nor consenting to it (see what happened to Brig. General Janis Karpinski for an example of this).

He then proceeds to present "two appalling failures," the first of which is....
....this administration's decision to subject our troops to a temptation no military force ever should be asked to withstand. Holding prisoners in secret — beyond law, without representation, without oversight — then demanding that they extract information from them, no matter the method, is something no American in arms should be asked to do. Making that demand is a betrayal of the young men and women who have embraced the duty of national service.

First of all, as suspected terrorists, fighting out of uniform and representing no legitimate government, those detainees who are not in possession of US citizenship are not subject to the rule of American or international law nor do they fall under the intentionally limited perameters of the Geneva Conventions for prisoners of war. Aside from their "right to life" they have no other rights. US courts have upheld this interpretation of the law for over a hundred years and US troops have been responsible for overseeing such detainees since the Revolutionary War.

Then comes the next lie: Accusing the Bush Administration of ordering that the US military "*extract information from them, no matter the method...*" While it is true that the life-or-death need for intel has resulted in extremely agressive interrogation techniques there is no evidence whatsoever that anyone at any level of military or civilian authority (including the CIA) has ever commanded US troops to "extract information from (*detainees*), no matter the method."

Virtually all incidences of prisoner abuse have been shown to be the result of individual misconduct in defiance of explicit orders and training to the contrary; over-zealousness as a result of intense emotion and anger generated by the stress of combat; or simply the lack of proper supervision and oversight by those in command.

To then aver that the Bush Administration has "(*betrayed*) *the young men and women who have embraced the duty of national service*" is to render judgement based on the premise of what is either a deliberately conceived lie or a lie that has proceeded out of ignorance or a predisposed bias.

According to Rutten, the second of the "appalling failures" "*...is that of the mainstream press, which has failed to keep this moral abyss directly and constantly under the public eye.*"

From where I stand, this is a curious "failure" indeed, seeing how the press has published, republished, editorialized and sensationalized every hint of detainee abuse whether real or imagined since the US invaded Afghanistan back in 2001. Recently, information made public over two years ago, was printed on the front page of the New York Times as though it was "new" news!

The failure of the press has not been their lack of coverage of the detention of suspected terrorists by the United States, but the lack of balance in their coverage.

We do not need to look any further than Tom Rutten and the LA Times for evidence in support of that conclusion.

First-Hand Update from Iraq

This past week I had another long personal visit with a soldier-friend recently returned from a 14-month deployment to Iraq. I value these conversations since they put me "on-site" (so to speak) and serve to validate or correct my perceptions and inform my understanding.

In this case, the soldier (an officer) was involved with intel gathering in the north-east corner of Iraq; essentially from Kirkuk and points east.

The area is primarily controlled by Kurds and my friend found that the Kurds were very supportive and grateful for the American presence in their country. They were also helpful in providing information about "suspicious" activities, details about conflicts and disputes between neighboring clan groups (and their often centuries-old origins), Iranian border traffic, etc.

The region under this command was also, apparently, a prime area for filling cars with explosives. Many such cars were captured or intercepted during the past year.

Kirkuk is populated by approximately 1/3 Kurds, 1/3 Sunni and 1/3 Shi'ite. Sadaam had initiated a severe Kurdish relocation program decades ago, forcing Kurds out of north-central Iraq towards Mosul and beyond. After the American Coalition invasion of Iraq many displaced Kurds have returned to cities like Kirkuk waving their property deeds and demanding their homes and land back. The Sunnis who replaced them have now lived and been settled there for a long time; some over 20 years. They are in no mood to be kicked off of what they consider to be their *own* property! After all, they have legal deeds, too!

Slowly but surely these disputes are being remanded to Iraqi judges to sort out. Because of the confusion of new laws and because of personal (often clan-related) bias among judges, many Iraqis would prefer to have the Americans adjudicate their disputes. It is clear that, although the United States is viewed as a foreign occupier, only the most radical of Iraqis really want the Americans to leave anytime soon.

Another interesting insight was offered concerning targeting suspected houses for armed searches. When the American troops did it the result was that often, an otherwise politically neutral family would be angered enough by the intrusion to begin leaning towards an anti-American view. House searching has now been turned over to the Iraqi security forces which has made life and community relations a lot better for our troops

Apparently the different branches of the military bring their own particular approaches to similar responsibilities. My friend said that there were four deaths among the forces that were within the area command structure (one of the more "safe" regions to be assigned to) during the 14 months of deployment. The Army's approach was to avoid conflict and build relationships, turning opinion positively towards both the United States and the new Iraqi government. The theory of this approach was that the cultivation of willing informants and the promotion of a general tide of positive opinion would, in the long run, eventually weed out those who were doing nasty things to other people.

When the Marines replaced an Army unit that had seen zero deaths over the previous 12 months, however, the new group suffered four deaths in their first two months. My friend didn't speculate on what the different approach might have been or why the Marines had experienced more armed confrontation than the Army troops had seen, but it was still a curious fact that was simply left dangling, unexplained.

My friend matter-of-factly stated that the Kurds did not seem to have any problem working with American female intel officers. Gender did not seem to be an issue with them. The Arabs were more cautious and hesitant but, after meeting and speaking with the women, became quite comfortable and trusting in their leadership during the months my friend was there. This odd bit of information was one of the more interesting and unexpected facts to emerge from our conversation.

Towards the end of our time together I asked my friend, based on a scale of one to ten (with ten being optimistic about the future of Iraq and one being pessimistic), what they would score, based on their personal experience.

I expected to hear something in the range of 7-8 but I was caught completely by surprise when my friend replied with an emphatic, "10!"

How this opinion squares with all of the doom and gloom media coverage I cannot figure out. Either my friend or the media is wrong....or else the truth lies somewhere in between.

I think I shall place my bets on my friend and become even more optimistic than I already am!

Given the size, diversity, history, and general political track record of Iraq in the past 30 years, the amount of violence and the number of Iraqis (& foreigners) perpetuating the current violence is remarkably small. Even the 1600 American troops killed in Iraq adds up to a relatively small number when compared to the number of folks who, for example, attend a single major league baseball game or a college football game. At Aloha Stadium, down the road a bit towards Honolulu, 1600 people would be considered a big disappointment for anything but a high school soccer game! While I do not wish to appear to diminish the sacrifice of these fine, brave soldiers (or the effect their deaths have had on their 3000 children), I simply want to assert the point that the "war in Iraq," while diverse, complex and difficult to fight against an enemy that wears civilian clothes, drives civilian cars, stores their arms in mosques and schools and initiates attacks from medical facilities and from radio-controlled remote explosive devices and employs suicide bombers, has already been won.

The rest of this "war," which will undoubtedly continue to involve (a declining number of) US troops for another 5-10 years, will be an ongoing game of "search and destroy," the tightening up of the national borders and the ironing out of potentially explosive relations with Syria (which continues to support the funding, training, harboring and deployment of Baathist-related terrorists/insurgents....don't forget that Syria's ruling political party, led by Assad, is also the same secular Baathist party that Sadaam Hussein espoused) and Iran (which continues to fund, support and advise al-Sadr and his Shi'ite gang of hoods and ruffians as well as trying to assist in creating and expanding rifts between Shi'ites and Sunnis in an attempt to destabilize the new Iraqi government).

Next week I will spend an hour or so each with two Army officer-friends and one Army enlisted-friend who have just returned from their 12-month deployment to Afghanistan. I will post summaries of those conversations, too.

Hiawatha Bray Calls Linda Foley's Bluff

Hiawatha Bray at Choose Honor has become the first member of the Newspaper Guild to publically challenge the Guild union President, Linda Foley, concerning recent comments accusing the US deliberately killing journalists.

Foley's comments, during a speech in St. Louis on May 13, were recorded on video (find video here at Jackson's Junction). The key paragraph in her speech has been transcribed as follows: *Journalists, by the way, are not just being targeted verbally or ... ah, or ... ah, politically. They are also being targeted for real, um ... in places like Iraq. What outrages me as a representative of journalists is that there's not more outrage about the number, and the brutality, and the cavalier nature of the U.S. military toward the killing of journalists in Iraq.* Her comments echo those of former CNN News Chief Eason Jordan who resigned last February after his accusations against the US military were challenged. Although Eason refused to allow a video of his comments to be released he did not offer any retraction, either.

Curiously, Foley's comments have received very little publicity in the MSM (the one exception being Thomas Lipscomb at the Chicago Sun-Times including a follow-up article here) although conservative bloggers, including Captain Ed, have been trying to get some traction on the matter. World Net Daily has covered the story as well but, until Hiawatha Bray gave his challenge today, Newspaper Guild members have been eerily silent.

"Prophet Yahweh" Prays Up a UFO for ABC Network Affiliate In Las Vegas

Prophet Yahweh, also known as Ramon Watkins, has been dealing with UFO's for years. He can even make them appear at will, at least that is what he claims. To back up his boasting, the Prophet contacted ABC affiliate KTLV in Las Vegas and told them that he would be glad to meet them at a time and place of their choosing.

So this morning, off went the camera and reporter, feeling a little bit foolish. But Mr. Yahweh read the Old Testament and prayed to God for the UFO to appear and.....apparently it did! Or something appeared.....and was captured on film. View the news coverage of the event **here** where it is linked by World Net Daily. And enjoy the obviously flustered news reporter when he realizes that his light-hearted outing has suddenly become exceedingly mysterious and confusing.

What does this all mean? I have no idea. But Prophet Yahweh predicts that there will be many more sightings in Las Vegas in the coming week, including one UFO that will descend low enough for everyone in Vegas to see it.

Only one thing is certain, of course....and that would be that the casinos are already taking odds on the prediction!

SUNDAY, MAY 29, 2005

Military Appreciation Sunday at Church

This morning's worship service was ordered on the theme of Military Appreciation. This was actually suggested and scheduled nearly a year ago when we realized that most of our deployed church members would have returned from their 12-month tours of Iran and Afghanistan by this Memorial Day weekend.

All active military were invited to wear their uniforms (which they rarely if ever wear to church events). Army, Air Force and Navy personnel were present as well as a mix of officers and enlisted.

During the service Worship Team Elder Wagnus invited all in active military service to stand and introduce themselves by name, by rank and by unit. Then the same was done with those who were no longer in active service.

Special cards with star stickers on them were available for folks to write down the names of family members or friends who had died while in in active service or following retirement. These were placed in the offering and later solemnly read by two uniformed church members. I included my late uncle, Jonathan "Jack", who passed away four or five years ago. Jack had served 3 tours of duty as a bomber pilot based in England during WWII. His survival, never having been shot down, is nothing short of miraculous. Towards the end of his service he flew General Eisenhower into France following the Normandy invasion and was subsequently asked by the General to serve as his personal pilot. My uncle, by that time, had seen enough. He turned down the offer and returned home.

Many of those whose names were read this morning undoubtedly had their own amazing stories to tell. Veterans of WWII, Korea, Vietnam, Desert Storm and Iraqi Freedom were all present today. But no stories were told. Not even that of my Uncle Jack. Soldiers introduced themselves and the names of those who have died were read.

From my experience with these men and women, this is how they like it. I have never met a soldier, either officer or enlisted, who wanted the spotlight to be on them, personally. Their stories are always inseperable from the stories of the rest of the men and women in their unit. In private conversation, perhaps especially with me as a friend and pastor, they will share personal and intimate stories.....some of which they have not even told their spouses or families.

Military service promotes an ironic mixture of personal confidence and personal humility that I wish could be easily transferred into the civilian population where far too many people exhibit arrogance and pride in order to hide their inherent lack of confidence in themselves or with the substance of their lives.

Sgt. Ron Wyatt, an Elder on our church Session, member of our Worship Ministry Team and recently returned from 12 months in Mosul, Iraq, gave a personal faith testimony. For Ron, his deployment was dreary, frightening and less than inspiring. He shared how he dealt with strong emotions of anger and hate towards both those murdering and killing and, at times, towards the Iraqi people themselves as a whole. Prayer, the reading of Christian books and the love and support of his church family here in Mililani helped him keep his Christian faith intact. His faith challenged his strong negative emotions and he became, over time, more at peace with turning things like his wife and children to the care of the Lord. Ron is the only member of my congregation to return from deployment with the opinion that things there are worse than that depicted in our American news coverage! He knows he is in a minority but he also feels comfortable speaking for himself and what he experienced. It says a lot for this church that people like Ron are able to be genuine and open without worrying what others will think or how they might respond.

This is part of what the Body of Christ is all about. Accepting, forgiving and loving one another for what we are.....with the common goal of following Jesus Christ as Lord and Savior together as family and friends.

Elder Laura also spoke, sharing her experience of coordinating our "care package" ministry during the past 1 1/2 years. She shared scripture from Proverbs and Psalms that she had included in each mailing; words of encouragement and trust in God.

The service was so full and complete with good things that the time was up before the scripture lessons were read and the sermon message preached. So I simply wrapped things up and said that I would deliver my sermon next Sunday and gave the Benediction.

Nobody complained!

MONDAY, MAY 30, 2005

Giant Teapot Terrorizes Malaysian Muslims

A giant teapot, vase, umbrella, "palace" and concrete boat, each symbolizing the common humanity of adherents to the world religions, are about to be torn down in Malaysia.

The structures stand on private land belonging to the "Sky Kingdom" *deviationist religious sect. Sect leader, 65 year old Ariffin Mohamad, says he will not contest the ordered destruction. "But," he added, "the action will seriously tarnish the image of the Government internationally."

The government alleges that the demolition is because it is illegal to build non-agricultural structures on agricultural land.

It is more commonly believed that the demolition has been ordered because the sect and its members have been outspokenly apostate from Islam and because the very existance of the sect and its highly visible structures are "humiliating" to Islamic teachings.

You can read more about this strange story here and at LGF (which receives a tip of the hat).

*The phrase, "deviationist religious sect" is used in the news story linked above. Although I have studied and taught on religious cults and sects for many years I do not believe I had ever heard this phrase until today. By googling I found that, with two exceptions, it was used exclusively for deviant Islamic sects. A definition of the term at the website for Apologetics research resources on religious cults and sects supported this view with this definition: "Deviationist: Alternative term for *heresy* (e.g. often used for those said to deviate from the teachings of Islam)."

It now appears that Islamic vocabulary is now entering our mainstream and academic English language vocabulary. This is not necessarily a bad thing. But we should think twice before using these terms since they may carry both specific and hidden meanings within Muslim communities of which we may not be aware.

Memorial Day 2005 Hawaii Style at Punchbowl

Memorial Day in Hawaii is a special day of remembrance with the central tradition being the decoration of graves at Punchbowl Cemetery (officially known as the National Memorial Cemetery of the Pacific).

Hundreds of Cub Scouts and Boy Scouts descend on the Sunday before Memorial Day Monday armed with thousands of small American flags and flower leis, lovingly made by a literal army of local volunteers.

Each grave is lovingly decorated and a brief service is held in preparation for the more public and official ceremonies on the holiday itself.

In recent years, as Punchbowl became filled to capacity, the state opened its own Veteran's Cemetary in Kaneohe. Here, it is primarily the Girl Scouts who continue the tradition of grave decoration. I can think of no better way to teach our children to honor and remember the sacrifices of those who have served...and died....in our US armed forces.

Amidst this year's ceremonies one stood out for me.

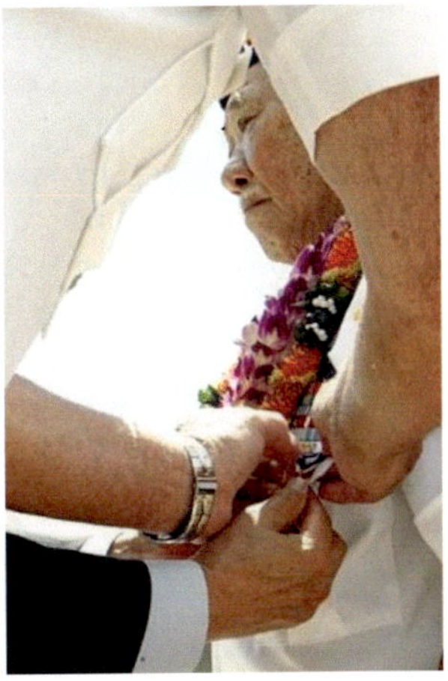

During the Korean War, Army Master Sgt. Clarence Young fell behind his platoon t to provide cover for their withdrawl from a heavy assault by the North Korean army. After using up all the ammunition for a 50-caliber machine gun mounted on a half-track, his companion ran to get more. After running some distance away he looked back to see the vehicle explode. Assuming that Young and the others had most certainly died in the explosion, he returned to the unit and reported Young's death.

Unknown to him and everyone else, Young survived and spent 30 months as a prisoner of war. Years later, when the full story became known, those who had served with Young recommended him to recieve the Medal of Honor for his heroic, selfless efforts that day. After military review it was decided that he would recieve the Silver

Star for valor. So, over 50 years later, Sgt. Young's bravory and ordeal was at last acknowledged in a special presentation ceremony let by US Senator Daniel Akaka (Dem. Hawaii).

Both the Honolulu Adverstiser and Honolulu Star-Bulletin published some good pictures of the Memorial Day decorations and presentation to Sgt. Young. I am reprinting them here although you can link back to their original context if you would prefer.

God Bless America, land that I love.
Stand beside her, and guide her,
Thru the night, with a light from above.....

Sports Authority Either Deceptive or Illiterate

I went to Sports Authority in Waikele this afternoon to by a new pair of tennis shoes. They had bins full of what were called "Clearance" items. Along the aisles piled high with all sorts of shoes (some marked down on sale and some at regular price) were big signs that said:

TOTAL STOCK CLEARANCE
Take 30% Off Lowest Price Marked

So, I pick out a pair of shoes on sale for $39.99 and go to check out to pay for them. I am charged $42.68. "Hold it a moment," I said. "I thought I would be given an extra 30% off."

No," she replied. "That is only for our clearance items."

"But," I said, "Your signs say that your entire stock of shoes is for clearance."

"I'm sorry," she said. "Only those shoes marked "clearance" are subject to the extra 30% off."

So I asked for the manager and, ten minutes later, I asked him the same question.

He said that the sign was clear about what was eligible for the discount. At the bottom of each sign in small letters was this:

"Items marked .97 eligible for discount."

Of course every shoe not in the bins was marked with a .99 ending price.

"But that doesn't make sense," I said. "How can the entire stock be clearance when only a few items are marked with the .97 price?"

"I'm sorry," he said, "that the way the signs are worded was confusing for you."

I figure that either the signs were so worded with a deliberate intent to mislead.....or else whoever made the signs did not know what "Entire Stock" means in plain English. I'm fairly sure it was the former. What do you think?

There....I feel much better now! Thanks for letting me blow off my frustration!

TUESDAY, MAY 31, 2005

Deep Throat: Hero or Heel?

W. Mark Felt aka Deep Throat

Today, at last, the mystery is solved. Deep Throat has publicly identified himself and confessed. Woodward and Bernstein have broken their silence and confirmed the identity of Deep Throat as being a former second in command of the FBI and spurned successor to the infamous Director Edgar J. Hoover.

Who is it? Well, it's 91-year old W. Mark Felt, who now lives with his daughter and grandchildren in Santa Rosa, California.

What was Mr. Felt's motivation in passing on the FBI's criminal investigation information on the Watergate break-ins to reporters for the Washington Post?

It would appear to have been nothing more than sour grapes.

Felt had been groomed as Hoover's successor as FBI Director. When Hoover died in 1972, however, President Richard Nixon passed him over and choose Justice Department official, L. Patrick Gray, instead.

Coincidently, the Watergate break-in occurred only one month after Hoover's death. Gray later admitted that he had turned over FBI files on the Watergate investigation to White House Counsel John Dean, even though there was widespread

suspicion that White House staff might have been involved in either the break-in itself or the subsequent cover-up.

In the midst of this mess, Felt contacted Washington Post reporters Bob Woodward and Carl Bernstein and began passing confidential information from FBI files to them....probably as a counter to what Gray was doing with the White House.

Bob Woodward & Carl Bernstein

There are those who, after learning today that Felt was Deep Throat, have criticized him for not taking the material to the Federal Prosecutor's office. I suspect that there were two reasons why Felt did not choose to do this:

First, it was probably unclear to him whether the Nixon appointees in the Justice Department (including Patrick Gray...whose nomination as Assistant US Attorney General was withdrawn by Nixon in order to appoint him acting FBI Director), could be trusted....especially with Gray passing this info on to the White House.

Second, he had personal reasons to "get even" with Nixon for being snubbed as Hoover's replacement.

The first reason, it seems to me, makes him out to be a sort of hero, performing an end run to expose the Nixon corruption in a way that Nixon could not control.

The second reason, it seems to me, makes him out to be a sort of heel, using the privilege of his law enforcement position to secretly release confidential federal investigative files to the public; something that appears to me to be most certainly illegal and worthy of criminal prosecution.

Ben Bradlee

Until today, only four men knew who Deep Throat was: Felt, Woodward, Bernstein and Post Editor Ben Bradlee. The mystery and its ongoing cache had brought both fame and money to Woodward, Bernstein and the Washington Post. Now that the secret is out it will be interesting to see the Post, the reporters and Deep Throat himself, fight over publishing rights and movie rights and all the other "rights" associated with making money off of public scandal.

The moral lesson to be learned from all of this would appear to be that a man can be both a hero and heel at one and the same time for doing one and the same thing. It is not inconceivable that Felt could receive a ticker-tape parade on his way to be booked by the FBI for his criminal offense. After 30 years, however, the statute of limitations has long expired. I say, skip the ticker-tape parade, too, and just leave the poor man alone.

Woodward and Bernstein, however, came out of this whole episode smelling like roses. Their integrity is intact. They have honorably protected the identity of their anonymous source until the end. We have yet to see, however, how honorably they will behave when the BIG BUCKS are at stake.

My guess is that Woodward & Bernstein have already written their book and will release it for publication within days. By the time the frenzy is all over we shall all be glad to go back to watching the latest news on Michael Jackson.

NY Times Shines Spotlight On CIA Transport Operations--Why?

Scott Shane, Stephen Grey and Margot Williams carefully researched public records, interviewed dozens of people and compiled a large and diverse amount of data into an expose of the CIA's covert transportation network, published in today's New York Times under the heading, "C.I.A. Expanding Terror Battle Under Guise of Charter Flights."

I do not consider this material newsworthy....unless you are a member of Al Qaeda or a some other group hostile to the United States.

Can you imagine the N.Y. Times publishing an article in 1944 headlined, "Eisenhower Expanding War Effort With Plans To Invade Normandy"?

I wouldn't have needed to know that bit of information, either. In fact, as an American citizen, I would not have *wanted* to know that information. "Loose lips sink ships," they used to say. I wonder what they say at the Times these days?

Ironically, the story serves no purpose other than to undermine national security. The irony is that the story is so senseless and damaging that the publishing of the story is a far bigger story than the story itself!

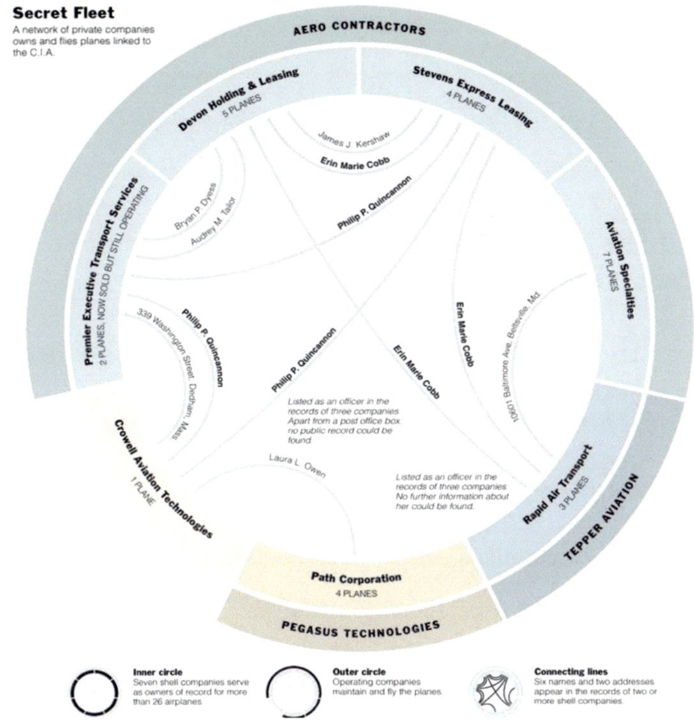

Why does the media feel that any secret they can reveal that hurts the Bush administration and its policy initiatives is a good thing, but the revealing of their anonymous sources is a bad thing?

I would hold that protecting the clandestine security activities of those engaged in a life and death struggle against people who want to destroy us is far more honorable than protecting the name of someone who leaks information that compromises our national safety and wastes a vast amount of taxpayer money invested into complex covert operations.

Although the CIA contracting with Aero Contractors is hardly a secret unbeknownst to the governments and militaries of the international community, it would be considered very bad form for even an Iran or North Korea to publish such information for propaganda purposes.

Apparently the Times does not feel the need to show even the same level of restraint shown to the United States by its sworn enemies.

I should think that the US Executive Branch would be justified by revoking all press privileges for the New York Times and cease from releasing any news of any kind to them. If anybody in the media ever deserved to be blackballed and marginalized I would imagine that the NY Times would find itself ranked very high on someone's list today.

Also listed in an attachment to today's Times article is a chart showing all the business fronts for the air carriers involved as well as the names of those listed as corporate trustees or board members of more than one of them. I wonder if this will put any of them in jeopardy of their lives? Does the NY Times care? No, of course not. They do, however, protect the names of the Iraqi "insurgents" that they embed themselves with. They wouldn't want to put *them* at risk, would they?

I'm afraid that this continuing trend in the MSM is making me and millions of other Americans consider revisiting the self-anointed absolute rights of a free press to print anything and everything without fear of penalty or consequences. Such thinking, however, scare me to death! The repression of the media by government edict would be disastrous.

By its unrestrained, intentional undermining of our government's efforts to conduct foreign policy and "provide for the common defense," however, the American MSM is sowing the seeds of the destruction of the very freedom that it cherishes.

True freedom carries with it the freedom to responsibly restrict one's own freedom to protect and preserve the freedom of all. What the MSM as a whole, and the New York Times today in particular, is practicing is not freedom, but anarchy.

FRIDAY, JUNE 10, 2005

Panhala: Where Poetry and Picture Capture Laughter

According to their website, www.Panhala.net/Archive/Index.html, the word "*Panhala* is Hindi for 'source of fresh water' (more or less). The purpose of this group is to share poems and prose that make the day a little brighter."

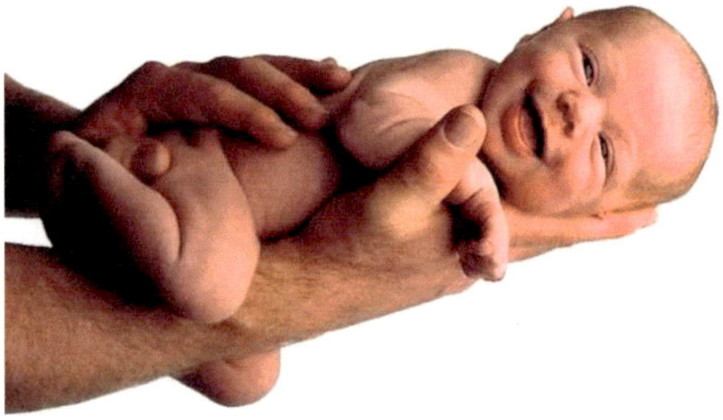

That explaination is followed by the following quote:
"There are two ways of spreading light: to be the candle or the mirror that reflects it." -- Edith Wharton
The postings on this site are excellent and beautiful "reflections" that will, indeed, make your "day a little brighter."

My favorite is simply entitled, "Laughter" and is illustrated by this very happy photo:

Take some time to browse around the Panhala site. It is truly one of the gems hidden in the vast tangle of the internet.

Sean Penn Visits Tehran

With a press pass certifying him as an official news correspondent with the San Francisco Chronicle, actor Sean Penn, an outspoken critic of the Bush administration and the war in Iraq, made a visit to Iran this past week Penn, apparently, is looking things over as the Iranian Shiite Mullahs make preparations for their predetermined, "slam dunk" general elections scheduled for June 17.

A photographer caught him standing "inconspicuously" amidst thousands of Muslims at prayer. Other photos of his visit can be found here.

According to Reuters, Penn visited a mosque for Friday prayers and listened to worshipers chanting enthusiastically for, "Death to America!"

Penn was seen scribbling in a notebook. Charles Johnson at LGF, apparently having access to a remote military surveillance drone, recounts some of Penn's scribbles that he thinks he might have maybe deciphered from the high-altitude photos.

King Kamehameha Day in Hawaii

This morning my wife and I drove to Ko Olina and sat on the beach. I snorkled around in the beautiful, clear water checking out the butterfly fish, Moorish Idols, blennies, sea slugs, needle gars, spotted Trunkfish, wrasses, a school of hundreds of Hawaiian Flagtails and, of course, the ubiquitous triggerfish known as Humuhumu-nukunuku-a-pua'a.

We then sat some more, read and talked and returned home by 11:30. Since King Kamehameha Day is a state holiday I was free to take a nap this afternoon. Tonight daughter #3 returns home from college in Seattle. Tomorrow we will go as a complete family of 5 to Kailua Beach for a relaxing afternoon ending in a BBQ dinner.

If you want to learn anything about King Kamehameha or King Kamehameha Day you wil\l have to click on the links. I'm not going to tell you anything about them since the only reason I wrote this post today was to make everyone not living in Hawaii a little bit jealous! Aloha!

SATURDAY, JUNE 11, 2005

Berlin Wants Next Year's World Cup Sex To Be "Hygenic"

According to BBC News, Berlin is anticipating lots of sex and prostitution during next year's World Cup Soccer finals. In order to make life easier for the hundreds of prostitutes who will be arriving from all over Germany, local health officials have prepared a leaflet listing 10 "rules" for the prostitutes' clients to follow.

Among the rules are, "Be polite and respectful towards prostitutes; maintain a high standard of personal hygiene; always use a condom and be clear about what you want."

This last instruction would appear to cover those unfortunate and awkward moments when the prostitute asks the john what he wants and gets that all-too-common response: "Ah.....I don't know......Do you want to play a little footie?"

To help everything go smoother they will also be distributing 100,000 free condoms to those soccer fans who absent-mindedly left theirs at home and spent so much money getting drunk that they can only afford either a condom or a prostitute, but not both.

Oh, by the way, it is rumored that there will also be some soccer being played. The ticket prices for the games, however, may be priced so high that only the prostitutes will be able to afford to attend.

Terry Schiavo's Autopsy...Where Is It?

Terry Schiavo died on March 31, 2005. Where are the results of her autopsy?

A news release from the following day, April 1, stated that the autopsy had been completed and that the "results of the autopsy may not be released for ***several weeks***," the medical examiner's office said. (emphasis added)

I read somewhere that, according to forensic pathologist Dr. Michael Badin, it takes around 6 weeks of preparation before a brain is able to be examined microscopically. Since the autopsy was performed on April 1st, that would bring us to May 13.

It is now four weeks past that date and still nothing.

Does anybody know what is going on? and why it is taking so long? and why the news media isn't pressing the question?

Oh, and while I'm at it, has there ever been any confirmation that Terry's "husband" ever buried her ashes as he promised he would do "in an undisclosed location near Philadelphia so that her immediate family (could) not attend and turn the moment into a media spectacle"?

Just wondering.......

Tyson Quits--Loses to McBride on TK After Six Rounds

Mike Tyson reaches new low

Mike Tyson "threw in the towel" when he did not come out of his corner for the seventh round of his comeback fight against unranked Irishman Kevin McBride in Washington D.C. tonight. The referee ruled a TK for McBride.

Tyson was either pushed or knocked to the floor as the sixth round come to an end. Two of the three judges had Tyson ahead 57-55 when the fight was called. The third judge had the same score, but for McBride.

After the fight, Tyson said, "I'm not going to fight again. I haven't got the fighting guts or the heart any more......I was just fighting to pay off the bills.... .I'm not an animal anymore."

Tyson did not appear to have improved his boxing skills very much after being warned for a low blow and having points taken away after a sixth-round head-butt opened up a cut under McBride's left eye. Perhaps Tyson's "inner goodness" will now have an opportunity to emerge.

Bomb Blasts Rock Tehran Today--At Least Nine Dead

A news article just released by Editor & Publisher gives the headline to Sean Penn ("Camera of Sean Penn, Journalist, Confiscated in Iran") but the meat of the story is this: The worst violence in ten years has broken out in Iran as the ruling Mullahs attempt to choreograph the Presidential elections scheduled for this coming Friday.

Numerous bombs have gone off in Tehran and elsewhere killing nine; and a gathering of several hundred women gathered in front of Tehran University demonstrating for a return to pre-revolution rights for women. Police and plainsclothed security forces kept others from joining the women. Cell phone service was also cut off from the area.

Women in Tehran demanded equal rights today

Poor Sean Penn even had his video camera confiscated for a brief time today. Could it be that the Mullahs are worried about all this international exposure to the growing evidence of domestic unrest and dissatisfaction with their iron-fisted, theocratic rule?
As always look to Regime Change Iran for the latest on this and other developing stories (one of which is that, according to US Representative Curt Weldon, Osama bin Laden has been in and out of Iran several times during the past several years.....).

Sorenstam Wins LPGA--Wie Second

Michelle Wie

It was another scripted performance for Anika Sorenstam as she ran away with the LPGA title today.

For me, however, the big story was that Sorenstam's *only competition came from a 15-year-old who just finished the 10th grade and is learning how to drive (a car).*

"(Michelle) Wie gave another big crowd at Bulle Rock a glimpse of the future with a 3-under 69 to finish in second place, the highest finish by an amateur in a major since 20-year-old Jenny Chuasiriporn lost in a playoff to Se Ri Pak in the 1998 U.S. Women's Open."

Out here in Hawaii we are all big Michelle Wie fans. It is

wonderful that the LPGA has waved restrictions and let her play in the big tournaments as well as lesser ones. Michelle has shown time and again that she is able to play with the "big girls."

Not all the older golfers appreciate this, however. According the the FoxNews report, "some players were riled that qualifications were changed to allow Wie into the field..." I can see why. Michelle cleaned their clocks! How embarrassing for them! On the other hand, as an amateur, Wie did not get to keep her $36,000 winnings which were divided up among those who tied for third.

Wie is out of school for the summer and will be getting in some serious and consistant tournament playing time over the next three months. It might be wise for some of the "older women" to keep their clocks in safe and secure places. Michelle is eager to clean them again.

For the record, Sorenstam finished with a -11 to Wie's -8. Not a bad showing against, perhaps, the greatest woman golfer of all time, playing in her prime!

2005 Paris Air Show Unveils Airbus A380

The annual **Paris Air Show**, which begins tomorrow, will feature the first public flyby of the new Airbus A380 Super-Jumbo passenger jet. The new plane dwarfs the current title holder of world's largest passenger jetliner, Boeing's 747 (see comparison **here**). Production delays have diminished hopes of contracting for 100 of the new airplanes. 50+ have already been claimed by major airlines (Note: They have to be major airlines....who else could operate and maintain them!).

The elegance and verstility of the A380's full-length double-deck seating areas is expected to lure passengers demanding more comfort and more leg-room in their long-distance air travel.

Hopefully, the A380 pilot at the airshow will not attempt to wow the crowd with the sort of aerial theatrics that destroyed the Soviet Union's TU-114 SST back in 1973 (see pictures here).

In any case, Germany and France have invested heavily in this behemouth and have bet the house on its commercial success. If it becomes standard fare in the airlines circuit one can only pray that it will prove its worth in both economy and safety.

Nebraska Senator Chuck Hagel Interrogates Mohammed al-Qahtani At Gitmo (excerpts)

Alleged photo showing Sen. Hagel w/al-Qahtani

Background: Today's Time magazine article on U.S. interrogation techniques used against suspected terrorist detainees at Guantanamo Bay has produced both outrage and yawns from its readers. Republican Senator Chuck Hagel from Nebraska weighed in on this subject the other night:

"It's not appropriate," Hagel said Sunday on CNN's "Late Edition.

"It's not at all within the standards of who we are as a civilized people, what our laws are. If in fact we are treating prisoners this way, it's not only wrong, it's dangerous and very dumb and very shortsighted. This is not how you win the people of the world over to our side, especially the Muslim world."

Rumors and unconfirmed anonymous sources have speculated on whether Hagel made a clandestine visit to Guantanamo Bay in recent days. One high-ranking government official, who did not wish either his ranking or his government to be revealed, has handed us apocryphal, verbatim notes taken during Hagel's personal interrogation of detainee, Mohammed al-Qahtani, who is suspected of being the 20th member of the terror group that launched the September 11, 2001 airline attacks on New York and Washington D.C.

Selected Excerpts

Hagel: Hi, there....I mean, salaam (or is it shalom? D**m all these Arab words sound alike!). I'm sorry to interrupt your evening meal.....is that "duck a l'orange?" Mmmmm......(D**m, all I got at the officer's club was chick peas and gravy!). Oh, where was I.....yes....have you got a few minutes? I mean, you're not too busy right now? Can I talk with you, please? You're not going anywhere tonight, are you? Hah, hah! That's a joke, son! Did you get it? ....."going somewhere?" That's funny isn't it?

al-Qahtani: Huh? What the....? Who are you? What do you want? Answer me right now or I'll slit your throat with this plastic spork!

Hagel: I am Senator Chuck Hagel from Nebraska and, within the appropriate standards of our civilized society I would like to try and win you over to our side.....You are Muslim, aren't you? You are? Good! That's even better!

al-Qahtani: Well? "Say it or slay it." That's what I always say. So get on with it. I don't have all day, you know. Oprah comes on at 7:00 pm.

Hagel: Ah, well, you see, yesterday, wearing my rubber gloves and using both hands I was reading my personal copy of the Koran......oops.......I mean, Qu'ran......and I became convinced that Islam is the "religion of peace." Am I right? I mean, you're more of an expert on this than I am.....

al-Qahtani: Peace? Peace will come when every camel-nosed infidel like yourself is either rotting in hell or converted, by the free exercise of personal faith and reason, to Islam. It will be your choice. Either way, peace will come. So, sure.....I guess in that sense Islam *is* a "religion of peace."

Hagel: Oh, really? Good! That's good! Really! You know, some of my best friends have been Muslims. Not that every Muslim is a terrorist, mind you, but some.....a few.....not very many of the terrorists I've heard about have allegedly been Muslims. Which is what you are, right? An alleged Muslim? No, I mean a terrorist? Be honest with me, please. If you are, you can have the strudel for dessert! Hah hah! Got you again! I wouldn't withhold your strudel! That wouldn't be.....well.....civilized, would it! No, of course you can have your strudel! But.....uh.....where was I.......?

al-Qahtani: Look, who are you, really? CIA? Special OPs? One of those American infidel goons from Abu Ghraib? What are you going to do? Shave my beard? Bring an attractive woman into my cell? Play another Christina Aguilera CD? Hah! You'll never break me!

Hagel: Heavens, no! That would be in violation of the Geneva Convention which I have never read in my life and actually have no idea what the h*ll the Geneva Convention is anyway but that doesn't matter because you have every right to be treated with respect and dignity while being held under illegal detention in this shameful gulag!

al-Qahtani: Are you for real? Guards! Guards! Get me out of here! This guy's nuts! He's talking like a madman!

Hagel: Shhh......it's OK......no one's going to hurt you.......you can trust me!

al-Qahtani: Trust you? You really *are* nuts! You know, if I could get my hands on a 747 right now I'd fly it right up your........

Hagel: Hold it.....stop right there......don't say anything that might incriminate you.....see.....I've got my fingers in my ears.......you have the right to remain silent.....

al-Qahtani: Stop it! Stop it! You're crazy! You're contagious! You're driving *me* nuts, too! Osama never told me about people like you! Guards! Guards! Get me out of here! I don't even like strudel! Get this psychopath away from me and I'll tell you anything! Really! I even know stuff about OJ Simpson! Just get this guy away from me!.......

Here, unfortunately, the excerpts come to an end. Military spokesmen have refused to confirm or deny whether Senator Hagel has visited Guantanamo or not (which proves, by the way, that President Bush knew there were no weapons of mass destruction in Iraq). But I do have it on very good authority that Mohammed al-Qahtani has ordered his lawyer to file a law suit alleging inhumane treatment and emotional suffering after being served blintzes and bagels for breakfast.

Phone calls to OJ Simpson's home in Florida have not been returned.

Update #1: Captain Ed discusses the same Hagel quotes here.

Update #2: Terrence, in a comment, correctly points out that Sen. Hagel was not quoted in the Time magazine article. I had conflated his quotation from numerous articles *about* the Time article. I have accordingly, rewritten my opening paragraph so as to be both accurate and fair. Thanks, Terrence

MONDAY, JUNE 13, 2005

Time Magazine Features Radical Muslim School in Illinois As a "Model"

Girls' "uniforms" are worn 6th grade & up

In the same Time magazine issue that turns Christina Aguilera CDs into instruments of illegal torture, a second article and photo essay presents the Bridgeview, Illinois, Universal (Muslim) School as a model for other Muslims to follow.

What "Time" forgets to tell us is that the Bridgeview Mosque, which runs the school, has been, in recent years, increasingly influenced by the radical Wahabbi sect and funded with $125,000 from the Saudi government, $369,000 from the government of Kuwait and $135,000 from the United Arab Emirates. The Saudi monarchy also pays $2,000 of the Imam's salary each month. Hundreds of other American mosques have also been built, "staffed" and funded by the same sources.

The Bridgeview mosque, which has been critically featured in numerous articles and blog postings (such as here, here, here, here and here) over the past several years, has also raised money "in memory of" Palestinian suicide bombers. According to one source, "Abdullah Azzam, bin Laden's spiritual advisor, visited Bridgeview in the 1980s and brought at least three Bridgeview men to fight in Afghanistan."

Students gather prayer once each day

According to Egyptian blogger The Big Pharaoh, Americans have been suckered by the MSM to believe that burkas, veils and complete separation of men from women is somehow normative in Muslim communities. Not so, he says.

> *Frankly speaking, I shouldn't be laughing really. I should be weeping because the Western mainstream media is telling the world that the only true faithful Muslims are those who wear the stupid cloth on their head (that was nonexistent 30 years ago) and separate boys and girls in schools. I should be weeping because Time magazine is showing us that only girls clad in black with no makeup on are the true Muslims who are struggling between*

their Islamic and their American identities. Meanwhile, those Muslims who disagree with the head veil, who think that Islam needs reform a la all major faiths, and who believe that we cannot live like our Muslim brethren did 1400 years ago are the "lesser Muslims" or the Muslims that are "out of the mainstream."

The wealthy, conservative and, yes, radical Muslims in the world, supported with money from Arab Muslim governments, are financing the spread of their version of Islam throughout Europe and the United States. Not every European or American Muslim is affiliated with these mosques and schools, of course, but many of them *are*. These are not folks who have any interest in pursuing the "American Dream." They have no interest in assimilating into American culture or society. Their interest is to set up Muslim communities/colonies which can operate autonomously under their own versions of sharia law, untouched and untainted by the "law of the land."

The Big Pharoah draws attention to the role of the Muslim Brotherhood in this expansion, entrenchment and consolidationon of conservative Islamic faith communities around the world. This "Brotherhood," founded in Egypt in 1926, has spawned Ayman Zawahiri (bin Laden's second-in-command), the assassins of Egyptian President Anwar Sadat, the blind sheik Omar Abdel Rahman (who was convicted in 1995 of plotting to blow up New York landmarks), the radical Palestinian group Hamas, and has been a close collaborator with both the Saudi Wahabbis and bin Laden's Al Qaeda.

Today there is a battle taking place for the soul of Islam...not only in the Middle East, Indonesia, South-East Asia and the Philippines....but also in Europe and North America. The brutality and single-mindedness of the financially powerful, radical Islamists have given them the upper hand in this conflict. Moderates are cowering in fear, even in the United States.

Somehow, in spite of this, the wars in Iraq and Afghanistan must be won so that the rise of successful democracies in the the Arab Muslim world will encourage other moderate, democratically-inclined Muslims to boldly reclaim their faith from the radical proponentsts of death and devastation within the Muslim world.

The central hallmark of Islam since its founding by Muhammad has been its sense of unity. It is not easy for Muslims to view their faith as being rent by schism. Even Shiites and Sunnis make their respective *hadj* to Mecca where they offer praise to Allah with one voice.

The reality, however, is that in recent years the radical Islamists have been killing their so-called "brothers" in the faith without any hesitation or restraint. Sooner or later this will force the hand of the more moderate Muslim individuals and nations to face up to the danger and declare war on those who consider them to be no better than infidels themselves.

In Iraq and Afghanistan, the United States has already kick-started the coming Muslim world-wide civil war. Slowly but surely, the radicals and moderates are separating like an amoeba dividing into two nearly identical halves. One group will not tolerate the other and, sooner or later, the other half will be forced to respond.

The United States should not be so naive as to doubt that this civil war will, in part at least, take place on our own soil. Whether mosques and Muslim schools such as those in Bridgeview, Illinois, will be part of the problem or part of the solution has yet to be seen. Accordingly, at this point in "Time," it is both foolish and irresponsible to elevate any one mosque or school to the status of being a "model" for other Muslims in the United States to follow.

At the same time, however, it should be considered to be prudent for our government and our own citizenry (both Muslim and non-Muslim) to keep a very close and vigilantnt eye on who is funding what and what is being preached and taught in the mosques and Muslim schools in America.

Michael Jackson Found "Not Guilty" On All Counts

Is it just me or does Michael Jackson look like he is stoned out of his mind? Could it be the "pain killers?"

Whether innocent or guilty of the abuse charges, Jackson looks like one of the "living dead."

One can only wonder if he is in any way, shape or form in control of his life at this point in time and, if he isn't, who is?

I will not be surprised if his life ends in the not-too-distant future in a manner reminscent of Elvis Presley. Two great talents, each destroyed from the inside out.

TUESDAY, JUNE 14, 2005

Quote of the Day--Innocence In Aruba

Antonius "Mickey" John, one of two hotel security guards released yesterday in connection with the disappearance of Natalee Holloway:

"I knew from day one that I was innocent."

The second guard, Abraham Jones, was not quoted as saying:

"I knew from day two that I was innocent."

Phil Jackson Returning as Lakers' Coach

We can expect a "centering calm" and the gentle murmur of "ohm" when the Los Angeles Lakers start suiting up in preparation for next year's season. Yes, indeed, that can only mean that Phil Jackson, the "Dr. Phil" of the NBA, has agreed to return as the "Shaq-less" Lakers' "Head Guru."

Rumors have it that Jackson's contract requires that he stand up, wave his arms in the air and scream at least once each game (as a preventive measure to keep courtside paramedics from mistaking the aura of his "inner child" for his having fallen into a coma).

"Christer" & "Christers"--Emerging Vocabulary to Demean Christians

(Welcome Hugh Hewitt fans. Feel free to browse around the site and maybe find a few things to smile about. Aloha, Bird of Paradise)

The word "Christer" (and "Christers") is used repeatedly in today's article in the LA Weekly entitled, "The New Blacklist," written by Doug Ireland. The word is not used in a complimentary fashion.

For me this is a new word. From the context of the article it appears that Ireland is using it as a synomym for "anti-gay Christian groups," a phrase that appears in the article's sub-title.

Elsewhere in the article he associates the word with "the Christian Right," specific organizations such as the "Rev. Donald Wildmon's American Family Association," the "Illinois Family Institute," "Focus on the Family," the "Family Research Council" and "similar national groups," "far right and theocratic fundamentalism," "local pressure campaigns and boycott threats," and initiators of "censorship and pressure campaigns" and individuals such as "Ken Hutcherson — a conservative National Football League linebacker turned preacher."

Martin Kaplan (director of the Norman Lear Center at the Annenberg School of Communication at USC), is quoted as identifying Christers as those who wish to move toward "theocratic oligopoly. The drumbeat of religious fascism..." (see Hugh Hewitt's reaction to this quote here).

Chip Berlet (senior analyst at the labor-funded Political Research Associates... and co-author of "Right-Wing Populism in America: Too Close for Comfort") identifies Christers as having

"an incredible dread, completely irrational, of a hodgepodge of sexual subversion and social chaos...motivated by fundamentalist Christian doctrines like Triumphalism and Dominionism, which order Christians to take over the secular state and secular institutions."

Berlet further describes Christers as "fundamentalist religious primitives," who see Bush's reelection "as a mandate from God" and who "see that the leadership of America is within their grasp."

Ireland also speaks of those who read and believe in the Bible as though they were from another planet. Here is one example:

The key to those doctrines is what fundamentalist religious primitives call the Great Commission, which is basically an injunction to convert everyone to Christianity. In the Bible (Matthew 28:19-20), it says, "Go ye therefore, and teach all nations, baptizing them in the name of the Father, and of the Son, and of the Holy Spirit: Teaching them to observe all things whatsoever I have commanded you . . ." The fundamentalist interpretations of these and other texts.....have incredible motivating power for the religious right, and help explain the vehemence of the Christers' intolerance of the freedom of others to think or act differently."
Wow. I had no idea that one word could mean so much!

A Google-search showed the earliest internet useage of this word to be in a beastiality story posted on June 14, 2004. The first time the word appears with the sense used by Ireland, however, seems to have been November 16, 2004 in a posting at Unknown News entitled, "Slouching Towards Gilead, where we find,

Fascists don't do elections. Christers determined to set up a Christer Nation don't do elections.
Next, dated March 25, 2005, during the Terry Schiavo vigil there is a headline at the blogsite Direland that reads, "SCHIAVO: NADER ALLIES HIMSELF WITH THE CHRISTERS."

The word also appears in an undated article that quotes the word as used by a member of the Church of Christ in a self-reflective manner--"Church of Christer."

It also shows up as the name of a fictitious "Christian Band" in the recently released "spoof" movie, "Never Been Thawed." In a **review of the movie** we find,

In the film, the Christers - made up of Anders and three local musicians - were created when a punk band called the Reach Arounds switched to contemporary Christian music purely for financial reasons, billing themselves as "the bad boyz of Christian rock.

"Their performances mix religion with profanity-laced banter by Anders' character, a frozen-food collector named Shawn, who's more interested in hooking up with "really hot Christian chicks" than finding salvation."

It would appear that the words "Christer" and "Christers" have been recently resurrected and re-constructed by liberal secularists so as to be used to lable and demean conservative Christians.

Curiously, neither of the words appear on any of the on-line encyclopedias (including Wikipedia, which is always ahead of the game on most things), dictionaries or thesauri. A few sites devoted to idioms and slang did produce the following citations:

The word appears as an idiom from Carleton County, New Brunswick, Canada,
christer \'kryz-tur\ n - Also: christler; Term of disapprobrium generally applied to minors and (ironically) equivalent to "li'l' devil"; "C'm'ere you little christer, and stop makin' such a racket." Etymology is obvious, and typical of the indiscriminately iconoclastic County dialect.
Also, according to Bartleby,

The word Christer has two meanings in England. It is used by printers to designate an exclamation point, and by other people in a sense which I can best explain by illustration. A Harvard professor, an Englishman, was discussing a certain English journalist then in this country, and he said to me: 'Oh, he's a simply fearful Christer; preaches in chapel every Sunday, and all that.'"

American poet, Allen Tate (1899-1976), used the word in his poem, "The Swimmers," as follows,

the horsemen came
Again, all but the leader: it was night
Momently and I feared: eleven same
Jesus-Christers unmembered and unmade,
Whose Corpse had died again in dirty shame.

Also, at the Canadian Webzine "Barbed Wire," in their final on-line issue described as "The Death Issue," a submission entitled, "Lady Dead Freshness versus the Greatest Race Driver Who Ever Lived," by William Harper, uses the word in this context (edited for obscenity),

WALLING: What kind of Celine f***g Dion fans do you take us for? Get out of here, Holy Man. Get out of my sight this instant or I'll f***g hammer you!
MONK: Good God!
WALLING: No. Angry f***g vengeful god. Now split, you stupid Christer!

The on-line Urban Dictionary does, in fact, have a definition of the word, "christer,"

*1. **Christer***
1. When you use the position in other words known as "doggystyle" (as in) "God i just christer'd that girl"
(Do you suppose this is in contrast to the "Missionary Position?")

A visit to the local library this afternoon took me to the Unabridged Oxford English Dictionary where I found this listing:

***Christer**--U.S. slang; a term applied disparingingly to anoverzealous, over-pious, or sanctimonious person.*

The OED lists the earliest known citation for the use of this word as, "1924 W. Fabian, Sailors' Wives vii 90 'You never were a Christer in college.'" Subsequent citations are listed for John dos Passos, Henry Miller and Ezra Pound.

I find it curious that this venerable tome finds the word to be of recent U.S. origin whereas Bartleby's offers two English usages for the word and none for North America! I suppose that more research is needed to determine the full etymology of this word.

In any case, it is clear that those who desire to demean and discredit conservative, evangelical Christians have now discovered a new set of words to work their verbal mischief. I fully expect the words "Christer" and "Christers" to rapidly become common usage in both the print and online media. Television will also soon be using these terms, first in cable shows but, not too far behind, network sit-coms as well.

In the New Testament we can read in Acts 11:26 that it was in Antioch (Syria) that Jesus' disciples were first called "Christians." I expect that the term, which means, more or less, "little Christs," was coined by local Jews or pagans to mock and deride those who had commited themselves to following the risen Jesus as Lord and Savior. In any case, the name stuck and was quickly worn by these disciples as a mark of honor.

Perhaps those of us who are Christians today should take the descriptive word "Christer" and wear it proudly, too! By embracing it and annointing it with the grace and power of the Spirit of Christ we will soon empty it of whatever imaginary power it may have to insult or demean us in the eyes of the world.

Maybe I shall wear a button reading, "I am a Christer! And I am not ashamed!"

I don't believe that Mr. Ireland has any idea what he has gotten himself into!

WEDNESDAY, JUNE 15, 2005

See You On Saturday

I'm taking a three night, two day midweek "weekend" with my family beginning today. We're driving up to a beach cabin on Oahu's North Shore, between Waiamea Bay and Sunset Beach. Pastors never get the real weekend off so it's kinda nice to squeeze one in somewhere else once in awhile! Aloha. Don't eat your hearts out or anything! Bird of Paradise

Waiamea Bay

Belated Thoughts On Senator Dick Durbin

For three days I have been blissfully unaware of anything except the gentle sound of waves lapping the beach on North Shore Oahu. Ignorance is indeed bliss....especially when my ignorance consists of being completely unaware of Senator Dick Durbin's existence.

Upon my return home this afternoon, imagine my dismay in learning that, not only does a Senator Dick Durbin actually exist, but that, like John Dean, he cannot seem to say what he "really means!"

What he actually did say on the Senate floor last Tuesday night was clearly designed to slam the Bush administration. Unfortunately, his aim was wide of the mark and he wound up beating up on the United States in general and the United States military in particular. By far, the best commentary on the matter I have read today is a letter written to the US Senate by former Senator Newt Gingrich, quoted in full at Powerline. (Homerun quote: *Moreover, Senator Durbin equates the terrorist detainees at Guantanamo with the millions of innocent men, women, and children exterminated by the order of evil dictators. The fact that he did so as a high ranking member of the Senate on the Senate floor makes his comparison all the more shocking*.)

While I believe that Durbin's misspoken words deserve every bit of criticism he has thus far received I cannot bring myself to agree with those who are calling for a vote of censure from his Senate colleagues. On the other hand, those who have failed to criticize his words deserve to be criticized as severely as he has been.

Although I do not find anything to laugh about in Senator Durbin's comparing US military interrogators with the Nazi SS, the Soviet KGB or Pol Pot's brutal, genocidal thugs, I do find one bit of related trivia to be at least mildly amusing.

According to Hugh Hewitt's quote from an article in the Chicago Tribune, since he became Senate Minority Whip, "(Durbin's) office budget has grown by almost $1.5 million, enabling him to hire a full-time speechwriter, two floor assistants and a third press secretary."

Let me see....Durbin gets a speechwriter and then delivers a speech which embarrasses both himself and his party, enrages the Republican opposition, slanders members of the US military during a time of war and is then happily and affirmingly quoted by Al Jazeera.

I'd hate to be Senator Dick Durbin's speechwriter.

Three Days of Paradise In Paradise

Well, I'm back from my mid-week weekend to Oahu's North Shore. I'll tell you this...beauty is never boring....no matter how much of it there is I never get tired of it. Consider these two photos. The first shows Thursday evening's sunset from the beach in front of our bungalow. The second shows Friday evening's sunset from the beach in front of our bungalow. Both are beautiful. Each is the same but different. Neither of them are boring!

What more can I say? Except that I did some more snorkling and found a rich variety of tropical fish including both varieties of humuhumu'nukunuku'apua'a swimming together in abundance along with tangs, unicorn fish, trunkfish, and a number of other varieties I have not yet been able to identify.

Two Humuhumunukunukuapua'as:
Reef Triggerfish (Left) Lagoon Triggerfish (Right)

Always fun is running into a green sea turtle and joining it as it "flies" through the water like a gentle giant, pausing from time to time to nibble on an appetizing piece of algae. (Note: No matter how tempting it may be, the urge to touch such a turtle must be resisted. Touching it can spread disease which can kill them. And I must say that I have seen many diseased and disfigured turtles over the years....I also wish these last three photos were mine...alas they aren't!)

I'll leave the images of salad topped with fresh mango and chopped macadamia nuts; chicken, pineapple chunks, onions and sweet peppers wrapped together in aluminum foil and BBQed on a grill; eaten under the swaying fronds of coconut palms framing the white sand and the blue, blue ocean......well, I'll leave these images to your imagination! Aloha!

The Last Word On Senator Durbin and "Torture"

Captain Ed posts an excerpt from Sunday's New York Times regarding what American and Iraqi troops discovered in Western Iraq along the Syrian border today. The NYTs graphically headlined the article with these words,

Iraqis Found in Torture House Tell of Brutality of Insurgents

The excerpt reads as follows:

> *Marines on an operation to eliminate insurgents that began Friday broke through the outside wall of a building in this small rural village to find a torture center equipped with electric wires, a noose, handcuffs, a 574-page jihad manual - and four beaten and shackled Iraqis.*
>
> *The American military has found torture houses after invading towns heavily populated by insurgents - like Falluja, where the anti-insurgent assault last fall uncovered almost 20 such sites. But rarely have they come across victims who have lived to tell the tale.*
>
> *The men said they told the marines, from Company K, Third Marines, Second Division, that they had been tortured with shocks and flogged with a strip of rubber for more than two weeks, unseen behind the windows of black glass. One of them, Ahmed Isa Fathil, 19, a former member of the new Iraqi Army, said he had been held and tortured there for 22 days. All the while, he said, his face was almost entirely taped over and his hands were cuffed.*

Captain Ed add comments of his own addressed, in part, to Senator Dick Durbin:

> *If Senator Durbin wants to get up on the Senate floor and rail against torture, perhaps he could start with these torture houses, where real cruelty took place, not the humiliation tactics at Gitmo that tried to save American lives.....*
>
> *The Gitmo detainees are the genocidal, sadistic, bloodthirsty freaks, Senator, not their*

jailers or the interrogators who try to protect the United States by getting them to talk. If you can't recognize that -- and so far, it appears that you lack the ability or the will to do so -- then you have no place in the Senate, especially during a time of war. Time for you to offer your resignation and salvage what's left of your honor.

Senator Durbin....are you listening?

SUNDAY, JUNE 19, 2005

Evangelical Outpost Has Hints & Tips To Make Your Life More Fun

Joe Carter, aka as Evangelical Outpost, has spent the past three months sharing his collection of hints & tips on odds and ends. He calls these "sort-of-bi-monthly" installments, "Yak Shaving Razor." Last week he added installment #8 to his collection. Consider the following:

#69 Dowload of the Week -- Want to create PDF documents but can't afford Adobe Acrobat? Try CutePDF Writer, a free version of commercial PDF creation software.

#38 Dead Pixel Test -- Is that spot on your monitor a speck of dirt, a scratch, or a dead pixel? Find out by using this simple test.

#37 Lost and Found -- Lost your keys again? Professor Solomon has an intresting method for finding lost objects. (HT: Lifehack)

Go ahead. Check it out. Who knows, you might even find a way to impress your date with some faux knowledge of fine wines! (Hint: See #48)

Oh, and by the way....this is what Joe has to say about "Yak Shaving Razor":

Yak Shaving -- [MIT AI Lab, after 2000: orig. probably from a Ren & Stimpy episode.] Any seemingly pointless activity which is actually necessary to solve a problem which solves a problem which, several levels of recursion later, solves the real problem you're working on. (From the on-line hacker Jargon File)

Anti-Syria Coalition Wins Majority In Lebanon's New Parliament

The votes are more-or-less in from Northern Lebanon, the last national region to vote in the first Parliamentary elections since Syria's withdrawl two months ago. According to BBC and ABC it appears certain that the alliance led by Saad Hariri (whose father's assissination triggered the street demonstrations in February that eventually toppled Syrian occupation) will have an absolute parliamentary majority in the new government. After today's vote the totals between the various parties and factions stand as follows:

Hariri-led alliance- 72	*Aoun-led alliance - 21*
Aman and Hezbollah – 35	*Full parliament – 128*

Saad Hariri waves to supporters during a recent political rally in Lebanon

Given the deep, sectarian divisions between the armed and radical Hezbollah in the south, the Christian-dominated Aoun in the center and Hariri's Sunni and Druze supporters in the north, it will be interesting to see if Hezbollah, in particular, will be willing to allow someone in Beirut to tell them what they should or should not be doing in their tightly-controlled domain.

For Lebanon to ever return to peace, stability and unity, and for Beirut to ever return to its former reputation as the Paris of the Middle East, Hezbollah must either be willing to exist as a cooperative minority party or else precipitate another civil war....fighting to the death to maintain its stranglehold on the south.

Personally, I do not anticipate Hezbollah giving up any of its "sovereignty" without a very physical and bloody fight. I pray that I am wrong.

In any case, the new government in Lebanon will serve to isolate Syria even further from its few remaining "friends." It would be a good sign, indeed, if these new political realities led Syria to have a change of heart concerning its tacit, if not active, support of the Iraqi "insurgency."

MONDAY, JUNE 20, 2005

Man's Best Friend?

Don't ask me why, but I came across this interesting item this evening.

A tombstone in Hoddom Cross Cemetary in Dumbriesshire, Scotland, reads as follows:
In memory of Jamesy Geddes, spouse of Andrew Black, who died at Ecclefechan, 13th June 1834, age 32yrs..Also their daug who died in infancy..

I never knew that the Scots (and I am one of them) spelled the word "dog" this way! lol

A Palestinian's Response to Compassion--"I Believe In Death"

Captain Ed's post and personal comments on this story cannot be improved upon. Accordingly, I am reproducing them in full. (Read it....and weep...)

No Good Deed Goes Unpunished, Palestinian Edition

"The title of this post is a proverb that keeps proving its wisdom over and over again, in large things and small, but in this particular case it has taken on a despicable hue. The Israelis agreed to admit a Palestinian woman to its country in order to treat her for severe burns after a kitchen explosion left her scarred and in great pain. What did they get for their compassion and generosity? A suicide bomber -- but fortunately, an incompetent one:

> *A badly burned Palestinian woman was alternately defiant and tearful Monday after Israeli soldiers caught her trying to enter Israel with 22 pounds of explosives hidden on her body. The woman, who suffered serious burns on her hands, feet and neck in a kitchen explosion*

five months ago, had been granted permission to cross into Israel from the Gaza Strip for medical treatment when she raised the suspicion of soldiers at the Erez checkpoint. ...

At the Shikma Prison in Israel's Negev Desert, where the Shin Bet security service allowed Israeli TV reporters to interview her, al-Biss said she was determined to carry out a suicide attack against Israel because of its occupation of the West Bank and Gaza.

"My dream was to be a martyr," she said, adding that she was recruited by the Al Aqsa Martyrs Brigades, a violent offshoot of Palestinian leader Mahmoud Abbas' Fatah movement. "I believe in death."

"Biss later changed her story, claiming that she had no idea that she carried 22 pounds of explosives until she was asked to undress for a security inspection at the border. Perhaps she thought she had put on weight, or maybe she likes to lift weights 22 pounds at a time. Either through her incompetence or that of her dressmaker, the Israelis discovered and dismantled the explosives before she could detonate them, sparing the lives of the people who had opened their arms to her to relieve her pain.

"In its twisted way, it provides a perfect microcosm of the entire Palestinian conflict. No matter what happens, no matter how much the Israelis and the West work to get the Palestinians what they need to heal and live peacefully, the Palestinians only appear interested in killing everyone involved, including themselves. They have sold themselves on death instead of life, and reason and compassion hold no attraction for them. (via the Corner, and Power Line also addresses this story)."

Update: Powerline's Scott Johnson also has a take on this story...and more details, too. And, of course, LGF weighs in as well.

Palestinians and Reuters News Service In Need of a Qualified PR Coordinator

Charles Johnson at Little Green Footballs has graphic and amusing evidence of what happens when too many people try to use the same props. Be sure to look carefully at the photos containing the "key" evidence!

TUESDAY, JUNE 21, 2005

Durbin Apologizes On Floor of Senate & Newt Offers a Brilliant Resolution To the Controversy

Senator Dick Durbin, who infamously compared the American treatment of terrorist detainees at Guantanamo Bay with the tactics used by the Nazi SS, Soviet KGB and Pol Pot's murderous thugs has now, on the floor of the U.S. Senate, publically apologized to those who were offended by his words.

Unfortunately, he did not clarify whether he did or did *not* mean to make that comparison in the first place. So, until he says something more definitive, we are left to wonder whether Durbin is simply sorry that some folks didn't like what he said.

I suppose that, for the mixed up and incoherent "Senate traditions," this apology will probably suffice.

Even former House Speaker, Newt Gingrich, speaking on Hugh Hewitt's radio show this afternoon, admitted that he is now recalling his demand for Durbin's censure by the Senate. Instead, he is urging the Senate to debate and vote on a resolution that would simply declare that the Senate rejects any proposition that equates the American treatment of terrorists at Guantanamo Bay with Nazi death camps, the Soviet gulag or Pol Pot's "killing fields."

This would, of course, give Durbin the opportunity to simply vote "yes" or "no," therefore clearing up the controversy once and for all.

The question now becomes, what Republican Senator will have the courage to sponsor such a resolution? Whoever does may provide evidence that they have the "right stuff" to be considered as part of the 2008 Republican nation ticket.

On the other hand, ***why hasn't there been a single Democrat*** who has stepped forward and said something like,

While Dick Durbin's comments may have been twisted and falsely criticized by the more unhinged fringes of the Republican Right Wing, I would like to make it perfectly clear that I would never agree with nor offer support of consolation to anyone....and I mean anyone....who would intentionally or by innuendo, compare American policies and practices towards even the most despicable terrorist detainee with even the most innocuous actions of the German Nazis, the Soviet Communists or the Cambodian Khmer Rouge. I hope I have made my personal opinion on the matter clear. Thank you.

The silence is not only deafening.....it is damning.

WEDNESDAY, JUNE 22, 2005

Was It U.S. Military Policy to Shoot Wounded & Surrendering Japanese Soldiers In WW II?

A friend of mine, now 83 years old, recently told me a story about being in the Marines during WW II. As he was about to be deployed to the South Pacific from a base in Southern California, the officer orienting them for the situations they would be facing stated that they would be required to shoot and kill surrendering or wounded Japanese soldiers they might encounter.

My friend indicated to the officer that he would not be able to comply with that order. He was subsequently written up for insubordination and wound up spending the next two years on an East Coast Marine base doing paper-shuffling word. All personal leaves were cancelled. He described the experience as similar to being under house arrest. Later, he did receive an honorable discharge.

This raised an interesting question in my mind.
Were U.S. Military orders issued during WW II requiring U.S. Marines and/or other soldiers to kill surrendering or wounded Japanese soldiers in the South Pacific?

I am well aware that many surrendering Japanese soldiers did so with the intent of "taking out" a few American GIs before they would be killed. Wounded Japanese frequently would blow themselves up along with Americans who attempted to come to their aid.

In personal accounts such as "My Private War" by Private Chester W. Nycum, I can read graphic accounts as to how U.S. soldiers began to routinely kill wounded and surrendering Japanese simply out of a sense of self-preservation. In this case, the untrustworthy and deceptive behavior by the Japanese brought this action upon themselves.

But nowhere, whether in Nycum's short reminiscence or in any other place, have I read where soldiers were explicitly ordered to do this as military policy.

Stanley Frankel's on-line book, "Frankel-y Speaking About World War II In the Pacific," suggests that in his unit, at least, the exact ***opposite*** was the order of the day:
Lieutenant Jones explained there was one infallible method of convincing a reluctant Japanese prisoner to tell all he knows: to tell him, via interpreters, that they will send his name and picture back to Japan. At that, the Japanese falls to his knees, begs forgiveness, and proceeds to spill enough beans to send a few squads of his brothers- in- arms to honorable ancestors. We might note that few Japanese ever attempt to hold anything back. Being taken prisoner is not in their handbooks. No Japanese is ever taken alive. Thus, they are not drilled in the "Name-Rank- Serial No- nothing more" routine. They usually reveal everything easily without any persuasion

For this reason, ***our men have been repeatedly warned that though all dead Japanese are good Japanese, a live Japanese prisoner is worth ten times his weight in American lives. The bravado with which some American soldiers cold-bloodedly shoot quivering, defenseless, even wounded Japanese, in this context, can be equated to treason****. The moral aspect of the situation is secondary; the significant point is that taking Japanese prisoners can save American lives.*

Can anyone help clear this up? Does it really matter?

An old posting on Free Republic, entitled "Film Exposes Allies' Pacific War Atrocities" presents an "expose" of WW II movie footage showing the sort of killings described by Private Nycum.

The article ends with these words:

One US marine, Steve Judd, based on the island of Saipan during some of the fiercest combat of the war, blamed repeated exposure to horrors for some of the Allied excesses.

Judd described how he was ordered to clear some caves. Aware of the Japanese tactic of pretending to surrender before blowing themselves and their captors up with a hidden grenade, he and his team decided to be indiscriminate. 'We just blew it all up. We don't know if there were women and children or whatever, we just blew them up,' he said.

'Some people today will tell you it was cruel and inhumane, but you weren't there - we were.'

This article generated some fascinating comments, including this one from someone named, Hobey Baker:

My Dad was in the infantry in New Guinea in World War II. He said neither side took prisoners, and the ***U.S. troops were TOLD not to take Japanese prisoners*** *because they were just too dangerous. The level of brutality on both sides was unimaginable.(My Dad said the Australians were the toughest troops on our side, because they'd been in the jungle the longest, hated the Japanese the most and were half-crazy from drinking quinine to keep the malaria symptomsdown.)*

*My Dad made it clear that no one in combat in the Pacific was in anything like a normal frame of mind. Everybody was terrified, brutalized and just prayed that they'd live long enough to go home and try to forget all the s**t they'd done and seen.*
This comment seems, at last, to corroborate my friend's story and even offers a partexplanationtion for why the order (if it was, indeed, an official order) was given. Even so, asanecdotalodal comment it does not actually "prove" that such orders were given.

I suspect that this particular question has more than a little relevance to our current national "discussion" over the treatment of "prisoners of war," "terrorist detainees" and "enemy combatants." The issue is always context, context, context.

This is chillingly captured by another comment on the Free Republic post, this one by someone named Ron C.:

"Pacific war atrocities" began with the Japanese.. as in the Philippines with the Bataan Death march, gang rapes of women and children and indiscriminate and frequent murder and robbery of tens of thousands of captives. The Japs did not hold with any of the "conventions" of war, and made that quite apparent to the allied troops who swore a "tit for tat" policy on the ground. Such "crimes" did not happen in the US war between the states, because the participants weren't savages - but in most wars savage things happen, and revenge became all to common in the Pacific, far worse than the European theater.

I've known about, and seen footage of WWII war that few have ever or will ever see - some of it the most brutal imaginable, committed by all sides in the war. But, the last line of the post tells it like is really is, "Some people today will tell you it was cruel and inhumane, but you weren't there - we were." My uncles were there, and what they brought home were tales of horror so far beyond common knowledge today that I doubt the public has any ability to comprehend what they had to face - they had to kill quickly in any way possible - or be killed. Did they kill unnecessarily and brutally? You bet they did, but their fiendish enemies did far more of it - many of their victims being non-combatant civilians.

At this point I have sort of run out of things to say. Perhaps it doesn't matter whether official orders to kill wounded and surrendering Japanese soldiers were given or not. In point of fact, it would appear that context even generated conflicting and mutually exclusive policies in this regard.

I suppose that, given the reality of the history of war, the prisoners held at Guantanamo Bay and elsewhere should count themselves lucky that they are still alive to defecate, sweat, tremble when cold and, yes, even to be interrogated under the watchful eyes of the FBI, the U.S. military, the CIA, the ICRC, Amnesty International and Senator Dick Durbin.

THURSDAY, JUNE 23, 2005

And the Poppies Grow......

The photo on the left will surprise you. It does ***not*** show opium poppies growing in northern Afghanistan! It is actually a BBC photo showing the "Flanders Field" type of poppy growing *en masse* in Hertfordshire, England.

If you want to see what opium poppies look like, the one on the right is the picture you should be looking at:

Gonzales To Replace O'Conner On High Court?

Yesterday, Hugh Hewitt posted this link: Bill Kristol writes that he hears it will be O'Connor stepping down next week, not the Chief, and that the Attorney General will be her replacement.

Alberto Gonzales is not the most conservative of possible nominees, but he is at least as conservative as O'Conner, who he would be replacing. At only 49 years of age, he would have at least a 15-20 year term of service.

In his favor is the fact that the Senate, without filibuster (although with great delay) confirmed him as Attorney General just this past February. It would be very difficult for the Democrats to justify his appointment to the Supreme Court as an extraordinary circumstance under this circumstance!

As Kristol suggests in his article, when the time comes for Reinquist to retire, the would be the time for Bush to nominate a more conservative judge to the court. That would undoubtedly bring the reality of a full-blown filibuster into the Senate once again.

Then again, as he admits himself, Kristol could be wrong about the entire thing!

A Funeral At Punchbowl Cemetery Tomorrow

Tomorrow morning I will officiate at a brief inurnment service for a member of my congregation. The service will take place at Punchbowl cemetery in Honolulu. The official name for the Punchbowl site is, "The National Memorial Cemetery of the Pacific." It is always an honor for a airman, seaman, soldier or Marine to be buried there.

Joe Hazard died last Saturday at the age of 83. He had been bedridden and confined to his home

with Parkinson's Disease for over 7 years, personally cared for by his loving and devoted wife, Karen.

Joe served in the U.S. Navy for over 32 years, a span of time covering World War II, the Korean War and Vietnam. He worked in the area of aviation maintenance. As a licensed pilot himself, he would never release a plane back into service unless he knew he would be comfortable flying it himself.

In his younger days he had been a Navy boxing champion and weight lifter.

He retired at the rank of Master Chief Petty Officer, the highest non-commissioned rank in the Navy.

When I first met Joe, he was already showing the first signs of Parkinson's. His one hand, in particular, shook uncontrollably....unless he was driving his car...when the shaking would stop as he clutched the steering wheel!

As his health declined I visited Joe and Karen at home each month and served the Sacrament of Communion to them both. Although baptized as a child, Joe had only attended Navy chapels as an adult, both before and after his retirement. Consequently, he had never had an opportunity to "join a church" or to publicly make a personal confession of faith in Jesus Christ as his Lord and Savior.

After many conversations and much prayer, Joe, now confined at home to his bed, made his confession of faith in my presence. His health did not permit other visitors to come into his home at that time. Soon after, Karen did not even allow me to visit as it made him too anxious and upset.

In any case, I reported Joe's confession of faith and desire to be received into the membership of our church to the church Session. They voted to receive him into membership on my recommendation alone, without meeting with Joe or hearing his confession shared publicly. This is the only time in my 26 years of ordained ministry that this has happened.

After receiving news that he had died last Saturday, I drove over to the house. He had passed away less than an hour before I arrived. It had been 5 or 6 years since I had last seen Joe. Karen, on the other hand, had, in the beginning, been able to attend worship on occasional Sundays. Eventually, however, she was unable to leave Joe for even that one hour each week.

At the house I prayed for Joe and Karen as I trusted his soul "to the care and mercy of almighty God." Because of his earnest and sincere affirmation of faith seven years ago, I was able to add those glorious words, "In the sure and certain hope for resurrection to eternal life."

Tomorrow I will share these words at his service. There will be full military honors as well, with the presentation of the American Flag to his wife, Karen.

Karen, born and raised in Japan and living through World War II as a child, has her own amazing story to tell. I hope to post it here soon.

FRIDAY, JUNE 24, 2005

Punchbowl Funeral

Yesterday I posted a story on today's funeral service at Punchbowl, National Memorial Cemetery of the Pacific. This morning the service took place as planned with around 20 people attending (not including the Navy Honor Guard).

As always there was a aura of solemn gratitude for those who lay at rest in that place. The photo at the top of this post was taken at the conclusion of the service as Karen was being handed the American Flag, a gift from "a grateful nation." Amen.

A Great Way to Say "Thank You" To Our Soldiers In Iraq & Afghanistan

"The Anti-Idiotarian Rottweiler" is promoting a great idea: A one-stop email site for distributing encouraging notes of thanks and appreciation to our troops deployed in Iraq and Afghanistan.

It appears than some soldiers have been writing home saying that, from what they read in the Main-Stream Media, they are begining to doubt whether Americans are aware of all the good stuff they are doing there or whether anyone is still supporting them in their efforts.

So.....if you would like to write a generic sort of "thank you" to our soldiers in harm's way, or if you would rather write a short note sharing some of the "good stuff" you know they have been doing....send it off to this address!)

rottmope@yahoo.com

Aussies Raid Muslim Bookstore In Melbourne

Muslim literature being sold in a bookstore adjacent to the Brunswick mosque near Melbourne, Australia, was the subject of a recent raid by the Australian Security Intelligence Organisation (Herald Sun (Victoria),

Books sold at the store attached to the Brunswick mosque tell Muslims they should "hate and take as enemies" non-Muslims, reject Jews and Christians, and learn to hate in order to properly love Allah.

Although Muslims are encouraged to engender hate towards Christians and other non-believers it appears that the major thrust of much of the literature centers on hatred of Jews. Examples are cited where the killing of Jews is not considered to be displeasing to Allah.

Perhaps the most revealing items in the article was this:

*One text says of devotion to Allah: "**As regards hatred for His sake this is an essential prerequisite for loving Him.**"*

I suppose that even we Christians are told to share in God's hatred of sin....("I hate divorce," says the Lord God of Israel..." Malachi 2:16).

Yet Jesus tells us that the hatred of others is strictly forbidden ("**You have heard that it was said, 'Love your neighbor and hate your enemy.' But I tell you: Love your enemies[i] and pray for those who persecute you, that you may be sons of your Father in heaven.**" Matthew 5:43-44).

The contrast between these two teachings, the first being the message of hate being blessed and required by Allah, and the second being the love of enemies as commanded by Jesus, is far too great to reconcile them one to the other. The god of Muhammad ("Allah") cannot say these things and still be considered to be the same god as the "Lord God of Israel."

I will stop short of saying that the literature uncovered in that Melbourne mosque's bookstore is representative of "mainstream Islam" (whatever that may be), but the fact that so-called "moderate" Muslim leaders do not condemn such ideas lends them an aura of legitimacy.

The teachings of Jesus lead his followers to build medical clinics and hospitals for Christians and non-Christians alike. We are required to be tolerant of the beliefs of others even thought, at the same time, we may feel compelled to speak against those same beliefs. Truth is to be discerned and then embraced as an act of freee, personal choice and conviction.

The harsher teachings of Muhammad, however, appear tcapable of leading his followers to murder and behead innocent people and to carry explosives under your clothing in order to blow yourself up in an "enemy's" hospital.

For a Christian, "God is love."

For a Muslim of the kind that writes the above-cited books, Allah is the source of both good and evil and permits his followers to do unto others what no Christian would ever tolerate being done to anybody!

Knowing personally two of the leaders of the Honolulu mosque, I very much doubt that they are encourging their brothers and sisters in Islam to read and follow such teachings.

Yet I can only wonder...and worry...over what is being preached, taught and encouraged at the mosques in other folks' neighborhoods.

Billy Graham, Billy Clinton & the Last Crusade

First it was President George Bush holding hands with his good friend, Saudi Crown Prince Abdullah. Today it was (former) President Bill Clinton holding hands with his good friend, the venerable Rev. Dr. Billy Graham.

Today's occasion was framed by the setting of a Billy Graham Crusade in New York....an event that may well prove to be Dr. Graham's final crusade appearance in the United States.

Clinton introduced Graham to a crowd estimated to be close to 80,000 people. He shared an anecdote concerning how impressed he was as a young boy when Billy Graham, scheduled to preach at a evangelism crusade in Arkansas, refused to speak because the event was segregated. As Clinton put it today, "I've loved him ever since. God bless you, friend."

I must confess that I am glad to see a senior member of the Democratic Party having something nice to say about an evangelical Christian. Hillary was at the event, too, but I do not believe she spoke on the dais as her husband did. This, I think, is to her credit.

It is also difficult to compare these two men:

One Bill worked his way up the political ladder to attain the highest office in the U.S. Government, serving for 8 years as the most powerful individual in the world.

The other Bill has done nothing much except tell people about Jesus Christ and then inviting them to receive him as their Lord and Savior.

For all his greatness, the first Bill will likely be remembered as only the second President to be impeached by the U.S. Congress...for attempting to cover up a sexual relationship with a White House intern by lying under oath.

For all his humility, the second Bill will likely be remembered as the preeminent American Christian evangelist of the 20th century; a friend of Kings, Queens, Presidents and Pope; a man polled repeatedly as the most respected man in America.

The first Bill, who was great, was made humble.

The second Bill, who was humble, was made great.

As **Jesus** once put it, "But many who are first will be last, and many who are last will be first."

All in all a moving witness to the sinner and the saint; the fallen and the redeemed; an example of what we should not be and an example what we should be; two people taken together forming a perfect illustration of the sort of multiple personalities at war within each one of us.

By God's wonderful providence, Billy Graham has lead more than a few Bill Clintons to the "throne of grace" during his 50+ years of personally practicing what he preached.

We are all better for having shared this world with the likes of Billy Graham. Bill Clinton would no doubt agree. It is somewhat ironic that, on that platform in New York today, it was a man who was once the most powerful person in the world who was looking up with admiration at a man who had never really had any power at all, except for a Bible and some Good News.

SUNDAY, JUNE 26, 2005

Nude Justice Statue Scores a Touchdown

Well, well, well...It appears that John Ashcroft's de-nuding of the front hall of the Justice Department Building has been undone. The once-draped figures of the Spirit of Justice and the Majesty of Justice have been, at long last, re-nuded to their former glory.

Seeing the now infamous photo of John Ascroft with the bare-breasted Spirit of Justice in the background reminded me of the (fully-clothed) mosaic of Jesus that hovers above and behind one end of the University of Notre Dame football stadium.

Both figures have their arms raised as if signalling a touchdown.

So, now we have both a "Touchdown Jesus" and a "Touchdown .....ah.... ...Justice? Spirit? .....ah ...." Can someone come up with a better name for the Justice statue? The winning suggestion will be awarded six points for the.....well.....you know....!

While on the subject of Jesus and sports, here is a nifty site where you can puchase these four little beauties: Jesus Plays Football: Jesus Plays Basketball; Jesus Plays Baseball; and Jesus Plays Soccer

And, last but not least, there is this Jesus in Cincinnati...either signalling another touchdown or suddenly forgetting how to walk on water!

You can read more about this Jesus here, here and here.
Hat Tip to Michael Homan for discovering those Jesus sports statues. He also has some funny things to say about them. Check him out!

Marriage In Paradise

I thought some of you might enjoy these two photos of a wedding that took place today between two members of my congregation. I officiated, of course, but also brought my camera along "just in case."

The groom is a good friend and church Deacon. He has served three tours of duty in the Middle East/Persian Gulf and was part of a P-3 crew who miraculously survived a dramatic ditching of their crippled and burning plane....the first time there had ever been survivors of such a crash. He has no doubt that God intervened to save the entire crew. I think that God had plans for him that included his new bride!

In any case, the ceremony eneded with a traditional U.S. Navy Wedding Sword Arch. As the newly married couple approached each pair of officers, the swords were lowered and they were not permitted to pass to the next pair until they had kissed each other. I took this photo during their third kiss. (It sort of gives new meaning to the phrase, "making a pass," don't you think?)

One Navy Wedding tradition that they skipped was the one where the bride gets a sword-slap on her behind after passing the last two officers. In this case, she got away with it because of her own prior service in the U.S. Navy.

The groom did not get a "swat" either....perhaps because he had his own Navy sword tucked away in my church office. Or perhaps because he out-ranked both of the officers at the end of the arch! (Good planning on his part!)

I am glad to say that the new husband and wife still appeared to be happy three hours later at the wedding reception. By God's grace that happiness will be "forever-after." Or , more precisely, "As long as we both shall live!"

MONDAY, JUNE 27, 2005

High Sierra Vacation

I'm afraid I will not be posting much of anything in the next three weeks. I am leaving one paradise for another.....heading to the beautiful Sierra Nevada Mountains to spend time with my extended family at Donner Lake over the Fourth of July.

Later, I will head to Southern California to help daughter #1 find housing for her upcoming move to that area for graduate school.

Then comes a Presbytery meeting in Los Angeles and, finally, a return to the Sierra for one more week; this time hiking and fly fishing with my brother.

If I run across a computer with an internet connection I might (if my wonderful wife is not watching) post a few thoughts or photos so don't abandon me forever!

To those of you who visit me often, thanks. I hope to see you again, soon. To the rest of you, take a look through the archives. There are things there that will make you smile....and a few things that might make you cry!

So, Aloha In Jesus to you all. Be sure to take some time out to enjoy your summer, too!

MONDAY, JULY 04, 2005

Comet Bulls-Eye for NASA

Although I am still on vacation in the middle of nowhere I did manage to stay up last night and watch scientific history unfold as NASA's Deep Impact probe struck "paydirt" in spectacular fashion. I want to congratulate NASA and the Jet Propulsion Lab for their success.

WEDNESDAY, JULY 06, 2005

One of Those Days

Well...Daughter #1 and I arrived in Los Angeles this morning as planned. What wasn't planned was getting on the Budget Rent-a-Car airport shuttle instead of the Dollar shuttle. So, after a trip to Budget we returned to the airport and, after a long wait, caught the right shuttle and picked up our car at Dollar.

After checking into our hotel and checking out apartment rentals in newspapers and the internet we drove to Santa Monica to register with West Side Rentals and search their listings.

After driving down to Palisades Park, overlooking the Santa Monica Beach, I got out of the car to put some quarters in the parking meter. Daughter #1 also got out of the car, being careful to make sure the doors were all locked properly.

Unfortunately, I had intended to get back into the car and had left my key on the dashboard. So...called Dollar "road service" and paid for a local locksmith over the phone. While we waited, we sat on a park bench, enjoying the late afternoon sun sparkling off of the Pacific Ocean as we sorted through all of the apartment possiblities and made phone calls.

Forty minutes later the locksmith arrived and, after struggling with our door lock for, oh, say...five seconds, got it unlocked and got us back on the move.

Nothing much to add except that we enjoyed a wonderful meal at my favorite Mexican Restaurant in Del Rey/Westchester, La Hacienda Del Rey (on Lincoln Ave.), and, after some more research and planning out tomorrow, are going to bed early!

Life is never dull.....and if a locksmith can open a locked car in five seconds I guess someone else could do it, too. What a happy thought! Buenos Noches!

SATURDAY, JULY 09, 2005

Farewell To Rehnquist & His Gold Stripes

I was sorry, but not surprised, to hear of Chief Justice William Rehnquist's resignation from the U.S. Supreme Court today. He has been a fine jurist whose opinions have been straightforward and clear, showing little of the "gray" logic of imprecision and ambiguity shown by other Court members in recent years.

He will not only be missed, he will be difficult to replace...in some ways more difficult to replace than outgoing Justice Sandra O'Conner.

One thing I will not miss will be the silly gold bands Rehnquist added to his robes to distinguish himself from his "non-Chief Justice" colleagues. The Chief Justice should view him/herself as the "first of equals." The emphasis should always be more on the "equal" part of the equation rather than on the "first" part. Those gold bands always appeared to me to signal a sort of "look-at-me" pride that, ironically, seemed to diminish, rather than increase, the status of this high office.

I sincerely hope that his replacement will return to the time-honored tradition of wearing a plain, black robe like every other American judge.

UPDATE: Well, as should be obvious, being on an extended vacation and trying to catch the news in bits and pieces has left me with more than a little egg on my face! Rehnquist is, of course, still on the court and may well be there long enough to welcome John Roberts, his former court intern, as a member of the Court by his own right! I continue to wish Chief Justice Rehnquist both life and health but still look forward to the day when those ghastly "stripes" are retired to the Smithsonian.

Three Thoughts On the London Bombings

1. I am baffled by the confusion of both law enforcement and the media regarding the timing of the explosions. Surely, the objective evidence of video surveillance cameras, Underground transport clocks and eyewitness accounts should have been reconciled within one hour of the blasts, showing a near-simultaneous detonation. An error of 26 minutes is a vast error and I remain mystified that it took nearly two days to correct it.

2. The effect of the bombings on the public psyche has been dramatically lessened for two reasons:

First, the attacks were not "new" or "innovative." In contrast to the attacks on 9?11 they were almost mundane, as in: "Oh, dear, not ***another*** bombing! How sad for the Brits."

Second, the three Tube bombings were deep underground, providing neither spectacular photographs of the explosions themselves (as with the jetliner impacts at the WTC) nor follow-up photos of the damage and carnage (as with the train bombings in Spain). Out of sight=Out of mind."

This is a welcome miscalculation on the part of the terrorists (thus far, the bus has been the only visual icon of the attacks).

3. The London attacks should remind us all how even small, simple explosive devices, when used with strategic precision, can paralyze a city of millions. Had there been any chemical or radioactive component to the bombs the casualty figures would have been in the thousands and the London Underground system significantly shut down for months, if not years.

Security concerns raised by the incident serve only to reveal the contents of the American "Patriot Act" to be tame and almost innocuous in the face of the threat that we face in a free and open society.

I suggest that vocal and strident opposition to even the more "controversial" aspects of the Patriot Act by members of Congress will, at this point in time, be political suicide...especially for those who might have an interest in pursuing national office.

Praise God for the Little Things

Daughter #1 and I have now completed our three-day visit to Los Angeles.

In this short amount of time we managed to locate and purchase a wonderful used-car for my daughter to drive and to sign a lease for an apartment where she can live when she returns at the end of the month to begin graduate school.

God made both possible, providing both when we had virtually run out of both ideas and time.

With the car, God brought us a salesman who happened to be a Christian immigrant from the Middle East. I mentioned that I had recently had the honor and privilege of meeting the world-wide spiritual head of his "denomination" in Hawaii. Tears immediately formed in his eyes, he asked me to pray for him and his family and promised to try and get us the car at no profit for hiself.

This he actually accomplished, with our purchase price ending up being nearly $1,300 under the sticker price and less than both wholesale and retail Kelly Blue Book listings....for a car that looked as though the previous owner had washed his hands every time before he drove it!

After the deal had been signed, I did pray with him. As my daughter got into her "new car" to leave, he leaned in the window and told her that if she ever needed anything while living in LA she should give him a call as, because of my faith, my ministry and my prayers, he would consider her as his own daughter!

What a witness to God's providence! And what a witness to my daughter regarding the Spirit who makes us one in Christ Jesus our Lord!

The apartment was a similar experience.

On the afternoon of our final day, we visited an apartment close by another one we had been disappointed in earlier. My daughter fell in love with it immediately. The Manager had moved in himself only four days earlier. It turned out that he had many family members in Hawaii. He and my daughter hit it off right away. He took her application and said that the management group would run a credit check this weekend and choose between applicants.

Soon after, we visited another apartment that was acceptable but not anywere near as attractive as the first. My daughter was essentially offered this apartment on the spot. What should she do? Take the sure thing? Or leave LA hoping to get the one she really wanted? She was told that the credit check would take ten to fifteen minutes. We drove away completely unsure what to do. We decided to phone the manager of the first apartment to explain the situation and see if he could expedite her application process in some way.

As my daughter picked up her cell phone to call him, the phone rang. We expected it to be the manager of the second apartment. Instead, it was the manager of the first apartment, offering her the lease. Apparently, he had been impressed with her, personally ran a quick credit check, phoned the management association and asked them to waive their review and allow him to offer it to her. They agreed and he had phoned to tell her!

Within seconds of the end of this call, she received two phone calls. I won't tell you who phoned, but I will tell you that they were from the two people that would have been the first two people she would have immediately phoned to tell them the good news.

My daughter was shocked, stunned and overjoyed all at the same time. God had worked another "miracle" that was almost beyond comprehension. She had been told that it would take a minimum of two weeks to locate a decent, affordable apartment in Western LA.

To add to the aura of mystery, I then mentioned to her that I had, for some reason I could not even understand myself, only prayed one time for God to provide a particular apartment. That afternoon, as we were nearing the neighborhood of a new apartment listing, I had asked God that this particular apartment, which we had not yet seen, would be the one that God had chosen for my daughter.

After attempting to contact nearly 100 apartment listings and after personally visiting more than 20 of them, this one apartment...the only one I had felt moved by God to pray for...was the one she wound up with.

In Hawaii we call this a "chicken skin" moment! Although I have experienced such things many, many times in my own life and ministry, it was something new for my daughter. I quoted to her my "life verse" from Proverbs, "Trust in the Lord with all your heart, and lean not on your own understanding. In all your ways ackownledge him, and he will make straight your paths."

That, I told my daughter, was exactly what had happened with both the car and the apartment.

Without a moment's hesitation, she replied, "Yes, and I think it fits my 'life verse' from Philippians, too!" And then she quoted,

I can do all things through Christ who strengthens me.

Amen! I couldn't have put it better myself!

SUNDAY, JULY 10, 2005

"Eyes Wide Shut"--Sleepwalking Through a War

John Daniszewski, writing in the Los Angeles Times this morning ("London Can Take It!"), somehow managed to find a way to sum up the entire political divide over the "war on terrorism" in one paragraph:

"It is one thing to face the future stoically," (historian Max Huston) suggests, "but not with eyes closed. **Even if Britain does not feel it is at war, the people who are bombing it do**, *and so it is necessary to be on guard."*

That, in a nutshell, is the whole point. The terrorists are at war with us and know that they are at war with us. Britain, Western Europe and Americans have not yet figured that out. Until we do we will be sleepwalking and in complete denial of the seriousness of the reality which we are facing....or, more precisely....the reality which is facing us!

Lord, keep us from the following description of Americans as cited in another LA Times article today written by Doyle McManus ("Afrter Flaggin Support Second Wind for Bush"):
The effect of a single event on public opinion--even a major terrorist event--is usually temporary.

People are worried about terrorism, but the edge comes off their concern as times passes, said Andrew Kohut of the Pew Research Center..

We cannot allow the "edge" to "come off." Whether we believe we are at war or not....those who wish to destroy us have no doubts whatsoever.

Is Toyota Promoting a New Morality?

Tell me if I'm wrong, but I heard an ad for Toyota on the radio this morning while returning my rental car at LAX. The ad zipped by me fairly quickly but what I thought I heard was this:

Everyone in my family drives a Toyota: My mother, my wife, ***my girl friend*** *and my kids.....*

Now, I may be a pastor but I do not consider myself a prude. On the other hand....please, someone....anyone...tell me I did not hear this ad correctly! Perhaps their new slogan should be:

"Toyota...Not Your Father's Family Car!"

MONDAY, JULY 18, 2005

Sen. Tancredo Does An "Oops!'

The good U.S. Representative Tom Tancredo of Colorado mispoke today. We all do it. But when a U.S. Congressman says something as dangerous and potentially incendiary as threatening to bomb Mecca in retaliation for future Islamic terrorist attacks on the United States, the Senator must rise above personal pride and admit that he erred......and erred badly.

One Hand Clapping has some good thoughts on this as does Hugh Hewitt. They both link to others who share their thoughts with various degrees of of passion and intelligence. Note especially the comments section at the end of One Hand Clapping's post. It appears that there are more than a few folks out there who are getting really sick and tired of this terrorism idea and are willing to cheer Mr. Tancredo's off-the-cuff suggestion.

As a Christian, I find such an idea abhorrent and morally untennable. It is our moral "high ground" that will ultimately overcome the evil that confronts us, not the bombs and bullets of a superpower.

The Japanese and Germans would still be our enemies today were it not for the forgiveness and generosity we showed them following their defeat in WW II. Even with the questionable (they will always be questionable) decisions to fire bomb Tokyo and Dresden and to drop nuclear bombs on Hiroshima and Nagasaki, it should be obvious that the United States and its allies demonstrated tremendous restraint and wise discretion in offering an open hand rather than a clenched fist to the citizens of those countries both during and following the years of conflict.

As a matter of practical policy, an action such as that suggested by Rep. Tancredo, would doom, not only the United States, but the rest of the non-Muslim world to an eternity of conflict that would never end until every Muslim was dead or until everyone left alive in the world was a Muslim.

I'm Back!

I'm back at last from my three week vacation. I had a good time. Before too long I will post some photos from this year's hiking and fishing in the Sierra Nevada with my brother.

The best news of all is that I can now climb up a very long set of stairs without huffing and puffing! A series of hikes to lakes with elevations of 9,000-10,000+ feet will generally have that effect...if one survives the hikes in the first place!

In any case, I can assure you all that the beauty of God's creation can still be seen in all its glory. Since no one has ever said it better, I'll let John Muir, speaking of the Sierra Nevada, have the last word here:
All the world lies warm in one heart, yet the Sierra seems to get more light than other mountains (OUR NP, pg.76).....The sunshine falls in glory through the colossal spires and crowns, each a symbol of health and strength, the noble shafts faithfully upright like the pillars of temples, upholding a roof of infinite leafy interlacing arches and fretted skylights (OUR NP, pg.99).

TUESDAY, JULY 19, 2005

Bush Nominates Judge John Roberts to Supreme Court

The nomination of US Court of Appeals (Washington DC) Judge John Roberts to the Supreme Court this evening appears to have pleased most of the conservative pundits. Hugh Hewitt calls the nomination a "home run." One of his talk-show guests one-upped him by calling the nomination a "grand slam."

Personally, I know nothing about Judge Roberts except what I am reading on the internet. I do know that there were many conservatives who were floating Roberts' name as a nominee nearly two years ago. On the other hand, I expect the Democrats to at least symbolically oppose his nomination with as much grilling and hand-wringing as possible....SHORT OF A FILIBUSTER!

Yes, short of a filibuster. Based on what I have read this evening, I do not believe that the Democrats will be willing to risk losing everything by detonating their own "nuclear option" over Judge Roberts. It appears that any opposition to this nominee will prove to be a lost cause from the beginning. It would be far more likely to find the Democrats letting this one ride and save their "big guns" for Rehnquist replacement and/or the appointment of someone like Clarence Thomas as Chief Justice.

Even so, over the next few weeks we will all learn more about this man than we have any real need to know. Will there be pubic hairs on his Coke cans? Playboy magazines on his coffee table? Or will he turn out to be a church-going Christian? An Atlanta Braves fan? Or, horror of horrors, perhaps it is discovered that he once tipped a public restroom attendant in Dallas who turned out to have been an illegal alien from Mexico....or, even worse....from Saudi Arabia!

I have already read criticisms based on opinions he wrote in his law school term papers! Wow! Wait until we hear from his preschool teacher who will vaguely remember that he might have made a little girl cry by tickling her during naptime.

If that won't disqualify him from the Supreme Court, what will?

High Sierra Vacation

I have just returned from four days in the High Sierra with my brother hiking and fly fishing (catch and release). We stayed at Lee Vining, on the shore of Mono Lake. Our daily hikes started with a short drive from there each morning.

On Day One, just to break ourselves in, we hiked up Yosemite Creek for about two miles....just to enjoy the beauty, fish a little, get ourselves acclimated to the higher altitude (app 8,000 ft) and to look at the pretty wildflowers.

On Day Two, we drove to nearby Lundy Lake and climbed 1700 vertical feet in four miles to Oneida Lake. The remains of the old Oneida Mine were very evident in the area around

Crystal Lake. On our way back down we met Forest Service personnel on their way up to "blow up" and collapse the mine entrance (which we had just visited). I suppose the reason for this was the fear of liability. In any case, the photos we took of the mine entrance were possibly the last ever taken!

On Day Three, we drove up Tioga Canyon to Tioga Pass (approx. 10,000 ft) and climbed up 1000 more and then down 200 in one mile to reach the Gaylor Lakes basin, one of our favorite places in Yosemite. I first discovered this spot 30 years ago and had the best day of fly fishing I have ever had in Middle Gaylor. The high meadow gives the illusion of being on top of the world! Upper Gaylor Lake was mostly frozen but we fished off of a snow bank, overhanging the water!

Afterwards we took a five mile hike up the Parker Fork of the Tuolumne River. The flowers were beautiful and I was surprised to catch several small Brown Trout in the high elevation where usually Brook Trout are to be found.

On Day Four, we took a long-anticipated hike to a lake with a name but no trail...at least there is no trail marked on any USGS maps, etc. that we researched. This lake was also still mostly frozen, due to the late and heavy winter as well as the lack of strong winds

(which usually break up the ice by the end of May or mid June each year).

The lake glimmered in a spectacular setting. Our guess is that only 20 or so people must visit this lake each year out of the 10s of thousands of hikers that pass close by heading for other lakes in other places.

I will not tell you the name or location of this lake...we don't want to let out our little secret! But, I would invite everyone to guess it's name! If you get it right I will do something nice for you (something I haven't thought of yet!).

Well, that's about it for this year. As always, I began to feel in good physical shape the day we stopped hiking and returned back to my brother's house in the San Joaquin Valley. While I was glad to return to Hawaii, my family and my congregation yesterday, I was glad to be gone for a few weeks, too!

WEDNESDAY, JULY 20, 2005

London Bombers May Have Been Duped?

Gee...who can a terrorist trust these days? According to London police, they may not be able to trust their "handlers" anymore.

According to News.com/au (HT to dogbarktree at Free Republic) London investigators are considering the possibility that the four "suicide" terrorist bombers might have been "duped" by the handlers into thinking that their bombs would go off with a timing device after they had "pushed the button" and gotten off of the train or bus they were on. Instead, the bombs exploded immediately when detonated. Evidence includes the fact that the bombers had paid the cost of their automobile parking fees and had purchased return tickets to Kings Cross Station where they first entered the subway.

Another odd piece of "evidence" is the report than none of the Muslim terrorists apparently cried, "Allah Akbar" ("God is Greatest") as they set off the bombs....something apparently quite normal and expected in such situations.

I wonder if they get their 72 virgins if they died, not by their own design, but by the machinations of other Muslims? Any ideas on this?

Austrailian Muslim Leaders Sponsor Anti-Terror Summit

According to today's Australian Herald, Muslim leaders in that country are organizing a "summit aimed at heading off extremist elements of the faith in Australia." They have even invited Australian Prime Minister John Howard (a bold critic of Islamic terrorism and strong backer of American policy in Iraq) to address the summit.

Why has the Council of American-Islamic Relations (CAIR), which purports to represent American Muslims, not called for such a summit in our country? Why have they not invited President Bush to speak to their assembly?

Why, in fact, are they still considered to be a major representation of American Muslims in spite of having had several of their leaders indicted, charged and/or convicted of supporting Islamic terrorist groups?

Whereas the Australian Muslims have demanded that all literature promoting Islamic terrorism be removed from every mosque and bookstore in their country, the Council on American-Islamic Relation has not even acknowledged that such literature exists in American mosques!

Is their something wrong with this picture?

American Soldier Shot By Sniper, Gets Up and Treats the Sniper's Wounds---Wow!

Pfc. Stephen Tschiderer, a U.S. Army medic in Baghdad, was shot in the chest by a sniper on June 9, 2005. According to the story released by the 256th Brigade Combat Team, Tschiderer, protected by his body armor, got up and directed his patrol's attention to the sniper's location in a nearby van.

The van was taken by the patrol but the sniper escaped, leaving a trail of blood. When finally located, lying on the ground groaning in pain, Tschiderer first applied handcuffs and then administered first aid to the man who, just a few minutes before, had been praising God ("Allah Akbar"), believing he had killed him.

Two men.....two Gods.....take your pick. I've already made mine!

P.S. The most surreal thing about this entire incident is that the sniper and associates were video/audio taping the whole thing. By clicking here you can watch Pvt. Tsschiderer being shot and listen to the celebratory words of his attackers. You can also, miraculously, watch Pvt. Tschiderer get up off of the ground, alive.

Scary....and creepy, too.

THURSDAY, JULY 21, 2005

Clarence Silva Ordained & Installed As Bishop of Honolulu

Although I am a Presbyterian pastor, I do have other friends who live in other "neighborhoods" of the Body of Christ. I even have friends who live outside of the Body of Christ......including Buddhist, Unitarian, Muslim, Mormons and Jewish. Tonight, however, I joined all of the above as part of an ecumenical and interfaith delegation invited to attend the ordination and installation of the new Roman Catholic Bishop of Honolulu.

The service was large enough to require the use of the Blaisdell Arena, a sort of combination convention center and venue for concerts, sports and other "events" like Ice Capades and the occasional large, traveling circus.

I believe there must have been at least 6-7,000 people there tonight.

The liturgy was long and unhurried, lasting more than 3 hours. It was virtually identical to the recently televised installation of the new Pope Benedict 16 as the Bishop of Rome......not surprising since both were being installed as bishops!

Among those who I processed in with were these three gentlemen who are leaders in the Egyptian Coptic Church in Hawaii.

During the service of ordination I found it interesting that each of the visiting bishops (there were two archbishops, 12 bishops and 3 auxiliary bishops present) layed their hands on the new bishop individually, one at a time. This is somewhat different from our common Presbyterian practice which involves all ordained pastors and elders laying on hands all at one time....often creating somewhat of a "traffic jam" around the person or persons being ordained!

The "Principal Consecrator" for the service was The Most Reverend William J. Levada, Apostolic Administrator of the Metropolitan Archdiocese of San Francisco. He is the man recently chosen by Pope Benedict XVI to take the new Pope's "old job" as Prefect of the Congregation for the Doctrine of the Faith in the Vatican.

Bishop Silva appears to be very much like his formal portrait, shown at the top of the post. He seems humble, pleasant and genuinely happy to be back in Hawaii where he was born and raised and where so many of his family still live. Unlike Pope Benedict XVI, he did not have the "deer caught in the headlights" look about him during his installation!

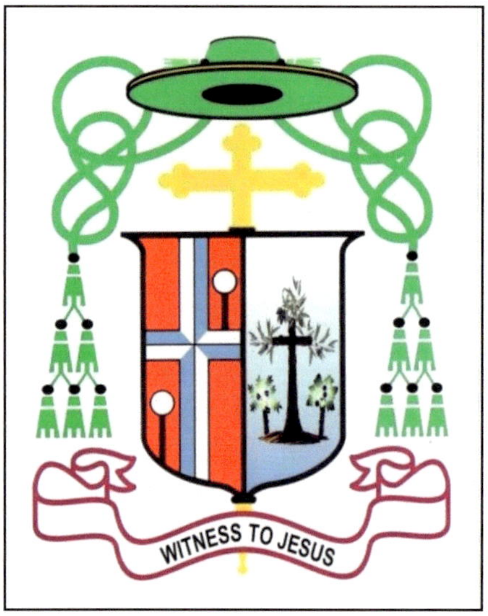

His official Crest shows, on the left, the symbol of the Diocese of Honolulu. On the right is the personal symbol he has chosen....three trees....chosen because his name, "Silva," means "trees" in Portuguese, the language of his forebears.

The little tree on the right is a Kukui tree, native to Hawaii and noted for the nuts that are not only processed to make beautiful leis, but also contain oil once used for "anointings" as well as for a fuel for lamps.

The little tree on the left is an oak tree, representative of Oakland, California, the Diocese where Fr. Silva has spent most of his previous ministry.

The central tree is, of course, the living cross of Christ...bursting with olive leaves, the symbol for peace.

The trees grow on an island, representing Hawaii, and surrounded by the blue waters of the Pacific Ocean, an ocean whose name, in Spanish, also means "peaceful."

Best of all is the motto chosen by the new Bishop: "Witness to Jesus."

I am hopeful that, as I continue to participate in "multi-faith" friendship building in Hawaii, I will have the opportunity to meet and establish at least some measure of personal relationship with Bishop Silva as I have done with other Christian and religious leaders. If my intuition is correct, I believe that I will find him to be not only a good Bishop, but a good man and a good brother in Christ, too!

While we may be divided by our "differences" in doctrine and tradition, what we will have in common will more than compensate for them.......for we will share one Spirit, one hope, "one Lord, one faith, one baptism, one God and Father of us all." And that will be more than enough as we "Witness to Jesus" in Hawaii together.

FRIDAY, JULY 22, 2005

Senator John Kerry Throws a Rock From His Glass House

Associated Press released this story today. **Seriously, I am not making it up**! Those who followed the story of repeatedly rebuffed requests for the full release of Democratic Presidential candidate John Kerry's military records during last year's campaign will get the irony.

Otherwise, just pretend you get it and fake the laugh.

Kerry: Release Records on Roberts
Friday, July 22, 2005

WASHINGTON — Democratic Sen. John Kerry urged the White House on Friday to release "in their entirety" all documents and memos from Supreme Court nominee John Roberts' (search) tenure in two Republican administrations.

"We cannot do our duty if either Judge Roberts or the Bush administration hides elements of his professional record," said the Massachusetts senator who was his party's presidential candidate last year.

;-)

Gunmen Kill Bride After Baghdad Wedding

That's the headline in an Associated Press release earlier today. Read the story here.....and weep.

Algerians Express Surprise At Diplomat's Kidnapping

Tucked away in the same article that contained the "murdered bride" story mentioned in my previous post, is a quote that verges on surrealism.

> *Algerian authorities, meanwhile, expressed surprise that two of their diplomats were abducted Thursday, saying Algiers has steadfastly refused to take part in the U.S.-led coalition.*

Surely, of all people, the Algerians should know better than this! After all, an Islamisists party actually WON the Algerian national election back in 1992. The existing government at that time quickly invalidated the elections and, to my knowledge, have not held any truly open or fair ones since.

This election debacle prompted both the military-supported government and the Islamisists to spend over ten years slitting the throats of men, women and children in small villages....terrorizing the weak and powerless and compelling them with murderous threats to adopt and support their particular visions of either a theocratic or secular Algeria governed under either a form of *sharia* or some variation of the present "constitutional" government.

According to the U.S. Department of State,
The country (Algeria) *is gradually emerging from over a decade of civil strife between proponents and opponents of an Islamic state. During that decade, actions by government authorities, insurgents and terrorist groups, some of which have ties to al-Qa'ida, deprived citizens of their fundamental right to security, created serious human rights problems, and set back the country's transition toward a democratic system. Fighting during the 1990s resulted in 100,000-150,000 estimated deaths.*

Why would the Algerian government be so naive as to think that the same sort of radical

Islamisists in Iraq would care whether the Algerian government had supported the American-led alliance or not?

In spite of the fact that the illusionary theory that Algerians (or Turks or Egyptians....) are somehow immune to terrorist attacks (because of what they have or have not done) has been repeatedly disproved, the kidnappings are nonetheless a sad and grievous affair and should be a serious concern for us all.

In the article cited at the top of this post, we read this poignant note:

> *A career diplomat and father of four, (the kidnapped Algerian envoy)Belaroussi has been in Iraq for about two years. He previously had served as financial director at Algeria's embassy in Paris from 1997 to 2002, Algerian officials said....*
>
> *Iraqi Deputy Interior Minister Ahmed Al-Khafaji told Al-Jazeera television that the Algerian envoy had refused Iraqi offers to provide him with bodyguards, saying he didn't need protection because "Algeria's relationship with the Iraqis is good."*

Is it just me or does it seem that nearly the entire world is living in some sort of denial over the actual existence of the tyrannical and fascist goal of world domination at any cost that motivates these radical Islamist terrorists?

Is George Bush the ONLY world leader who understands this situation or is he somehow deluded, too?

(Note: In all fairness, I suppose I should also include UK's Tony Blair, Australia's John Howard and Spain's ex-President Jose Maria Aznar as leaders who seem to more or less see things in a way similar to President Bush).

At the moment, I still think that Bush has got it at least as correct as anyone else in the world.....and far better than most!

But....although the Algerians were "surprised" by the lack of proper decorum and respect shown by the terrorists I, for one, was not. In fact, I cannot think of any horror, no matter how obscene, that would surprise me, coming from the corrupted souls of those who sincerely believe that they will be rewarded by God (Allah) for blowing up children.

SATURDAY, JULY 23, 2005

We Are Not Afraid

Michelle Malkin linked to this great site....We Are What Not Afraid...where there are hundreds....thousands of photo submissions bearing the words...."We are not afraid." Such submissions are regarded as acts of defiance against the acts of terrorism sweeping the world. My own submission today is this.

There are many more (and better) on the site. Check it out, be inspired and encouraged, and add your own!

Yard Sale? Garage Sale? Lanai Sale!

In Hawaii we have Yard Sales and Garage Sales.....but they are often given the local-style name, Lanai Sale! Whatever you call it, we had one today.

The sale was in "honor" of daughter #1 who is moving to Los Angeles next Saturday. She's been cleaning out her apartment stuff and all the other stuff she has had stored in our garage during the past 4 1/2 years. Her sisters and parents have done the same and, with everything collected into piles and boxes, we woke up at 6am this morning and started setting everything up outside.

I borrowed a tent-pavilion from some church friends and we put all the books inside to protect them from the rain showers that came and went all morning.

The large furniture items were just inside the garage and the clothes and odd-items were on tables in the driveway, which we covered up with old table clothes and bed pads every time the rain showed up.

Here in Hawaii, a lot of people worship at the lanai sale ritual every Saturday morning. Beginning at 7am, a steady stream of folks, rich and poor alike, came by to help redistribute the wealth and recycle both the profound and mundane items that come and go, masquerading as our "possessions" in life.

Jesus said, "Do not store up treasures on earth where moth and rust consumes them and where theives break in and steal."

Lanai sales are graphic examples of what Jesus was talking about! We had so much stufff that was once important to us....almost considered to be invaluable....that we now regarded as unnecessary, unneeded and unwanted!

Even so, one man's junk is another man's treasure....so, in exchange for a lot of quarters and one-dollar bills, we made a lot of treasure hunters happy this morning.

We even sold off two large items, a large futon/sofa and a five-piece dining room set (that had belonged to my wonderful wife's mother)....sold at the original asking price....no haggling today! Wonder of wonders!

When it was all over, and all the signs we had posted up and down the streets had been taken down, we added up the money and found that daughter #1 and her parents had each earned almost the exact amount of money. For my daughter, this meant that she had earned almost 1/3 of her first month's rent at her new LA apartment!

I told her she only needed to have four yard sales like this every month and she'd not only be able to pay her rent but have some money left over to burn.

Not surprisingly, the thought of another lanai sale was more than daughter #1 was willing to handle this afternoon.

Her mother and two sisters would no doubt agree.

Actually, me, too!

SUNDAY, JULY 24, 2005

Nothing To Be Upset About

It seems like too many blog entries I read (including my own) relate to subjects the writers are upset about....

I have spent over an hour this evening searching the news and other blog sites to find something to be upset about. I have considered the needs of my family and friends and checked the local news here in Hawaii, and I'll be darned if I can't find a single thing to be upset about!

I suppose that there is a psychological term for someone like me...something like, "psychonormative" or "anupsetive" perhaps.

In spite of my best efforts I'm afraid that today was a good day. A nice day. I led worship with friends this morning, received two new members and celebrated the Sacrament of Baptism for baby Jack.

I came home and fell asleep on the sofa for 2 1/2 hours. I woke up, washed dishes and cleaned up around the house. Picked up daughters #2 & #3 from church youth group (daughter #3 is interim youth minister intern for the summer). Went with my wonderful wife to some friends home for fondue....and to watch their video and digital "slides" of a recent trip to Italy, France, Switzerland, Germany, Austria and (as my friend said, "Don't forget.....") Lichtenstein! All in 11 days.

They spent two days with dear friends in southern Germany (who I had married here in Hawaii over 10 years ago and, five years ago, baptized their first child). I especially enjoyed seeing pictures of this family. They appeared very happy, maybe because "Daddy" had just returned from a one-year deployment to Iraq.

Maybe the closest I came to being upset all day was realizing that my friend's photos were every bit as good as mine....maybe (and this is hard to admit) even somewhat better!

This borders on violating the 10th commandment: "Thou shall not covet." So, instead, I'll just be happy that I didn't have to endure an hour or more of BAD pictures! There....that's much better...I don't feel inclined to be upset about this any longer!

So that wraps it up for today. Nothing to complain about. Nothing to be upset about. Nothing to even blog about. Sorry.

MONDAY, JULY 25, 2005

The Perfect Sermon

Here are some central thoughts gleaned from my sermon this past Sunday. I would welcome any comments

The Perfect Sermon

Jesus' first public sermon, as recorded in Mark 1:15, is The Perfect Sermon. Here it is and then I'll explain:

"The time has come. The kingdom of God is near. Repent and believe the good news!"

Things we all need:

1. We need to have a **Vision** of how things should be. (The vision must be from God). "Without a vision (from God) the people perish" Proverbs 29:18

This is a vision of the Kingdom of God, the Kingdom of Heaven. It is Paradise and Eden restored and much, much more. It is the Peaceable Kingdom, the Way It's 'Sposed to Be. Such a vision of limitless love, mercy, forgiveness, justice and peace between all people is from God. It is God's plan for us all.

2. We need to have a **Desire** to bring that vision into reality. (The desire must come from our heart...this is ***Love***). "Blessed are those who hunger and thirst after righteousness; for they will be filled." Matthew 5:6

We must really want this! If we don't, then we don't want Heaven, either. Why? Because Heaven is exactly what this vision is all about! After all, we pray, "Thy Kingdom come, Thy will be done on earth and it is in heaven."

3. We need to **Realize the Impossibility** of bringing that vision into reality by our own efforts alone. (When accompanied by sorrow and regret, this is ***repentance*** and ***confession of sin***). "For all have sinned and fallen short of the glory of God." Romans 3:23

This is where virtually every other "religion" and "philosophy" goes wrong. Apart from God, we can do nothing! We can know what is right and good. We can even want what is right and good. We can even "taste" it and see it as though it were "at hand!" But we can't reach it experience it in its fullness by our own strength alone.

4. We need to **Make the Effort** to bring that vision into reality anyway....Why? Because it is the right and good thing to do. (This is ***Faith***....the sort of faith that God "credits to us as righteousness"). "Love the Lord your God.....and Love your neighbor as yourself. On these two commandments hang all the Law and the Prophets." Mark 12:28-34

This is a command from our Lord. It is not optional.

5. We must **Know** that God will, at the "right time," bring this vision into reality and establish it forever even in spite of all evidence to the contrary. (This is ***Hope***). "Thanks be to God, who gives us this victory in Christ Jesus our Lord." I Corinthians 15:57

We are able to put our trust in God because we know Jesus and serve him as our Lord and Savior., It was Jesus, after all, who taught these truths, lived them out in his own life, willingly died on the cross and then rose from the dead to demonstrate that the power of God is with those who Live this Love, who Claim this Faith and who Hold this Hope.

This is what Jesus meant when he said,

***"The time has come. The kingdom of God is near.
Repent and believe the good news!"***

This word from Jesus, when taught to us by the Holy Spirit through our prayerful reading and hearing of Scripture, is, for us, The Perfect Sermon.

This is The Perfect Sermon because it contains all that we need to know in order to receive forgiveness and salvation in Jesus Christ and to enjoy the Faith, Hope and Love that will be the minimum daily requirements for our spiritual life in the Kingdom of Heaven.

Claim the Vision. Desire it in your heart. Confess and Repent of your inability to bring it about without the help of God. Even so, live out the Vision no matter what! And believe in your heart that God, who raised Jesus from the dead, will also one day raise you to eternal life with God in the Kingdom of Heaven.

Why Haven't We Caught Bin Laden?

OK. I gave it my best shot. I was patient. But I'm done with that now.

WHY HAVEN'T WE CAUGHT BIN LADEN?

Back in 2002, President George W. Bush said that he really didn't care one way or the other about catching Bin Laden:

"I don't know where bin Laden is. I have no idea and really don't care. It's not that important. It's not our priority."- G.W. Bush, 3/13/02

But when bombs go off in London.....the connection is made between Al Qaeda and Bin Laden.

When bombs go off in Egypt...the connection is made between Al Qaeda and Bin Laden.

When India sentences a man who claimed to be part of a larger Al Qaeda plot on 9/11 where planes were to be flown into the British Parliament buildings and Tower Bridge as well as the parliament buildings in India and Australia....the name Bin Laden comes up again.

In Iraq, the most grotesque terrorist attacks are master-minded by Zaraqawi, the self-described ally of Al Qaeda and.....you guessed it.....Bin Laden.

Bin Laden-inspired Taliban remnants continue to gather in the border regions between Afghanistan and Pakistan, wrecking havoc among both military, business, government and civilian populations from Kabul to Kandahar.

Terrorists are arrested in Jordan, planning to blow up 5-star hotels in that country. They, too, are linked....with Zarqawi.....and Bin Laden.

For nearly three years I have been patient, knowing the political tight rope being walked with the United States and Pakistan. An American incursion into Pakistan would more than likely bring down the Musharraf government and place that nation's nuclear weapons in the hands of the radical Muslims who might well seize some measure of power amidst the social chaos that would follow the fall of the government.

But I have run out of patience. GET BIN LADEN!

If we know where he is......or even THINK we know where he is.....we should go in and get him.

Who would fault us for this, given the increasing attacks and threats of attacks in Europe, the Middle East, the United States and elsewhere?

As long as Bin Laden and Zarqawi remain alive, we will continue to be seen as failures and losers in the eyes of Muslim extremists. The continued existence of these two men encourages the recruitment of young people who see Zarqawi and Bin Laden's survival as evidence that Allah is protecting them because their cause is just and right!

Is it possible that these fanatics are actually correct? Is it possible that the West is either *unwilling* or *unable* to catch these mere mortal men of flesh and bone?

If we are ***unwilling***, then we must be weaker than those who threaten us.

If we are ***unable***, then we are pathetic fools, unworthy to bear the label of "superpower."

Either way, the "small fish" continue to blow themselves up with anarchistic abandon while the two "biggest fish" in the terrorist pond remain at large, growing in mythological and symbolic stature every day.

THE MYTH MUST BE SHATTERED....AND THE SOONER THE BETTER!

Sadaam became small and pathetic as he crawled out of his hole in the ground.

Sadaam's sons became less than pathetic as they lay broken and dead in an Iraqi morgue.

Zarqawi and Bin Laden must also become small, pathetic, broken and dead if we are to move forward in the GWT.

President Bush needs to rethink this matter. And Pakistan and Musharraf need to stand aside so that we can finish the job we started nearly four years ago.

As a Christian I would much prefer that these two men repent of their sins and "get new hearts" that beat as one with the heart of God. I do "love them" and pray for their redemption and forgiveness often.

But as long as they "point the gun" at free and peaceful nations, it is the God-given obligation of our government to protect us from people like these.

TUESDAY, JULY 26, 2005

Statistics Sometimes Just Don't Add Up

According to a U.S. Census report printed in the Honolulu Advertiser this morning, 53% of unmarried and single Americans are women and 64% of unmarried and single Americans are men.

Uh.....doesn't that add up to 117%?

Go figure!

WEDNESDAY, JULY 27, 2005

Letter to a Muslim Friend

Dear -------,

Last week I read a news report that raised many new questions for me concerning Islam.

The news story concerned Imams and Islamic scholars who had gathered to determine whether such individuals as Osama Bin Laden and Zarqawi were to be considered Muslims or not.

The conclusion was that, as long as they fulfilled the Five Pillars of Islam, they must be considered to be Muslim.

This struck me as technically correct, since the Qur'an offers no other criteria for being or not being a Muslim.

Yet, while the "letter of the Qur'an" was met, I wondered if the "spirit of the Qur'an" was considered? Or whether there even was a "spirit of the Qur'an?"

In the Christian faith we hear our Lord, Jesus, say, "Not everyone who cries, "Lord, Lord," will enter the Kingdom of Heaven."

By this we understand Jesus to mean that the outer trappings of a person's life do not determine their eternal destination. Our Gospel declares that God knows and judges the heart of every person and is not fooled by what a person says they believe or whether they go to church every week or tithe or know the Bible by memory or even outwardly seem to live a good and decent life.

None of this, we are taught, can save a man from his sin. The attitude of his heart must be inclined towards the things that belong to God.

Jesus said, "It is not the things that go into a person that defiles them, but what comes out from them."

By this we understand Jesus to mean that the best evidence of what is in a person's heart is found in how they live out their life. Just as the health and value of a tree is measured by the quantity and quality of its fruit, Jesus says, concerning people, "By their fruit you shall know them."

The Apostle Paul, in Galatians, states that, "The fruit of the Spirit is love, joy, peace, patience, kindness, goodness, faithfulness, gentleness and self-control."

Jesus commands his followers to "Love one another as I have loved you." We are told that our love for God is measured by how we love our neighbor. Indeed, Jesus even commands his disciples to, "love your enemies and pray for those who persecute you."

We are commanded to "turn the other cheek' and to forgive others seventy times seven times. If we have something against our brother, or if our brother has something against us, we are told to stop going through the motions of worshiping and praising God until we have made peace with our brother.

It is not so much the doctrine of the Christian faith that sets a Christian apart from the rest of the world as it is the way in which the light of God's love shines in their life, especially as it pertains to their relationships with others.

A Christian who does not "walk the talk" or "practice what they preach" is a poor example of a Christian! More than this, if a person persists in behaving in ways contrary to the Christian law of love, they are to be confronted, disciplined and, if necessary, removed from the Christian community until such time as they may repent and seek forgiveness.

All this is captured under the idea of Christian "morality" or "ethics." It is impossible for a Christian to separate their faith from their behavior.

This is, I think, the issue that confuses me concerning Islam. Is there such a thing as Islamic "morality" or "ethics?"

According to the Muslim council I cited at the beginning of my letter, it is participation in the Five Pillars that makes a person and Muslim......regardless of whether they blow up children or encourage even the killing of other Muslims! Where is the ethics in this?

Christian morality requires us to critique and sometimes condemn even our own nation's soldiers when their actions do not conform to the established boundaries of decency.

What boundaries of decency guide and constrain a Muslim, whether in war or in peace?

Did Mohammed offer no guidelines on how the behavior of one Muslim is to be judged by other Muslims?

Is there nothing in Islam that can condemn the teachings and behavior of Bin Laden, Zarqawi and the followers of such "radical" organizations as Al Qaeda?

Is there nothing in Islam that can allow for the condemnation of a Muslim who boards a city bus and blows themselves up along with dozens of innocent men, women and children....some of whom may even be Muslims themselves?

Please help me with these questions. For a Christian the answers to these questions may be complex, but they are nonetheless clear. Where is the clarity in Islam?

In I Corinthians 13, the Apostle Paul writes that, "If I speak in the tongues of men and of angels, but have not love, I am only a resounding gong or a clanging cymbal. If I have the gift of prophecy and can fathom all mysteries and all knowledge, and if I have a faith that can move mountains, but have not love, I am nothing. If I give all I possess to the poor and surrender my body to the flames, but have not love, I gain nothing."

For a Christian, love is the measure of all things. In I John 4 we read, "Dear friends, let us love one another, for love comes from God. Everyone who loves has been born of God and knows God. Whoever does not love does not know God, because God is love."

From a Christian standpoint, Osama Bin Laden's attitude and behavior does not demonstrate love. Therefore the Christian comes to the conclusion that he "does not know God...."

What is the "measure of all things" for a Muslim? What evidence does one look for to determine whether a Muslim is reflecting the heart of God in their own life or not?

Is God all things to a Muslim? Good? Evil? Cruel? Merciful? Can a Muslim be all these things, too? If God is all things and the source of all things, is there nothing (apart from denying one or more of the Five Pillars) that can disqualify a person as a Muslim? Is there ultimately no basis upon which one Muslim can judge the actions or behavior of any other Muslim?

Please help me. Nothing I have thus far read (and I have read a great deal lately) has helped me answer these questions. Nothing I have heard from respected Islamic scholars or Imams has helped much, either. All is confusion. Please straighten me out!

Yours Sincerely,

Bird of Paradise

Please Walk, Not Run, To the Nearest Exit

Little Green Footballs has just posted this bittersweet photo along with a few words of comment:

> *A reader with a friend in Britain forwarded this photograph of a sign posted in the Notting Hill Gate Tube Station:*
>
> *I am assured that this is a real image, not a Photoshop remix.*

Oh....and please be sure that any loose or exposed wiring is safely and securely tucked out of site beneath one's clothes.....

THURSDAY, JULY 28, 2005

American Muslims Issue "Fatwa" Against Terrorism & Terrorists

Several days ago I expressed dismay that the Council on American-Islamic Relations (CAIR) had done little or nothing to take a stand against Islamic terrorism against civilians and to urge their contituency to do the same.

Well, thankfully, I cannot say that anymore.

Today the U.S. Muslim Religious Council held a press conference in Washington D.C. and announced the release of a Fatwa Against Terrorism.

The text of the "fatwa" (or religious edict) includes the following declarations:

The Fiqh Council of North America wishes to reaffirm Islam's absolute condemnation of terrorism and religious extremism.

Islam strictly condemns religious extremism and the use of violence against innocent lives. There is no justification in Islam for extremism or terrorism. Targeting civilians' life and property through suicide bombings or any other method of attack is haram – or forbidden - and those who commit these barbaric acts are criminals, not "martyrs."

In the light of the teachings of the Qur'an and Sunnah we clearly and strongly state:

1. All acts of terrorism targeting civilians are haram (forbidden) in Islam.
2. It is haram for a Muslim to cooperate with any individual or group that is involved in any act of terrorism or violence.
3. It is the civic and religious duty of Muslims to cooperate with law enforcement authorities to protect the lives of all civilians.

We issue this fatwa following the guidance of our scripture, the Qur'an, and the teachings of our Prophet Muhammad – peace be upon him. We urge all people to resolve all conflicts in just and peaceful manners.

We pray for the defeat of extremism and terrorism. We pray for the safety and security of our country, the United States, and its people. We pray for the safety and security of all inhabitants of our planet. We pray that interfaith harmony and cooperation prevail both in the United States and all around the globe.

Read the full text here which also includes the names of those who sat on the Fiqh Council which issued the "fatwa" (but also the names of all the many Muslim organizations, mosques and other leaders (including CAIR) that have so far endorsed it. The list is long and impressive.

Is it at last possible that the Muslim community in American will actually begin to deal with this matter internally? If so, this could prove to be a historic and major turning point in the GWT...at least as far as the safety of the United States is concerned.

P.S. Conspicuously absent among those signing the document is the infamous Bridgeview Mosque in Bridgeview, Illinois. I could find no evidence that any of that mosque's leaders signed the fatwah, either. Hmmmm......

HT: Power Line

FRIDAY, JULY 29, 2005

Second Thoughts On Fatwa

In yesterday's post I celebrated the release of an American Muslim "fatwa" condemning Islamic terrorism of every kind. The document was signed by a large number of well-known and influential organizations and individuals.

Some people, including Steven Emerson at **The Counterterrorism Blog**, are calling the *fatwa* a "fake."

In fact, the fatwa is bogus. Nowhere does it condemn the Islamic extremism ideology that has spawned Islamic terrorism. It does not renounce nor even acknowledge the existence of an Islamic jihadist culture that has permeated mosques and young Muslims around the world. It does not renounce Jihad let alone admit that it has been used to justify Islamic terrorist acts. It does not condemn by name any Islamic group or leader. In short, it is a fake fatwa designed merely to deceive the American public into believing that these groups are moderate.
Judea Pearl, the father of Daniel Pearl (who was butchered and murdered in Pakistan) has declared the *fatwa* to be

"....vacuous because it does not name the perpetrators of Islamic terrorist theologies and leaders of Islamic movements like Yousef Al Qaradawi, Osama Bin Laden, Ayman Al Zawahari, Hamas, Islamic Jihad, etc." Pearl told (Emerson) that these groups are "trying to perpetrate a deception on the American public."

I'm not an expert in Islamic *fatwas* but I gather from Emerson's article that a legitimate fatwa must be specific to a particular person, organization or discernable entity (such as the Ayatollah Khomeni's infamous *fatwa* against Solomon Rushdie). If this is true, then this particular *fatwa* would appear to ring hollow, if not to those of us too naive to understand the subtleties of Islamic jurisprudence, then most certainly within the American Muslim communities it is addressed to.

Emerson also points out that many of the organizations and individuals (including the leader of the council that issued the *fatwa*) have been accused of supporting the very sort of terrorism and terrorist organizations addressed by their declaration.

Please read Emerson's article yourself and decide whether to be skeptical or not. I, for one, will be pondering the old question concerning whether the leopard can change its spots.......

New Ideas Worth Reading From a Muslim Writer

Hugh Hewitt recently linked (w/ht to John Mark Reynolds) to a blog site maintained by Professor Reynold's Muslim colleague Mustafa Akyol. The site is called The White Path and contains some refreshing perspectives on international politics, terrorism and matters of faith from the perspective of a Turkish-American Muslim.

My only criticism is that Akyol does not appear to be posting very much lately. This is too bad. He appears to have much to say to us and I, for one, would like to hear more from him.

I have perma-linked to his site and would encourage everyone to "check it out."

I Thought This Was a Christian Blog? Why All the Muslim Stuff?

Looking back at my postings during the past week I noticed an interesting trend. They all involved the Muslim faith.

There are many other things to write about, of course, including Air America, Judge Roberts, the tragedies at this year's Boy Scout Jamboree, follow-ups on the London bombings, etc. But, because I am, heart and soul, a person of "faith," it is the issue of Faith, more than any other, that interests and intrigues me.

The intricacies and subtleties of Islam have long captivated me. For many years, the historic oppression of non-Muslims in the Arab world has challenged me to pray for an outpouring of the Holy Spirit with the Gospel of Jesus Christ in those dark and dismally depressed countries. Long before 9/11 I felt that the 21st century would be marked by great spiritual upheavals in India and the Arab/Muslim world. (Upheavals in China will spring from more of a political/social/economic foundation than a spiritual one.....at least in this century).

One thing I have never liked is "not knowing" something that is influencing my daily life. Islam, with all its glories, strengths, history, divisions, sects, inner conflicts, unity, disunity, cultural distinctions, weaknessess and failings, is influencing the Western world today more than at any other time since the late Middle Ages.

As a spiritual leader of a Christian congregation, I believe I must always be able to speak the **truth** in love about other faiths and religions as I teach and comment in classes, sermons and conversations. To do so, I must be informed. Indeed, my goal, as I have studied Christian sects and cults, Mormonism, Buddhism, Hinduism, Judaism and Islam, is to understand them so completely that I can see them through the eye of a believer.

Many Christian foreign missionaries have commented that they were not able to gain the respect of other faith groups until they could demonstrate that they not only understood that faith but could demonstrate respect and tolerance of it in their words and actions. Only then, they say, are the people they came to share the Gospel with willing to listen to what they have to say.

After living in Utah for over 6 years of ministry, I came to understand the Mormon faith far better than most Mormons. I still enjoy a visit to my home by Mormon missionaries so I can ask them questions they cannot answer and tell them things about their history and doctrines that they had never heard before! I may annoy them, but I certainly do gain their respect! And, yes, sometimes they even give me a chance to share the Christian Gospel with them...along with a glass of iced tea on a hot day.

I yearn to understand Islam in the same way. But the subject is far too vast for me to grasp with any measure of authority. Yet I continue to try. And I want my congregation and others who may read my postings, to grow in their understanding of Islam as well.

As Paul wrote to the Corinthians, "For I received from the Lord what I also passed on to you." The Christian Gospel is never "passed on" to someone in a vacuum; there is always a non-Christian context. Sometimes the context is that of another faith. It is always best to understand the context so that the contrast with the Gospel can be clearly made.

In the present time, I believe that God has allowed the Muslim faith to "rise up," with all of its contradictions and confusions, to challenge the world with a clear alternative to the Christian faith.

The present conflict, which will continue long beyond my children's generation, will, in the end, provide a wonderful opportunity for the Christian Gospel of Jesus Christ to spread to places previously closed to it. Any informed Christian would happily engage an informed Muslim in debating the merits of their respective faiths. The verbal exchanges that result may or may not change anyone's mind, but the result will be a sharing of the Gospel.

The West has freedom and access to everything the Islamic world has to offer. In the Arab world, the Christian Gospel is suppressed. Current world unrest has allowed movies like, "The Passion of the Christ," to be shown in Arab Muslim countries. The more the Christian faith is shared, and the more it is allowed to be compared side-by-side with the faith of Islam, the better it will be for the Christian faith.....and for the world.

My interest in the Muslim faith have also been helpful insofar as more than 15 of my church members have, so far, been deployed to the "radical Islamic" wars in Afghanistan and Iraq. Although it is not politically correct to say so, these are, without any doubt, at their core, religious conflicts. Conflicts between secularists, radical Muslims, moderate, liberal and conservative Muslims, Sunni and Shiite Muslims, and the Western, Christian culture of democracy and freedom of "life, liberty and the pursuit of happiness," unalienably given to all people by Almighty God.

My only concern is that the Western world will become so separated from its Christian roots that it will descend into a moral and ethical malaise that will mark it as indistinguishible from the forces arrayed against it.

Regardless, God is sovereign. Nothing will come to pass unless God wills it or permits it. And God will not allow the Gospel to be crushed or oppressed forever. For we have his revealed word and promise that, in the end, Christ will rule victorious, and every knee shall bow and every tongue confess him Lord, to the glory of God the Father.

SATURDAY, JULY 30, 2005

London Bombing Suspect Says He Was Careful Not To Hurt Anyone

Osman Hussain, one of the suspected July 21 London bombers, is telling interrogators in Rome (where he is being held) that the bombing he participated in was not designed to hurt anyone, just grab attention.

"Muktar" (the leader of the group who is being held in London) "urged us to be careful" (Italian Newspaper) La Repubblica quoted Hussain as telling his interrogators. "We didn't want to kill, just sow terror."

According to Hussain, there wasn't even enough explosives to "harm people nearby."

Golly gee whiz! Compassionate terrorism!

Hussain is NOT reported to have said,

"I love the people of London. I would never, ever dream of doing anything that might hurt anyone. I mean, if the bomb was bigger, it might have injured or killed a small child, or a woman...or even a fellow Muslim! If something like that happened I don't know how I could live with myself. My conscience would eat me alive! Allah would judge me harshly for that, I'm sure. After all, in the Qu'ran, it is written that, "Whoever kills a person [unjustly]...it is as though he has killed all mankind. And whoever saves a life, it is as though he had saved all mankind." (Qur'an, 5:32)

I am not a terrorist. Neither are my friends. We simply got together during a white water rafting trip and decided that we wanted to exercize our right of free speech to protest the treatment of Muslim prisoners at Abu Ghraib and Guantanamo Bay and the disrespect that has been shown to the Qu'ran by American infidels who deserve death...ah...I mean unbelievers....ah....who, well, you know, should have been wearing rubber gloves when they urinated into the air vent.....and....uh....you know, flushed the Qu'ran down the toilet or something like that. You understand what I'm saying, right?

Hey, in any case, no harm was done to anybody! Not even to us! See, I'm still breathing. I wasn't blown up into little pieces, splattered all over nearby buildings like Hasib when his bomb went off on the bus.....uh....did I say "Hasib?" Who's Hasib? I don't know anyone named Hasib! What are you trying to do, frame me? Is this a trick? Well, if it is, I don't think it's very funny!

Now, where was I......oh, yeah.....white water rafting.....white water.....uh....that reminds me, did I tell you that I once almost met Bill Clinton?.................

Senator Schumer: "Americans Are Not Proud of New York"

Yes, that's what U.S. Senator Chuck Schumer (Democrat, NY) told New York Times writer Deborah Solomon is an otherwise lighthearted interview dated Sunday, July 31.

In response to a question concerning homeland security protection for the New York subway system, Schumer replied,
The president should be a leader on this. Englishmen are proud of London. And Frenchmen are proud of Paris. But Americans are not proud of New York.
Uh...Mr. Schumer...if I remember correctly, the terrorist attacks on New York City (and Washington D.C.) on September 11, 2001, created the greatest outpouring of American patriotism and pride since World War II. Mayor Giuliani and the New York Police and Fire Departments became national symbols of what is good and right about America. During a time of national trauma, we all became New Yorkers in some deep spiritual or emotional sense....at least for a time.

No pride in New York? You've got to be kidding! Of course Americans are proud of New York City.....especially after a *Republican* Mayor took on the sleeze and corruption that had turned Manhattan into a rotten apple and a national embarrassment, cleaned the place up and restored the city to its rightful, prideful place in the eyes of Americans.

On the other hand, it *is* true that Americans are not proud of New York City in the same sense as the English are of London or the French are of Paris. That's because the comparison is bogus and specious to begin with!

Is New York the capital of the United States? London and Paris are national capitals.

Is New York the only city in the United States worthy of being proud of? London and Paris have no competition in their countries.

Is New York the residence of Queens, Prime Ministers and Presidents? Sure, New York has Queens....but none actually live there! Paris, on the other hand, has the Elysee Palace and London has 10 Downing Street and Buckingham Palace (And don't even *try* to compare these to Gracie Mansion!).

Did New York City survive the Blitz? Was it lost to, and then liberated from, Nazi occupation? Until 9/11, had any blood been shed on its streets from foreign invasion since the Revolutionary War?

Americans have much to be proud of. We have far more to be proud of, in fact, than all the pride in England or France combined!

Americans are proud of New York City. But New York City is only one of the cities and one of the national treasures we are proud of. While London and Paris stand alone, New York must share the spotlight of American pride with Boston, Chicago, San Francisco, Los Angeles, Seattle and, of course, Washington D.C. (to list just a few). Pride also falls on Yosemite, Yellowstone, Everglades, the Grand Canyon, the Mississippi River, the Great Lakes and Niagara Falls (to list just a few).

Even the subway system in New York is not as unique as that in Paris or London. It is not the only one worth mentioning in our country, for one thing. It is not even the oldest subway system we have! While it is by far the largest, it is not the only one worthy of attention by Homeland Security.

As one of two Senators from the state of New York, Senator Schumer is, of course, expected to be a national cheerleader for the city with the largest voter base in his state!

But he verges on arrogance when he expects all Americans to feel towards New York City the same level of "pride" that the English feel towards London and the French feel towards Paris.

Memo to Chuck: The United States is bigger than New York City. The Big Apple is a nice place, perhaps, to spend $400 on theater tickets and a dinner but, besides that......just get over it!

SUNDAY, JULY 31, 2005

Zimbabwe: Land is For Blacks Only

That's the headline at CNN today: "Zimbabwe: Land Is For Blacks Only."

It seems that the white European colonial settlers in the late 1800's who took undeveloped land in what was then called Rhodesia; and invested their sweat, blood, experience and wealth to turn agriculture into the largest sector of the Rhodesian/Zimbabwean economy; are now officially *persona non grata* as government policy.
"The land here is for the black people and we are not going to give it back to anybody. We are not inviting any white farmers back," Security Minister Didymus Mutasa, also in charge of Lands, Land Reform and Resettlement, told the state-owned Sunday Mail.
Only 700-800 of what were once nearly 3000 white farmers remain on their land. Based on the policy stated by Mutasa it would appear that their tenure is also running out.

The result of this forcible land transfer has been to reduce agricultural output to the point that the country is on the verge of massive food shortages. Export income from agricultural products is also declining meaning that the government has even fewer financial resources to meet the needs of its once-prospering people.

I suppose that, if the theory is to give back the land to the original black inhabitants of the land, it would follow logically that the land should be returned to them in the condition it was in before the white colonialists improved it.

Although that is obviously not the intent of the Mugabe land policy, it appears that, like Uganda and other countries that turned their backs on their colonial developers, Zimbabwe is essentially "killing the goose that laid the golden eggs."

I am reminded of the old anti-colonialist dictum:
When the white men came they had Bibles and we had the land. Now the white men have the land and we have the Bibles!
I suppose that does reflect some measure of injustice. But, when the economy collapses and the people begin to starve as a result of supposedly "righting a wrong," I would suggest that perhaps the people were better off with the "injustice."

Sudanese Vice President John Garang Dies In Helicopter Crash

Dr. John Garang, former Sudanese rebel leader and the best hope for keeping the peace between Northern and Southern Sudan apparently died today in the crash of his helicopter while returning to Sudan from a personal visit to Uganda just three weeks after being sworn in as the Sudanese Vice President under a new national constitutional written expressly for him.

According to FoxNews online and the AP, bad weather caused the helicopter to turn around and attempt to return to Uganda. The cause of the crash has not yet been established (although the AP article notes that "an Ugandan rebel group, the Lord's Resistance Army, operates in the area and has shot down Ugandan military helicopters in the past."

Even though the troubles in the Western region of Darfur continue to make headlines, the peace settlement reached with the Southern region (with significant and quiet help from the Bush administration) after over 25 years of violence (mostly suffered by the Black poplulation in the South) was viewed by many as an extraordinary step towards removing Sudan from the list of international pariahs.

There appears to be literally no one with any stature equal to Dr. Garang to step up and replace him in the Sudanese government. Although the story is still breaking (his death has not even been officially announced by Sudan) I would say that there will undoubtedly be those in both North and South Sudan who will try to take advantage of the situation to settle old scores and try to return to the former bloody status quo.

It will be a true test of Sudanese President El-Bashir's leadership for him to hold the peace agreement together in Garang's absence.

Pray for the people of Sudan. This is a sad day, not only for Sudan, but for a world that yearns for peace.

Saudi King Fahd Dies

Major news services are headlining a breaking story reporting that King Fahd of Saudi Arabia has died after a long illness.

Since the Saudi Government is "family owned and operated" and has not missed a beat during the King's long illness, there should be little effect from his death.

There have, however, been some unconfirmed reports of a division of opinion within the royal family as to who his successor will be. Regardless, we should not expect too much of a change in government policy....unless the Wahhabi religious leadership decides to take advantage of the "transition" to stage some sort of a "coup d'etat" or other show of power. Al Qaeda might also conceivably attempt some sort of response.....we'll just have to wait and see.

Space Shuttle Discovery Spacewalk

Astronaut Steve Robinson was "hanging out" earlier today as he did some outdoor chores around the space shuttle and the International Space Station.

Here is my favorite photo (yes, it is right-side up!) with Robinson's feet attached to the end of the shuttle's robotic arm.

Cool, yes?

SATURDAY, AUGUST 06, 2005

Morality & Hiroshima In the Context of the Evolution of Warfare

Yesterday was remembered as the 60th anniversary of the dropping of the first atomic bomb on the Japanese city of Hiroshima. Next week we will remember the dropping of the second atomic bomb on Nagasaki.

Few events of the past century have generated so much controversy, soul searching, second-guessing and moral introspection as the decision made by US President Harry Truman to drop those two bombs.

Somehow, in remarkable fashion, after many millennia of human warfare, those two bombs struck most of the world simultaneously as having crossed a line that should never again be crossed.

This unusual and nearly unprecedented reaction is worthy of note.

When the first man with a bow and arrow shot down an enemy at 20 yards, did the world cry, "foul?"

When English archers at the battle of Agincourt launched ten thousand arrows at once, obliterating and routing the French army, did the world cry, "foul?"

When besieging armies starved cities into oblivion, did the world cry, "foul?"

When gunpowder and cannon made the thick, stone walls of castle fortresses useless, did the world cry, "foul?"

When two cannon balls were tied together with chain and shot at the legs of charging troops, slicing off dozens of legs in the process, did the world cry, "foul?"

When aeroplanes began strafing and dropping bombs did the world cry, "foul?"

The answer to all these questions is, of course, "No."

In fact, advances in military power and effectiveness throughout history have been met not only with eager imitation by everyone else, but with admiration as well.

This unbroken evolution of destructive firepower proceeded across history with hardly a hiccough.....until World War I. Even then, it wasn't the trenches that posed a moral difficulty. It wasn't the diseases and infections that produced most of the casualties that posed a moral difficulty. It was the mustard gas.

Somehow, the world was, for perhaps the first time, almost universally repulsed by this new innovation in warfare. It is doubtful that ***before*** it was actually used, anyone would have considered it to be any less "moral" or "ethical" than any of the other methods of "mass killing" that were being implemented and used in that grotesque parody of war.

But, having been used, the world took a good hard look at where this particular military technology would lead them. And said, "Never again!"

The moral judgment came ***after*** its use. Not before. And that moral judgment has effectively restricted and condemned its use ever since.

A similar situation took occurred with the dropping of the two atomic bombs on Japan.

Before they were actually used, Germany and the United States were both working hard to find a way to control the power of the atom. Germany surrendered before unlocking the secret. The United States succeeded.

Whether to use this power to bring a swift and conclusive end to the war with Japan was seriously debated within both the scientific and political communities at the time.

The moral issues, however, did not revolve around the use of the bomb itself, but regarding *how* the bomb should be used. After the bombings of Dresden and Tokyo, there had been a loud outcry of disgust from many in America....even from within the military itself (subesquently, some pilots reportedly refused to fly bombing missions targeting civilians).

The debate primarily concerned whether it was morally acceptable to target a large civilian population area or not.

In retrospect, it was clearly a mistake, both militarily and ethically to have chosen to drop those bombs in the locations chosen. Prior moral outrage over such tactics should have been sufficient to have led President Truman and his advisors to have chosen differently.

In this, however, the moral issues concerning the atomic bomb were no different that those which concerned the more conventional fire- and blanket-bombings that had preceded them.

The moral judgment on the atomic power itself did not fully emerge until, as with the mustard gas, ***after*** it had been used

.

The effects of radiation on human life, and the vast wasteland created instantly by the concussion and heat, stunned the world into near speechlessness.

As with the use of mustard gas in World War I, the world took a good hard look at where this particular military technology would lead them and said, "Never again!"

I believe it is unfair to read that moral judgment back into those years, months and days before the detonation of those bombs. We know today what those who made the decision to drop those bombs did not. We cannot hold them guilty for the use of this technologically marvelous weapon that virtually guaranteed the end of World War II.

As with mustard gas and other chemical and biological warfare technologies, the genie of nuclear bomb technology has been kept in the bottle by international common consensus and the grace of God.

Those who use such technologies after the moral verdict has been made will always be guilty of a far greater sin than those who used them for the first time.

In the **New Testament, the Apostle Paul** tells us that sin did not appear until after "the Law" was revealed. Before the Law and its sworn acceptance by individuals and nations, there was a certain innocence from ignorance. But, having heard the Law and its judgments, there was no more excuse. Behavior that had once been, at best, "controversial," now became banned, forbidden, tabu, kapu.....sin without excuse......condemned by all.

Such, I believe, is the case with nuclear weapons.

They have been used once......twice.....the judgment has been made and the verdict unsealed......"Never again!"

And, by God's grace, this will remain the Law of the Land until the end of time.

It does us little good to curse the past and render judgments based on what we learned and understood after the fact.

On the other hand, it does us a great deal of good to apply that knowledge and understanding to our present times and be guided by them as we follow history into the future.

MONDAY, AUGUST 15, 2005

Blogosphere Needs MSM to Keep Us Honest....Honest!

I believe I have read this elsewhere but cannot recall where. But I know for sure that I read it today in the August edition of Readers' Digest, page 130, under the page heading, "MediaTrendLets."

Those of us who inhabit the blogosphere know the value of fact-checking and holding the MSM accountable for whatever it is they choose or do not choose to print or broadcast.

With links we can check sources immediately and make up our own minds if we consider them to be credible or not. We are not morons who believe everything we read, either on the internet or in the newspaper!

As I read this snippet in RD the only thing I could think of to say was, "Huh?"
"Don't confuse me with the facts!" That could be the motto of those of us who rely on the blogosphere, rather than traditional media, for our news. What's the future of newspapers and networks in this all-opinion world? Tom Rosenstiel, who directs the Projhect for Excellence in Journalism, told USA Today that **traditional media will evolve into "authenticators" telling people what information they can trust**. *(emphasis in original)*

Somehow this reminds me of the old fox-guarding-the-henhouse story.....

TUESDAY, AUGUST 16, 2005

"The Great Raid"--A Review

This afternoon I had the numbing privilege of seeing the movie, "**The Great Raid**," at the Mililani Theater Complex.

Having previously read (some years ago) one of the two books on which the movie was based ("**Ghost Soldiers**," by Hampton Sides) I was well familiar with both the details of the raid that rescued 500 Americans from the Japanese prisoner of war camp at **Cabanatuan**and the historical context in which the raid took place (Note: An estimated 1200 Americans died at Cabanatuan before its liberation on January 30, 1945).

The movie was a faithful, step-by-step adaptation of the book I had read. Just as I had remembered, the movie captured the business-like planning, the meticulous timing of the logistics, the crucial participation and sacrifice of the Filipino "underground" army, the merciless and ceaseless abuse of the American prisoners by their Japanese captors, the selfless and heroic efforts of an expatriate American nurse to maintain a clandestine flow of smuggled medicine for the prisoners and, of course, the bravery and discipline of the American Rangers who led and carried out the raid. As the ending credits explain, the raid remains the largest successful rescue operation in American military history.

The movie opens with segments of film from contemporary WW II archives intermixed with "antiqued" segments shot during the filming of the movie itself. These black and white images eventually segue into full color until, at the end of the movie, the black and white format returns.

This "framing" of the film suggests that what we are about to see is simply a "snapshot" of one incident among many others. As the black and white morphed into color, I found myself transported back in time to 1945 where I was present and contemporary with the events taking place.

While the movie explicitly address several serious themes (in particular the question of what constitutes "glory") there was little or no preaching. The moral evil of the Japanese policies and attitudes towards prisoners of war were simply depicted as they were with no narrative comment added....nor was any necessary.

The film was graphic and emotionally wrenching. The violence was comparable in its authentic explicitness to that shown in the now infamous opening scenes of D-Day in "Saving Private Ryan." The depiction of the prison camp and the surrounding geography of the Philippines (although filmed in Queensland, Australia) and even the recreation of Manila under the Japanese occupation were meticulously and convincingly portrayed.

The characters (and those who portrayed them) were shown as normal men and women placed in extraordinary circumstances. The lack of "big name" actors with easily recognized faces allowed the film to take on an almost documentary realism.

There is irony in this since (although the movie makes no mention of it) the Rangers really were accompanied by an army film crew complete with a movie camera. Actual images taken on the raid were smoothly integrated into the movie, especially at the end, and certainly helped to enhance the sense of authenticity that permeates the film.

There is a somewhat contrived love story woven into the fabric of the film. While it served to add a "human touch" to what was otherwise a grueling and exhausting two+ hours of violence and suspense, and while it provided a motivations for the American nurse to risk her life and for one of the forsaken and abandoned prisoners to cling to life and hope, it was too small a matter to counterbalance the overwhelming gravity of the actual drama of the raid. Even so, while the movie might have been historically better without that sub-plot, the final effect would not have been as complex and compelling.

The difficult and fateful decision by President Roosevelt and his military advisors to abandon the 20,000+ American troops (and 50,000 Filipino soldiers) following the siege of Corregidor and their heroic but futile withdrawal to **Bataan** was rightly understood by those prisoners of war to be a tragic betrayal unprecedented in American history.

In the end, however, the soldiers who risked and sacrificed their lives to ensure the freedom of these same prisoners three years later, demonstrated not only that they had not been forgotten but also provided a fitting sense of atonement and redemption as the film came to an end.

While I would not recommend this movie for anyone younger than high school age, I would also hope that any adolescent that might go to see the movie would have, at the very least, an opportunity to discover where the Philippines and Cabanatuan are located on a map of the world and also have some understanding of the raid's historical context before they enter the theater.

Like "Schindler's List" and "Saving Private Ryan," I believe that "The Great Raid" is of sufficient quality and stature to continue to refresh and sharpen our memories of a time that is fast fading into a slough of revisionism. "The Great Raid" represents a time, a place and a group of people who represent far more than just themselves. The good and the evil depicted in the various characters remind us of the choices being made by people and nations today....and their consequences.

The movie offers those who have the eyes to see, both a word of warning and a word of hope. It also affirms that personal and national philosophies and beliefs have moral consequences and that some beliefs lead to consequences that are, morally speaking, vastly superior to others

SUNDAY, AUGUST 21, 2005

Pope Benedict XVI Tells It Like It Is In Cologne

Pope Benedict XVI (who will, no doubt, soon be known as Pope Ben) came home to Germany and proved that he can speak from his heart as well as his head.

Perhaps as many as 1,000,000 young people from around the world have gathered for spiritual renewal and the opportunity to see the new Pope in person and hear what he had to say to them.

Whereas his predecessor, Pope John Paul II, frequently wrapped his Christian message in the larger context of world events, Pope Ben seems to prefer to wrap world events into the larger context of the Christian faith!

According to the (London) TimesOnLine,

The main theme (of his visit).....was the assertion that Christianity was not a faith that could be adopted Ã la carte. Addressing himself particularly to his European audience, the Pope said religion was not a consumer product, whose difficult rules could be disregarded at will. And he chided the materialist mentality that found it "inconvenient" to attend Sunday Mass regularly.

As a Presbyterian pastor I could not have said it any better (except, perhaps, for changing the word "Mass" to "worship and communion.")

To be a Christian is to enter into a package deal that requires the embrace of each part as being essential. No picking or choosing allowed!

--One body? Check.
--One Spirit? Check
--One Lord? Check.
--One Faith? Check.
--On Baptism? Check.
--One God and Father of us all? Check.
--Jesus the Way, the Truth and the Life? Check.
--No way to come to the Father except through Jesus? Check.
--To follow him means to become like him? Check.
--To call him "Lord" means to be obedient to him in all things? Check.
--To call him "Savior" means that there is no other name under heaven by which you must be saved? Check.
--If a person does not love others in the same way that Christ loved us then God is not in them, because God is love? Check.

That's just the beginning of a long list of essentials for the Christian believer.

The role of scripture, the Church, the sacraments, the resurrection, and the central concepts of righteousness and justice, sin, forgiveness, reconciliation and the sharing of the Good News in word (evangelism) and deed (missions) are also imperative for anyone who would consider calling themselves a Christian, regardless of the branch or denomination upon which they find themselves to have been grafted.

The Christian faith stands or falls as a whole. Each part, while good and true in and of itself, is true only in relation to the other truths of the faith. Truth is truth. The tablecloth is clean or it is stained, not thread by thread, but taken as a whole. To separate the warp and woof of the Gospel is to rend what was designed to be a seamless garment.

Pope Ben has got this very right, indeed. He was, at least publicly, also refreshingly silent concerning the veneration of Mary and other matters that might have otherwise separated a non-Roman Catholic from a Protestant or Orthodox believer.

As a former unenthusiastic conscript into the Nazi Youth program, the Pope was especially eager to meet with German Jews in their rebuilt synagogue in Cologne. There, in only the second visit to a synagogue by a modern Pope (one must assume that St. Peter ventured into one now and again as well!), he expressed the contrition and remorse which he, and all Christians, must feel for the "unimaginable crime" of the Holocaust.

At another location, Pope Ben met withrepresentativestives of the Muslim community in Germany. According to the Times report,

> *The Pope acknowledged the bloodstained history of atrocities committed in the name of religion. But this did not prevent him from speaking out unambiguously on the need for Muslims to combat the "cruel fanaticism" of terrorism that poisoned ties between their*

faiths. He told Muslim leaders that there was no room for apathy and disengagement, even less for partiality and sectarianism. But he balanced this harsh message with an insistence that Christians should not yield to prejudice and negative pressures. All religions had to treat each other with mutual respect.

According to other reports, the Muslim leaders, while appreciative of the Pope's meeting with them, did express some distaste for the implication that they were somehow responsible for curbing the "cruel fanaticism" that none of them supported in the first place! The question was also raised as to why this Pope met with Jewish leaders in a synagogue but did not meet with them in a mosque? After all, Pope John Paul II had visited a mosque during his tenure? (UPDATE: LGF has a link that possibly explains why the Pope skipped a visit to a mosque in Cologne.)

All this seems to show that Pope Ben, while perhaps more bold and blunt than his predecessor, is still eager to reach out and extend the hand of the Christian Church to those of other faiths....not as a sign of solidarity, of course, but as a sign of humility and respect.

Every Roman Catholic is, whether they admit to it or not, is a "Pope watcher." Whatever the Pope says or the Pope does becomes the model of behavior for every other member of the RC Church.

These seemingly small gestures will empower Roman Catholic priests and laity alike to follow his example in establishing better relationships with the leaders and members of other religions in their neighborhoods.

Those who persist in defying and ignoring the Pope's example will soon become marginalized. I have no doubt that this Pope will keep the people guessing as to what he will say or do next. Jesus said that the (Holy) Spirit blows wherever he chooses. I sense a fresh blowing of the Spirit through this first, major international sojourn by this new Pope.

I also appreciate his independence in asserting himself as a different and distinct personality from Pope John Paul II.

A small departure from one of John Paul's personal habits was noted during Pope Ben's arrival and disembarkment from his plane at the Cologne airport. Where JP II had always tried (when physically able to do so) to kiss the tarmac upon arrival in a new country, Ben XVI simply smiled, greeted Herr Schroeder, and went on his merry way.

John Paul had, of course, a wonderful smile and a friendly, gregarious natural disposition to go with it. Ben, on the other hand, is a quiet, private man not generally attracted to large crowds or the "spotlight."

Even so, John Paul always carried a tangible intensity in his demeanor, even in the lightest of moments. Pope Ben, on the other hand, has eyes that "twinkle," as though betraying some hidden mischief. His smile is genuine and warm. He is no longer the "man behind the curtain." Having been pushed forward into center stage by the hand of God and the voice of his Church, he has revealed himself to be more than capable of thoroughly enjoying playing the role of the Chief Servant among servants in God's household of faith on earth.

When blessed with a loving Master, a good servant will always submit to his will in all things. When the Master is the Lord, such submission will always bring peace. And, indeed, there is a peace within this man.

Although I am not a Roman Catholic, I believe that I will be a "Pope watcher," too. I expect that the view will be entertaining, enlightening, inspiring and even, on occasion, pleasantly surprising. Just like what we have seen on his trip to Cologne!

Harvard Re-Creates Embryonic Stem Cells from Adult Cells

For months everyone and their wives (read "Diana" and "Nancy") have been blasting President Bush on his unwillingness to approve Federal funding for new lines of embryonic stem cell research. I wrote about this matter last May in a post entitled, "What's the Big Deal About Embryonic Stem Cell Research."

Today, however, that entire point may well become mute.

According to the Associated Press in an article just posted on FoxNews, Harvard researchers are claiming that, by "fusing" an embryonic stem cell with a skin cell from an adult, the adult cell appeared to have been "reprogrammed" to return to it's original embryonic stem cell state.

If an effective procedure can be developed so that the fused cells can be separated and if the resulting new cells prove to be identical to embryonic stem cells, then the need to destroy human embryos in order to harvest their stem cells for research and medical use will likely become unnecessary.

This would remove a very contentious moral issue from the public debate over the ethics of this particular line of scientific research and effectively end the political debate over whether such research should or should not receive support from Federal grant money.

If this Harvard study proves to be true, then we will hear a vast, collective sigh of relief....with the possible exception of those researchers who have staked their professional reputation and financial future on their need to destroy frozen human embryos. Oh, and also those who may have invested large chunks of money into this venture. Like the State of California, for example!

The entire issue begs the question as to which came first in the evolutionary cycle, stem cells? or the specialized cells they create? Can there, in reality, be one without the other? If not, then where did they come from and how did they acquire this remarkable ability to change from one thing into another (and now, apparantly, also have the ability to change back again!).

It seems like another good argument for the Intelligent Design folks. Just like the "design" of the eye and other inter-dependent biological systems, this stem cell to specialized cell and back to stem cell cycle appears to have no credible naturalistic explaination for its origin.

For the past five years or more I have predicted great advances in therapeudic and restorative therapies over the span of my children's generation. I envision burned skin restored, lost fingers regrown and even damaged internal organs such as the liver, kidneys and even, perhaps, the heart and nerve cells in the brain and spinal column being repared as a result of stem cell research. Never did I believe that these breakthroughs would of necessity require the destruction of human embryos.

It appears that GW was right to defer the spending of our tax dollars on this line of research. Not because it was morally wrong (which I still believe it is) but because it was not necessary.

MONDAY, AUGUST 22, 2005

Pat Robertson Shames the Body of Christ

When I think of embarrassing Christian leaders, the Rev. Ian Paisley of Northern Ireland comes to mind. His militant, hateful and violent approach to Roman Catholics caused him to be condemned and disavowed by the Presbyterian Church of Ireland (of which he has never been a member. In 1946 he was "ordained" without the authorization of any recognized ecclesiastical body and has paraded himself around the world as a "Presbyterian" minister ever since. By any stretch of the imagination the title, "Rev.," which always appears in front of his name, should be, if not deleted entirely, at least be put in quotation marks!

Now, joining Paisley in the pantheon of "Embarrassing Christian Leaders," is the Rev. Dr. Pat Robertson. Now Robertson has been in and out of the pantheon for many years. Who can forget his claim that his prayers were responsible for steering hurricane Gloria away from the Atlantic coast ("*It was extremely important because I felt that if I couldn't move a hurricane, I could hardly move a nation*");

Or his claim to have been a "combat Marine" in Korea (when it turned out he had been nicknamed, "the liquor officer" who never got near the front lines).

Well, today on his "700 Club" television program, Robertson called for the assassination of Hugo Chavez, the President of Venezuela. Here is the transcript of what he said (courtesy of Captain Ed):

ROBERTSON: There was a popular coup that overthrew him[Chavez]. And what did the United States State Department do about it? Virtually nothing. And as a result, within about 48 hours that coup was broken; Chavez was back in power, but we had a chance to move in. He has destroyed the Venezuelan economy, and he's going to make that a launching pad for communist infiltration and Muslim extremism all over the continent.

You know, I don't know about this doctrine of assassination, but if he thinks we're trying to assassinate him, I think that we really ought to go ahead and do it. *It's a whole lot cheaper than starting a war. And I don't think any oil shipments will stop. But this man is a terrific danger and the United ... This is in our sphere of influence, so we can't let this happen. We have the Monroe Doctrine, we have other doctrines that we have announced. And without question, this is a dangerous enemy to our south, controlling a huge pool of oil, that could hurt us very badly. We have the ability to take him out, and I think the time has come that we exercise that ability. We don't need another $200 billion war to get rid of one, you know, strong-arm dictator. It's a whole lot easier to have some of the covert operatives do the job and then get it over with. (emphasis added)*

It would be considered madness for a politician to suggest such a thing openly. But for a prominent Christian minister to declare, apparently without a single moral qualm, that for the sake of America's need for oil and the insane idea that Chavez is inviting Al Qaeda into his country, we should sent in covert operatives and murder a Head of State simply for the sake of convenience?

Has he completely forgotten the lesson of scripture?

In John 11:49-50 we read that, when the Jewish leaders in Jerusalem were debating what to do about Jesus of Nazareth, "one of them, named Caiaphas, who was high priest that year, spoke up, 'You know nothing at all! You do not realize that it is better for you that one man die for the people than that the whole nation perish.'"

Now that sounds like an idea that would easily elicit a hearty "Amen!" from Pat Robertson.

Unfortunately, the strategy that Robertson seems to favor is the same one that led to the arrest, suffering, crucifixion and death of his own Lord and Savior, Jesus Christ ("go get 'em, Caiaphas!")

In retrospect, perhaps saying that, "the Rev. Dr. Pat Robertson Shames the Body of Christ" was not really an appropriate thing for me to have said. More appropriate would have been for me to have said that, "It appears that the Rev. Dr. Pat Robertson has lost his mind....and that he has shamed the Body of Christ as well!"

This time, when he enters the pantheon of embarrassing Christian Leaders, will somebody please close and lock the door behind him?

The Iraqi Constitution Is Still "On-Track"...Barely

A Draft Constitution for Iraq was completed today....but without the support of the Sunni members of the committee. Instead of trying to ram it through the legislature, thereby disenfranchising every Iraq Sunni, the committee majority carefully considered the matter and, bravely and intelligently, decided to **wait three more days** to find some way to bring the Sunni's "on board."

There are, of course, many different ways to "read" this unfolding drama.

For me, the most remarkable thing is that all three major political groups, Sunni, Kurd & Shi'ite, all seem to agree that they are all Iraqis and that the unity of the nation represents a higher priority than squeezing out the last, minute concession to benefit their own particular constituency.

Power Line's **John Hinderocker** has posted a brief, succinct and, I believe, correct analysis of what is taking place in Baghdad. He is optimistic and, until I discover something that proves me wrong, I am, too!

TUESDAY, AUGUST 23, 2005

Who Is Iraq's George Washington?

Every nation has a hero, whether mythical or historic, who symbolically sums up the nation's pride, purpose and personality.

--The United States has its George Washington.

--Numerous countries in South American have Simon Bolivar.

--England has its Winston Churchill (as a contemporary icon).

--Scotland its William Wallace, Robert Bruce and John Knox.

--Every world religion, as well, has their founder and "saints."

But what about the emerging democratic and free nation of Iraq? Who will one day be their George Washington?

Who will they honor with a statue in the town square?

Who will personify their overthrow of Saddam Hussein and their victory over murderous terrorism?

Who will be the lynch-pin that rises above sectarian differences and becomes the leader, respected and trusted by all sides and who inspires others to rise above their differences and sacrifice for the good of the nation as a whole?

I submit that there is, at the moment, no one who remotely stands in such a place of stature at this critical moment of Iraqi history.

When the textbooks are written, what will they say?
While we stood by, powerless and oppressed, the United States invaded our country and cast off the yoke of the dictatorial tyrant Saddam Hussein and his evil Baathist Party.

After the Americans (assisted by the British in the south) created some semblance of security, rich and educated Iraqis who had lived outside of Iraq for many years were flown back into Iraq by the United States. These men, hand-picked by American military and CIA operatives, soon coalesced to form the nucleus of our emerging government.

While many Iraqi men signed up to serve in our new armed forces and police units, it was the United States who screened them, trained them, paid them and, for a time, actually led them in missions against the insurgent terrorists.

While many Iraqi civilians and police officers were killed in terrorist attacks and others killed in crossfire between American troops and Al Qaeda operatives, it was the American soldiers who bore the heaviest burden to secure our freedom.

These soldiers, with the help of foreign civilians paid by the United States, literally rebuilt our country from the bottom, hiring and training Iraqi citizens to take over the management, maintenance and operation of the many components of the new and technologically advanced industrial, economic, educational, security and utilitarian infrastructure.

Our interim government was protected by American troops who also oversaw the logistics and successful completion of our first, free national election in decades. The men and women who we elected to our new parliament eventually framed a new constitution for Iraq. They did so in the area of Baghdad called the "Green Zone" which was a safety area secured by hundreds of American soldiers.

*We are a proud people and we salute the brave and visionary leadership of (***fill in the blank***) who inspired us and who heroically stood head and shoulders above everyone else during this most difficult period of our nation's new, emerging history.*

This mentor and role-model for our nation will always be revered as the Father/Mother of a democratic Iraq.
How inspiring this will be! How Iraqi hearts will fill with pride as they remember how they stood by and watched as the United States freed them and paid the price in money, material and blood for the freedom we enjoy today

The Iraqis will stand tall as they remember that they were completely unable to achieve this by themselves.

How, I ask, can a nation become forged into unity of vision when they do not have either a George Washington, Thomas Jefferson, Benjamin Franklin, Paul Revere, John Adams, John Hancock or even a Patrick Henry?

Al-Sistani the "Father of Iraq?" Al-Sadr? Chalabi?

A genuine nation evolves like the Beatles, through strong will, hard work, trial and error, vivid personalities, personal sacrifice, good luck and gifted talent.

The emerging Iraq appears to be more like the Monkees.
WEDNESDAY, AUGUST 24, 2005

No Liquor In My House

It's not just liquor; my house does not contain any alcoholic beverages at all.

This was a decision by my wife and I from the time we were married. Outside the house I would have maybe one beer and one glass of wine every 12 months or so.

When our first daughter turned 2 years old I gave that up, too. Parents set a very important example for their children and we wanted to set an example of a good life that did not require alcohol to have "fun" or to be "happy" or even to "celebrate" things.

Neither of us passed any judgment on others we knew (whether members of a Christian church or not) who either had a beer or glass of brandy once in a while. That was their decision but, if they came to our house for dinner and brought a bottle of wine along as a gift, we would quietly thank them but explain our household policy without seeming to be critical of their own.

Today, the newpaper printed the results of a national survey made by the American Medical Association. It is a very small sample (701 U.S. Teens) so I would not be comfortable describing the survey as "authoritative." Even so, the figures were very interesting:

In response to a question concerning where & how they, as teens, get alcohol....

At a party: 80%
From their home (w/out parents' knowledge): 67%
From relatives or a sibling older than 21: 65%
From someone else's parent(s): 40%
Using a fake ID: 36%
From their parents (w/their parents' knowledge): 32%

It seems to me that having alcohol sitting around your house will all too often wind up being too big a temptation for many teens to walk away from.

If a person has a genetic predisposition to alcohol addiction, a few drinks at a young age could lead quickly to a life of misery. Even one overdone binge with parents out of the house could lead to serious threats to both health and life.

My wife and I decided that it would be better to remove that temptation from our home, at least as long as our children were growing up. Our oldest is now 23 and can choose to buy or not to buy alcohol on her own as an adult. Daughters number 2 & 3 are 19 and 16.

Perhaps the day will come when I will share a beer or a glass of wine with one or more of my daughters. Should such a day ever come, they would have learned long before that it wasn't something I needed to have in order to enjoy life.

Hopefully, they will learn to do the same.

Woman's Attempt to Foil Car Theft Fails....Bare-ly

Here in Hawaii, we are used to the whimsical side of life. On Monday morning, for example, a woman, camping at Mokuleia on Oahu's North Shore heard suspicious sounds coming from outside her tent. As she peeked out she saw a man about to steal her car and drive off.

She dashed out of the tent and jumped onto the hood of her car, hoping to startle the man and cause him to stop. We can only assume that the man was, indeed, startled when he saw a completely naked woman jump onto the front of the car he was trying to steal!

The man kept his composure long enough to swerve back and forth until he threw the nude former car owner onto the side of the road and drove away, chased by another car driven by a friend of the woman. Eventually he got clean away by smashing into the pursuing car and leaving it behind.

The woman, whose name was discretely withheld from the public record, was treated at the Wahiawa Hospital and later released with minor injuries.

The woman was a visitor from Washington state. When she gets home and her friends ask her how her trip to Hawaii went......I would love to hear what she tells them!

Man Abandons Wife,Dies, Falls & Suffocates Daughter; Huh?

According to the AP article on CNN, Hollywood producer, Terry Carr drove off with his nine-year old daughter, Arieka, leaving his wife, Chikako, behind in a grocery store restroom in Ashland, Oregon. He then drove 280 miles south to Clearlake Oaks, California, where, the following morning, his body, lying on top of his suffocated daughter, was found in the back of his SUV in a convenience store parking lot.

The body was found on August 1st. His wife has no idea why he drove off without her. He dumped a box of belongings, including important personal papers and photos, in a pasture on the outskirts of Ashland a few days before he disappeared. His brother, John, lives in Clearlake Oaks but said he had not heard from Carr. Police now say that Carr died of a heart attack.

Hmmm. Sounds like a case for Miss Marple. Lots of questions here....

Who died first, Carr or his daughter?
Was her death accidental or intentional?
Had Carr suffered from depression?
Was he bi-polar?
Had he evidenced any indication of being suicidal?
Was he taking medication for depression, high blood pressure, etc?
Had he stopped taking any medications?
Had he and his wife had any arguments recently?
If so, what were the arguments about?
Why couldn't a 52 pound, 9-year old girl at least turn her head to the side and breathe, even with a 212 pound man on top of her?

I guess it took 3+ weeks to complete the autopsy. I wonder what else they found....such as medications, etc. in his body?

Something just doesn't add up with the story as I read it. I'm not usually a suspicious sort of guy, but this is almost too weird for me to swallow whole!

New Hampshire Physician May Lose License For Being Honest

Dr. Terry Bennett told his patient that she was overweight. She was. She got upset. Now he's in trouble and being asked by the State Attorney General's Office that he needs to take sensitivity training. What?

According to **FoxNews**,
"I told a fat woman she was obese," Bennett says. "I tried to get her attention. I told her, 'You need to get on a program, join a group of like-minded people and peel off the weight that is going to kill you.' "

He says he wrote a letter of apology to the woman when he found out she was offended.

Her complaint, filed about a year ago, was initially investigated by a panel of the New Hampshire Board of Medicine, which recommended that Bennett be sent a confidential letter of concern. The board rejected the suggestion in December and asked the attorney general's office to investigate.

Bennett rejected that office's proposal that he attend a medical education course and acknowledge that he made a mistake.

Wait....here's the best part....
Other overweight patients have come to Bennett's defense.

"What really makes me angry is he told the truth," Mindy Haney told WMUR-TV on Tuesday. "How can you punish somebody for that?"

Haney said Bennett has helped her lose more than 150 pounds, but acknowledged that the initially didn't want to listen.

"I have been in this lady's shoes. I've been angry and left his practice. I mean, in-my-car-taking-off angry," Haney said. "But once you think about it, you're angry at yourself, not Doctor Bennett. He's the messenger. He's telling you what you already know."

My guess is that it is the complaining patient who should be required to take a class...."What class and Why?" you ask. Hey, I report....you decide!

Iraqi Sunnis Debate Whether To Wield Constitutonal "Nuclear Option"

Lost in all the commentary about the current impasse in the Draft Committee for the new Iraqi Constitution is that the minority Sunni group (less influential due to their boycott of last January's elections) holds a very powerful ace up their sleeve.

When Thursday rolls around and the final deadline arrives to present the Draft Constitution, the Sunnis know that a "very bad thing" will happen if it is not approved. What would happen, according to the current laws adopted to govern this interim stage of political formation, is that the existing parliament would be dissolved and all political progress would halt until new parliamentary elections could be held.

The "bad thing" would be a major setback in law and order and a major boost for Sunni-led terrorist groups. This is a great threat that can be used as leverage by the Sunni committee members to hold the Kurds and Shi'ites "hostage" to their demands for getting what they want.

There is also the reality that, if new parliamentary elections were to be held, the Sunnis would not boycott the second time around. Enough Sunnis would likely be elected to prevent any alliance of Kurds and Shi'ites to hold absolute power in the legislature (as they do now).

There is, however, also the possibility of this "threat" backfiring on the Sunnis. If the Draft Constitution is presented to the Parliament on Thursday without their endorsement, the Kurds and Shi'ites have the votes to pass it without the Sunnis at all.

This outcome would move the Constitutional process forward, of course, but it would marginalize the Sunni participation in future planning even more. They would be faced with living with a Constitution they did not endorse while serving in a government in which they hold virtually no power.

The Sunni population would then, once again, be faced with either boycotting the Constitutional vote (a tactic that backfired in January), voting for it (which would be to support a document not endorsed by their elected Sunni representatives) or vote against it (which, while most likely preventing its implementation and moving the process back to square one, would strain the attempts at national reconciliation, cooperation and political power-sharing to the breaking point.

Who will blink first? I do not think that the Shi'ites or Kurds will back off much more than they already have.

Although the outcome of a Sunni rejection might possibly empower the Sunnis in the short term, all other scenarios are less pleasant. Not only would their rejection destabilize national security, but it would likely significantly diminish their influence in the future government. Shi'ite and Kurdish anger and distrust towards the Sunnis (already present but suppressed) would show itself in their coordinating power in ways that would leave the Sunnis sidelined as a super-minority opposition party as opposed to being a contributing member of a coalition government.

My guess is that it will be the Sunnis who will blink on Thursday. If they don't, they, and the majority Sunni populations in central Iraq, will be the losers. I believe that they know this and will endorse the final draft.

Then again.....I could be wrong!

THURSDAY, AUGUST 25, 2005

The Proposed Draft of the Iraqi Constitution (as of 8/25/05)

Click HERE (PDF file) if you would like to read the actual Draft of the Iraqi Constitution being debated this week.

Key issues of concern for the Sunni minority members include:

Federalism: I'm sure what the key sticking points are in the document. I know that the Sunni participants are concerned that the current Draft provides the opportunity for "Regions" and "Provinces" to exercize a wide range of discretionary authority. For example, "Article (133): It is permissible to delegate the federal government's authorities to the provinces or vice versa, with the two parties' approval, and this is regulated by law." It seems that here, certain "provinces" could be granted powers otherwise granted only to the federal government in the constitution. I don't know what this means. It almost sounds that, by agreements, certain areas of Iraq could legislate and govern almost independently of Baghdad?

A related concern is that generated by "Article (150): Laws legislated in Kurdistan since 1992 remain in effect, and decisions made by the government of the Kurdistan region--including contracts and court decisions--are effective unless they are voided or amended according to the laws of the Kurdistan region by the concerned body, as long as they are not against the constitution."

The fact that the constitution also permits existing "provinces" to join together by common consent and form larger "regions" means that all the northern Iraqi provinces could join to form one vast region comparable to a "Kurdistan" and the southern provinces could unite as one vast region dominated by Shi'ites. In these two powerful regions, minority citizens would have little influence on regional affairs which would also, of course, include the two sections of Iraq's vast oil reserves.

The few provinces with sunni majorities (I believe there are three of them) could also unite to form one region as well, but there would be little economic wealth or even large swaths of productive agricultural land in these areas. Sunnis have a good reason to feel threatened by these possibilities.

Division of Federal Power

Sunnis are concerned over the amount of power being granted to the president and his/her cabinet. Since it is unlikely that a Sunni will ever hold this office, their only hope to wield influence over policy and power will be through the council of representatives (where they one day might be able to block legislative matters requiring a 2/3 majority.) Accordingly, the more power granted to the council of representatives, the happier the Sunnis will be.

Former Baathist Party Members

The Constitution specifically targets former Baathist Party members for ostracism from the new government. Articles (7) & (145-3rd) & (148-3rd-c & d) and continues the de-Baathification Committee until dissolved by law. Article (145-1st & 2nd).

It is notable that Article (7) specifically names "the Saddamist Baathist Party" as the pariah. Being a "Baathist" in and of itself will not disqualify anyone. Syria, for example, is governed by a Baathist Party. This appears to allow for a little bit of wiggle-room for folks who worked for Saddam's party or government but was not a member of his party.

Other Matters

I am still somewhat baffled over the lack of specificity in the second legislative body called the Council of Union in Article (63). It seems as though this will be a body that reviews proposed legislation that may affect a particular region and make recommendations of some sort to who? The Council of Representatives? The President?

I am also baffled by Article (151) that reads, "A proportion of no less than 25% of the seats in the Council of Representatives is specified for the participation of women."

Since the Constitution states that each member of the Council of Representatives will represent approximately 100,000 Iraqis, that means, with a population of over 26,000,000, there will be 260 members + or - in that Council. The Constitution requires that at least 65 (25%) of them be women.

If the Representatives are freely elected as per Article (48) "by general, direct secret ballot" how in the world can they legally require that at least 65 women get elected?

Overall Impression

I feel that the opening general, foundational principles and rights laid down in in the Preamble and in Articles (1)-(48) are extremely commendable and, indeed, visionary. Even with the provisions designating that "Islam is the official religion of Iraq and is a basic source of legislation" (Article 2) the rights of other religions are also fully affirmed (note that it says, "a" basic source..... and not "the" basic source of legislation. This is a very big distinction).

I also do not feel threatened by the inclusion of experts on Sharia being included on the Supreme Federal Court (Article 90) although I could change my mind should future legislation designate them as a majority of this Court's members).

In any case, read the text for yourself. By next Monday, God willing, Iraq will have a Draft Constitution endorsed by Kurds, Shi'ites *and* Sunnis to present to the Iraqi people for their approval.

FRIDAY, AUGUST 26, 2005

Michael Yon's "Gates of Fire" Tells It Like It Is On the Ground In Iraq

Michael Yon, who blogs at *Michael Yon: Online Magazine* is, in his own words, "an independent, informed observer chronicling the monumentally important events in the efforts to stabilize Iraq." His gritty, graphic and startling writing and photography have been earning the respect of a **broad swath of the blogosphere**.

His latest entry, dated August 25, 2005 and entitled, "Gates of Fire," will surely go down as one of the most dramatic reports from the ground that we have yet seen from Iraq.

The American media is very good a showing up burning cars and rubble caused by terrorist bombs. Every terrorist attack seems to get more coverage than any of the successful, daring and courageous missions led by our own American troops or even those led by the Iraqis themselves.

The reality of the war against the terrorists in Iraq seems never to get told. Why, I don't really know. We do ocassionally receive copies of the military incident reports filed after a firefight. Even these sterile, "tell-it-like-it-was"-in-the-tersest-possible-manner reports, convey drama and tragedy and heroism and even a moral insight or two in a way that simply can't be concealed by the "facts."

How much more telling when the writer is a gifted story-teller, free to speak of the anger, fear, confusion and admiration experienced in a moment when life and death intersect in the blink of an eye.

Read Yon's posting. Let his own words tell you about LTC Erik Kurilla, CSM Robert Prosser, Jose L. Ruiz and SGT Daniel Lama. Let him explain this photograph....

this photograph......

and this one, too....

And be proud of these men. Pray for them. Email them. And, if you are willing and able, send a little money to Michael Yon who is paying for his efforts with his own money. You will find a PayPal link at his site. Take a moment and use it. I did.

Church Block Party In Hawaii

Every year, for the past six years, my congregation has thrown a "Block Party" for our neighbors and community of Mililani. Today we had our 7th. *(Click on pictures to enlarge)*

We throw the party for several reasons: 1. To show our neighbors that we're glad to have them around! 2. To give a chance for folks to get to know us better, and 3. To share the good news of God's saving love in Jesus Christ.

This last reason is the best one, of course. Since God's love is free, we offer everything at the Block Party for free, too! The entertainment, the children's activities (face painting, crafts, "pond

tic-tac-toe," sponge throwing and a real dunk tank), bibles, the "Jesus" video, devotional materials and, of course, food....lots of food. Hot dogs, beef & long rice, white & brown rice with chili, raw veggies and lots of chocolate brownies.

It's a lot of work but a lot of fun, too. We're helped out by the Korean, Samoan and Micronesian congregations that worship and meet in our facilities each week (we do not charge any rent....after all, the Gospel is free, right?). Other local congregations also help out in various ways.

At the end of the day (6:30-7:0 pm) everyone (and I mean everyone) gathers on the church lawn for a big party dance! "We are family!" "Electric Slide." "Macarena" and more. Old and young and just about everrace you can think of, dancing for the sheer joy of it. I tried to explain it to a rather distinguished visitor from South Korea..."Just think of it as being like the wedding reception at Cana.....but without the wine!"

As usual I had a good time, too. I didn't have to sit in the dunk tank this year!

.

Tomorrow we will celebrate our 35th Anniversary with a special worship service in the morning and a catered dinner, more entertainment and fire-crackers in the afternoon. Yes, the day will literally end with a blast!

SUNDAY, AUGUST 28, 2005

Hawaii's Ewa Beach Wins Little League World Series

Michael Memea celebrates winning homer

It has been a dream season for a bunch of boys who live and play baseball just a few miles from my home here on Oahu.

Today, the dream of nearly every American boy came true for them as they defeated last year's World Championship team from Curacao in the **final game** of this years Little League World Series.

The team from Ewa Beach, Hawaii, took the early lead, gave it up and fell behind 3-1 in the top of the third inning. Back-to-back homers in the bottom of the third tied the score at 3-3.

In the fifth inning, Curacao took back the lead with two home runs of their own and held that lead, 6-3, going into the bottom of the sixth inning.

A bunt, a single and a potentially inning-ending double play ball that arrived at first base just half a step too late, allowed Hawaii to tie the game 6-6 going into the seventh and last inning.

Ewa's pitching held the defending champs scoreless in their half of the seventh.

The dramatic game then came to a sudden end as Hawaii's Michael Memea walked up to the plate and hit a lead-off, walk-off home run over the left field fence.

Hawaii is very proud of her boys from Ewa Beach. The coaches and parents have been "class acts" and have shown the world that the word "aloha" can be used in the same sentence as "World Champions!"

Will New Orleans Die Tonight? Hurricane Katrina Takes Aim

Note: Best bets for on-line updates, The Irish Trojan's Blog and the Times-Picayune Online. Also, Michelle Malkin has links to a number of other valuable sites.

As Hurricane Katrina, now a category 5 storm (sustained winds of 160+mph), aims straight at the heart of New Orleans, a series of near-apocalyptic scenarios are being seriously discussed.

The blogosphere is centering on two matters:

1. The levees protecting New Orleans along Lake Pontchartrain are 18 feet high. The hurricane, however, is predicted to produce a storm surge of as high as 20 feet. If such a surge takes place, it would be very likely that the levee would give way, plunging the Big Easy (which sits 15 feet below sea level) under 30 feet of water. Associated Press and others are predicting that, if such a disaster should occur, as many as 10,000 or more people could perish in the flood and the city, as we have known it, could well disappear forever. Fetid, polluted water could potentially take as long as 10 months to drain, leaving a layer of toxic waste across the entire historic center of New Orleans.

2. The second issue concerns the New Orleans Super Dome, which has become the shelter of choice for, perhaps, 30,000 of the area's homeless and those who had no way to flee the city. Concern is being expressed as to whether the facility will be able to withstand the sustained winds and rain of Katrina. If the roof does not hold, where will the 30,000+ people go? Also, if the city does indeed flood, the two lower floors of the Dome will be under water. Electricity will be essentially cut off and so will tens of thousands of people, stranded on what will be an artificial island will only three day's food supply and no apparent way to be evacuated.

Katrina has been described as perhaps one of the three most powerful hurricanes in American history. A recent satellite photo shows it virtually filling the Gulf of Mexico from Yucatan to Florida to Louisiana.

From those blogging from the New Orleans area I am getting a sense of genuine fear and doom. One has placed the likelihood of a worst case scenario as high as 70%.

I, for one, will be praying mightily for the people of New Orleans and the surrounding Gulf coast. The many bayous and general low-lying areas are particularly susceptible to the dangers of this kind of storm. It is almost certain than many historic communities will be completely swept away by tomorrow afternoon. Any people foolish enough (or not given sufficient warning) will also be swept away.

Even if the worst does not happen, and the levees hold, the damage will be horrific. The old infrastructure of the New Orleans metropolitan area, especially the sewer system, will not be able to weather the storm. Avoiding a flood does not necessarily assure that the city will remain inhabitable after the storm passes.

I will be up tonight, reading the on-site blogs and watching what information can be gleaned from television sources. I do not expect, however, that we will really know the facts until the sun comes up tomorrow morning.....or whenever the storm passes far enough along to allow it to "shed some light" on the situation.

May God have mercy on New Orleans, the Gulf Coast and all who dwell therein during the next 24 hours.

MONDAY, AUGUST 29, 2005

Global Fund Cancels Uganda's AID Funding...Could It Be Because Uganda's abstinence Approach Is Working?

Cheat-Seeking Missiles has a series of posts here, here and here in response to last Thursday's announcement by the Global Fund to fight AIDS, Tuberculosis and Malaria that it had cancelled all grant funding for Uganda, due to a discrepancy in accounting after grant dollars had been converted to Ugandan currency.

What is ironic in all of this is that Uganda has had more success in reducing the incidence of AIDS in their population than any other African nation.

Also ironic is the fact that Uganda has taken an approach to the AIDS epidemic that is contrary to the policies of the United Nations, the Global Fund and every other participating country in Africa. What is so unique about Uganda's approach? It has declared that Abstinence, self-control and the instilling of a responsible national sexual morality is key to any long-range strategy to reduce the epidemic.

Every other agency and nation puts their priority on "safe sex" education and the massive distribution of condoms. The obvious fallacy in this way of approaching the problem is that AIDS is primarily spread through frequent sexual activity among multiple partners. The number one guaranteed way to reduce the spread of AIDS would be to.....ta dah!...reduce the amount of polygamous sexual activity, right? According to the international community, apparently, that is the wrong answer.

The correct answer is....ta dah!...condoms! Yep. Condoms. Safe sex is the answer! And apparently Uganda has been taken to task for failing to adhere to the politically correct approach to the AIDS situation.

The fact that their approach is works does not, it seems, make others happy. It appears, if fact, to have made some very influential people very angry.

Cheat-Seeking Missiles "theorize(s) that the true cause for the suspension is pressure from anti-abstinence, (anti-)morality and (anti-)monogamy groups like George Soros' Human Rights Watch, which said:

Human Rights Watch accused[Ugandan] President Yoweri Museveni and his wife, Janet Museveni, of falling under the influence of U.S. Christian conservatives and placing millions of young Ugandans at risk of contracting HIV, the virus that causes AIDS.

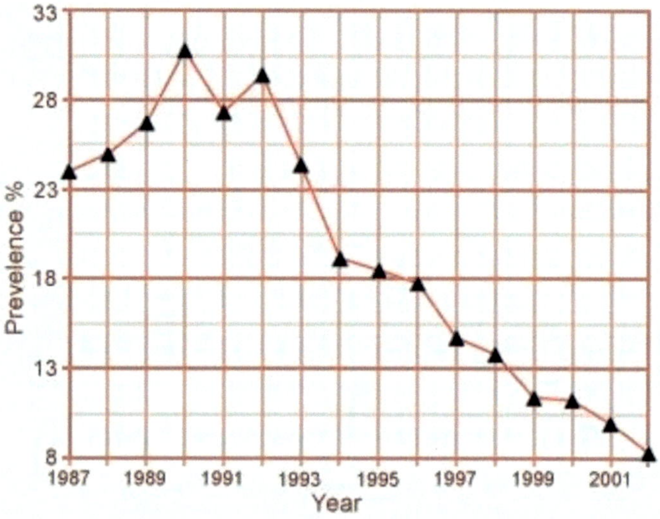

"Risk?" Take a look at this chart, showing that the rate of AIDS has been reduced from 30% in 1990 to 8% in 2002.

Unconvinced? Here, taken from "Cheat's" site is the Global Fund's own assessment in their own words from a 2003 news release showing the success of their grant program:

Uganda, one of first countries in Africa to experience the impact of HIV/AIDS and still one of the countries most affected by the virus, is also one of the continent's great success stories in terms of reducing high HIV infection rates. HIV prevalence among pregnant women in urban areas has declined from a peak of 30 per cent in 1992 to 6 per cent in 2001. This and other successes in the field are widely acknowledged to be the result of high-level political commitment to HIV prevention and care, involving a wide range of partners and effected through an aggressive anti-HIV/AIDS campaign involving virtually all sections of society. Nevertheless, Uganda is still confronted with a serious HIV/AIDS epidemic, including rising numbers of people needing care and support.

Compare Uganda's success performance with what is going on in many of Uganda's neighbors which follow the UN/Global Fund protocols of "safe sex" education:

Very high HIV prevalence, often exceeding 30% among pregnant women is still being recorded in four other countries in the region, all with small populations: Botswana, Lesotho, Namibia and Swaziland. There, comparisons of prevalence levels at selected antenatal clinics have shown no evidence of a decline. In Swaziland, for example, HIV prevalence among pregnant women was 39% in 2002, up from 34% in 2000 and only 4% in 1992. Elsewhere in the subregion, HIV infections in pregnant women appear to be stabilizing at lower levels; around 18% in Malawi (2003), 16% in Zambia (2003), and 25% in Zimbabwe (2003); but there is little evidence of an impending decline. (source)

Now, of course it may be true that money destined for Uganda's AIDS program is unaccounted for. But this allegation has not even been proven yet.

One has placed the likelihood of a worst case scenario as high as 70%.

I, for one, will be praying mightily for the people of New Orleans and the surrounding Gulf coast. The many bayous and general low-lying areas are particularly susceptible to the dangers of this kind of storm. It is almost certain than many historic communities will be completely swept away by tomorrow afternoon. Any people foolish enough (or not given sufficient warning) will also be swept away.

Even if the worst does not happen, and the levees hold, the damage will be horrific. The old infrastructure of the New Orleans metropolitan area, especially the sewer system, will not be able to weather the storm. Avoiding a flood does not necessarily assure that the city will remain inhabitable after the storm passes.

I will be up tonight, reading the on-site blogs and watching what information can be gleaned from television sources. I do not expect, however, that we will really know the facts until the sun comes up tomorrow morning.....or whenever the storm passes far enough along to allow it to "shed some light" on the situation.

May God have mercy on New Orleans, the Gulf Coast and all who dwell therein during the next 24 hours.

MONDAY, AUGUST 29, 2005

Global Fund Cancels Uganda's AID Funding...Could It Be Because Uganda's abstinence Approach Is Working?

Cheat-Seeking Missiles has a series of posts here, here and here in response to last Thursday's announcement by the Global Fund to fight AIDS, Tuberculosis and Malaria that it had cancelled all grant funding for Uganda, due to a discrepancy in accounting after grant dollars had been converted to Ugandan currency.

What is ironic in all of this is that Uganda has had more success in reducing the incidence of AIDS in their population than any other African nation.

Also ironic is the fact that Uganda has taken an approach to the AIDS epidemic that is contrary to the policies of the United Nations, the Global Fund and every other participating country in Africa. What is so unique about Uganda's approach? It has declared that Abstinence, self-control and the instilling of a responsible national sexual morality is key to any long-range strategy to reduce the epidemic.

Every other agency and nation puts their priority on "safe sex" education and the massive distribution of condoms. The obvious fallacy in this way of approaching the problem is that AIDS is primarily spread through frequent sexual activity among multiple partners. The number one guaranteed way to reduce the spread of AIDS would be to.....ta dah!...reduce the amount of polygamous sexual activity, right? According to the international community, apparently, that is the wrong answer.

The correct answer is....ta dah!...condoms! Yep. Condoms. Safe sex is the answer! And apparently Uganda has been taken to task for failing to adhere to the politically correct approach to the AIDS situation.

The fact that their approach is works does not, it seems, make others happy. It appears, if fact, to have made some very influential people very angry.

Cheat-Seeking Missiles "theorize(s) that the true cause for the suspension is pressure from anti-abstinence, (anti-)morality and (anti-)monogamy groups like George Soros' Human Rights Watch, which said:

Human Rights Watch accused[Ugandan] President Yoweri Museveni and his wife, Janet Museveni, of falling under the influence of U.S. Christian conservatives and placing millions of young Ugandans at risk of contracting HIV, the virus that causes AIDS.

"Risk?" Take a look at this chart, showing that the rate of AIDS has been reduced from 30% in 1990 to 8% in 2002.

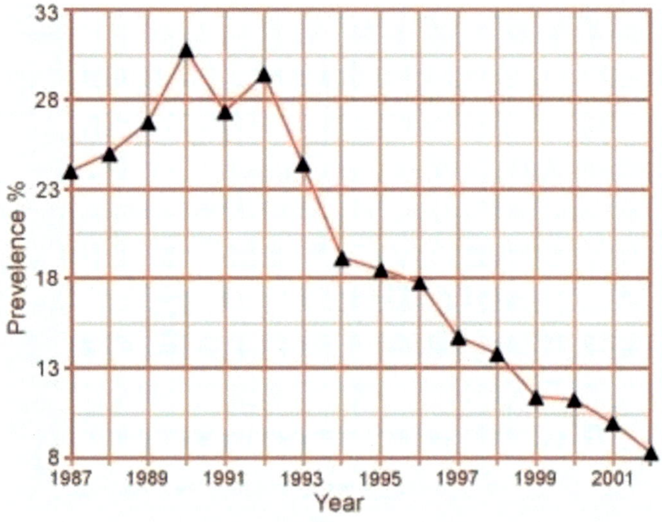

Unconvinced? Here, taken from "Cheat's" site is the Global Fund's own assessment in their own words from a 2003 news release showing the success of their grant program:

Uganda, one of first countries in Africa to experience the impact of HIV/AIDS and still one of the countries most affected by the virus, is also one of the continent's great success stories in terms of reducing high HIV infection rates. HIV prevalence among pregnant women in urban areas has declined from a peak of 30 per cent in 1992 to 6 per cent in 2001. This and other successes in the field are widely acknowledged to be the result of high-level political commitment to HIV prevention and care, involving a wide range of partners and effected through an aggressive anti-HIV/AIDS campaign involving virtually all sections of society. Nevertheless, Uganda is still confronted with a serious HIV/AIDS epidemic, including rising numbers of people needing care and support.

Compare Uganda's success performance with what is going on in many of Uganda's neighbors which follow the UN/Global Fund protocols of "safe sex" education:

Very high HIV prevalence, often exceeding 30% among pregnant women is still being recorded in four other countries in the region, all with small populations: Botswana, Lesotho, Namibia and Swaziland. There, comparisons of prevalence levels at selected antenatal clinics have shown no evidence of a decline. In Swaziland, for example, HIV prevalence among pregnant women was 39% in 2002, up from 34% in 2000 and only 4% in 1992. Elsewhere in the subregion, HIV infections in pregnant women appear to be stabilizing at lower levels; around 18% in Malawi (2003), 16% in Zambia (2003), and 25% in Zimbabwe (2003); but there is little evidence of an impending decline. (source)

Now, of course it may be true that money destined for Uganda's AIDS program is unaccounted for. But this allegation has not even been proven yet.

Other nations supported by the Global Fund, such as South Africa, have also had "account discrepancies." But South Africa's funding has not been cut off. On the contrary, the Global Fund has been working with them for over three years to return them to full compliance.

As insult to injury, not only did the Global Fund cut off Uganda's AIDS grants, but also grants for their tuberculosis and malaria programs as well. Even though there is no evidence of any of that money being misused. This action is unprecedented in the Global Fund's history.

According to their own site, the Global Fund's largest contributor is the United States. It is even more ironic, therefore, that the Bush administration has touted Uganda's "abstinence first" program as a model for the rest of African and, indeed, for the world.

Note that Uganda does distribute condoms and does provide education on how the disease is spread and how "safe sex" can reduce its spread. Somehow, it is the idea of abstinence and personal self-control that sticks in the craw of the funding elite. Perhaps the thinking goes like this:

"Does it sound like morality? Then it must be Christian. If it's Christian then it must be fundamentalist Christianity. It may also have Republican support which means it does not play well with Democrats so......it must be wrong!"

Also of interest is that Islamic countries, which have, by law, strict penalties and cultural restrictions on "free sex" also have the lowest rate of AIDS in the world. But it isn't politically correct to say, either!

Perhaps the United Nations and the Global Fund can be pressured by the Bush administration to reconsider this matter. Much of it is, of course, our money to begin with. If they cannot distributed it in a way that encourages success, then perhaps the United States should find a new way to distribute the money.

Other nations supported by the Global Fund, such as South Africa, have also had "account discrepancies." But South Africa's funding has not been cut off. On the contrary, the Global Fund has been working with them for over three years to return them to full compliance.

As insult to injury, not only did the Global Fund cut off Uganda's AIDS grants, but also grants for their tuberculosis and malaria programs as well. Even though there is no evidence of any of that money being misused. This action is unprecedented in the Global Fund's history.

According to their own site, the Global Fund's largest contributor is the United States. It is even more ironic, therefore, that the Bush administration has touted Uganda's "abstinence first" program as a model for the rest of African and, indeed, for the world.

Note that Uganda does distribute condoms and does provide education on how the disease is spread and how "safe sex" can reduce its spread. Somehow, it is the idea of abstinence and personal self-control that sticks in the craw of the funding elite. Perhaps the thinking goes like this:

"Does it sound like morality? Then it must be Christian. If it's Christian then it must be fundamentalist Christianity. It may also have Republican support which means it does not play well with Democrats so......it must be wrong!"

Also of interest is that Islamic countries, which have, by law, strict penalties and cultural restrictions on "free sex" also have the lowest rate of AIDS in the world. But it isn't politically correct to say, either!

Perhaps the United Nations and the Global Fund can be pressured by the Bush administration to reconsider this matter. Much of it is, of course, our money to begin with. If they cannot distributed it in a way that encourages success, then perhaps the United States should find a new way to distribute the money.

Mililani Congregregation Celebrates Its 35th Anniversary

Today the church I serve as Pastor celebrated its 35th Anniversary.

Nine ordained PCUSA pastors (three of whom have served as pastor of this congregation and two of whom became ordained while members of this congregation) participated in the morning worship.

Seven of the Nine Pastors

There was so much sharing and talking story and worship and special music and the Sacrament of the Lord's Supper and a Children's sermon and the introduction of special guests (including our State Senator) and a farewell to one of our dear church families and a wonderful retrospective "slide show" and two sermons and...and...well...it went for almost 3 hours! Now that's more like an Assembly of God or a Baptist type of worship.....Presbyterians are supposed to worship by the clock, aren't they? Well, today our clock broke! But God was praised and we all had a good time, too!

Hungry.....and waiting to be fed!

In the afternoon we had our Anniversary Luau. Kalua Pork (I said I wouldn't come if they didn't serve Kalua pork!), white rice (there's always white rice in Hawaii), fried rice, frozen fruit, fish, teryaki chicken and haupia dessert!

The Luau Line

There were anniversary shell/kukui nut leis for everybody and enough fresh pineapples for every family to take one home! Fresh tropical flowers from our members' homes and gardens decorated the tables and a small stage provided a focus for the entertainment.
Special guests included our original architect, two current and one former State Representatives plus a personal, handwritten letter of congratulations from President George Bush (actually, I made the last one up......sorry).

In good local fashion we all sang our State Song/Former Hawaii National Anthem "Hawaii Ponoi" and "Hawaii Aloha." (I was proud of Rick, who spotted a typo in the last song. Three letters were missing. You grow up here and you KNOW these songs by heart! Rick helped out with the singing by adding his ukulele to Tony's and my guitars.)

Not "Sister Act" but Mom & Daughter!

Mom and daughter sang and left us all with "chicken skin," and then the daughter sang "Hero," which she had also sung at our 25th Anniversary when she was only 13.

Grace Being full of grace!

Grace shared her beautiful hula and then Randy and Gay Hongo, wonderful local Island Christian entertainers (with at least six Na Hoku awards) shared their music along with three dancers from a Christian hula halau.

Randy & Gay Hongo.................. and friend

After the closing benediction we ended things with a "bang" as John and Mike set off a string of "10,000" firecrackers (a string that really only has 2,500 of them.....but that's still plenty to make a lot of noise for a very long time!)

The grand finale

It was hot, and rainy, and humid and sunny and wonderful. As always, we gave thanked God for bringing us all together in this final corner of his creation....you know, the place he made after he had practiced trial and error on all the rest! We don't call Hawaii "paradise" for nothing!

In fact, you could say that, at least in our little spot in Mililani, the Kingdom of God was alive and very, very well indeed! Amen....BANG!

Toe-To-Toe With Hugh Hewitt

Radio talk-show host, Hugh Hewitt, should patent his latest media creation.

Distrustful of interviewers who take comments out of context and morph them into something very different when they appear in print, Hugh has come up with the idea of the "before" and "after" interview analysis. The idea works like this:

Hugh allows himself to be interviewed by a journalist, but the interview is taped for later broadcast on his show (and the transcript printed on the web)....*after* the article or column has appeared in print. His radio listeners and blog readers can than compare the one with the other and draw their own conclusions as to whether or not Hugh's comments were represented accurately or not.

It's a win-win situation for Hugh, who gets to fill air time and make money off of someone else's interview. It also allows for the manly art of "tit for tat" and thrust and parry that he practices with such skill and relish.

Hugh's first excursion into this new media genre took place last week in an interview with LA Times columnist and Associate Editor, Tim Rutten., who was researching a column on the future of conservative talk radio.

To begin with, Rutten deserves a lot of credit for being willing to go along with Hugh's eccentric interview demands. After reading the interview transcript posted at Radioblogger.com, Rutten also generates respect for being a good sport with a granite jaw!

Now in most interviews, the interviewer asks the questions. In this instance, however, I counted where Hewitt asked Rutten somewhere near 58 questions compared to Rutten's 42. When I subtract the 16 questions where Rutten is either repeating one of Hugh's questions or asking for clarification, the interviewer's questions are reduced to no more than 26, less than half the number of those asked by the one being interviewed!

At times the verbal exchanges gave the appearance of Hugh, as a criminal attorney, cross-examining a hostile witness. Questions flew like combination punches in a boxing match. Hugh's constant flurries of one question followed by another kept Rutten off-guard and off-topic for most of theirOccasionallyer. Ocassionally, Rutten would attempt to counter-punch or throw something like a short uppercut in a futile attempt to regain control of the bout.

Hugh took full use of his "home court (meaning radio talk show venue)" advantage and came away a winner by unanimous decision.

Hugh managed to win points by pounding incessantly on the subject of liberal bias in the media, both in general and at the LA Times, in particular. Every attempt by Rutten to respond was immediately met by a maelstrom of facts, opinions and sheer chutzpah that kept him off-balance and back on his heels.

Once back on his own turf, Rutten tried to regain some of his top ranking by lobbing dismissive names and labels at Hugh from long-distance in his column; indirectly calling Hugh a fool, a bore and a narcissist. He also continued to affirm that a good journalist (such as himself) is able to separate his/her personal political bias from their "craft" and create fair, unbiased and trustworthy reports. Thus ended the final round.

This judge, while impressed with Rutten's confidence and courage, had to give the fight to Hugh on points. There were no knockdowns and Hugh has already offered his opponent a rematch. Don't hold your breath.

Iraq's Constitution Flap--Yes, There IS a Good Side

I am personally surprised and deeply disappointed in the failure to achieve a sectarian consensus on the proposed Iraqi Constitution.

The list of negative repurcussions is long and potentially dangerous and destablizing for the future of a unified and peaceful Iraq. I have spelled out some of those issues in my previous posts, The Proposed Draft of the Iraqi Constitution (as of 8/25/05) and Iraqi Sunnis Debate Whether To Wield Constitutonal "Nuclear Option."

ON THE OTHER HAND.......There are some very good things shining through in the midst of this otherwise very bad thing.

Most importantly, there is now a national consensus that the future of Iraq is enexorably tied to participatory democracy. It is recognized by all major groups, Kurd, Shi'ite and Sunni, that political power no longer resides in terrorism, armed militias or strident ideological intransigence.

This new reality is demonstrated by the realization of the Sunni political and religious leadership that the only effective way to express their opposition to the proposed constitution is to GO OUT AND VOTE!

Yes. Really! For sure! Sunnis right and left are urging their people to go out an register to vote! What a contrast from just nine months ago when the Sunni mantra was "Boycott....Boycott...Boycott." That futile attempt to discredit the national elections backfired miserably, leaving the Sunnis with minimal representation in the resulting interim national assembly.

If, however, they can rally three of the four majority Sunni provinces to reject the proposed constitution, they will have achieved a tremendous victory on two fronts--One for themselves and Two, for democracy.

For themselves, they will have forced a return to a new interim government in which they will be able to elect a more representative Sunni presence. This will give this second interim government far more legitimacy than the current one.

For democracy, they will have demonstrated that, even as a "not-very-respected" minority "party," they can still wield a more legitimate influence over national affairs with the ballot than they could ever hope to gain through bullets.

While the insurgents and terrorist cells in Iraq clearly are pleased with the Sunni leaders rejection of the proposed Constitution, they will, in the long run, come out as losers no matter what transpires in the weeks and months to come.

The Iraqi people have turned a very important corner. They have seen their future. And that futurewill be in the ballot box and not in car bombs.

The current dispute may be viewed as a severe and serious stumble, but the momentum towards freedom and democracy has now passed the point of no return. For most of us, including most Iraqis, this is the answer to prayer!

Good News From Iraq? Really!

Arthur Chrenkoff has now posted Good News From Iraq #34. If you are tired of seeing pictures of blown up cars and reading about the failure of everything in Iraq, here's your chance to catch up on all the good stuff that the mainstream media doesn't want you to know. Or, could it be that they don't think you'd be interested? Prove them wrong!

P.S. But be warned. There is a LOT of good news here. The equivilent of 39 pages of good news!

TUESDAY, AUGUST 30, 2005

Katrina Fails To Achieve "Worst Case Scenario"

UPDATE: New reports are coming in suggesting that the "worst case scenario" for the city of New Orleans may indeed be unfolding. See my latest posts here and here and, as always, check Irish Trojan's Blog for the latest updates.

As Hurricane Katrina passes into both history and legend, it leaves behind what may become the most devestating and expensive natural disaster in American history.

Tens of thousands, perhaps even more than 100,000 homes have been effectively destroyed. Thousands of square miles of agricultural, industrial, commercial, business and residential areas have been flooded. Power grids have been destroyed. Colleges and Universities closed. Public schools leveled. Water and sewage systems ruined. Roads and bridges washed away. Tourism crushed. Transportation and distribution of food and other essential products in chaos.

But it could have been worse.

The loss of life, while tragic, will be small compared to the potential worst-case estimates of tens of thousands had the New Orleans levees been breached.

In the "nick of time" Katrina dropped from a category 5 hurricane to a category 4, just before reaching the coast.

In the "nick of time" Katrina lost significant power on its west flank.

In the "nick of time" Katrina veered slightly to the east, sparing New Orleans the full force of her fury.

Had these three "nicks in time" not occurred as they did, we could well be a nation in mourning today.

Instead, we are faced with three Gulf states, Louisiana, Mississippi and Alabama that are knocked down, but not knocked out. Recovery will be long and hard.....but not impossible. Life in the region will eventually be reborn rather than cremated and scattered. In the darkness, there remains light and hope for a new tomorrow.

Insurance and oil-related costs will take their toll on all of us in the United States, whether we live in the effected areas or not.

But there is an immediate need for food, shelter, communication, electricity, transportation, public services, health care, sanitation and so much more.

Government funding and insurance payments will help in the long run, but the need for charitable donations to the American Red Cross and other front-line help agencies is massive.

If you are reading this, prayerfully consider clicking on the Red Cross link and making a generous gift towards hurrican relief. Or contribute to any reputable agency that you personally support.....as long as it has an established presence in the region.

If you attend a Christian church or are a member of any other religious community, speak to your spiritual leaders and ask them to take up a special offering for Hurricane Katrina Relief when you gather for worship or fellowship this coming weekend.

My congregation will be doing that this Sunday. As a Christian, giving out of love and compassion for others is neither optional nor required.....it is essential.
This is how we know what love is: Jesus Christ laid down his life for us. And we ought to lay down our lives for our brothers. If anyone has material possessions and sees his brother in need but has no pity on him, how can the love of God be in him? Dear children, let us not love with words or tongue but with actions and in truth. 1 John 3:16-18

Katrina/New Orleans Update: Bad News

It appears that my previous post on the effects of Hurricane Katrina, while horrific, was too optimistic.

Late reports indicate that there has occurred at least one major levee break in the line of defense between the city of New Orleans and adjacent Lake Pontchartrain. The Army Corps of Engineers along with state and local officials is desparately trying to fill the breach to prevent the below-sea-level city from turning into a giant lake.

As the following reports recently posted by Brendan Loy at Irish Trojan's Blog indicate, it is no exaggeration to describe today's desparate struggle as the second "Battle of New Orleans." Unlike the first one, however, this is a fight for the life and death of the city itself.

The view from St. Amant
8/30/2005 01:05:00 PM EST
Posted by Brendan

Bill Crews reports in from St. Amant, southeast of Baton Rouge:

Still w/o power here in St. Amant. I've been tuned into WWL 870 AM. They are transmitting w/an approximate 28 day supply of propane to generate their transmitter. Still operating out of the Omni (?) Building, located next to the 'S-dome. That's one of the buildings w/all the glass & doors blown out of it. Here are some comments I've heard in the last few hours: "City still continues to flood due to levee breach...""Lower half of Plaquemines Parish has been reclaimed by Gulf of Mexico and Miss. River...""North shore of Lake Ponchartrain now extends (N) to Old

Spanish Trail Rd...""The Ponchartrain Causeway was completely submerged except for the 'hump' in the middle...""Martial law has been declared...""The Miss. River levee was beached from Belle Chase, southward...""Search and rescue efforts still continue..." BTW, officials are now asking all refugees to go to the Lamar Dixon Expo Center, near my home, in Gonzales, LA. We may go volunteer later; they are expecting thousands.

BOWL WILL FILL IF LEVEE BREACH CONTINUES
Officials to attempt sandbag airlift
8/30/2005 11:30:00 AM EST
Posted by Brendan

WWL-TV: "Break in 17th Street Canal Levee is now 200 feet wide and slowly flooding the City of New Orleans. Huge sand bags are being airlifted to try to stem the rush of water in that area. The expectations are that the water will not stop until it reaches lake level." In other words, we are talking about something that very closely resembles the worst-case scenario -- flood waters completely filling the bowl, turning Lake Pontchartrain and New Orleans into one big toxic lake. This will will happen, unless the airlift works or officials can find some other way to stem the flood.Anthony sums up the situation succinctly:

"assuming no additional storm surge, or Mississippi floodwaters, the water level in the 'bowl' will end up being effectively equal to the level in Lake Ponchatrain."

Cliff, a hydrologist, gives an excellent, more detailed explanation of why that's true.Does anyone know what the typical water level in Lake Pontchartrain is, in comparison to the various regions of the city? How many feet above the French Quarter? How many feet above Tulane University? etc.Regarding whether the sandbagging plan will work, Cliff writes:

It's difficult to say without knowing exactly how deep the breach actually is. The fact of the matter is, even if they can reduce the width of the breach from 200ft down to 100ft or 50ft, then they will potentially slow down the amount of water coming into the city. The depth of the breach also determines how fast the water is moving across it, and if the velocity is high enough, it's possible that the sandbags won't hold. Blocking the actual canal with sandbags/barges is a good alternative I think, but it obviously requires a lot more volume of stuff to block it with. From the one photo I've seen, if the breach is actually 200ft wide, by scale, the canal looks to be at least 3x as wide as the breach, and if it's 10ft deep, that's a lot of volume to try & block. Like I said, it's difficult to make an estimate not knowing all the information. But if they only need to block a couple of feet in the breach, then that would require far less material than blocking the canal.

On a more hopeful note, "The LSU researchers [speaking on WWL-TV] indicated that they thought the breech could be sealed," according to another commenter.

Photos of Katrina/New Orleans Aftermath

Aerial photo of levee break

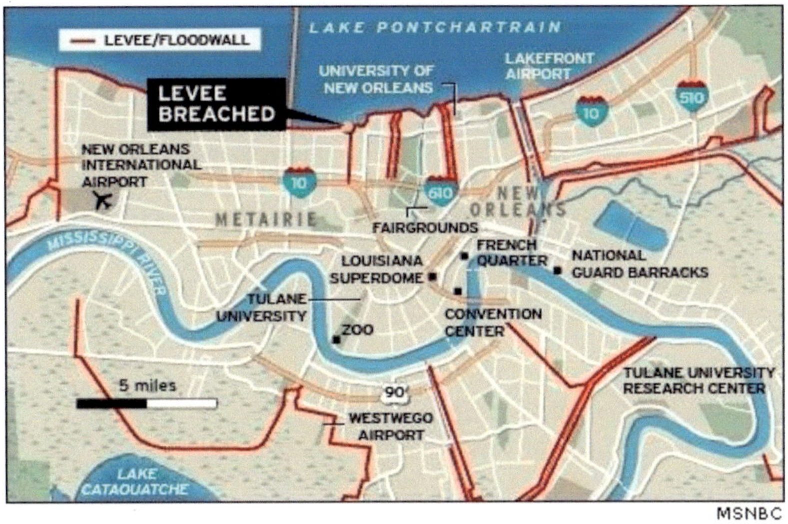

Apparent location of levee break

Downtown New Orleans w/Super Dome in distance

New Orleans filling up with water

New Orleans: More Bad News

Brendon Loy at Irish Trojan's Blog shares some very unsettling news:

But before you read it, click here, and you will find the very **best map of New Orleans showing what parts are above sea level and the parts that will be under water for a very long, long time.**

Sandbag efforts fail; 12- to 15-foot flood expected
8/30/2005 07:24:00 PM EST
Posted by Brendan

Very bad news from WWL-TV:

6:41 P.M. - Efforts to stop the levee break at the 17th Street Canal have ended unsuccessfully and the water is expected to soon overwhelm the pumps in that area, allowing water to pour into the east bank of Metairie and Orleans to an expected height of 12-15 feet.Essentially, everything that is below sea level in New Orleans will be submerged. The Gulf of Mexico is slowly but surely reclaiming the Crescent City.

Photo of the Island of Super Dome

Water surrounds the New Orleans Super Dome where, according to reports, at least 10,000 people continue to suffer with no toilets, no electricity and little food. At least two people are reported to have died in the Dome and today, another died after falling from an upper level, apparently a suicide.

Other reports indicate that fights have broken out

and people are demanding to be let out even as more refugees are being brought to the shelter from surrounding areas.

On another sober note, prisoners at Orleans Parish Prison have rioted and taken hostage a prison deputy, his wife and four children who had been brought to the prison to take shelter from the storm.

WEDNESDAY, AUGUST 31, 2005

Looters Disrupt Rescue Efforts

This piece posted at Irish Trojan's Blog, demonstrates just how bad the looting is getting in New Orleans (Note that major looting is also being reported in Biloxi).

Mayor Nagin orders police to focus on looters
8/31/2005 08:22:00 PM EST
Posted by Guestblogger

As looters get way out of control, the New Orleans mayor told the police to abandon their search and rescue efforts and crack down on the lawlessness in the city. Nagin says, "They are starting to get closer to heavily populated areas -- hotels, hospitals, and we're going to stop it right now."

"Abandon search and rescue efforts" because of the looting? What a disgrace! The so-called "social contract" is being destroyed by antinomian anarchists in the damaged areas. Don't get me wrong, but these people are "thugs" of the worst kind. Every one of them belongs confined in an area surrounded by very high fences...not to punish them...not to help reform them...but to protect the lawful population from their penchant to terrorize.

There are even reports that looters are trying to break into the Children's Hospital, where 100 children are being cared for by terrified medical staff. Police and National Guard troops have been called but have not been able to respond.

Should the order be given to shoot these people in self-defense? Or would that simply lead to outright war in the flooded streets of New Orleans? Can you imagine urban warfare like Falluja here in the United States? How does a "civilized" society respond to such a riotous threat? Sadly, it appears to be true...."the enemy is within."

Thoughts On Looting In New Orleans

Looting has turned both the flooded and the unflooded streets of New Orleans into states of lawlessness. There are even reports of New Orleans Police driving looters out of stores and then piling merchandise into their own vehicles. Police have also been reported to have broken into car dealers and driven off with SUVs, supposedly commandeered for their "police work."

In some precincts 30-40% of officers have reportedly "quit" and simply stopped doing their job at all, leaving the isolated and besieged citizenry to fend for themselves.

What is it that drives men and women to act in such a way? Sin? Of course. But the nature of that "sin" is complex and convoluted.

If I was protecting my family under the circumstances we are seeing in New Orleans, and if my family was going hungry, I would "loot." Of course I would.

I would justify this as follows: Normally I would go down to the store to buy what I need. Today, there is no one there in the store to take my money. I will take what I need, keep track of it and try to pay the owner back later.

Well, that's probably what I would do. Is this really stealing? Technically and legally, yes. Morally? I'm not sure. Jesus' disciples plucked wheat from a field and ate it. This was done on the Sabbath, which got him a lot of criticism for having allowed his disciples to "thresh" wheat on the day of rest. I doubt, however, that Jesus owned the field from which he took the wheat. Was this stealing? Did Jesus sin?

Even David took the shew bread from the presence of the Lord when he was hungry. Was this sin? Or was it morally right to use available food to satisfy hunger that cannot be satisfied in any other way?

Is it morally right for someone to hoard food...far more than they need for themselves...while others are starving nearby? Do those who are starving have a moral "right" to force their way into the person's home and take that food in order to survive?

Do the "rights" of ownership and possession always trump the "right" of others to live? After all, our own founding documents say that "life" is an unalienable right, given to us by our creator.

It has been said that possession in 9/10s of the law. I suppose that the need for sustenance might be at least a part of the other 1/10.

But looters in New Orleans are not simply taking those things necessary for life. They are stealing drugs from pharmacies, electronic items like TVs and computers. One woman was seen carrying a vacuum cleaner through the flood waters. To vacuum what????

Here we have clearly stepped over the line between "needing" and "wanting."

The when we "want" something but do not "need" it, the Bible describes this with the word, "covet." As in "Thou shalt not covet." This is, of course, the last of the 10

Commandments. The eighth Commandment is also worthy of mention here...."Thou shalt not steal."

Coveting is to stealing what "committing adultery in your heart" is to adultery.

The looting and stealing in New Orleans has its origins in the hearts and minds of those doing it. When the opportunity came to act on their thoughts and desires, they did so.

Arresting these people and putting them in jail might protect the rest of us from their larceny but will not necessarily change their hearts and minds for the better.

It will take months and years of sweat and toil, along with billions of dollars, to reclaim the city of New Orleans from it present polluted and defiled condition.

Yet this will be a far easier task than trying to change the hearts and minds of people who would take a shopping cart full of Nikes home from a store without paying for them simply because they were able to.

SATURDAY, SEPTEMBER 03, 2005

Homeland Security Head Chertoff Plays the Fool

U.S. Homeland Security Chief, **Michael Chertoff**, said today, in response to a question about preparedness for the New Orleans disaster, that the "'perfect storm' of a combination of catastrophes exceeded the foresight of the planners, and maybe anybody's foresight."

Chertoff is wrong, of course. Planners were very aware of the potential dangers in having a category 4 or 5 hurricane hit New Orleans. Indeed, after Hurricane Betsy, a category 2 hurricane, hit the city in 1962, the levees were strengthened to withstand a category 3 hurricane. Apparently the cost of making them strong enough to hold under the surges of a category 4 or 5 storm were more than the politics and budgets of the day could afford. So, everyone settled for "second best" as being better than nothing. Until this past weekend, that decision had seemed like a good bet.

Both the city and the Army Corps of Engineers knew full well what would happen if the levees were breached. I suspect that they even knew how many inches or feet of water would stand in every block of New Orleans should such an event occur. For 24 hours after Hurricane Katrina had passed by, folks were breathing a big sigh of relief. The levees had appeared to have held, almost as if by a miracle of God.

Ironically, the largest breach that occurred took place on a section of a canal levee that had just been rebuilt and strengthened recently.....strengthened to withstand a category 3 hurricane.

Chertoff may have just misspoke, as can happen at a press conference during a period of emotional stress and physical exhaustion.

But his foolish answer greatly diminishes his credibility as an "expert" on this sort of thing. He is not an expert on hurricane disaster response planning in New Orleans and should have said so and then kept his mouth shut.

TUESDAY, SEPTEMBER 06, 2005

Barry Bonds Returns...Steroid Free

Bonds last March

Well, I guess that enough time has passed for Barry Bonds to show a negative result on a steroid test.

After lots of time to correct a "knee problem" Bonds took batting practice yesterday and plans to rejoin the San Francisco Giants as early as next Tuesday.

He looks just a little bit thinner and gaunter than he did last March when he announced the first of his knee surgeries. Now we just wait and see if he can still hit a ball into McCovey Cove!

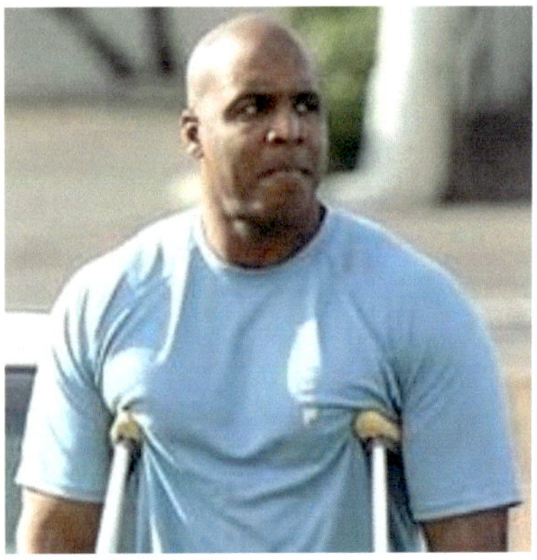

Michael Jordan took two years off from the NBA to play minor league baseball, supposedly to dodge a charge of gambling on games. He came back to have some good seasons and keep his image as the greatest basketball player of all time.

We'll see if Barry can do something similar. He is a good player....one of the best. If he can finish his career without steroids and still pass Hank Aaron on the home run list I have no doubt that he will get into the Hall of Fame.

I don't know whether to wish him well or not. As a Giant's fan, that hurts more than my knee.

WEDNESDAY, SEPTEMBER 07, 2005

Newsflash: Louisiana Told Red Cross to "Stay Out" of New Orleans

Yes, the headline is correct. Earlier today, Fox News reporter Major Garrett broke a story that claims that the Red Cross was fully deployed with food, sanitation and medical supplies to assist those left behind in New Orleans (including, presumably, the Super Dome and the Convention Center) but were barred from entering the city by the Louisiana Homeland Security who claimed that they wanted people to leave New Orleans and, if the Red Cross went in there, people would feel they did not need to leave, making the evacuation more difficult.

What is really galling is that they were ready to enter New Orleans on Monday afternoon, BEFORE the levees broke, flooding the city.

Even more mystifying is that, as the days past and the suffering, death and sanitation crisis became a national disgrace, the interstate access to both refugee facilities remained intact.

Why did the state of Louisiana deny the presence of the Red Cross and the supplies so desparately needed by thousands of suffering people?

Hugh Hewitt has something to say about this and **Radioblogger** has the complete transcript of Hugh's radio interview with Major Garrett this afternoon.

Read....and don't forget to scratch your head while you weep.

FRIDAY, SEPTEMBER 09, 2005

Illusionists Create Controversy Over Flight 93 Memorial Plan

Brave men and women died on September 11, 2001, when Flight 93 crashed in a rural spot in Pennsylvania. Those who took action knew that they were going to die so they acted to prevent the terrorists from carrying out a devestating crash into what was most likely supposed to be the White House.

For several years the National Park Service and others have been working with survivor's families and others to create a suitable and lasting monument at the crash site.

Finally, the design shown below was chosen (click to enlarge).

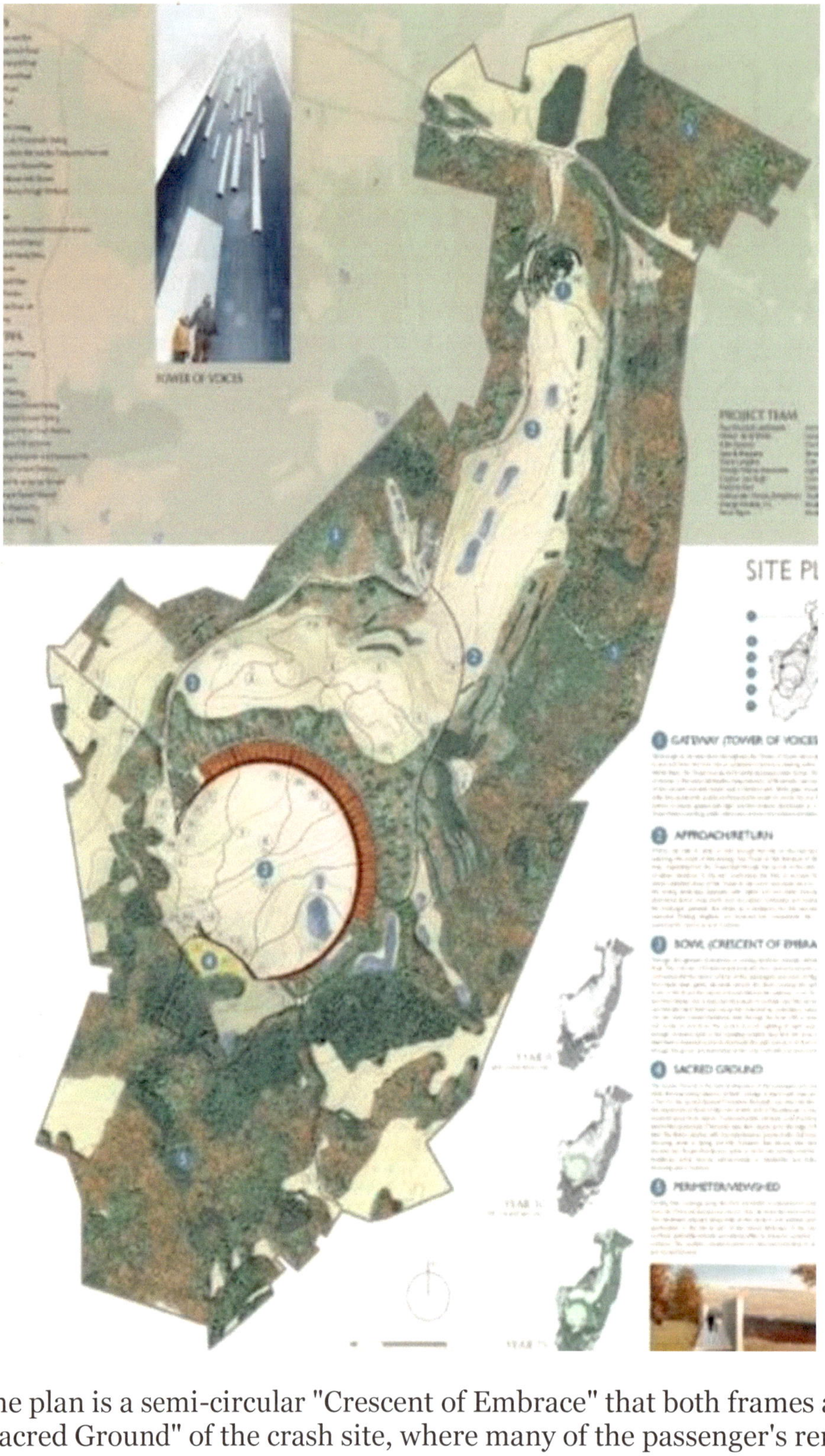

Central to the plan is a semi-circular "Crescent of Embrace" that both frames and sets apart the "Sacred Ground" of the crash site, where many of the passenger's remains are interred.

To some, however, including the normally sane Captain Ed, Michelle Malkin and Charles at Little Green Footballs, that "Crescent of Embrace" looks far too much like the crescent moon on the Muslim logo (minus the star, of course).

Their superimposed crescent makes the monument design look like this:

For Captain Ed

the crescent suggests that either the designers had no idea about the event they intended to memorialize, or that they want to turn this memorial into a multicultural scolding for America in the same way that the World Trade Center memorial designers attempted earlier....As long as that crescent remains in the design, I'm not donating a red cent to the memorial.

After reading all the hoopla over this matter I began to smell a ***conspiracy*** lurking....slinking about throughout history, sneaking the "crescent menace" into some of our most famous historical and architectural sites and, even more disturbing, into some of the most mundane items in our daily lives.

After a brief sabbatical of somewhere around 60 minutes or so, I uncovered the following sinister symbols of Islamic serruptitiousness:

The symbol for the Royal Canadian Navy Ship, "Crescent"

The state flag of South Carolina

Spielberg and Geffin's DreamWorks logo

Fake Roman coins

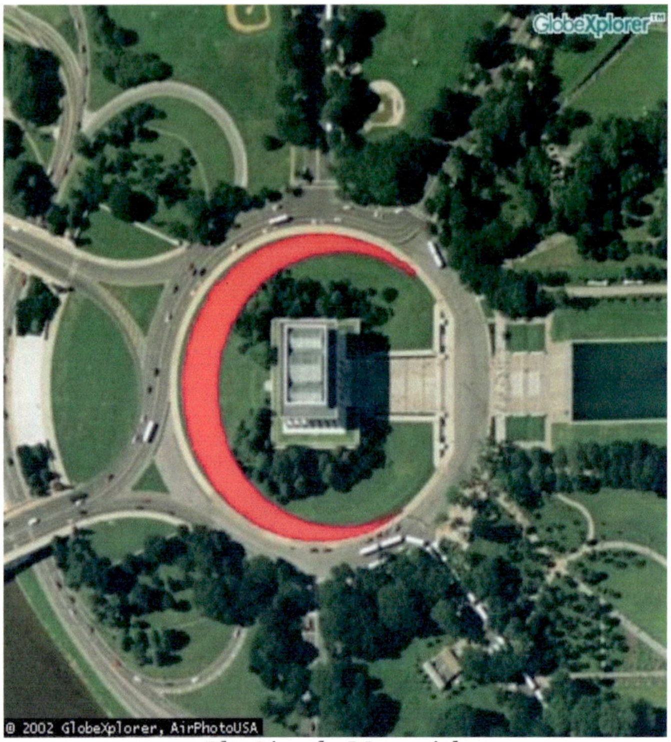

The Lincoln Memorial

St. Peter's Square in Rome

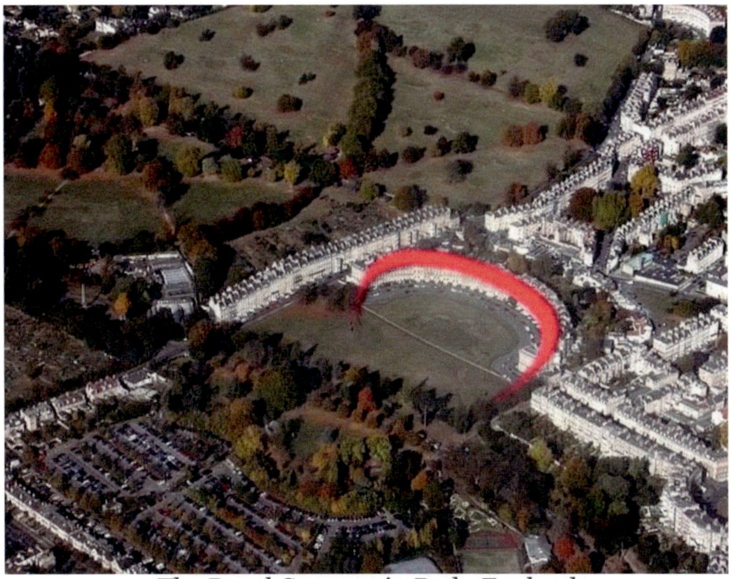

The Royal Crescent in Bath, England

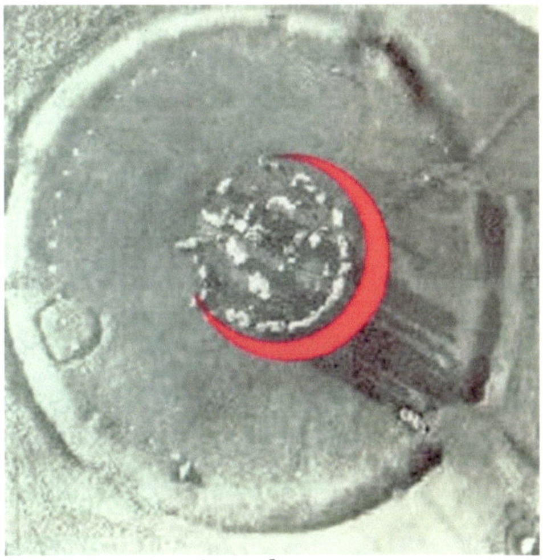

Stonehenge

And, the most nefarious of all……

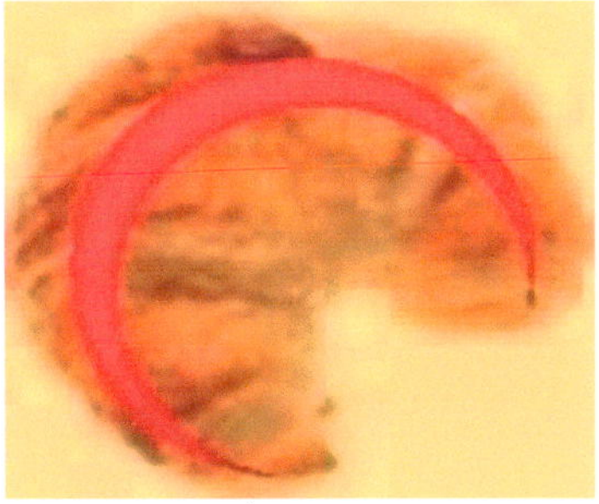

The Croissant

Clearly this all leads us back to the French!

The next time I dine at **Le Bernardin's** in New York I will be sure to order "Freedom Rolls" instead!

As for those who find Muslim terrorists hiding under every semi-circle, I say,

HAVE A NICE DAY

SUNDAY, SEPTEMBER 11, 2005

9/11 Four Years Ago Today--Lest We Forget

I Remember....

....the shock....

....the fear....

....the horror....

....the anger....

....the defiance....

....and the hope....

I will not forget.

Made in the USA
Las Vegas, NV
03 November 2026

57421892R00193